THE SKILLED
LABOURER
1760–1832

THE SKILLED
LABOURER
1760–1832

J.L. HAMMOND
AND BARBARA HAMMOND

First published by Longmans, Green, and Co., London 1919

This edition is published by arrangement with Longman Group
Limited, London.

This paperback edition first published 1995
Fraser Stewart Book Wholesale Limited
Unit 3B Colwell Drive · Abingdon · Oxon · OX14 1AU
Produced by Alan Sutton Publishing Limited

British Library Cataloguing-in-Publication Data applied for

ISBN 0-7509-0967-6

Library of Congress Cataloging-in-Publication Data applied for

Cover photograph: detail from Industry of the Tyne: Iron and Coal *by
William Bell Scott (Wallington Hall, Northumberland; photograph The
Bridgeman Art Library)*

Printed in Great Britain by
The Guernsey Press Company Limited
Guernsey, Channel Islands

PREFACE

In the *Town Labourer* the writers tried to give a picture of the social conditions created by the great changes of the Industrial Revolution. They described the general character of the new life of town and factory, the ideas and difficulties of the class in power and the outlook and the temper of the workers. This book treats the same period from a different aspect. Its aim is to present the detailed history of particular bodies of skilled workers during those changes. It would be impossible to cover all industries in a book planned on the scale of this volume : the industries chosen are those for which the fullest records were available.

The writers owe a substantial debt to Professor George Unwin, who has helped them liberally from his large store of special knowledge of industrial history. They are under obligations to other friends, notably Mr. A. Clutton Brock, Mr. G. D. H. Cole, Professor L. T. Hobhouse, Mr. R. H. Tawney, and Professor Graham Wallas. Mr. G. W. Daniels has been kind enough to make some valuable suggestions on the subject of the early history of the cotton trade, on which he speaks with special authority, and Mr. T. W. Hanson of Halifax, who is steeped in the exciting history of the West Riding, has given important help for the chapter on the Yorkshire Luddites. The Appendix is due to Mr. A. G. C. Lloyd of Capetown.

The writers published in the *Town Labourer* a list of their principal authorities. It seems unnecessary to reproduce that list, but a few books on which they have drawn more specially for this volume should be mentioned. They are : *Annals of Coal Mining*, by R. L. Galloway; *History of the*

Cotton Manufacture, by Edward Baines; *The Lancashire Cotton Industry*, by Professor S. J. Chapman; *Yorkshire Past and Present*, by Thomas Baines; *The History of Wool and Woolcombing*, by James Burnley; *History of the Worsted Manufacture in England*, by John James; *A History of Machine-Wrought Hosiery and Lace Manufactures*, by William Felkin; and *The Risings of the Luddites*, by Frank Peel.

HEMEL HEMPSTEAD, *November* 1919.

CONTENTS

CHAP   PAGE

I. INTRODUCTION 1

II. THE MINERS OF THE TYNE AND THE WEAR . . 12

III. THE MINERS OF THE TYNE AND THE WEAR . . 31

IV. THE COTTON WORKERS, 1760-1818 47

V. THE COTTON WORKERS, 1818-1832 94

VI. THE WOOLLEN AND WORSTED WORKERS:

    I. INTRODUCTION 136

    II. THE SPINNERS 143

    III. THE WOOLLEN WEAVERS 156

    IV. THE SHEARMEN OR CROPPERS 167

    V. THE WORSTED WEAVERS 190

    VI. THE WOOLCOMBERS 195

VII. THE SPITALFIELDS SILKWEAVERS 205

VIII. THE FRAME-WORK KNITTERS 221

IX. THE NOTTINGHAM LUDDITES 257

X. THE LANCASHIRE LUDDITES 271

XI. THE YORKSHIRE LUDDITES 301

XII. THE ADVENTURES OF OLIVER THE SPY . . . 341

CONCLUSION 377

APPENDIX 382

INDEX 385

CHAPTER I

INTRODUCTION

THE history of England at the time discussed in these pages reads like a history of civil war. This is the impression produced by the speeches and the policy of Ministers, the letters and the conduct of magistrates, the records of the Courts of Justice, the system on which our military forces were organised and the purposes they were designed to serve. Critics and partisans of the established order alike take this war for granted. It produces an atmosphere more intense and more absorbing than the great war that was raging from one end of Europe to the other, and it persists long after that war is over.

What was this civil war about ? It was not a quarrel over religion nor a quarrel over rival claims of Parliament and Crown. The issue that now divided the English people was in one sense less simple, in another sense it was simpler than the issue that had provoked the better known civil wars of the seventeenth century. It was less simple because it assumed various and changing aspects and one side in the struggle was not always articulate. Yet it was simpler because it arose from the fundamental instincts of human nature, for the question that it put was this, whether the mass of the English people were to lose the last vestige of initiative and choice in their daily lives.

The last vestige ; for so much had been lost already that the upper classes came readily to think of the surviving elements as an anachronism. For two centuries there had been a steady concentration of economic power in the hands of a small class. The historian traces the growth of this power through its different stages : the appropriation of the monastic lands, the decay and disappearance of the guilds, the enclosures, the changes in school and university, the rise in one trade after another of capitalism in a form that enables the few to control the productive energy of the many. In the medieval village all over Europe, here as elsewhere, the normal man had certain rights. On the dissolution of that old village society in England these rights were lost, and the peasant disappeared in a social revolution that created a proletariate ready for the service of the owners of capital, whether they employed their capital in agriculture or in one of the new industries.[1]

So much attention has been bestowed on the development of capitalism before the Industrial Revolution, that there is perhaps a tendency to underestimate the importance of the changes that accompanied the Revolution. ' Long before 1776 by far the greater part of English industry had become dependent on capitalistic enterprise in the two important respects that a commercial capitalist provided the actual workmen with their materials, and found a market for the finished goods.' [2] This is true, though readers of these pages will do well to note that among the exceptions Professor Ashley names the Yorkshire Woollen Industry. The men whom Arthur Young described as working on their little farms round Leeds bought their own wool and sold the cloth that they made to merchants in the Cloth Hall. But if it is true that the majority of domestic workers were dependent on capitalist enterprise, it does not follow that the changes the Industrial Revolution produced were unimportant in their consequences to the worker. They were so important that when the weaver in Oldham or the cropper in Halifax or the woolcomber in Bradford looked back in 1820 or 1830 to the beginning of his life, he thought he could remember a time when the worker was in all senses a free man.[3] We can see that the fate of the worker at the Industrial Revolution was predetermined—unless some miracle had happened to change the temper of English society—by the social changes that preceded the Revolution, for those changes had made it difficult for the workers, deprived of all the machinery and traditions of co-operation, to obtain a share in the control of the new power.[4] But it would

[1] For an excellent account of the fate of the peasant in the different countries, see Professor Ashley's address to the International Congress of Historical Studies, 1913, *Comparative Economic History and the English Landlord*.

[2] Ashley, *Economic Organisation of England*, p. 141.

[3] The cotton handloom weaver often preferred famine to the discipline of the mill.—Chapman, *Lancashire Cotton Industry*, p. 46.

[4] Mr. Belloc goes too far surely in suggesting in his book *The Servile State* that the capital for the new industries came exclusively from the rich, for Gaskell (*The Manufacturing Population of England*, 1833) tells us that the most suc-

be wrong to conclude that their fate was any the less terrible on that account.

Within certain limits the ordinary workman had still a large margin of freedom in his daily life at the beginning of the period discussed in this volume. We have Felkin's picture of the Frame-work Knitters of Leicester: ' Each had a garden, a barrel of home-brewed ale, a week-day suit of clothes and one for Sundays, and plenty of leisure.' We have Bamford's agreeable picture of the Lancashire weaver at the end of the eighteenth century drawn from his uncle's home at Middleton. The domestic worker was not like the modern domestic worker who usually supplies the worst examples of sweated conditions. He was not hopelessly and despairingly poor. He had some say in his own life : he could go out and dig in his garden or smoke as he pleased : he was in some cases a farmer as well as a weaver or a spinner : he was in short not quite disinherited from the old village economy in which a man did not merely sell his labour but had some kind of holding and independence of his own.

The industrial changes that occurred at this time destroyed this social economy with its margin of freedom and choice for the worker. To the upper-class observer those changes seemed to promise a great saving of human labour. To the worker they seemed to threaten a great degradation of human life. And the worker was right, because the saving of human labour did not mean that the worker worked less or received greater compensation for his toil, but that the capitalist could draw greater profits from the labour of the workers he employed. What happened during this period was that the power of the owners of capital to control the energy of mankind was so immensely increased by the industrial changes that in many parts of England it spread over the entire life of a society. The worker had to surrender his freedom to this power: he had to surrender his home as well. His wife who in the old days brewed the ale, cleaned and cooked, and helped with the loom, had now to spend the day in the mill : the child had to be sent or carried to the mill as soon as it could walk. Robert Owen told Peel's Committee in 1816 that he could remember in the days before the advent of factories that the

cessful were men who started from very small beginnings. Robert Owen was in this sense no exception. But Mr. Belloc seems to us to be perfectly right in his conclusion that the disastrous form that the new society took was determined by the moral atmosphere of the time.

children looked as well fed as at that time, though few of
them were employed before they were twelve or thirteen. A
few years' experience of the new system made this seem incredible, for it was supposed that no home could be kept going
unless the children of five or six went to the mill. Under
that system the owners of capital could decide not only
how the worker spent his life, but how he brought up his
children. In other words the weaver or spinner or carder
could call less of his life or his time his own than the humblest peasant in the old village, who worked so many days
for his lord and so many days as farmer or as weaver for
himself.

The workers were in the main ignorant men, but they were
not so perverse or so foolish as they appeared to the philosophers who wrote *The Results of Machinery*. They felt that
the grasp of the new power was closing on them, and they
resisted instinctively every change that could hasten that
process. They considered about each invention not whether
it meant that a piece of work could be done in one hour instead
of ten—the only consideration for the reasonable and enlightened people of the time—but whether it brought their
final enslavement a day nearer. They were fighting as literally
as ever men have fought ' pro aris et focis.' Something of
the atmosphere of a tragedy—the tragedy that seemed to set
science in the lists against happiness, and knowledge against
freedom—clings to the villages and the grey hills of the West
Riding. The bleak and sombre landscape that gives its sad
tone to the life and the art of the Brontës seems to speak of the
destinies of that world of combers and croppers and spinners
and weavers on whom the Industrial Revolution fell like a
war or a plague. For of all these classes of workers it is true
that they were more their own masters, that they had a wider
range of initiative, that their homes and their children were
happier in 1760 than they were in 1830. Surely never since
the days when populations were sold into slavery did a fate
more sweeping overtake a people than the fate that covered the
hills and valleys of Lancashire and the West Riding with the
factory towns that were to introduce a new social type for
the world to follow.

It was not only those workers whose art or skill was superseded by the developments of the factory system that suffered
in these changes. The strengthening of the power of capital
which followed the introduction of machinery told disastrously

on the position of those home workers whose industry remained a domestic industry. The hand-loom weaver sank steadily more and more as the power-looms increased, until, as one of them said to Oastler, they were reduced to living on their children. The Frame-work Knitters were in a different case, in the sense that no factories were started until after our time to do the work that was done in their homes, but as we shall see, their fortunes declined almost as tragically as those of the hand-loom weaver. Felkin gives a most interesting review of the changes in their conditions as recalled by an old man who had been apprenticed in 1755 : [1] ' When a lad, the work-people laboured ordinarily ten hours a day, five days a week, the Saturday being always left open for taking in work to Nottingham, gardening, etc. : through the middle of his life they worked about twelve hours a day ; but of late years they work by necessity fourteen to sixteen hours a day. . . . For the first thirty years or thereabouts of his being in the trade, or from 1755 to 1785, fluctuation in wages was almost unknown ; taking work in, he describes as being as regular and well under-stood in the general rate of wages, as to be like going and paying 1d. for a penny loaf.' It is interesting to note that a Leicester witness, speaking of the conditions of this trade in 1833, said, ' We have no factory bell : it is our only blessing.' [2]

The new industrial system which robbed this society of its freedom robbed it also of its pleasures. If the introduction of machinery had taken place under a system that allowed the workers to control it, that system would have increased leisure and so made the life of man happier : it would in fact have done what the philosophers claimed for it. But machinery was introduced under a system that placed the workers at the disposal of the owners of capital, who valued machinery as a means, not to a larger and richer life for the workers, but to greater and quicker profits for their enterprise.[3] There were of course many thinkers, politicians, and magistrates before the Industrial Revolution who thought that the mass of men and women ought to spend their lives in hard toil without relief or distraction. But the Industrial Revolution gave a great momentum to this view and increased the power of

[1] Factories Inquiry Commission, 1833, c. i. p. 180.
[2] *Op. cit.*, c. ii. p. 10.
[3] See *William Morris*, by A. Clutton-Brock, pp. 226 f., for an admirable discussion of this aspect of the industrial system.

those who held it.   Take for example the way in which the
average manufacturer regarded the introduction of labour-
saving machinery.   He never thought of it as a means to
increasing leisure.   On the contrary ; if one machine could do
ten men's work, there was all the more reason for not allowing
so valuable an instrument to be idle a moment longer than
was necessary : in other words, the machine was an argument for lengthening rather than shortening the working day.
There were honourable employers, chief among them the
illustrious John Fielden, who contended as ardently as any
workmen's leader against this vicious monomania, but the
spectacle of the immense and sudden expansion of trade was
so intoxicating that the educated classes were led to forget
every other side of life.

   This aspect of industry, as an unrelenting and slave-driving
master, was emphasised by the general atmosphere of competition that dominated this new world.   During a war a
nation is obliged to concentrate all its resources on one aim,
to regard everything in its bearing on the efficiency of a society
for one particular purpose.   Everything is seen in a special
perspective which is false if once you take your eyes off that
exclusive end.   The Industrial Revolution had an effect like
this on the imagination of England, for it made people think
that their society was to be judged solely by its commercial
success in a struggle of which the whole world was now the
arena.   The test of success was the test of profits : if a society
could make its social and political conditions favourable to
the earning of high profits that society was prosperous.

   Under this influence there grew up the idea which more
than any other branded the workers as servile : the idea that
they were to be treated as the instruments of this power, and
not as citizens with faculties and interests of their own for
which society should make some provision.   This fixed idea
rules the outlook of the age on religion, politics, philosophy,
and   all   the   arts   and   pleasures   of   social   life.   The
optimism created by the new discoveries mingled with as
dark a disbelief in a wide range of happiness and freedom as
the world had ever known.   The majority of educated men
renounced the hope of adapting human life and human power
to their new surroundings in such a way as to satisfy the
nobler instincts of human character, content to think of the
mass of their fellow-countrymen as concerned only with a
routine of working, eating, and sleeping.   It was as if men

had deliberately turned their backs on 'the master task of civilised mankind.'[1]

The towns that belonged to this age are steeped in its character : they are one aspect of an industrial system that refused to recognise that the mass of mankind had any business with education, recreation, or the wide and spiritual interests and purposes of life. The age that regarded men, women, and children as hands for feeding the machines of the new industry had no use for libraries, galleries, playgrounds, or any of the forms in which space and beauty can bring comfort or nourishment to the human mind. The new towns were built for a race that was allowed no leisure. Education, it was believed, would make the workers less passive and therefore less useful instruments : therefore they were not to be educated, or to be educated only within the narrowest limits. Recreation was waste : the man who was kicking a football or playing a fiddle might be wielding a hammer at a forge or superintending a spinning machine. In some parts of Lancashire it was the custom to forbid music in the public-houses, and parsons and magistrates were found who thought that the worker would be demoralised by hearing an oratorio in a church on a Sunday. A witness before the Factory Commission gave his impressions of the factory system in a vivid phrase : 'Thinks they are not much better than the Israelites in Egypt and their life is no pleasure to them.' It is significant that we find in the pages of Crabbe, of Cobbett, and of Bamford the same lament that the games and happiness of life are disappearing. The rich might win their Waterloos on the playing-fields of Eton, but the rivals who were trying to shake our grasp of the new wealth could only be conquered by a nation that shut up its workers in mill or mine or workshop from the rising to the setting of the sun.

For with the Industrial Revolution the long working day becomes the rule in all industries, factory or domestic, old or new. We have an example of a new domestic industry in the case of lace-running, which employed over 180,000 women and children at the time of the Reform Bill. In this industry the worker paid the penalty of these hours in blindness. A girl worker before the Factory Commission, who worked from six in the morning to ten at night, with two hours off for

[1] See Graham Wallas's powerful chapter on 'Disposition and Environment' in *The Great Society*.

meals, described the trade as one that made you subject to
headache, and said in contrast to another witness who was
no longer able to see the clock at all, that she could see the
clock but could not distinguish the figures from the hands.
She added a grim touch from the manners of the time : ' I
went a long way to see a man hanged t'other day, and couldn't
see him a bit after all. I heard folks talking : that was something. I got very near at last. A man asked me couldn't I see
him now. I said I could, I was so ashamed, but I could not.' [1]
For workers and rulers alike the harsh dilemmas of the
new world were sharpened and embittered by the Great War.
Some historians think that England found in that war the
golden opportunity for her new industries, and that while
the armies of the Continent were tramping to and fro over
Europe, and Napoleon was allowing her peoples no respite
from his rapid stratagems in politics and war, she was laying
the foundations of her commercial supremacy. There is a
contrary view that the artificial conditions created by the war
encouraged a premature expansion of the cotton industry,
and that it would have been better for that industry had it
developed more slowly and more naturally. The advocates
of a minimum wage for weaving were on this view recommending a measure that would have been a public benefit,
apart from its effects on the social life of Lancashire, because
it would have steadied the wild speculation of the early years.
At any rate it is certain that the war aggravated every problem
that the Industrial Revolution presented to the age.
It is a commonplace that that Revolution introduced pro-
foundly disturbing elements into the economic world from the
scale on which trade was now conducted : a development
that made nations and industries dependent on a series of
delicate relationships spreading like a net all over the globe. [2]
The war added a new and terrible element of disorder to the
uncertainty and caprice of demand which marked the introduction of ' great industry ' with its world-wide markets. At
times it was conducted directly by economic weapons : the
spinners and weavers suffered grimly in the great duel between
the Berlin Decrees and the Orders in Council. Nobody can
read the evidence given before the Committee on the Orders
in Council in 1812 without appreciating the difficulties of an
employer who suddenly found himself denuded of orders for

---

[1] Factories Inquiry Commission, 1833, c. ii. p. 18.
[2] See for a full discussion, Smart, *Economic Annals*, vol. i. p. 606.

his five or six hundred workers.[1]   And the cause that increased the miseries of the workers and brought serious embarrassments to the traders hardened the mind of the ruling class against all liberal ideas by making them more afraid than ever of the very name of reform.   Thus it came to increase not only the distress but the discord of the time, for it was now, as the industrial changes pressed more and more on their habits and daily life, that the workers became conscious of their wrongs as citizens.

In the early days of this period there was no general sense of grievance in the industrial districts on the subject of political disabilities, for at that time there was no sharp conflict in political ideas between the workers and their rulers.   So long as the politics of the Birmingham workers took the form of a strong desire to pull Dr. Priestley's house to pieces, their rulers had no undue inclination to bridle their energy.   Bamford gives an amusing account of the experience of the unhappy reformers who tried to hold a meeting at Thorpe, near Royton in Lancashire, in 1794.   The reformers had assembled in a public-house and the mob attacked it with great violence ; the house was wrecked and the reformers very savagely handled. 'The constables of the place had been called upon by the peaceably disposed inhabitants to act but they declined to interfere and the mob had their own way.   Mr. Pickford, of Royton Hall, a magistrate, never made his appearance, though he lived within a few score yards of the scene of the riot, and was supposed to have been at home all the time during which the outrage was perpetrated.   He was afterwards known as Sir Joseph Ratcliffe, of Milnes Brig, in Yorkshire.   Such of the reformers as had the good fortune to escape out of the house ran for their lives, and sought hiding places wherever they could be found ; whilst the parson of the place, whose name was Berry, standing on an elevated situation, pointed them out to the mob, saying, " There goes one : and there goes one ! That's a Jacobin, that's another ! " and so continued till his services were no longer effectual.'   Twenty years later the

---

[1] Sadler pointed out in the House of Commons that so long as there was no regulation of industry the fluctuations to which trade and manufactures are subject fell on the workers. 'Thus if the demand and profit of the employer increase, the labour of the operatives, most of whom are children, augments till many of them are literally worked to death ; if that demand diminish, the children are thrown partially or wholly out of work and left to beggary and the parish.'—House of Commons, March 16, 1832.

magistrates took a very different view of popular demonstrations, because popular demonstrations were now directed not against reformers but against the conduct and the privileges of the class in power. If Lancashire had sent 80,000 people to St. Peter's Fields to demand the suppression of the Radicals, or to support the Combination Laws or the Corn Laws, there would have been no Peterloo. As the working classes came to want things that the ruling class had no mind to give them, they became acutely sensible of political disabilities which had formerly seemed of no account, and the more they felt those disabilities, the more harshly did the ruling class enforce them.

Thus there is a growing strain and tension, the workers finding their lives more and more hemmed in, their surroundings more and more forbidding, their place in the society that regulated their arrangements more and more insignificant. Their rulers were becoming at the same time more and more preoccupied with the danger of yielding any point to their impatience. They sought to maintain every monopoly, to keep Manchester under the rule of the county magistrates, to preserve a system which gave two members to a ditch in Wiltshire and left the large industrial towns unrepresented, to strengthen and perpetuate by every device the control of the new world and the new wealth by a small class. They seemed bent on withholding from the workers all initiative in every direction, politics, industry, education, pleasure, social life. For they had come to look on civilisation as depending on the undisputed leadership of this small class and on the bondage of the workers in the service of the new power by means of which they hoped to make and keep England the mistress of the commerce of the world. A jingle put into the mouth of Wellington at the time of the Reform struggle summed up the philosophy of this class :

> If I say A I must say B,
> And so go on to C and D ;
> And so no end I see there 'll be
> If I but once say A B C.[1]

Here were all the elements of a mortal struggle. And so we see on one side strikes, outbursts of violence, agitations, now for a minimum wage, now for the right to combine, attempts, sometimes ambitious and far-sighted, to co-operate for mutual

[1] Wallas's *Life of Place*, p. 246.

aid and mutual education, the pursuit from time to time of projects for the reform of Parliament : on the other, Ministers and magistrates replying with the unhesitating and unscrupulous use of every weapon they can find : spies, *agents provocateurs*, military occupation, courts of justice used deliberately for the purposes of a class war, all the features of armed government where a garrison is holding its own in the midst of a hostile people. It is not surprising that a civil war in which such issues were disputed and such methods were employed was fierce and bitter at the time or that it left behind it implacable memories.

CHAPTER II

THE MINERS OF THE TYNE AND THE WEAR

THE miners of the Tyne and the Wear are a specially interesting study, because it is possible to collect from local papers and pamphlets a fairly consecutive history of the workmen's point of view. For a study of the history of the mining industry in general, it would be necessary to examine the various experiments of the time in organisation : such as the system of letting mines to small labour contractors that prevailed in Derbyshire, or the leasing of mines to groups of workmen. But the miners of the Tyne and the Wear represent the normal mining society, and the struggle in these districts is a good example of the efforts of the workmen to secure by combination some share in the profits of the industry, and some degree of independence and assurance.

The degrading serf system by which the mining population in Scotland [1] was bound to the soil had not obtained in England for several centuries,[2] but in Northumberland and Durham a system of yearly bond was customary down to 1844, and was a constant source of disputes between the binders and the bound. By this bond the men bound themselves to serve for the coming year at a certain rate of pay. The masters were not bound to provide them with constant work, but the men were bound to descend into the pit when required. The usual time for this ' binding ' was October, but in early days, at any rate, the masters were careful not to bind all the men at one time ' lest it should be in their power to distress the trade, by refusing to work till their demands were satisfied.' [3]

In 1765 a combination of masters endeavoured to turn this system of a yearly bond into a slavery nearly as gross as that

[1] The workers in mines and salt works of Scotland were nominally released from bondage in 1775 (15 George III. c. 28), but as this measure was not effective a further Act was passed in 1799 (39 George III. c. 56).

[2] Galloway, *Annals of Coal Mining*, Series I., pp. 75-76, suggests 1460 as the date when miners were emancipated.

[3] *Annual Register*, 1765, p. 130.

22

which was legal in Scotland. The occasion for this attempt was, strangely enough, the scarcity of pitmen due to the rapid increase of the coal trade. An apologist for the masters explained that in 1764 some colliery owners near Newcastle attracted workers by offering them two, three, or even four guineas as ' binding money ' in place of the customary shilling, with the result that the men in other collieries became discontented, and as their year of service drew to a close showed signs of readiness to quit their respective masters, and to offer themselves where golden guineas were to be had.[1] Another account explained that it was the owners of the more hazardous pits who started the scheme, because they found the bounties which they were forced to give to attract workers a serious expense.[2] Whatever the origin of the idea, the result was that the coal-owners of the Tyne and the Wear met and entered into an agreement ' that no coal-owner should hire another's men, unless they produced a certificate of leave from their last master ; and, as no coal-owner would grant such a certificate, it was by the pitmen called a binding during the will of the master.'[3] The men's position was described as follows : if they wanted to move and go to another pit they ' now find that no other Owner will hire them, but that they must be forced to work at pits which perhaps they do not like, and at what Wages the Master pleases, starve, or go to other parts.'[4] The men in fact found themselves faced with the prospect of virtual slavery.

To protest against this agreement of the coal-owners the men all struck work on August 25, the date when, as they thought, their year's bondage expired. The masters retorted by declaring that they were bound till November 11, a discrepancy that can only be explained by the supposition that the masters had inserted a clause to that effect in the bonds without the knowledge of the men. It is clear that it was the usual custom to bind the men for eleven months and fifteen days in order to prevent them from gaining a settlement in the parishes where their masters lived. Whatever the rights or the wrongs of this particular point, the men's action had a very rapid effect on their masters' policy, and the scheme of introducing virtual serfdom collapsed, as

[1] *Annual Register*, 1765, p. 130.
[2] *Lloyd's Evening Post and British Chronicle*, September 20-23, 1765.
[3] *Annual Register*, 1765, p. 130, and *London Chronicle*, September 21-23, 1765.
[4] *Lloyd's Evening Post and British Chronicle*, September 20-23, 1765.

we learn from a handbill preserved among the Home Office Papers.[1] It is dated August 31, and runs as follows : ' The Gentlemen in the Coal Trade, on the Rivers Tyne and Wear, earnestly recommend to the several Pitmen to go immediately to their work, as they are obliged by Law to do, till the Expiration of their present Bonds, at which Time they do assure them, that each Pitman shall receive a Discharge in Writing if he shall require it, that he may be at Liberty to engage in the Service of any other Master : and that no Agreement is entered into by the Gentlemen of the Coal Trade, to refuse employing any Pitman on Account of his having served in any other Colliery the Year before.' These assurances, however, came too late, and the only pit where the men would work was the Hartley Colliery owned by Thomas Delavel : ' a very remarkable Instance,' so the newspapers called it, ' of the Gratitude of the common People,' for Mr. Delavel was conspicuous as a humane employer, and the strikers sent him assurances that his pit should not be in any way molested.[2] On the other hand, when Sir Ralph Milbanke started some of his pits on September 13, in the middle of the strike, a body of men came and broke up the machinery, and three troops of dragoons were sent for to protect the colliery district.[3] With this exception the men do not seem to have done any actual damage, though we read afterwards, ' Mr. —— of Fatfield has been obliged to keep soldiers and a Justice of Peace in his house night and day for this fortnight past. . . .'[4]

The reason why the masters did not test the legality of their claim that the binding extended to November 11, by summoning their recalcitrant servants before a magistrate, and having them sent to prison for a month,[5] is explained in a letter, dated September 13, from Mr. J. B. Ridley to the Earl of Northumberland.[6] The letter is interesting as showing the solidarity of the men. You may wonder, he writes, why no proceedings have been taken under 20 George II., ' this

[1] S.P. Dom. (George III.), vol. iv.

[2] *Annual Register*, 1765, p. 131.

[3] *London Chronicle*, September 17-19, 1765 ; Home Office Papers, S.P. Dom. Entry Book, 194, September 17.

[4] *Lloyd's Evening Post*, September 30-October 2.

[5] By 20 George II. c. 19 a workman could be sent to prison for a month if a master satisfied a J.P. that the workman was guilty of 'a misdemeanour, miscarriage or ill-behaviour' in his service.

[6] S.P. Dom. (George III.), vol. iv.

is very well, where two or three or a dozen men desert their
service, and has been many times properly executed with good
Effect, but where there is a general Combination of all the
Pitmen to the Number of 4000, how can this measure take
Effect ? in the first place it is difficult to be executed as to
seizing the men, and even if they should not make a formidable
Resistance which scarce can be presumed, a few only can be
taken, for upon the Face of the thing it is obvious that the
whole persons guilty can not be secured, so the punishment of
probably twenty or forty by a month's confinement in a House
of Correction, does not carry with it the least Appearance of
Terror so as to induce the remaining Part of so large a Number
to submit, and these men that should be so confined would
be treated as Martyrs for the good Cause, and be supported
and caressed, and at the end of the time brought home in
Triumph, so no good effect would arise. . . .'

The coal-owners accordingly thought it the wisest course to
obtain military help and to insert the following advertisement in the Newcastle papers :

'Whereas most of the Bound Pitmen, of the Gentlemen of the
Coal Trade on the Rivers Tyne and Wear, have lately deserted
their respective Employments before the Expiration of their
Bonds and refuse to return to serve out the respective Times for
which they were bound, as they are by Law obliged to do : The
said Gentlemen therefore earnestly desire all Persons not to retain
or employ any of the said Pitmen till they have performed their
bound Services to their present Masters, as they have not till then
a Right to serve any other.' [1]

The pitmen in answer to this drew up and published [2] a
declaration so remarkable for its spirit of independence and
for its outspoken language that it deserves to be given in full :

'Whereas several scandalous and false reports have been and
still continue to be spread abroad in the Country, concerning the
Pitmen in the Counties of Durham and Northumberland absenting
from their respective Employments before the Expiration of their
Bonds : This is therefore to inform the Public, that most of the
Pitmen in the aforesaid Counties of Durham and Northumberland
were bound the latter End of August, and the remainder of them
were bound the Beginning of September 1764, and they served
till the 24th or 25th of August 1765, which they expect is the
due time of their Servitude ; but the honourable Gentlemen in
the Coal Trade will not let them be free till the 11th of

[1] *Newcastle Chronicle* and *Courant*, September 14 and 21.
[2] *Ibid.*, September 21.

November, 1765, which, instead of 11 Months and 15 Days, the respective Time of their Bonds, is upwards of 14 Months, So they leave the most censorious to judge whether they be right or wrong.   For they are of Opinion that they are free from any Bond wherein they were bound.   And an Advertisement appearing in the Newspapers last Week commanding all Persons not to employ any Pitmen whatever for the Support of themselves and Families, it is confidently believed that they who were the Authors of the said Advertisement are designed to reduce the industrious Poor of the aforesaid Counties to the greatest Misery : as all the Necessaries of Life are at such exorbitant Prices, that it is impossible for them to support their Families without using some other lawful Means, which they will and are determined to do, as the said Advertisement has caused the People whom they were employed under to discharge them from their Service. Likewise the said honourable Gentlemen have agreed and signed an Article not to employ any Pitman that has served in any other Colliery the year before ; which will reduce them to still greater hardships, as they will be obliged to serve in the same Colliery for Life ; which they conjecture will take away the antient Character of this Kingdom as being a free Nation.   So the Pitmen are not designed to work for or serve any of the said Gentlemen, in any of their Collieries, till they be fully satisfied that the said Article is dissolved, and new Bonds and Agreements made and entered into for the Year Ensuing.'

The Gentlemen of the Coal Trade meanwhile repeated with greater emphasis their denial of the existence of the obnoxious agreement not to employ each other's pitmen, and issued further handbills and advertisements to that effect :

‘ Whereas an opinion still seems to remain, that an engagement is subsisting among the gentlemen of the coal trade, or some of them, not to engage any pitman who shall have been employed in any other colliery : It is therefore hereby declared, in the most public manner, that there is no such agreement, nor any agreement intended to be entered into ; or is it meant by the gentlemen of the coal trade to refuse employing any pitman on account of his having served in any other colliery ; and that they require no more from the pitmen than that they shall perform the conditions of their present bonds.' [1]

The pitmen, however, were not satisfied with this declaration from their employers, and they seem to have taken the opportunity to improve their position with respect to wages before their return to work, which finally took place on October 4. It is interesting to notice from the newspapers of the time

---

[1] *Newcastle Chronicle* and *Courant*, September 21.

that the question of government interference to settle the wages was raised. Why should not the Privy Council intervene before the meeting of Parliament : ' it is imagined there would be no greater difficulty to settle these unhappy men's wages than it was to fix a price for the labour of the journey-men taylors.' [1] The terms on which the men returned are nowhere stated ; all we can learn is that the contest was settled amicably and that they resumed work ' in great spirits.'

A striking feature of the accounts of this episode in the Press is the sympathy shown to the miners. The local papers indeed give no comment, but the London papers—and London was seriously affected by the shortage of coal, which went up from under 30s. to 40s. a chaldron—published many letters from the district, showing that the men had public opinion on their side. What is perhaps most remarkable is that protests were made against the employment of the military. ' Impartial people,' ran one letter, ' think the masters have brought this upon themselves, by endeavouring to break through an old custom ; however, in a country which boasts its Liberty, it is an odd way of deciding differences between masters and servants by Dragoons.' [2] Again, ' The sending a body of troops against them [the pitmen] is a measure but little approved by the considerate part of the people ; every-body thinks that some expedient to reduce the price of pro-visions, would have been the best means of quieting the tumult ; and many persons say, it is rather an extraordinary circum-stance to knock a set of poor men on the head, because they will not quietly submit to be starved.' [3]

The conditions of the colliers' lives and of the hardships under which they suffered were described in some detail and with much feeling in a letter published in two London papers [4] by a certain Richard Atkinson during the strike. This letter is particularly interesting because it shows that the familiar charge of extravagance was levelled against the miners even in these early times. Mr. Atkinson's indignation had been roused by the masters' assertion that the troubles were due to laziness and not to distress. The men's wages he tells us

[1] *London Chronicle*, October 1-3.
[2] *Lloyd's Evening Post*, September 16-18.
[3] *Lloyd's Evening Post*, September 18-20. See also *London Chronicle*, September 28, for letter of protest from Y. E. against use of military.
[4] *Lloyd's Evening Post*, September 25-27, and *Public Ledger*, September 26.

are 7s. a week.[1] ' Cut off from the light of heaven for sixteen
or seventeen hours a day, they are obliged to undergo a
drudgery which the veriest slave in the plantations would
think intolerable, for the mighty sum of fourteen pence.'
Further, they cannot spend even that sum as they like, for the
overseer, appointed by the proprietor to keep the men to their
duty, and to pay them their wages ' constantly keeps a shop
contiguous to the Pit, where he lays in every necessary both
for the belly and the back, and obliges the poor men to buy
whatever they want from him, stopping it out of their wages,'
and keeping them constantly in his debt. ' Such, Mr. Printer,'
he exclaims, ' is the real situation of the Colliers. To be sure
it is the business of the Proprietors to represent them as a
set of lazy, disorderly fellows, who want only to increase their
wages, for the sake of extending their extravagancies ; the
more they are kept down, the more their Masters will be
enabled to venture ten thousand guineas on a favourite horse,
or the accidental turn of a card. But the sensible part of
the kingdom, who will always judge for themselves, must
immediately see, that when Butter in the northern parts of
England is at sixpence and Butcher's meat at threepence a
pound, a man who has but seven shillings a week to support
himself, a wife, and four or five children, can have no mighty
matter to squander away at an alehouse, or at any other place
of recreation, which happens to agree with the casual bent
of his inclination.'

From the letters of Mrs. Montagu, the famous blue-stocking,
herself a colliery owner, we learn the impression the colliers
made on their employers in these early days. ' The Tyne Vale
where I live,' she wrote in 1775,[2] ' used to look green and
pleasant. The whole country is now a brown crust, with here
and there a black hole of a coal-pit, so that I cannot boast of
the beauty of our prospects. As to Denton, it has mightily
the air of an ant-hill : a vast many black animals for ever
busy. Near fourscore families are employed on my concerns
here. Boys work in the colliery from seven years of age. I
used to give my colliery people a feast when I came hither,

[1] The employers' view (*London Chronicle*, September 21-23, and *Annual
Register*, 1765, p. 130) was that they earned from twelve shillings to fourteen
shillings a week. Arthur Young, who got his figures from employers, in his
Northern Tour, vol. iii. pp. 8 and 9, gave the earnings as one shilling to four
shillings a day with firing.

[2] See *A Lady of the Last Century*, by Dr. Doran, pp. 199 ff.

but as the good souls (men and women) are very apt to get drunk, and when drunk, very joyful, and sing, and dance, and holloo, and whoop, I dare not on this *occasion*,[1] trust their discretion to behave with proper gravity ; so I content myself with killing a fat beast once a week, and sending to each family, once, a piece of meat. It will take time to get round to all my black friends. I had fifty-nine boys and girls to sup in the court-yard last night on rice pudding and boiled beef ; to-morrow night I shall have as many. It is very pleasant to see how the poor things cram themselves, and the expense is not great. We buy rice cheap, and skimmed milk and coarse beef serve the occasion.'

Mrs. Montagu goes on to explain that she will also ' bestow some apparel ' on the most needy. Self-interest and benevolence blend in a happy concord over the cheap rice and the skimmed milk : ' Some benefits of this sort, and a general kind behaviour gives to the coal-owner, as well as to them, a good deal of advantage. Our pitmen are afraid of being turned off, and that fear keeps an order and regularity amongst them that is very uncommon.' But Mrs. Montagu was a woman of sensibilities, and even the promise she made to herself to start a spinning school for the girls, if profits continued good for two years, failed to quiet her scruples ; ' I cannot yet reconcile myself to seeing my fellow-creatures descend into the dark regions of the earth ; tho' to my great comfort, I hear them singing in the pits. . . .' [2]

Arthur Young gave in 1768 an unfavourable picture of colliers as ' a most tumultuous, sturdy set of people, greatly impatient of controul, very insolent, and much void of common industry.' [3] Their characters indeed were not of a kind to endear them to their social superiors, and as the eighteenth century went on and the coal trade increased, the manners of the pitmen altered ' materially for the worse.' There is little mention of them in the records of the time beyond references to their turbulence. Thus a petition from the Magistrates and Principal Inhabitants of Sunderland in 1785 asks for a permanent military force as a protection not only against the disobedience of the Seamen and Keelmen, but against the unruly behaviour of ' another description of Men called Pitmen,' amongst whom, ' from their numbers and habits of

[1] Her husband had lately died.
[2] *A Lady of the Last Century*, p. 202.
[3] *Northern Tour*, ii. p. 261.

Life, discontents frequently arise which call for the inter-
position of the Civil Power aided by a Military force.' [1]

In the first volume of the Reports of the Society for
Bettering the Condition of the Poor [2] there is a long and
serious account of the situation and shortcomings of the
mining poor, and of the provisions made for the benefit
of the Duke of Bridgewater's colliers near Manchester, by
the Rev. Thomas Gisborne, written in 1798. ' It is to high
wages,' he informs his readers, ' that many of the criminal
habits, so often ascribed to the character of a collier, may in
part be ascribed. . . . To economy, he is, in general, an utter
stranger.' When first his wages are paid the collier and his
family may be seen ' indulging themselves in the use of animal
food three times a day.' The week after, it is true, they have
to descend to a diet of rye bread with oatmeal and water,
till ' the next receipt of their wages enables them to return to
a course of luxury.' A contrast is drawn between the luxurious
and riotous pitman with his wage of 16s. (or with the family's
labour of 20s. or even 30s.) and the decent and frugal agricultural labourer who, on his wage of 9s. a week, would certainly never be able to succumb to the wild debauchery of
meat three times a day. Drunkenness, profane language,
deceit, ' riotous dispositions, impatience of supposed grievances, and discontent inflamed by the contagion of turbulence
and clamour,' are amongst the charges brought against the
miners. The chief remedy proposed by the Rev. Thomas
Gisborne was that the colliers should by religious education
be led to ' a just sense of revealed religion, and of the rewards
and punishments of a future state.' Failing this the possession of gardens and other property was to be encouraged as a
corrective to bad habits ; [3] and the truck system and ' tommy-

[1] H.O., 42. 6. In 1793 the Mayor and magistrates of Newcastle asked for
barracks to be built (H.O., 42. 25).
[2] Pp. 170-73, and pp. 223-6.
[3] The effects on miners' characters of giving them some land above ground
had been noticed by Arthur Young in his *Northern Tour*, 1768, vol. ii. pp. 262 ff.
A certain Mr. Danby, who owned a colliery at Swinton in the West Riding,
tried the expedient of allowing the colliers to enclose bits of the barren moor.
The effect was magical : ' the whole colliery, from being a scene of idleness,
insolence and riot, is converted into a well-ordered and decently cultivated
colony. It has become a seminary of industry ; and a source of population.
One of these model colliers in particular roused Arthur Young's keenest admiration. This man, James Croft by name, after working from midnight till noon
every day in the colliery, cultivated seventeen acres without outside help. He

shops' instituted near Manchester by the Duke of Bridgewater were praised. By such a method 'the collier always
has credit for necessaries and reasonable comforts; and, at
the same time, is not able to squander the mass of his gains,
to the injury of himself and his family.'

The unsatisfactory behaviour of the miners created a good
deal of uneasiness amongst their neighbours. The Bishop of
Durham, who as Lord of the Manor had been given the mineral
rights of the district by a legal decision early in the century,
when the growth of the mining industry made the question
vital, now urged the creation of additional chapels in populous
districts. 'I hope,' he had written in 1793, in reference to a
dispute between coal-owners and men, 'the good sense of the
People will in a little time prevail and convince them of the
happiness which they enjoy.'[1] But so little did the expedient
of additional chapels succeed, that seventeen years later, in
1810, the Bishop's stables were requisitioned to hold three
hundred recalcitrant strikers, for whom there was no room in
the Gaol and House of Correction.

The dispute in 1810 was not connected with wages.[2] It
was concerned primarily with that persistent cause of friction,
the yearly bond, and incidentally with certain special grievances, including fines. The history of the dispute is briefly
as follows.[3] In October 1809, just before the annual binding,
the masters agreed amongst themselves to bind the men for
a year and a quarter instead of a year, that is till January
1811, so that after that time the yearly binding should be in
January instead of in October. This they did because, October
being a very busy time, the men could force up the binding
bounty. The new plan was propounded to the men at the
binding; they agreed to it and were bound for the year and
a quarter. Afterwards, on thinking it over they realised the

never took more than four hours' sleep, and on moonlight nights less. Arthur
Young raised a subscription of £100 to free him from colliery work, so that his
twenty hours' toil should be in future devoted to the land alone. It is not
surprising to read that Croft's industry brought him to an early grave. See
Autobiography of Arthur Young, edited by M. Betham Edwards, p. 55.

[1] H.O., 42. 23.

[2] Wages were estimated to have risen thirty or forty per cent. in 1804, and so
great was the demand for men that bounties of twelve and fourteen guineas on
the Tyne, and of eighteen guineas on the Wear were given (Galloway, *Annals*,
i. 440; *Victoria County History of Durham*, vol. ii. p. 347).

[3] See Sykes, *Local Records*, ii. p. 403, and *Tyne Mercury*, December 11,
December 18, 1810; January 1, January 15, 1811.

disadvantages, and determined that in October 1810 they
would strike, unless the masters consented to bind them for
a year as usual. The men had some sort of 'brotherhood'
or confederacy, possibly formed now, possibly of earlier date.
Its existence was publicly known about July.[1] In October
the masters refused to grant the demands made on them, and
all the men on the Tyne and the Wear struck work. The delegates from the different collieries held frequent meetings, but
'they were hunted out by the owners and magistrates, assisted
by the military, and committed to prison.'

The hunt for strikers continued for several weeks, and the
overflow of prisoners from the Gaol and the House of Correction at Durham filled the Bishop's stables, without any
effect being produced on the strike itself. At last, when
matters were at a deadlock, a parson magistrate, the Rev.
Mr. Nesfield, Rector of Brauncepeth, and Captain Davis, in
charge of the Caermarthen militia, who guarded the prisoners,
intervened as mediators. The stable prisoners, to whom they
appealed as the leaders of the strike, refused to make terms,
'leaving it entirely to their partners at liberty.' The result
of the negotiations was that the pitmen returned to their
work, and promised to fulfil their present bonds, that is up
to January, whilst Mr. Nesfield pledged his word to them that
he would act as mediator and bring forward proposals to
improve their position in future. The main proposal, to
which they are said to have agreed at the time, was that
by a compromise the binding time should in future be neither
October nor January, but April. As soon as the prisoners
were released they published in all the Newcastle papers [2]
a dignified message of thanks to the inhabitants of Durham,
for their 'kindnesses and favours' during their confinement
in the stables, to the soldiers who did their duty over them for
their 'good behaviour,' and to Captain Davis, Mr. Nesfield, and
others for the trouble and interest shown in befriending them.
This message was signed by four leaders on behalf of 159
prisoners.

After the men had gone back to work, Mr. Nesfield found
the path of the peacemaker a thorny one. He addressed
the coal-owners on the River Wear, inviting them and two
men from each colliery to meet him at Chester-le-Street on
December 20, and offering to submit for their consideration

---

[1] Committee on Combination Laws, 1825, p. 2 ; and *Tyne Mercury*, February
26, 1811.   [2] *Tyne Mercury*, December 4, 1810.

such regulations as would remove the peculiar cause of the present discontent. But the coal-owners refused his overtures; they argued first, that the River Wear did not constitute the coal trade, but that the River Tyne, Hartley, Blyth, and Cowpen were integral parts of it, and that therefore they could not make any separate arrangements; secondly, that the plan of inviting two men from each colliery was objectionable ' lest such Meeting should hazard a Recurrence of the late Disturbances.' They further hinted that his interference was uncalled for, and that if his services were needed he would be informed, in which case the coal-owners would ' attend with Deference to your Recommendation as far as they can do consistently with what is fit to be observed on such an important Occasion; at the same Time keeping in view the Duty they owe to themselves, their Workmen, and the Peace of the Country.'

Mr. Nesfield's goodwill was not daunted by this cold reception, and he proposed a new meeting on January 3, inviting this time all the coal-owners of the Tyne and Wear districts to attend. Whether it was the near approach of the new binding time and the fear of riots, or some other motive that changed their attitude, the coal-owners now accepted the invitation, the conference took place, and Mr. Nesfield brought forward proposals under twelve heads. On this occasion it was the men who thwarted Mr. Nesfield's good intentions of acting as peacemaker; the masters, after notifying the fact that some points did not meet with their approval, accepted his proposals as a whole for the sake of peace and quiet. The pitmen agreed to the clauses which enacted that the conditions, apart from the bond under which they were hired, should be clearly set down in a book, that a copy of the bond should be handed to a representative appointed by them, that fines should lapse if not demanded at the ensuing pay day, and that if fined when they were voluntarily idle they should be paid when they were compelled to be idle: but they now rejected, though not unanimously, the proposal they had originally accepted that the binding time should be on April 5. They also rejected the proposals designed to meet their grievances about fines for deficient measures, and foul coal, and payment when the pit was made unfit for working by an accident to the engine.

The conference accordingly broke up without arriving at any agreement. The negotiations that followed can only be

guessed at. This much is certain : that the men were ultimately forced to accept the proposals, and when their bonds
expired in January, were bound peaceably for 1¼ years.
The 5th of April henceforth remained the regular binding
day till the bond system came to an end in 1844. The coal-
owners were afterwards said to have adjusted the business
' by the assistance of legal weapons,' [1] and as no records of
actual prosecution exist, threats of prosecution under the
Conspiracy and Combination Laws were probably sufficient.

A curious glimpse into the scenes of the binding time is afforded
by a correspondence in the *Tyne Mercury*.[2] That paper on
January 29 inserted a paragraph explaining that the reluctant
pitmen at Jarrow were urged by a Methodist preacher to
accept their bonds, under pain of hell fire if they refused.
' At the time appointed, the pitmen WERE bound, the fear of
hell vanished, and they got comfortably drunk, as usual upon
such occasions.' Next week a correspondent wrote on behalf
of the Methodist preacher, impugning the truth of this account,
and declaring that the fulminations from the pulpit were
directed against the combination or Brotherhood with its
oath. ' This Oath is illegal ; and because Christianity teaches
subjection to the laws it is unchristian and immoral.' This
version of the affair roused violent protests from a voluminous
writer signing himself ' No Methodist,' who quarrelled with
the Methodists, not because they had used unfair pressure
in urging the pitmen to return to work, but because after
being ' the principal founders, supporters, and propagators of
the combination,' they now posed as its destroyers, whereas
in reality they had not declared their opposition till it was
already ' annihilated by the strong arm of the Law.'

The use of the strong arm of the Law to put down the
pitmen's combination possesses a certain piquancy from the
fact that the masters themselves were formed into an illegal
combination commonly known as the ' Newcastle Vend.' [3]

The Vend, which had existed ever since 1786, and possibly
before, was an agreement made between the different coal-
owners that no pit should sell or ' vend ' more than a certain

---

[1] *Tyne Mercury*, February 12, 1811.

[2] *Ibid.*, January 29, February 5, February 12, and February 26, 1811.

[3] For particulars of the Vend during this period, see 1800 Reports of the
House of Commons Committees on the Coal Trade (specially App. 41 to the First
Report, which shows how it was worked), and the 1829 Report of the House of
Lords' Committee on the Coal Trade.

fixed amount of coal. At the beginning of the year a rough and liberal calculation was made of the whole amount for which there was likely to be a demand, and the proportion in which each individual colliery might supply it was arranged. The price of the coal of different collieries differed according to its quality, and that too was fixed at the beginning of the year. By this arrangement the collieries with inferior coal were ensured a certain sale, and if any owners shipped more than their stipulated quantities they were bound at the end of each year to make an allowance to those who had shipped less.[1]

From the men's point of view the Vend gave them more or less regularity of employment by equalising the work. 'One great Consideration,' said a coal-owner to the 1800 Committee, in speaking of the system, 'is, I believe, the Peace and good Order of the Country.' He went on to explain that if the inferior pits were to stop work the men would go and call out the workers in other pits.

In the troubled days of 1816, when the iron trade was almost at a standstill, and the Staffordshire and Shropshire miners were wandering about the country starving, the pitmen of the Tyne and Wear suffered much less severely. The mines which, like those in Northumberland and Durham, supplied coals for the London market were, of course, less affected by the depression of trade than the mines whose output was mainly consumed by neighbouring furnaces. On the Wear indeed there was a small strike 'upon the ostensible ground of their present wages being inadequate to their support, while the price of bread-corn continues so very much higher than it has been,' but the magistrates and the soldiers soon sent the strikers back to work.[2]

It is clear that the system of a yearly bond, guaranteeing the men a certain minimum of work at a fixed rate of pay,

---

[1] A case was begun in 1794 against the Duke of Northumberland's agent and five others, principal members of the Vend, for wickedly conspiring, combining, and confederating to cheat the public, by a certain Mr. Errington who had inherited an interest as lessee in a coal mine belonging to the Duke of Northumberland, and had found the output limited below a profitable amount by the agreement, but after obtaining the removal of the trial from Newcastle to York Mr. Errington's ardour cooled and the matter was dropped. See First Report on the Coal Trade, 1800.

[2] *Annual Register*, 1816, *Chronicle*, p. 73, quoting the *Tyne Mercury*. See H.O., 42. 151, for the Rev. Mr. Nesfield's views on this strike. He thought the men unjustified.

gave a certain protection to the Northumberland and Durham miners in sudden depressions of trade during the year. It also gave them facilities for concerted action which the Combination Laws might check but could not destroy. Their well-known ' turbulence ' acted also as a protection against any attempt actually to lower the money wages at the time of binding. Mr. Buddle, the well-known colliery manager,[1] was asked in 1829,[2] whether a reduction in wages could ' be effected without danger to the tranquillity of the district, or risking the destruction of the mines, with all the machinery and the valuable stock, vested in them ? ' ' I should think not,' he answered ; ' but the coal-owners have not the power of reducing the wages till April next.' . . . ' Is it possible another year to hire the workmen at lower wages, if the present prices of coals continue ? '—' I should conceive not without great disturbance and perhaps not succeeding in the end.'

The system of paying wages in goods or truck instead of in money was prohibited by law in 1817.[3] The truck grievance seems never to have been so acute in the Northern as in the Midland mines,[4] although its existence is mentioned from time to time.

In 1819 the wave of excitement about Reform which spread over the country after Peterloo affected the pitmen in the north.[5] ' Until within these few weeks,' wrote Mr. John Buddle on October 25,[6] ' our Colliers and the body of Labourers, of every description, connected with the Coal Works, never troubled their heads with politics.' The mischief he ascribes to the publications, the *Black Dwarf* and the *Black Book*. ' They are to be found in the *Hat Crown* of almost every pitman you meet.' This zeal for politics was combined with discontent about their lot, and restiveness about the bond. ' Their constant cry,' he writes some weeks later, ' is that they work

---

[1] He invented the system of 'splitting the air.' See Galloway, *History of Coal Mining*, p. 146.

[2] 1829 Lords' Committee on the Coal Trade, pp. 68, 69.

[3] 57 George III. c. 122.   [4] See *Town Labourer*, 1760-1832, pp. 66-71.

[5] For an interesting estimate of the numbers of men and boys employed in 1819, see H.O., 42. 198.

	Underground.	Above ground.	
Tyne . .	6,000	2,800	8,800
Wear . .	4,000	1,850	5,850
Hartley and Blyth	500	250	750
			15,400

[6] H.O., 42. 197.

" far too hard for their wages," and cannot exist upon [them].
One fellow at Heaton, after having solemnly made this declaration last say Friday, gave 6s. 10d. next day for a White Hat.' [1]

The men's grievances are fully set out in a pamphlet entitled
*A Voice from the Coal Mines, or a plain statement of the various
grievances of the Pitmen of the Tyne and Wear, addressed to the
Coal-owners, their head agents and a sympathetic public, published
by the Colliers of the United Association of Northumberland and
Durham in 1825*,[2] a publication made possible by the repeal
of the Combination Laws. A clear account is given of the
conditions of employment.

Foremost among the grievances was the system of fines.
Without entering into tedious technicalities, the men's fines
can be briefly described as follows :

(1) When the hewer's coal was measured, if there was any
deficiency in any particular corf or basket, he forfeited the
whole corf. There was great uncertainty as to the standard
measure, and hence the system gave ' rise to much injustice
and oppression.' [3]

(2) If foul coal, flint, or stone was found mixed in any corf
the hewer was fined 3d. a quart for it, and if there were more
than 4 quarts he was guilty by law of a misdemeanour. Under
the term foul coal, it was said, ' the master classes whatever
part of the strata he pleases.' [4]

A second grievance was what may be called the ' three-days
grievance.' A stipulation that a minimum of work of nine
days a fortnight must be provided, was inserted in the bond,
but by the arrangements drawn up by Mr. Nesfield in 1810, if
an accident happened to the engine which made the pit unfit
for working, after three days the men were to be paid 2s. 6d. a
day. Later on the clause was amended in such a way that the
arrangement applied if a pit was rendered unfit for working
by an accident to the engine, ' or any other cause.' Some of
the coal-owners interpreted these words ' or any other cause '
very liberally ; and when work was slack they would lay the
pit idle for three days, resume work for one day, lay it idle for
three days again, and so on, thus cheating the men not only

[1] H.O., 42. 199. Although the name of the writer is scratched out the letter
is clearly from Mr. Buddle.

[2] This Union was founded after the Repeal of the Combination Laws, 1825.
Cf. Galloway, *Annals*, i. p. 465, and Buddle's Evidence before Committee on
Combination Laws in 1825, p. 1.

[3] *A Candid Appeal to the Coal-Owners and Viewers*, 1826.   [4] *Ibid.*

of their stipulated minimum but of their 2s. 6d. a day as well. The men who were thus cheated when work was slack were themselves fined half a crown a day if they were absent when their employers wanted them.

A grievance which was to play a more important part later was the length of hours worked by the boys, seventeen in some pits; and another grievance was the hardships caused by the use of the Davy lamp.[1] Owing to this lamp, declares the pamphlet, the miner has now ' to suffer the most awful agony in an exceedingly high temperature.' Complaints with reference to wages were mainly connected with shortage of work and with fines and deductions. Detailed estimates from two pits put these fines and deductions at a little over 2s. a week. Thus in one pit where not more than nine days' work a fortnight was provided and the weekly earnings were about 13s. 6d., the deductions were reckoned as follows :

	S.	D.
Candles	0	7½
Caller and smith	0	1
House rent and fire . . .	0	3
Picks and pick handle . . .	0	3
	1	2½
Fines and forfeits	1	0
	2	2½

The estimate of the wages which would produce ' reasonable comfort ' to the collier's family, we give elsewhere ;[2] they are high compared with the actual wages. The colliers in fact had no intention of being reduced to subsistence level, and appeals to them to remember that mine owning and mine working were expensive occupations, which left little margin for wages, met with a blunt response : ' We are not ignorant of the great expense incurred in the working of the mine ; yet princely fortunes have been amassed by both our employers and their ancestors ; and even men from our own ranks, have grown rich by the emoluments arising from the coal mines. . . .'

According to the 1842 Mines Report, a great impetus was

[1] See *Town Labourer*, 1760-1832, p. 25.
[2] *Town Labourer*, 1760-1832, pp. 34-35. It works out at £1, 6s. 3¼d. a week.

given to the Miners Association in 1826 by the refusal of the masters to give the customary hiring bounty, and 4000 men are said to have joined the Union.[1] 'The Union of the Pitmen,' wrote Lord Londonderry that same year, February 26, 1826,[2] 'is entirely established, and if the Coal-Owners do not resist their Combination they must surrender at Discretion to any Laws the Union propose.' He enclosed an interesting pamphlet called *A Candid Appeal to the Coal-Owners and Viewers*, . . . *from the Committee of the Colliers United Association*, from which we learn particulars of some attempted negotiations between the Pitmen's Union and the Coal-Owners. When the Colliers United Association, as it called itself, approached the Coal-Owners Union Committee with the suggestion that a meeting should be held by representatives of both sides 'in order the better to adjust the exceptionable parts of the Bond,' the coal-owners 'refused to take any notice of it on the ground that we were not a corporate body, and the Coal-Owners Union Committee knew nothing of and therefore would not recognise or treat with such a body of men as the Colliers Union Association.'[3]

It is interesting to notice in the *Candid Appeal* that the men claim a certain share in the management of affairs that directly concern them. Thus they object to the clause in the customary Bond which refers 'the settlement of differences and disputes between the contracting parties to two viewers,' and ask that a body consisting of two viewers appointed by the proprietors and two hewers appointed by the men should be set up for the purpose. They also object to a proposed scheme for a Benefit Society: 'It has long been a favourite object with the rich and opulent to desire and promote plans for making the poor maintain the poor, and the funds of Benefit Societies have generally been made to aid the poor rates, and thereby relieve at the same time both the poor and the rich. . . . We view therefore with some jealousy and suspicion a recommendation lately submitted to us from the colliery viewers, or some of them, to institute a general fund for the relief of colliers, their widows and families, etc. We can hardly hope that those who have refused to attend to our complaints or make any reply to our just remonstrances, will be prepared to lay aside all partiality and sinister views and

---

[1] First Report of Commission for inquiring into employment of children in mines and manufactures (Appendix, Part i.).

[2] H.O., 40. 19.   [3] See *A Candid Appeal*.

interest themselves sincerely in the management and direction of a fund solely for our benefit.   Besides, any plan proposed for our benefit, to which we should be called on to contribute, must be under our own special management and direction.' [1]

Lord Londonderry's alarm at the power of the Union was unnecessary, for during the next few years the men lost ground rather than gained it.   In 1828 the 15s. a week guaranteed them by the Bond was reduced to 14s., and in 1830 ' it was withdrawn altogether by a section at least of the coal-owners, with the result that in many collieries wages fell very low, as low as 8s. or 10s. per week, owing to want of work.' [2]

[1] *A Candid Appeal*, pp. 4, 5.   [2] Galloway, *Annals*, i. p. 465.

CHAPTER III

THE MINERS OF THE TYNE AND THE WEAR

The Strikes of 1831 and 1832

THE men, unable to improve their position by peaceful persuasion, determined to join battle with the coal-owners. On February 26, 1831, about 10,000 pitmen [1] of the Tyne and Wear met near Chester-le-Street and resolved to obtain redress for their grievances, and on March 21 a mass meeting of about twenty thousand persons, attended by the workers from forty-seven collieries, was held on the Town Moor of Newcastle, at which a policy was formulated. Amongst other things the system of ' tommy-shops ' was condemned. To the Lord Mayor of Newcastle, who had offered to act as mediator, they sent on March 23 a letter detailing their grievances.[2] First and foremost comes the three-days grievance, which we have already described. 'An article in the bonds empowers the Owners to limit the working days to only nine in the fortnight, in which nine days we are allowed as much work as will yield us 28s. at the prices for working which is mentioned in the bond ; but there is another article the former part of which reads as follows : if through any accident happening the engines or pits, rendering them unfit for working, or any other cause, the pits be laid off work for more than three successive days, we are to be paid 2s. 6d. per day, but not until we have laid idle three successive days. But, sir, that clause in this article which reads thus, or any other cause the pits be laid off work, does, we think, destroy the virtue of the former article : for if the owners chooseth to keep the coals and not send them to market, they may assign it as a sufficient cause for laying the pits off work for three days, and if we be set to work upon the fourth, we have no claim of any allowance

[1] In 1831 the Mayor of Newcastle estimated that the total number of pitmen employed on the Tyne and the Wear was 30,000 to 40,000 (H.O., 52. 14). Mr. Buddle before Lords' Committee on Coal Trade, 1829, gives 20,954 as the number.

[2] *Tyne Mercury*, April 12, 1831.

31

for the loss of such time. . . .' [1] The second grievance was the length of the hours worked by the boys : 'Again, another article binds the boys to work fourteen hours from starting at the crane and until ending at the same, which through the distances the crane is underground, keeps the boys sometimes seventeen hours from home, leaving them only seven or eight hours a day for every other purpose of life.'

The third grievance was the system of colliery houses by which the men and their families were dependent for shelter on signing the bond, for if 'we are not agreed for the ensuing year, or if we be legally discharged from the colliery, the owners, their agents or servants are empowered to enter such dwelling, turn us with our families and furniture to the door, without having recourse to the legal proceedings of the law.'

The fourth grievance was the system of fines already described. 'These measures we wish to have softened'; put in blunter language, the men wished for protection from fraud, especially with regard to false corves, for 'if the corves be made ever so much above their measurement, we are not allowed to have them adjusted, so that we have to guess when there is a sufficient quantity of coals in her, but if, when sent to bank, any corf be deficient, we lose the price of that corf altogether.'

Into the grievances connected with the 'tommy-shop' system the men did not enter; probably they felt strong enough to settle that question by themselves, on the lines of the resolution passed at their meeting. It is important to note that they did not actually threaten to strike, if their demands were not granted; they expressed their determination to refuse to be bound till they were satisfied, but were willing to continue working unbound, whilst their original plan was to send two delegates to London to state their case before the House of Commons. As the Mayor of Newcastle had offered to 'intercede' for them, they turned to him first.

The result of the Mayor's mediation was that the coal-owners passed certain resolutions on March 28.[2] They conceded a twelve-hours day for boys at the crane, ignored the three-day grievance, merely reiterating that a minimum of 28s. a fortnight should be guaranteed as before, suggested that in future the binding contract should be entered into in January, three months before it took effect, so that the men should have time to arrange about their houses if necessary, and refused to make any concessions in the matter of fines or honest dealing; the

[1] *Tyne Mercury*, April 12, 1831.   [2] *Ibid.*

fines ' being a necessary protection to the owners against negligence, or frauds.' No change in reference to the size of the corves, they said, was required, since a measure existed at the top of the pit. On the subject of the truck system they passed the following curiously worded resolution : ' That the workmen be paid their wages in money as has hitherto been the custom, and remain at liberty to supply themselves with candles, gunpowder, and shop goods, wherever they may think proper.' It is noteworthy that the *Tyne Mercury*, which represented the views of the coal-owners, forgetting that the week before it had denied the existence of any grievance on the ground that such a system would be illegal, hailed this abolition of ' tommy-shops' as an important concession. Finally the coal-owners resolved not to carry on any colliery after April 5 with unbound men.[1]

In answer to this, the pitmen replied that the masters had not met their point about the ' three-day' grievance, and they asked a question which showed that they had now raised their minimum terms, ' Is it unreasonable to ask for employment for eleven days in a fortnight at 3s. per day ? '[2] The masters retorted by an ingenious denial of the three-day grievance, showing that on paper it could not exist; however, they practically conceded the men's demands, agreeing that as there was some ambiguity in the wording, ' the intentions of the parties being the same,' the clause might be more clearly expressed.[3] This point settled, the dispute was narrowed down to two questions: (1) the demand for a 33s. minimum a fortnight ; (2) fraudulent fines. On the first question the coal-owners with bewildering logic affirmed in the same breath, first that the men already made higher wages than 33s. a fortnight, and could count on as much for the ensuing year, and secondly that if the men were bound on those terms only three-quarters of them would be engaged. Further, comparisons were drawn with the wages of other miners and those of other occupations. The fines they could not dispense with, ' but they may state that they are levied

---

[1] The Mayor of Newcastle told Sir H. Ross, who was in command there, that the coal-owners did not wish for an immediate settlement, but wanted the price of coals enhanced and hence offered terms unlikely to be accepted. Ross wrote : '. . . The terms they have offered to the pitmen are such as to be very beneficial to themselves if accepted, and if rejected (which they will be) they will be well content ' (H.O., 40. 29).

[2] *Newcastle Chronicle*, April 9.   [3] *Tyne Mercury*, April 12.

unwillingly and with every proper discrimination and for-
bearance.' Again the men demanded protection from fraud;
they asked not to be fined till the fault was shown before
witnesses on both sides, and to have ' the privilege of measur-
ing the Corves at any Time without previous Notice of their
Intention,' a demand which speaks for itself.[1]

For several weeks the dispute went on and the pits lay idle ; [2]
eleven magistrates not connected with the coal trade offered
their services as mediators without success, an offer deprecated
by the *Tyne Mercury* [3] as ' liable to produce an impression on un-
educated men that their complaints are well founded and must
be attended to.' In vain Lord Londonderry offered 30s. a fortnight to his pitmen, asking that the fines should ' be left to
his honour, and that of his agents.' [4] ' I conceived my colliers,'
he wrote afterwards [5] ' were really attached to the family and
their old establishment. I tried by addressing them (as well
as Lady Londonderry) to work upon their sense of justice and
regret as well as their affections.' At last both sides agreed
to a minimum of 30s. a fortnight, and the fines remained the
only point at issue. The *Tyne Mercury* [6] made the novel but
unfruitful suggestion that they should be used for a fund for
the education of the pitmen's children. Ultimately towards
the end of May it was decided that the several collieries should
treat separately with their own men. Lord Londonderry
started concessions ; [7] other coal-owners followed suit, and
by the middle of June all the pits were at work again.[8] The

---

[1] *Newcastle Chronicle*, April 16.   [2] See H.O., 52. 12, and 52. 14.
[3] April 12.
[4] *Newcastle Chronicle*, May 14. Lord Londonderry was criticised by the
Tyne Mercury (April 12) for joining with two other J.P.'s in issuing a warning
to the pitmen against assembling, acting violently, and deterring others from
working: 'it is not very decorous of the Marquis of Londonderry to put his
name as a magistrate to such a notice, when he is himself interested as a coal-
owner.'   [5] *Newcastle Chronicle*, June 11.
[6] May 3.   [7] H.O., 52. 14, and 40. 29.
[8] The Duke of Northumberland wrote to the H.O. on May 26 that work had
been resumed—' the occupiers having made their own terms respectively with
the refractory workmen, and thereby departed from the Union which they had
recently established in their own defence; whilst the original and imposing
Union of the Pitmen is in full authority and force. In many cases new covenants
have been made upon fair and tenable principles, abrogating some hard and
indefensible customs and giving an advance of wages upon an average of £10
per cent. In some cases a precipitate and absolute concession has been made to
the demands of the pitmen—more I apprehend in the eagerness of mercantile
zeal than from any positive and impending intimidation ' (H.O., 52. 14).

Tyne Mercury[1] thus summed up the result of the negotiations : ' Though it be true that the owners of each particular colliery have made the best terms they could for their own concern, it is quite clear that the servants have triumphed over their masters in the struggle.' The men in fact had won a twelve-hours day for the boys and for the inferior grades of labour, had raised their own guaranteed minimum 1s. a week, and had secured themselves against a system of fraud. For a few months there was peace.

The hero of the fight was Thomas Hepburn, a pitman at Hetton Colliery. The Union which had won the victory is commonly called Hepburn's Union, for he was its moving spirit, but it was not till August of this year (1831) that he was appointed a paid organiser to visit the different collieries.[2] Hepburn's watchwords which he reiterated to his followers at every meeting, with almost wearisome emphasis, were moderation and abstention from violence. On their orderly behaviour public sympathy depended, and public sympathy was an important factor, especially when it took the form of credit allowed by tradespeople to pitmen earning no wages. During the 1831 strike Hepburn was on the whole successful in enforcing orderly conduct ; some machinery indeed was destroyed at Blyth, Bedlington, and at Jesmond Dene, and soldiers were called out to protect the pits when blacklegs were working, but considering that 17,000 men were idle, and for the most part hungry, the absence of serious outrage was remarkable. Hepburn was a politician and he took a prominent part in the Reform agitation, speaking both at the dinner of the Northumberland Political Union in September, and at the great meeting in October on Newcastle Town Moor when 50,000 persons gathered together to demand Reform. The pitmen themselves, in all the pride of their recent victories, met in August at their usual meeting place, Boldon Fell, to the number of 10,000 or 12,000, and resolved to send a loyal address to the King ' thanking him for his beneficent attention to the wants of his people, for the Reform Bill, and for the support he had given to his ministers.' [3] The address which was dispatched to Lord Melbourne was signed by 11,561 workmen from fifty-seven collieries.

To understand the events of 1832 it is necessary to consider

---

[1] May 31.   [2] Sykes, *Local Records*, ii. p. 308.
[3] Sykes, *Local Records*, ii. p. 308; *Newcastle Chronicle*, August 20; *Tyne Mercury*, August 23.

the position of the coal-owners and their outlook on life. They
had been beaten and they dreaded the future. As early as
June 21, 1831, the perils of their position were put very ably
by an anonymous writer, under the pseudonym of ' Vindex,'
in the *Tyne Mercury*. The men, he reasoned, by the very
orderliness of their conduct, had shown themselves to be
powerful antagonists. ' Their minds were bent upon the
attainment of certain rights which they esteemed due to them,
and during a season of abject poverty and great distress they
have maintained those rights more by arguments and reason-
ings, than by tumults or disorders.' The delegates, he urged,
had been chosen with ' infinite discrimination,' and their
appeals to the public distinguished by art and ability. The
coal-owners, on the other hand, had played an ignominious
part : if the prosperity of the coal trade was not to pass away
they must rouse themselves and ' resist the exorbitant demands
of the pitmen. If the spirit of intimidation ever stalked abroad,
and if revolt was ever brewing, it is now.'[1]

The coal-owners, moreover, had lost something more substantial than prestige. During the year that followed April
1831 their profits fell, partly, no doubt, in consequence of the
strike ; partly, if unkind critics are to be trusted, in consequence of the new Coal Act, under which London coals were
sold by weight and not by measure.[2] By the use of false
bottoms in the boats masters had often packed on a boat,
supposed to carry 21 or 22 tons, as many as 27 to 30, thus
cheating the pitmen, the canal companies, and also the royalty
owners.[3] Another cause of diminished profits was the stricter
supervision of the men's corves or baskets. A writer who gave
the men's version of affairs in the *Newcastle Chronicle* of January
7, 1832, estimated that by the ' adjustment of corves ' after the
strike, from three to four keels a day less were frequently
wrought in a colliery: in other words, formerly ' the men were
frequently cheated out of three or four keels a day.' This
means, of course, that the men by working at the same piece
rates could now make the required sum in a shorter time.

With the object apparently of distributing the work equally
over different days and amongst the different workers, the

---

[1] Compare H.O., 40. 29 (H. Morton Lambton to General Bouverie on June
8, 1831): ' . . . the business of mining cannot be carried on for a great length
of time if the men remain in the present state of insubordination.'

[2] 1 & 2 William IV. c. lxxvi.

[3] *Tyne Mercury*, January 10, 1832, quoting from *Birmingham Journal*.

Union laid down a rule that no hewer should make more than 4s. a day.[1] On this the coal-owners seized as a serious grievance, attributing their losses largely to this diminished output. They stated boldly that two-thirds of the hewers made their 4s. in six hours, a statement vehemently denied by the men. Since the guaranteed minimum was 30s. for eleven days, and the owners admitted that eight hours was the customary day for a hewer, the statement on the face of it seems improbable. However this might be, many of the coal-owners believed that the men had passed that ' limit beyond which wages cannot be raised, because beyond it the employment of labour ceases to be profitable.' [2] The pitmen, wrote Mr. James Losh, a prominent colliery owner, on January 28,[3] have forced from their employers higher wages for shorter hours, consequently many collieries have made no profit, and many masters will soon cease employing men at all unless the men show a more reasonable spirit. Mr. Losh who represented, so to speak, the reasoning faculty on the employers' side, basing his arguments on large generalisations of political economy and on quotations from Holy Scripture, never wearied in assuring the pitmen that their own and their masters' interests were inseparably united, the masters being presumably the only judges of those interests. Comparisons with the wages of other occupations in the district and elsewhere fortified the belief that the pitmen were overpaid, and that by the law of supply and demand their remuneration must be reduced; thus we find Mr. Losh pointing out [4] that sailors and fishermen are worse paid for more dangerous occupations, lead, tin, and copper miners paid only half as much for as dangerous work, whilst the lot of South-country agricultural labourers should make the pitmen thankful for the many blessings they enjoy. Even the coal miners at Bilston were said to make only 8s. 7½d. a week when rent was deducted.[5]

Apart from these theoretical considerations the natural man in the employer was tempted by the supply of cheap labour available from the neighbouring lead mines, where 7s. or 8s. a week was the usual wage for men, who, if not engaged in precisely similar tasks, were at any rate working underground. Indeed the masters soon persuaded themselves that it was a positive charity to give these distressed lead

[1] H.O., 52. 14.   [2] *Tyne Mercury*, May 31, 1831.
[3] *Newcastle Chronicle*.   [4] *Newcastle Chronicle*, April 23, 1831.
[5] *Times*, December 9, quoted in *Tyne Mercury*, December 27, 1831.

miners work, and the objections of the pitmen to this course
were 'a heartless combination against their industrious but
starving fellow creatures.'[1] 'How absurd it is,' wrote Mr.
Losh,[2] 'to attempt to hinder men who are working for 8s. or
9s. per week, from removing thirty or forty miles, to places
where they can earn, with less labour, more than twice that
sum.   I will only add,' he went on, summing up the position
with obvious sincerity, 'that whoever advises the pitmen
to seek for unreasonable wages far above the average of the
district in which they live, or in any way to interfere with the
property or controul the operations of their employers, must
be very ignorant or very wicked ; and I think one may safely
conclude that they can neither be good Christians nor honest
men, who act themselves, or advise others to act, contrary to
the scripture rule of "doing unto others as you wish they
should do unto you."'

In the autumn of 1831 the cholera came creeping on towards
the North of England from Russia.   About the end of October
it appeared in Sunderland, from December till March of the next
year it devastated Newcastle, Gateshead, North Shields, and the
neighbouring colliery villages.   'It raged principally amongst
the lower orders whose dissolute habits and poverty rendered
them speedy victims to its direful attacks, most of them only
surviving a few hours.'[3]   At Newburn-on-Tyne out of a population of 550, 424 persons were attacked, of whom 57 died.
Public subscriptions were opened for the relief of the sufferers;[4]
but in spite of this the epidemic proved a severe drain on
the resources of the young Union, and left it without any
reserve funds to face the next conflict with the masters.   By
March 1832 no less than £10,000 had been paid out by the
Union for the relief of the sick and destitute ; in Hetton
alone £700 was subscribed by the men for the relief of the
sick.[5]

Meanwhile trouble of another sort was brewing.   At Callerton,
Coxlodge, and Waldridge lead miners were imported and the

[1] 'Publicola' in *Tyne Mercury*, December 13, 1831.

[2] *Newcastle Chronicle*, January 28, 1832.

[3] Sykes, *Local Records*, ii. p. 323.

[4] To the Sunderland Fund Lord Londonderry sent £100 with 'a very feeling letter,' Lord Durham £100 and 1100 tons of coal.   'Such philanthropy,'
wrote the *Tyne Mercury*, December 20, 1831, 'better becomes their rank than
the brightest coronets they can boast.'

[5] See account of Union Meeting of March 3 in *Newcastle Chronicle*, March
10, 1832.

pitmen refused to work with them ; at Waldridge the angry
coal miners stopped the engine and endangered the lives of the
lead miners working below. The Union had nothing to do
with any of these affairs ; indeed at Waldridge the delegates
did their best to prevent mischief, and the Union sided with
the masters in the original matter of dispute : the refusal of
the pitmen, in defiance of their bond, to accept the prices fixed
for a new seam. The Union's policy was clearly stated by
Hepburn : ' It was wrong for men to combine and prevent
others from working, when they had got work in a legal manner.
. . . By the articles into which they had lately entered, though
they bound themselves to the maintenance and support of
each other, they could not hinder any one from working with
them.' [1] Again he urged strongly that when once the bond
was entered into it must be kept, and whoever broke it would
be punished.[2] The law indeed provided penalties, and various
pitmen from the above-mentioned collieries were sent to prison
for three months' hard labour because they had deserted their
work.

The case of Coxlodge was particularly hard. By an oral
agreement at the binding time, it was arranged that as
more workmen had been bound than could be employed at
Coxlodge, the surplus men from Coxlodge should go to Gosforth (a less profitable pit for the workers), but that they should
have the first claim if extra labour was required at Coxlodge.[3]
In defiance of this understanding, when extra labour was
wanted at Coxlodge, the owner imported low-paid lead miners.
The pitmen already employed at Coxlodge, finding their remonstrances ignored, struck work. Some were sent to prison, the
rest had their indentures cancelled, and soldiers were called
in to evict them from their houses. When the doors of
their cottages had been nailed up, they at last appealed to
the Union. Delegates from that body made an investigation and passed the following unheroic resolution : ' That the
dispute having terminated in a manner highly prejudicial to
the men, and in a way which cannot but be also injurious
to the masters, a deputation from this meeting be appointed
to wait on the Rev. Mr. Brandling, the owner, to solicit him to
continue to employ those men who may be willing to remain.' [4]

[1] *Newcastle Chronicle*, August 20, 1831.
[2] *Ibid.*, March 10, 1832.
[3] *Ibid.*, January 17, 1832.
[4] *Ibid.*, January 28, 1832.

But the men concerned rejected this proposal by 108 votes
to 34. ' Is it to be believed,' urged the Union Committee in
its appeal to the public, ' that a large body of sober, industrious
men (and in the whole district there is not a more sober and
industrious body than was lately at Coxlodge) would without
provocation, without ill treatment, without witnessing violation
of contracts, wantonly abandon their work, to experience,
with their families, all the misery of houseless penury ? ' [1]
It is not surprising that bitter words were uttered about the
minister of the Gospel who had so merged the Christian in
the employer as to turn these families adrift at a time when
cholera was raging.

Into the intricacies of the 1832 quarrel between masters
and men it is unnecessary to enter; overseers and pitmen gave
their different versions of the same affair, anonymous writers
on both sides sent long letters to the Press, charge was followed
by countercharge, statement by denial with bewildering
rapidity. Conditions varied at different pits, and technicalities often obscured the issues. Early in the year some of
the masters began to threaten the deputy overseers and others
with a loss of their places at the next binding unless they
consented to leave the Union. The policy of the Union, as
formulated by Hepburn on March 3, was to support all those
who lost their places from the caprice of their masters and to
refuse to supply their places ; [2] but not, as was often afterwards stated, to refuse to be bound altogether.

On March 10 a general meeting of coal-owners on the Tyne
and Wear, with Robert W. Brandling in the chair, issued what
can only be described as a provocative manifesto in view of
the approaching binding time.[3] After a fantastic computa-
tion of the loss to the coal trade by the 1831 dispute and the
diminished output, they described the introduction of the
lead miners, their happiness, and the excellence of their work.
' These facts are most important, as they prove beyond the
possibility of doubt, that the Pitmen formerly employed could
have been neither overworked nor ill-paid.' Their disputes
in fact were due not to grievances but to a secret combination, and the Waldridge affair was cited as an illustration.
Beyond issuing this declaration, the coal-owners seem to have
taken no concerted action at the binding time. In about half

---

[1] *Newcastle Chronicle*, January 28, 1832.
[2] *Ibid.*, March 10, 1832.
[3] *Ibid.*, March 17, 1832.

the pits, including Lord Durham's and Lord Londonderry's, the men were bound as usual on the same conditions as the previous year.   In the other half, difficulties arose, with the result that April 5 passed and the pits lay idle and eight thousand men were out of work.   The point of dispute at most pits was the refusal of the owners to bind 'the deputies, shifters, bankmen, and enginemen,' or the more prominent members, unless they deserted the Union.   In some cases their comrades refused to be bound without them.   At some pits the men tried, as was the custom at binding time, to get some particular grievance remedied.   In some, no doubt, unreasonable demands were made, as at Hetton, where some of the younger men asked for the dismissal of the viewer.

It is clear that there was no uniform demand for higher wages or better conditions : the Union's policy was to keep what had already been won.   As the dispute went on it became a commonplace on the masters' side that the quarrel had begun because the men demanded higher wages : the men invariably denied this ;   the explanation of this contradiction is perhaps to be found in a sentence in the *Tyne Mercury*,[1] where after repeating that the men had struck for higher wages the writer naïvely adds : ' This they have not said in words, but they have required more privileges than they previously had, which is equivalent to demanding a higher price for their labour.' On the other hand, the men declared that various collieries were offering reduced wages, a fact which the *Tyne Mercury* admitted might be true, excusing it on the grounds of reduced profits.   But whatever the original causes of dispute at the various collieries, by the middle of May the issue had become clear and simple ;   the policy of all the coal-owners whose pits still lay idle became identical ;   they refused to bind any men unless they deserted the Union.   It was a life and death struggle for the right to combine.

In the early days of the strike the men's hopes ran high. They were as confident as the coal-owners that God was on their side.   A resolution at one of their meetings in April was worded thus : ' That as oppressed people, in every age of the world, when united, had confounded their enemies, we act in conjunction with the example of such ancients and moderns, as have withstood and overcome their enemies.' [2]   At the same meeting one speaker outlined a proposal for a great

[1] April 10, 1832.   [2] *Newcastle Chronicle*, April 21.

general union to spread over the whole country.[1] 'It would
be an excellent thing if this could be brought about, union
would go forth, and religion would follow, and moral degradation be banished from the earth, and the world become
evangelised.' When several weeks had passed their growing
bitterness was expressed in somewhat grandiloquent language :
'That as our opponents are all alive to our destruction, we,
the objects of their antipathy, resort to every auxiliary within
our reach to frustrate their diabolical design.'[2]

How were the eight thousand unemployed pitmen supported
during their long struggle ?   As we have seen, the cholera had
depleted the Union funds, but half the pits were still at work,
and in them the Unionists, out of every £1 earned, contributed
6s. to the support of their comrades :[3] a further proof in the
masters' eyes, if one were wanted, that the wages paid were
excessive.

Meanwhile lead miners and others were being brought into
the district to take the place of the Unionists in pit and
cottage.   Evictions were carried out with the aid of soldiers
and angry passions let loose.[4] At Hetton, where ejections
first took place on an extensive scale, a pitman Errington,
who with two others had deserted the Union, was found
murdered.   At Friars Goose the ejection was accompanied by
a serious affray.   The signal was given by a pitman's wife,
Elizabeth Carr, who refused to move, was carried to the door
on a chair, seized the hat of a policeman, flourished it above
her head and cheered on the exasperated mob.   The justice
dispensed by the authorities was rough, and the indignities
suffered by the rioters were not likely to pacify the feelings
of men already embittered by the loss of home and work.
Special constables were sworn in and instructed to arrest
miners whenever they found them standing together, and to
lock them up in the colliery stables or empty houses.   'Some
of them were bound hand and foot against the mangers in
the stalls all night, with neither food nor water, and if they
attempted to make the least resistance, a cutlass or pistol
was held to their faces.   It was not the riotous and disorderly
persons that were mostly punished, but chiefly those who had
been taking leading parts in the union, and who had taken

---

[1] They seem to have had no connection with the National Association for the
Protection of Labour. See *Town Labourer*, pp. 311 f.

[2] *Newcastle Courant*, June 2.

[3] H.O., 40. 30.   [4] *Ibid.*

no part whatever in the disorders.'[1] It was in vain that Hepburn urged the unbound men not to go near the collieries where other men were at work, and above all to keep their wives from interfering in matters with which they had nothing to do.[2] The wives might well have answered that they were pretty intimately concerned with measures that turned them out of house and home, and they certainly showed their feelings in vigorous fashion : thus when some lead miners were being marched to their new abodes at the Tyne Main and Friars Goose they were ' assailed in Gateshead by the pitmen's wives, who not only " cudgelled " them with their tongues, but threw stones at them.'[3] In many cases the owners added to the hardships of eviction by publishing at the same time the clauses in the Vagrancy Act which proclaimed penalties for encamping in the open air or under a tent.[4]

Whilst the unruly strikers were breaking the heads of the lead miners, the orderly strikers were publishing accounts of their incompetence, which were promptly contradicted by the masters. In this connection it is interesting to read in the 1842 Mines Report[5] that the newcomers are said to have been unsatisfactory, and that by 1842 hardly one remained in the district.

Competent or incompetent, the tide of supplanters flowed steadily in from Wales, from Staffordshire, and from Yorkshire ; by June about two thousand had already entered the district.[6] Still the strikers kept up a bold front, and at their meeting on June 16, when the strike had lasted ten weeks, Hepburn declared that they must be out for another ten, after which their services would be needed at the busy time, and they would win.'[7] Meanwhile a tragic event which struck the public imagination prejudiced their cause. On June 11, Mr. Fairles, an old magistrate of seventy, was accosted when on horseback by two pitmen who asked for money for a drink. Angry words passed, blows followed, and in the end Mr. Fairles was left brutally wounded in the ditch. Eleven days later he died. Jobling, the man who had first addressed him, was arrested and afterwards hung. His corpse was exposed in chains on a gibbet until, to the public relief, it was

---

[1] Fynes, *Miners of Northumberland and Durham*, pp. 28, 29.
[2] *Newcastle Chronicle*, June 2.   [3] *Tyne Mercury*, May 8.
[4] *Newcastle Chronicle*, May 26.   [5] Appendix, Part i.
[6] Losh in *Newcastle Chronicle*, June 2.   [7] *Newcastle Chronicle*, June 23.

stolen away. Armstrong, who had committed the actual assault, was never found, though tradition said he was at large in the district till after Jobling's execution. Like all other crimes and misdeeds this assault was attributed to the Union. 'I am afraid,' said Mr. Justice Parke, in sentencing Jobling,[1] 'that this is one of those melancholy circumstances which are occasioned by that combination which has prevailed in this county so long—one of the unlawful effects, and we have witnessed many—arising out of a combination, alike injurious to the public weal and the private interests of all who are concerned in it. It is to that combination that I attribute that utter want of moral feeling which induced you to stand by and assist another in inflicting that mortal wound which led to the death of the deceased.' George Weddle, a policeman who had killed a miner named Skipsy, was sentenced at the same Assizes as Jobling to six months' imprisonment.[2] Skipsy had been trying to make peace in a quarrel between miners and constables when Weddle shot him dead.

Perhaps the most striking illustration of the heavy odds against which the Union was fighting for recognition is conveyed in the letter from Lord Melbourne to the magistrates of the district:[3]

WHITEHALL, *July* 16, 1832.

SIR,—I am commanded by his Majesty to call your most serious and immediate attention to the state of the colliery districts in the county of Durham.

It appears that, for some time past, extensive and determined combinations and conspiracies have been formed and entered into by the workmen, for the purpose of dictating to their masters the rate of wages at which they shall be employed, the hours during which they shall work, the quantity of labour which they shall perform, as well as for imposing upon them many other regulations relating to the conduct and management of their trade and concerns.

In pursuance of this system, and in furtherance and support of these demands, which are as unwise and injurious to the authors of them as they are violent and unjust in themselves, tumultuous assemblages of people have been gathered together, to the great danger of the public peace, at which the most seditious and inflammatory discourses have been delivered, and the most illegal resolutions adopted.

The natural consequences of such proceedings have shown

[1] *Newcastle Chronicle*, August 4.   [2] *Tyne Mercury*, August 7.
[3] *Newcastle Courant*, July 28, 1832.

themselves in outrages of the most atrocious character, in menaces and intimidation, in the injury and maltreating of peaceable and industrious labourers, so as to endanger their lives,—and in the commission of murder in the face of open day.

In these circumstances I am commanded by his Majesty to express his confident expectation, that all who hold the commission of the peace will act with the promptitude, decision, and firmness which are so imperatively required, and that they will exert themselves for the prevention and suppression of all meetings which shall be called together for an illegal purpose, or which shall, in the course of their proceedings, become illegal; for the detection and punishment of all unlawful combination and conspiracy, as well as of all outrage and violence; and for the encouragement and protection of his Majesty's peaceable and well-disposed subjects.— I have the honour to be, sir, your humble servant,   MELBOURNE.

As the summer passed secessions became more frequent, and the ardour of the contributors to the strike fund cooled. Six shillings in the pound was a heavy tax when no end seemed in sight.   By August 28 one hundred men in Lord Durham's pits refused to pay any longer.[1]   Others soon followed suit.   On September 1 the Union held its last meeting at Boldon Fell. They were willing to alter their rules to meet the employers' wishes provided they might continue as a society.   But no compromise could be accepted, the 'monstrous System of Violence and Insubordination' must cease to exist.   'By the Introduction of Workmen of more upright Principles, and with more correct Notions of the Rights and relative Duties of Masters and Servants,' the coal-owners, they were told, hoped to prevent the recurrence of these disgraceful scenes.[2] The Union was beaten; on September 20 it was formally dissolved.[3]

All through that summer and autumn over Northumberland and Durham there were rejoicings for the passing of the Reform Bill, public dinners, the ringing of bells, and a proud display of banners with appropriate mottoes: 'A day of liberty is worth an eternity of bondage.'   'United we stand, divided we fall.'   'Fortune follows the Brave.'   As winter approached, Hepburn, shunned by those men whom he had led to disaster, spurned by the men who had proved faithless to their cause, wandered about in the bitterness of failure,

[1] *Tyne Mercury.*
[2] R. W. Brandling to J. Losh, *Newcastle Chronicle*, September 8, 1832.
[3] H.O., 40. 30.

a ragged hawker of tea whose wares no one would buy.   Driven by hunger, he sued for work at the Felling colliery, and was told it would only be given him if he promised to have no more to do with Unions.   He paused, consented, and kept his word.[1]   Perhaps the darkness of his days was lightened by the vision of the future pictured in almost his last public speech : ' If we have not been successful, at least we, as a body of miners, have been able to bring our grievances before the public ; and the time will come when the golden chain which binds the tyrants together will be snapped, when men will be properly organised, when coal-owners will only be like ordinary men, and will have to sigh for the days gone by.   It only needs time to bring this about.' [2]

[1] He lived till 1873 ; see Fynes, *op. cit.*, p. 36.
[2] Fynes, *op. cit.*, p. 36.

CHAPTER IV

THE COTTON WORKERS

1760-1818

THE history of the cotton industry is often regarded as an epitome of the Industrial Revolution, for it presents in a clear and striking form all the features of that Revolution. Unlike older industries it was unhampered by traditions or restrictions —except such restrictions as its rival the woollen trade could succeed in imposing on it—for ancient industrial regulations were discredited by the time it grew up; it rose in an incredibly short time from a small struggling trade to become England's leading industry; it was centralised in the Lancashire district, changing the whole character of that district; it was the chief field for the application of the mechanical inventions of the period. A few figures will illustrate the rapidity of its growth.

In 1764 the import of cotton wool into Great Britain was 3,870,392 lbs.; in 1833 it had risen to 303,726,199 lbs.[1]

At the Coronation of George III. in 1761, representatives of the principal trades of Manchester walked in procession through the streets; tailors marched in that pageant, worsted weavers, woolcombers, shoemakers, dyers, joiners, silk weavers, and hatters; but there were no cotton weavers or manufacturers,[2] and yet by 1774 there were probably about 30,000 persons in and round Manchester engaged in the cotton industry.[3] By 1787 some 162,000 persons were employed in that industry in Great Britain:[4] by 1831 these numbers had risen to 833,000.[5]

It is with this multitude of workers and with the vicissitudes of their fortunes that we are concerned, and we shall deal with the development of the industry and the application of mechanical inventions only in so far as they affected the workpeople.

The early history of the use of cotton is largely a history of

---

[1] Baines, *History of Cotton Manufacture*, pp. 109, 111.
[2] Aston, *A Picture of Manchester*, p. 19.
[3] Chapman, *The Lancashire Cotton Industry*, Manchester, 1904, p. 3.
[4] Baines, *op cit.*, p. 219.   [5] Baines, *op cit.*, p. 218, quoting M'Culloch.

the attempts of the old-established woollen trade to strangle its young rival.   In the seventeenth century only coarse cotton fabrics were made in England, but with the development of colonial commerce in the latter part of the seventeenth century fine cotton goods were imported in considerable quantities from India and the East.[1]   Indian calicoes, muslins, and chintzes took the fancy of the elegant world and ' the liberty of the ladies, their *passion* for their *fashion* ' [2] was blamed as destructive to the old silk and woollen manufactures of England.

The vagaries of fashion are amusingly described by Defoe in 1708 : ' . . . such is the power of a mode as we saw our persons of quality dressed in Indian carpets, which but a few years before their chambermaids would have thought too ordinary for them ; the chints was advanced from lying upon their floors to their backs, from the foot-cloth to the petticoat ; and even the queen herself at this time was pleased to appear in China and Japan, I mean China silks and callico.' [3]

The appeals that were made to patriotic sentiment on behalf of silk or wool were unsuccessful, and to protect the woollen trade against this competition an Act was passed in 1700 prohibiting the introduction of Indian silks and printed calicoes for domestic use, either as apparel or furniture, under a penalty of £200 on the wearer or seller.[4]   But this drastic Act was ineffective ; goods were smuggled in or else calicoes were manufactured in India and printed or dyed in England.   In 1720 another attempt was made to destroy the trade.   An Act [5] was passed which entirely prohibited the use of any ' printed, painted, stained, or dyed calico ' for clothing or for furniture under the penalty of £5 in the case of clothing, £20 in the case of furniture.   Cotton goods made with warp of another material, if printed or dyed, were prohibited.   Calicoes dyed all blue and muslins, neckcloths, and fustians were excepted.   Now English cotton goods were in those early days made with linen or woollen warp, for the English fingers could not match the suppleness of the fingers of the Hindoos or spin a sufficiently fine strong thread for the warp ; they could only produce in fact a ' mongrel manufacture.'

Doubts arose as to the scope of this Act, and it was argued

---

[1] Mantoux, *La Révolution Industrielle au xviiie siècle.*
[2] *A Plan of the English Commerce,* 1728, quoted by Baines, *op. cit.,* p. 80.
[3] Quoted by Baines, *op. cit.,* p. 79.
[4] 11 & 12 William III. c. 10; see Baines, *op. cit.,* p. 79.
[5] 7 George I. c. 7 ; see Baines, *op. cit.,* p. 166.

by some that fustians came under it. These doubts were set at rest in 1736 by an Act which legalised the use of fustians.[1] Pure calico goods if printed or dyed were still prohibited and remained prohibited till 1774 when, owing to the exertions of Arkwright, who was producing pure cotton goods of this description, and in spite of the opposition of the other Lancashire manufacturers, the prohibition was repealed.[2] The efforts of the woollen trade to retain its position had failed and cotton had to a great extent superseded silk, so that by 1785 it could be said 'Women of all ranks, from the highest to the lowest, are clothed in British manufactures of cotton, from the muslin cap on the crown of the head, to the cotton stocking under the sole of the foot.'[3]

The New Machinery

Our period is the period of the great mechanical inventions that revolutionised trade and the workers' lives, and it will be necessary to give some account of them. In 1760 cotton was carded and spun by hand in the spinsters' own houses, and woven at hand-looms in the weavers' houses. By 1830 hand-spinning was dead, and all the processes previous to weaving were carried on by complicated machinery in factories, whilst weaving was partly done in factories, by power-looms worked by girls, but partly still by hand-loom weavers in their own houses.

In 1733 John Kay, a native of Bury but an inhabitant of Colchester, had invented the flying shuttle,[4] a device by which the weaver could pull a string and so send the shuttle on its course through the web, without throwing it himself by hand. By this invention one man could manage a wide loom alone whereas previously it was necessary to have a man each side of the loom. Kay's invention, like many other inventions, was unpopular with the workers, but it made its way, and by 1760 it was in general use for cotton weaving, causing a considerable increase in the demand for yarn. The weavers in fact wanted more yarn than the spinners could supply.[5] New markets were opening in Germany, Italy, and North America; the merchants pressed the weavers, the weavers in their turn

---

[1] 9 George II. c. 4; see Baines, *op. cit.*, p. 167.
[2] 14 George III. c. 72; Baines, *op. cit.*, p. 168.
[3] Macpherson, *Annals of Commerce*, quoted by Baines, p. 336.
[4] Mantoux, *op. cit.*, p. 198.
[5] Ure, *Cotton Manufacture of Great Britain*, i. p. 192.

pressed the spinners.   The system of production at this time is described by Ure :

'The workshop of the weaver was a rural cottage, from which when he was tired of sedentary labour he could sally forth into his little garden, and with the spade or the hoe tend its culinary productions.   The cotton wool which was to form his weft was picked clean by the fingers of his younger children, and was carded and spun by the older girls assisted by his wife, and the yarn was woven by himself assisted by his sons.   When he could not procure within his family a supply of yarn adequate to the demands of his loom, he had recourse to the spinsters of his neighbourhood.   One good weaver could keep three active women at work upon the wheel, spinning weft.' [1]

The troubles of the weaver trudging round several miles to procure his yarn are described : ' he was often obliged to treat the females with presents in order to quicken their diligence at the wheel.' [2]

This was a satisfactory state of things for the spinsters but it did not last long, for three inventions, Hargreaves' spinning-jenny, Arkwright's water frame, and Crompton's mule turned the tables, and unworked yarn was soon produced faster than the weavers could consume it.   Instead of being scarce and a prize, yarn became an important article of export.   These inventions must be briefly described.

The spinning-jenny invented by James Hargreaves about 1765, though not patented till 1770, was a multiplied wheel. One spindle alone was worked by the ordinary spinning wheel, but Hargreaves' invention made it possible to work first eight and afterwards as many as one hundred spindles by a single wheel.   The output was enormously increased, but the structure of the industry was not altered as the jennies could be worked at home.   Arkwright's water frame, on the other hand, patented in 1769, revolutionised the character of the trade.

It is impossible here to give even in outline the remarkable story of Arkwright's career, how he rose from a travelling barber who bought country girls' locks, dyed them with a special secret dye and sold them to wig-makers, to be a knight and a High Sheriff worth half a million ; nor can we discuss the vexed question of the precise credit due to him, how far he picked other men's brains, how far the inventions he patented

[1] Ure, *op. cit.*, i. p. 191.   [2] Ure, *op. cit.*, i. p. 193.

were his own. As it has been well put, his history as an inventor is obscure, his history as a manufacturer is clear.[1]

A process of spinning by means of passing the material to be spun through rollers had been invented and patented by Wyatt and Paul as early as 1738, and establishments where the process could be worked had been set up, but they had all failed. Those establishments can be regarded as the real ancestors of the cotton-spinning factories. No attempts were made for many years to introduce the process, and roller spinning remained an idle discovery till Arkwright took out a patent for a roller-spinning frame, worked by water power, in 1769. This water frame, as it was called, produced a stronger thread than the wheels or jennies, a thread that could be used for warp ; thus it was now possible to manufacture pure cotton goods, unmixed with linen, and, as we have seen, Parliament was petitioned to withdraw the prohibition on these goods.

In 1775 Arkwright took out another patent for a series of machines, for the subsidiary processes of carding, drawing, and roving. In the lawsuits which Arkwright brought later against rivals whom he accused of infringing his patents, each of the several methods he patented was claimed by some other inventor, and in the final trial the verdict was given against him. Whatever his claims as an inventor, he possessed at all events an unrivalled power of working other people's ideas, and it was he, more than any other single man, who brought the cotton-spinning industry into the factory system. For some time water frames in factories producing warp, and jennies in houses producing weft, worked on side by side. ' The jenny,' it has been well put, ' simply multiplied human hands, while the water frame was a substitute for human skill,'[2] but not for human skill exercised in the cotton industry, since the warp produced by the frames had previously been made of linen or wool.

The third of the inventions, the mule, was invented by Samuel Crompton in 1779. Crompton was the antithesis of Arkwright. A quiet man of inventive genius but without any administrative or business ability, he devised his new machine after some years' work in his ancestral yeoman's house near Bolton. The machine was called a mule because it borrowed features from the water frame and from the jenny. It had both rollers and spindles, and produced a finer and

[1] Mantoux, *op. cit.*, p. 214.   [2] Chapman, *op. cit.*, p. 53.

stronger thread than any that could be spun before. It made
the production of fine muslins possible, and thus established
a new branch of the cotton industry in England. Crompton
worked his mule by hand in his garret, but the quality of the
yarn he sold was so excellent that neighbours soon began to
pry into his secrets. Ladders were placed against his house,
and holes were made in the walls for inquisitive eyes. Crompton
lacked the money or the business enterprise to take out a
patent, and was persuaded to give up his secret in return for
a voluntary subscription. The story of Crompton's career
reflects little credit on his hard-headed rivals. The original
subscription list amounted to £67, 6s. 6d., but not all of this
was paid ; after the mule had been brought into general use,
when the new muslin industry had grown up in Bolton, Paisley,
and Glasgow, and was making huge fortunes for others, a
further subscription of £500 was raised for Crompton. In
1812, Parliament, treating him much less generously than the
undistinguished relative of a successful politician, voted him
the sum of £5000, but the several business enterprises in
which he invested his money came to grief, and he died a
poor and disappointed man.

The original mules, as we have said, were worked by hand ;
gin-horses were sometimes used and water power was applied
to them about 1790, but it was only slowly that jennies or
mules passed into factories, and ' for many years the typical
jenny- or mule-factory remained small,' [1] and men would
start with one mule in a loft, adding others gradually.[2] For
Arkwright's water frames, on the other hand, water power, large
mills, and considerable capital were essential. It must be remembered that any new invention takes time to supersede its rivals,
the structure of an industry does not change in a day or a year,
and the introduction of the mule did not mean that jennies
disappeared, though it ultimately took their place and, in a
perfected form, superseded the water frame. Hence during
the last twenty years or so of the eighteenth century, whilst
the cotton industry was increasing by leaps and bounds, there
were large mills or factories, built where water power was
plentiful on country rivers, producing warp by means of
Arkwright's water frames, whilst jennies and mules were pro-

[1] Chapman, *op. cit.*, p. 59.
[2] Robert Owen, for example, in 1789 started by taking a factory and sub-
letting all but one room where he employed three men on three hand-mules
(see Chapman, *op. cit.*, p. 60).

ducing the weft in dwelling houses or small establishments. Larger businesses, however, were gradually replacing the smaller and steam power was also beginning to supplant water power. Meanwhile the weavers, a growing and a prosperous body of men, were working in their own houses, turning the yarn into cotton goods.

The class of labour required by the different machines varied. Before the inventions already described, spinning, as we have seen, had been a woman's industry with children helping in the subsidiary processes. The factories or mills were now worked by child labour, chiefly prentice labour, with a few unskilled men or women ; in the case of the jennies and mules, on the other hand, skilled men's work gradually replaced the labour of women and children. Jennies with eight or twelve spindles were worked by children, but when jennies were larger and mules more complicated, it became more economical to employ skilled men ; hence we have, side by side with the exploitation of child labour, the growth of a small skilled aristocracy of spinners, who followed the machines into the factories. Their conditions, wages, and outlook present a marked contrast to those of the weavers.

The conditions of the child labour in the factories are discussed elsewhere ; [1] we must here consider the attitude of the adult workers to these new inventions.

Men and women who see their livelihood taken from them or threatened by some new invention, can hardly be expected to grow enthusiastic over the public benefits of inventive genius. A larger view and a vivid imagination may teach them that the loss to their particular occupation may be temporary only ; but then, as it has been remarked, man's life is temporary also.[2] The indignant spinsters of Blackburn with their friends broke open Hargreaves' house and destroyed his jennies, and Hargreaves was thus driven from his native county to find a more peaceful home for his inventions at Nottingham. In 1779 there was a more systematic attack upon the new machines, directed especially against the new series of machines for carding, roving, etc., patented by Arkwright in 1775. Trade was depressed in consequence of the war with America, and the new factories and the jennies that turned a number of spindles were looked on as partly responsible for

[1] See *Town Labourer*, chap. viii.
[2] Hobson, *Evolution of Modern Capitalism*, 1906, p. 328.

the want of work. Arkwright, who had started his career as
an organiser of factories at Nottingham where he found the
necessary capital, had afterwards set up mills in Derbyshire.
For his different enterprises he enlisted different partners but
he was careful to manage the whole business himself. About
1776 he tried his luck in Lancashire, providing the machinery
for a mill erected at Birkacre near Chorley. But the people
of Lancashire were hostile. ' Upon the fourth day of October
last,' stated one of the proprietors in a petition for redress to
Parliament, ' a most riotous and outrageous Mob assembled
in the Neighbourhood, armed in a warlike Manner, and after
breaking down the Doors of the Buildings, they entered the
Rooms, destroyed most of the Machinery, and afterwards set
fire to and consumed the whole Buildings, and every Thing
therein contained.' [1] The damage he estimated at £4400,
the sum actually spent on the undertaking.

At the first attack, on Sunday, the proprietors put up a
fight and two of the assailants were killed and eight wounded,
but the mob returned next day in overwhelming force.[2] Josiah
Wedgwood, who happened to be travelling through the district
at the time, estimated their numbers at eight thousand, and
noted that the Duke of Bridgewater's miners were amongst
them.[3] The works of the elder Peel (father of the first
Baronet) at Altham were also visited, and the machinery constructed on Arkwright's processes destroyed. Peel retired in
disgust to Burton-on-Trent and built mills there instead.[4]
Wigan, Bolton, Blackburn, Preston, and Manchester were all
visited or threatened by mobs who destroyed in those districts
all jennies with more than twenty spindles, leaving those with
twenty and fewer spindles, which they held to be a ' fair
machine ' as it could be used in a cottage.[5] Ultimately the
rioters were stopped by the appearance of military force, but
it is clear that there was much private sympathy with
their objects. It was alleged by the *Edinburgh Review* many
years later [6] that the Birkacre mill was destroyed ' in the
presence of a powerful body of police and military without
any one of the civil authorities requiring them to interfere to

[1] *House of Commons Journal*, June 27, 1780.
[2] *Annual Register*, 1779; *Chronicle*, p. 229.
[3] See Mantoux, *op. cit.*, p. 418.
[4] W. Cooke Taylor, *Life and Times of Sir Robert Peel*, pp. 7-9.
[5] Chapman, *op. cit.*, p. 76; Baines, *op. cit.*, p. 159.
[6] *Edinburgh Review*, June 1827, p. 14.

prevent so scandalous an outrage.' This may be a myth, but it must be remembered that Arkwright was intensely unpopular with other manufacturers, and that the landed class were afraid that the poor rates would be burdened with persons thrown out of work by the new inventions.[1] At Wigan the magistrates, principal inhabitants, and manufacturers met and agreed to suspend the use of all machines and engines worked by water or horses for carding, roving, or spinning, till the determination of Parliament on the subject was known.[2] The Quarter Sessions at Preston, however, passed resolutions on the advantages of machinery and the dangers of competition from other counties if its progress were checked. They went on to ask for a special commission to try the rioters lying in Lancaster gaol.[3] The request was refused, as the Law Officers reported that there were only two persons, Richard Haslam and Samuel Parkinson, against whom it was possible to bring a capital charge.[4]

The extent of public sympathy with the rioters is illustrated by the tone of the petition sent up to Parliament next spring by the cotton spinners and others of Lancashire. The petition is interesting, as it is perhaps the only document expressing the workers' opinions about the new changes. The petitioners explain that in addition to the distress caused by the American dispute and by the war with Spain, events which have caused a ' casual Diminution of Commerce,' ' a Domestic Evil of very great Magnitude ' has sprung up during the last few years in the form of the introduction of patent machines threatening the petitioners with a total loss of employment. They do not hesitate to avow their share in the Riots ; last September, they declare, their sufferings became so ' intolerable as to reduce them to Despair, and many Thousands assembled in different Parts to destroy the Causes of their Distress ' and demolished one of the largest patent machines together with some smaller ones. They recall the resolutions of the magistrates and manufacturers of Wigan, declare that the work produced by machines is inferior to hand work, and call the machines a mere monopoly ' for the immense Profits and Advantages of the Patentees and Proprietors.'[5]

[1] Baines, *op. cit.*, p. 160.
[2] *House of Commons Journal*, April 27, 1780 : Petition of Cotton Spinners.
[3] *Annual Register*, 1779; *Chronicle*, p. 233.
[4] H.O. Dom. (George III. 13).
[5] *House of Commons Journal*, April 27, 1780.

A Parliamentary Committee investigated their complaints and reported in favour of machinery.[1] The cotton masters gave evidence of the enormous increase in the cotton manufacture during the last ten years ; the looms, they said, had increased to three times their former number, and the weavers could not be supplied with warp if the machinery were stopped, whilst a jenny spinner could make 2s. or 2s. 6d. a day in contrast to the 3d. or 4d. a day made by a spinner with one spindle. The spinners, on the other hand, stated that though a woman could now only make 3d. or 5d. a day with one spindle, sixteen years ago she could earn from 10d. to 1s. 3d. a day, whilst the earnings on jennies of twenty-four spindles had also gone down. They reiterated their belief that the work was better done by small jennies than by large ones, and added a significant complaint that marks the rise of the new order of capitalism: ' the Jenneys are in the Hands of the Poor and the Patent Machines are generally in the Hands of the Rich.'

After these riots in 1779 the workers made no more attempts to check the introduction of machinery for spinning. The reason no doubt lies in the fact that whenever any labour was displaced by the introduction of any particular species of machinery for spinning, it was soon absorbed by an expansion of trade.[2] Many of the economists of the day, with this example before them, came to think that the introduction of machinery would be a similarly painless process in every case. The weaving trade offered employment to any surplus labour from spinning. The mills with ' patent machines ' to which the petitioners of 1780 objected continued to grow in number and size. Not only did Arkwright set up new establishments, but he sold his machines or permission to use them to ' numbers of adventurers, residing in the different counties of Derby, Leicester, Nottingham, Worcester, Stafford, York, Hertford, and Lancaster.'[3] By 1782 Arkwright estimated that ' a business was formed, which already employed upwards of five thousand persons, and a capital on the whole of not less than £200,000.' In addition to this there were numbers of unauthorised mills set up in defiance of the patent. In the lawsuit over the validity of the patent the counsel opposed to Arkwright

---

[1] See *House of Commons Journal*, June 27, 1780.

[2] Chapman, *op. cit.*, p. 74.

[3] Baines, *op. cit.*, p. 183, quoting Arkwright's 'Case.' These attempts to localise the cotton industry in other counties were a failure.

described these unauthorised mills as employing 30,000 persons and a capital of some £300,000.[1]

It will perhaps be convenient to trace here briefly the further changes in the cotton-spinning industry during our period. The cardinal change is the introduction of steam power to work the machinery. When Watt's steam engine was perfected, and it was no longer necessary to place mills on streams, machinery was attracted back to towns. The first mill to use Watt's engine was one at Papplewick in 1785 ; the engine was first used in Manchester in 1789, in Oldham in 1798.[2] It did not of course supersede water power at once, but early in the nineteenth century its superiority was so manifest that water mills ceased to be built, whilst steam factories rose on all sides. Mules and jennies were gathered more and more into factories and worked by steam power. The self-acting mule was a later development ; many unsuccessful experiments were made with it, and it was not in satisfactory working order till about 1825.

We can summarise the results of these changes by saying that whereas at the beginning of the nineteenth century the bulk of the master cotton spinners were still small men, as the century advanced the small establishments could not hold their own against the large establishments worked by steam, and employing many hundreds or even thousands of hands. This development had an important consequence in the history of the workers, for in these establishments the men spinners formed a compact body with common aims among whom combination was easy.

The Weavers and the Combination Act

We must now turn to the cotton weavers. In their case we shall find no startling changes in the structure of the industry, for at the time of the Reform Bill weaving is still in the main a domestic industry, though the power-loom and the factory system are rapidly gaining ground. But though there was no startling change in the structure of the industry, there was a lamentable change in the conditions of the weavers.

Before the invention of the spinning-jenny, the weavers suffered from a shortage of yarn. After that invention and the introduction of Arkwright's water frame, yarn was abundant, and by 1780 it was said that the number of looms had

[1] See Baines, *op. cit.*, pp. 183, 184.   [2] See Chapman, *op. cit.*, p. 57.

increased threefold.[1] It is probable of course that many of these looms were looms that had been converted from linen or woollen looms to cotton looms. When the mule came into use the demand for more looms grew rapidly, and the almost feverish prosperity of the trade is graphically described by William Radcliffe.[2]

He calls the years from 1788 to 1803 ' the golden age of this great trade,' and describes how ' the old loom-shops being insufficient, every lumber-room, even old barns, cart-houses, and out-buildings of any description, were repaired, windows broke through the old blank walls, and all fitted up for loom-shops. This source of making room being at length exhausted, new weavers' cottages, with loom-shops, rose up in every direction.' Of the ' operative weavers *on machine yarns*,' he says, ' both as cottagers and small farmers, even with three times their former rents, they might be truly said to be placed in a higher state of " wealth, peace, and godliness," by the great demand for, and high price of their labour than they had ever before experienced. Their dwellings and small gardens clean and neat,—all the family well clad,—the men with each a watch in his pocket, and the women dressed to their own fancy,—*the church crowded to excess every Sunday*,— every house well furnished with a clock in elegant mahogany or fancy case,—handsome tea services in Staffordshire ware, with silver or plated sugar-tongs and spoons,—Birmingham, Potteries, and Sheffield wares for necessary use and ornament, wherever a corner cupboard or shelf could be placed to *shew them off*,—many cottage families had their cow, paying so much for the summer's grass, and about a statute acre of land laid out for them in some croft or corner, which they dressed up as a meadow for hay in the winter.'

The golden age was not so golden nor did it last so long as William Radcliffe suggests.[3] Early in 1799 the weavers were complaining of the decrease in the price of labour and forming themselves into an Association for mutual protection and for obtaining Parliamentary relief. At the end of April a correspondent wrote from Wigan to the Home Office to say

[1] See p. 56 above. Radcliffe (quoted Baines, *op. cit.*, p. 338) denies that there was any increase till 1788.

[2] William Radcliffe, *Origin of Power-Loom Weaving*, 1828, pp. 59-67.

[3] Nor did all weavers enjoy its blessings, for Prof. Chapman points out that the fustian weavers were not in this happy case (*op. cit.*, p. 39). See also *The Cotton Trade during the Revolutionary and Napoleonic Wars*, by G. W. Daniels (Manchester Statistical Society).

that numbers of societies were being formed in that and the neighbouring counties, and that ' when the sum of five hundred pounds is collected by the grand central committee at Manchester consisting of three persons . . . they are to pay it into the hands of some great person in London who hath engaged to procure them an act of parliament for an advance of wages.' [1]

On May 27 the same correspondent sent to the Home Office an address that had been issued to the public by the newly formed association of weavers.[2] It is worth quoting at some length. The address is to be printed and distributed in different towns in the name of the general committee assembled at Bolton, May 13, 1799. John Seddon is president, James Holcroft is secretary, and the committee is composed of representatives from different towns as follows : from Bolton and the neighbourhood six, from Manchester and Salford three, from Stockport, Oldham, Wigan, Warrington, Blackburn, Chorley, Newton, and Bury two each, from Whitefield, Chowbent, and New Chapel near Leigh one each.

The writers begin : ' The present existing Laws that should protect Weavers, etc., from imposition, being trampled under foot, for want of a union amongst them, they are come to a determination to support each other in their just and legal rights, and to apply to the Legislature of the country for such further regulations, as it may in its wisdom deem fit to make, when the real state of the cotton manufactory shall have been laid before it.' They talk of the ' mutual interest of both employers and employed ' and ask for a ' candid consideration how every necessary of life has increased in price, while the price of labour has undergone a continual decrease. . . . And ye who are our enemies, do you not blush to hear these facts repeated—Great Britain holding the reins of universal commerce, is it not shameful that her sons should be thus imposed on ?—are you afraid that we should approach Government, and there tell the truth ?—that ye use the mean artifice of stigmatising us with the name of Jacobins, that ye raise your rumours of plots, riots, etc.' They disclaim all connection with attempts to undermine Government, and in their dread

---

[1] H.O., 42. 47.

[2] H.O., 42. 47. This address is printed by William Radcliffe, *op. cit.*, p. 76 He also gives a later one of June 29 which shows that the Association was trying to join with the masters in advocating the prohibition of the export of cotton twist.

of any misunderstanding on this point go so far as to declare
the 'late law on meetings[1] appears to us to be only intended
as a bridle to that wild democratical fury that leads nations
into the vortex of anarchy, confusion, and bloodshed.' They
give particulars of reduced payment; supposing a man to
be newly married in 1792, he would then be receiving 22s.
for forty-four yards of cloth; in 1799, surrounded by four or five
small children, he would be receiving only 11s. for sixty yards,
worked with a finer weft. 'It is in vain,' they conclude, ' to
talk of bad trade; if goods are actually not wanted, they
cannot be sold at any price; if wanted, 2d. or 3d. per yard
will not stop the buyer; and whether does it appear more
reasonable that 2d. or 3d. per yard should be laid on the con-
sumer, or taken from the labourer?' The official endorsement on this document is interesting. It is in the handwriting
of the Duke of Portland (Home Secretary): 'Can anything
more be done in this case than calling the Attention of
the Magistrates to the Facts by a Letter to the Chairman
of the Sessions, or some intelligent Magistrate in that part
of the County which is indeed all or at least the principal
part of the manufacturing district.'

The correspondent (Mr. John Singleton of Wigan) who sent
up the weavers' address denied that the weavers had grounds for
complaint; the labouring class he declared was ' fully employed
and *well* very well paid for their labour and before these arts
were us'd to disturb their peace and make them discontented
was both happy and contented.' He throws an interesting
sidelight on the introduction of women into the trade : in
spite of the war the number of looms have increased, 'for if
a Man enlists, his Wife turns Weaver, for here the women are
weavers as well as the Men, and instructs her children in the
art of weaving—and I have heard many declare that they
lived better since their husbands enlisted than before.'[2]

The action of the weavers in associating together was speedily
followed by the first Combination Act, passed July 1799. It
seems probable, indeed, that their association was a cause
of its introduction. The paper containing their manifesto was
sent up, as we have seen, to the Home Office on May 27.[3] On
June 17 Pitt obtained leave to bring in the Workman's
Combination Bill, and in his speech referred specially to the
combinations in the northern part of the kingdom.[4] The

[1] Probably the Seditious Meetings Act, 36 George III. c. 8.
[2] H.O., 42. 47.   [3] *Ibid.*   [4] See *Town Labourer*, p. 119.

Combination Act, however, was not the sort of answer that
the weavers wanted or appreciated. A general meeting of the
acting magistrates within the hundred of Salford in November
even thought it necessary to publish a handbill of warning to
the discontented : ' We, the undersigned, taking into consideration the various and repeated Attempts that have lately
been made, to excite a spirit of Dissatisfaction amongst the
Weavers and others employed in the Manufactures of this
County, and by violent Hand Bills, and other inflammatory
Publications, to encourage an illegal Opposition to the Act
passed in the last Session of Parliament " To prevent unlawful
Combinations amongst Workmen " do hereby signify our
determined Resolution to maintain, as much as in us lies,
due Obedience to the Laws . . .'[1]

The passing of the Combination Act did not deter the weavers
from pressing Parliament next year for a regulation of their
wages. The journeyman weavers of Chester, York, Lancashire, and Derby sent up a petition[2] praying for a more speedy
and summary mode of regulating abuses ' and for the settling
of the Wages, Pay and Price of Labour from time to time.'
The Combination Act, it must be remembered, nominally
prohibited combination amongst masters not less than amongst
men, and the weavers take the opportunity to point out that
their evils are due to ' a powerful Combination of the Master
Weavers or Manufacturers, and that the Petitioners scarcely
earning a bare Subsistence by their daily Labour, are totally
unable to seek the Suppression of Combinations of so much
Secrecy, Wealth and Power, or any Redress of their Grievances,
by any existing Law.' Some of the master manufacturers,
however, were on the men's side, for on the same day came a
petition from master manufacturers in Chester, York, and
Lancashire stating that their difficulties were due to the fact
that there was no power to settle wages. A special Committee
of the House of Commons was appointed to take evidence,
and on May 8 it published the Minutes of Evidence.[3] James
Holcroft, weaver of Bolton, who had been secretary of the
Association the year before, stated the men's object clearly.
' Is it the wish of the Weavers,' he was asked, ' to have any
Standard Price or not ? ' ' We wish for no particular Wages,
but what may be fixed upon mutually between the Manufacturers
and Workmen, or by the Quarter Session.' ' Is it not regu-

[1] H.O., 42. 48.   [2] *House of Commons Journal*, March 5, 1800.
[3] *Ibid.*, May 8, 1800.

lated at present by the Manufacturers and Workmen ? ' 'No, we wish to be regulated similar to the Silk Manufacturers.' [1]

The Cotton Arbitration Acts

The weavers did not obtain their desired regulation, but they were given instead an Act [2] providing for arbitration in the cotton trade. Richard Needham, weaver of Bolton, who had been one of the general committee in 1799, gave the history of this Act both before the Committee on Artisans and Machinery in 1824 [3] and also before the Committee on Hand-loom Weavers ten years later, in 1834. [4] We will quote the latter account : ' At that time Mr. Pitt was prime minister and chancellor of the Exchequer as well ; I was not here but another person was here at the time we were applying for it. Mr. Pitt stopped Colonel Stanley from moving any further in the business ; he sent to the weavers' solicitor, and sent him down to hold a delegate meeting to consult the weavers as to the plan he had to suggest, which was a principle of arbitration, and if we would give up the application for a regulation of wages at that time, he would give us that in lieu of it.'

That Pitt had seriously considered the question of granting a minimum wage seems probable. Mr. Bayley, the Lancashire magistrate, as early as 1798 wrote to the Home Office urging the adoption of some such measures as ' indispensable to keep quiet the lower Orders and to conciliate their good Will. . . . If the great Mind of Mr. Pitt would give it *five Minutes* Con-sideration, I am sure the Bill would pass.' [5] Amongst the Home Office papers for 1800 is an undated and rather illegible paper probably belonging to the year before, which seems to be a memorandum on the subject prepared for Pitt by Mr. King, then Under Secretary of the Home Office. [6] ' On look-ing into Burn's Justice Title *Servants*, head 4 *Rating of Wages*, Mr. Pitt will see the Authority given to Magistrates to settle the wages of all artificers and labourers by the day, week or month. If any thing can be done as suggested by Mr. Bayley it appears to Mr. King that it must be grounded on the acts there mentioned.' The memorandum points out that the

[1] See Chapter VII.   [2] 39 & 40 George III. c. 90, passed July 28.
[3] Fifth Report, p. 544.
[4] Report from Select Committee on Hand-loom Weavers' Petitions, 1834.
[5] H.O., 42. 45.   From this letter it seems that Rose had a Bill on the subject in his charge.   [6] H.O., 42 55.

existing Acts apply to cases where employment is uniform ; in manufactures of great extent and employing great numbers the only remedy seems to be ' to leave it to the call for employment to regulate the wages. . . . I know not what Rule Mr. A. Smith or anyone would desire to lay down.'

If Pitt played with the idea of an Act for regulating wages, he rejected it and gave the weavers instead the Arbitration Act. This Act [1] provided that in all cases of dispute over wages or hours each party could name an arbitrator, and if the arbitrators could not agree either arbitrator could require them to submit the points in dispute to a Justice of the Peace whose decision would be final. The Act had some success for a short time as a device for settling disputes and protecting the men from actual frauds, but before long the masters put their finger on a fatal flaw in the drafting. The Act obliged the masters to appoint an arbitrator, and made provision for cases of disagreement between the arbitrators, but it contained no provision to compel an arbitrator to act. The masters having discovered this hiatus amused themselves by appointing an arbitrator living in London or some other distant place who had no intention of acting, with the result that the arbitration went no further.

The working of the Act and the grievances of the weavers are described very fully three years later in the evidence before a Select Committee of the House of Commons.[2] Thomas Thorpe, who had acted as arbitrator in some two hundred cases (in a few he was chosen by the masters), said so long as the Act was carried out it worked well. Of the cases in which he had acted eleven had been referred to a magistrate, and of those eleven all but one had been settled in the men's favour. James Holcroft, who had acted in some three hundred cases, said that only four or five had been referred to a magistrate. He described in detail a case which throws light on the scope of the Act and the persistent desire of the men for a minimum wage. At Whitefield, where wages had been reduced some time before from 6½d. to 3½d. a yard, the men, hoping to use the Act to raise their wages, wished to arbitrate in a body, but they were advised by Mr. Gurney that they could only act individually. Consequently some nine hundred applications for arbitration were made, but the magistrates treated

[1] 39 & 40 George III. c. 90.
[2] Minutes of Evidence taken before the Select Committee on the Cotton Weavers' Petitions, 1803.

the demand as if it were an attempt by the men to fix wages, and said that the Act gave no such power. This interpretation of the Act, which of course made it worthless as a protection to the men against anything but actual fraud or breach of agreement, was supported by the legal opinion of Law, afterwards Lord Ellenborough ; Gurney, who advised the men, taking the opposite view that the reduction of wages on this scale was a proper subject for the operation of the Act. When Holcroft was asked if it was the favourite wish in Whitefield that there should be a regulation of wages, he replied : ' It was not only the favourite Wish of the People at Whitefield, but the favourite Wish of the Four Counties of Lancaster, Cheshire, York, and Durham.'

Another witness, James Draper, gave an instance of the dismissal of a workman because he had appointed an arbitrator, and it came out very clearly in the inquiry that the masters thought it beneath the dignity of an arbitrator of their class to meet a workman, that they resented workmen being allowed to administer oaths, and that dishonesties and frauds of the meanest kind were very common on the part of the employers. One master, Richard Cliff, in defending his conduct in choosing a remote and non-effective arbitrator, said, ' I don't know who I could have got to attend against the People who were appointed on the Weavers' Side.'

It is clear that there was a good deal of uneasiness amongst the authorities about the attitude of the weavers, law-abiding and even anti-Jacobin though the latter at this time were. Prices were leaping up, food riots were occurring all over the country, and sedition of the stomach and sedition of the mind were often confounded by the anxious friends of law and order. When hunger prompted the composition of the many doggerel rhymes [1] sent up by the recipients in alarm to the Home Office during these years, it was in truth difficult to distinguish the two. Any attempt of the working classes to assist themselves in the ' Wants and Distresses arising from the various Events which Divine Providence may permit to chasten us ' [2] was regarded with suspicion, hence it is not surprising to find Mr. Bayley, who at this time wrote constantly

[1] *e.g.*   ' The Bishops, Vicars, Curates,
                 Parliament and Kings
                 Not only Evils are
                 But worthless Things.'—H.O., 42, 55.

[2] Salford magistrates' handbill, H.O., 42. 48.

to the Home Office, declaring that 'much of sedition has mixed itself with the Weavers' Petition and Bill. It will not have escaped your Observation,' he adds, ' that Mr. Gurney is their Counsel and Mr. Foulkes their Solicitor.' [1]

' Cavalry should be stationed near Bolton and an eye kept on whole quarter' is the official endorsement of an enclosure in Mr. Bayley's letter. The enclosure, from Mr. Fletcher of Bolton who figures in our pages elsewhere, had amongst other things urged the taxation of the export of cotton twist, a measure which was constantly being pressed by the weaving interest, and as constantly opposed by the spinning interest. Mr. Bayley's fears were not allayed by the receipt of an anonymous threatening letter a few weeks later.[2] There is of course no reason to connect this letter with the weavers or their organisation, but as a type of the letters that were showered upon the magistrates all over England wherever famine was rife, it is worth while to quote part of it. These letters are interesting as showing how far the poor were from taking the same view as their betters about the chastening mercies of Divine Providence. We have altered the spelling and punctuation. ' And the people said unto Joshua, the Lord our God will we serve and His voice will we obey. You Magistrates and Gentlemen of old England, by God's laws and the church we mean to stand, and men's laws to destroy. Unless the price of provisions comes to a fair price, a famine appears in the midst of plenty. Betwixt the Badger and the huxter the poor do starve. As a caution take this writ. For a fare living on our bended knees to God we will call.' Unless this comes about the writer threatens ' a civil war' and ' your fine halls and your pleasure ground we will destroy either by fire or sword.'

Throughout the year 1801 there was great distress among the workers in the cotton district, and great alarm among the authorities. There seemed indeed cause for alarm lest hunger should drive the manufacturing population, ill-policed as it was, into open rebellion against law and order.[3] There were rumours that the cotton factories at Bolton would be burnt, tales were told of large bodies of men, some said fifty

---

[1] H.O., 42. 50. [2] *Ibid.*
[3] The sums paid for the prosecution of felons in the county of Lancaster rose from £583 in 1798 to £1429 in 1799, and £2764 in 1800. Of these sums nearly two-thirds were paid at Manchester. H.O., 42. 55 (Mr. Bayley, October 21).

thousand, bound together by illegal oaths. The magistrates were not the only alarmists. Thomas Ainsworth, the manufacturer, wrote to Sir Robert Peel (1st Baronet) from Bolton :[1] 'There is nothing to fear from Jacobinism further than availing themselves of the distracted state of the country and the common saying of the poor is better to die in a battle than be starved in our houses.' With reference to a rising he adds : 'If ever there is an invasion or other commotion to employ the regular force of the country I make no doubt but that opportunity will be seized.' Mr. Yates, Peel's partner, wrote in equal alarm two days later, giving an account of food riots at Bury :[2] 'I am sorry to say that what I have seen and heard to-Day, convinces me that the Country is ripe for rebellion and in a most dangerous situation, and I firmly believe that if provisions continue at the present high prices, a Revolution will be the consequence . . . my heart bled this morning,' he adds, 'to see so many Children not more than half Fed.' Both these gentlemen share the magistrates' doubts of the Volunteers. In the Bury food riot it was thought wiser not to call them out. Mr. Ainsworth went so far as to declare ' great doubts are entertained as to Volunteers acting and some are supposed to be corrupted. I am of opinion not one Corps in Lancashire would [act][3] in their own Towns against their neighbours and perhaps relatives.'

Under these circumstances it is not surprising that the magistrates were alarmed. Seditious language was not wanting,[4] but more dangerous than mere seditious language, doctrines subversive of the foundations of society were being circulated in the cotton district,[5] and opinions unfavourable to the Government seemed to be gaining ground. This was the belief of Mr. Fletcher of Bolton, who wrote that he had ' encouraged several loyal masters who employ great numbers of servants in different Branches of the Cotton manufacture, to examine into the political opinions of their workmen, and to discharge such as are known to be Jacobin from their employ.'[6]

---

[1] H.O., 42. 61, March 12, 1801.   [2] H.O., 42. 61.   [3] Torn out.

[4] *e.g.* One Dyson was sent to the Salford House of Correction for saying 'Damn the King and Country.' When told he would be informed against, thinking perhaps he might as well be hung for a sheep as a lamb, he not only damned the magistrates but damned the volunteers for a set of damned fools. He had further announced that it was 'time to take Billy Pitt's head off.' H.O., 42. 62.

[5] See *Town Labourer*, p. 315.   [6] H.O., 42. 62.

It is in the year 1801 that the first mention is made in the
Home Office Papers of that unhallowed band of informers and
spies, of whom the magistrates henceforth made continual
use. The Rev. Mr. Hay, J.P., who will figure later in the
Luddite chapters, rejoices in having found an informer to
attend the secret meetings, although it cannot be said that
the information he furnished was very exciting.[1] Mr. Fletcher
of Bolton also begins to send up informers' tales.[2] It is in this
year that we first hear of Mr. Bent, alias ' B.,' so long the
trusted informer of Mr. Fletcher and the trusted confidant of
the discontented.[3]

Meanwhile the organised weavers directed their efforts to
obtaining by lawful means an amendment of the Arbitration
Act. Now an application for amendment involved concerted
action, and concerted action, however law-abiding, in this
atmosphere of suspicion and fear, was at once attributed by
the magistrates to sedition and Jacobinism, and hence the
weavers worked under difficulties. Their meetings, too, were
constantly stopped or dispersed.

' The intention of a second application to Parliament to
amend what is called the *Weavers' Bill*,' wrote the Rev. Mr.
Bancroft of Bolton,[4] ' has I believe been made a means of
combining and stimulating the People. It was mentioned
before that Correspondencies were carried on between a Leader
here (Holcroft) and the People of Scotland. I expect that
Holcroft has of late abated in his exertions.'

Mr. Fletcher of Bolton wrote to the same effect early next
year :[5]

' In this neighbourhood (Bolton) the seditious seem to be
mostly occupied about the intended application to Parliament
for regulating the cotton manufacture. This application
(although perhaps some small alteration may be necessary
in the existing Laws as to that Trade) certainly originates in
the *Jacobin Societies* and is intended as a means to keep the

---

[1] H.O., 42. 62. [2] H.O., 42. 62, and 42. 65.

[3] See Chapter X. B.'s name occurs in some papers sent up to the Law
Officers about the prosecution of persons for sedition. The suspected persons meet
in public-houses to redress grievances ; they talk vaguely about the regulation of
wages, and Bent the chairman, who always dealt in large figures, declared that
he could raise 50,000 women and children in three days. The Law Officers
discouraged the idea of prosecuting without more facts than those disclosed.
H.O., 42. 61.

[4] May 2, 1801, H.O., 42. 62. [5] April 3, 1802, H.O., 42. 65.

minds of the Weavers in a continual Ferment, and as a Pretext to raise Money from them which will probably be employed in part at least, to seditious purposes.'

Parliament was less suspicious of the weavers' intentions than were the magistrates, and a Special Committee, from whose report we have already quoted, heard evidence from both masters and men. The result of the inquiry was the passing of an amending Act designed, not as the weavers had hoped, to oblige the masters to carry out the law, but to soften their hearts towards it by removing some of the features that were particularly repugnant to them.

In the course of the debate Rose made a significant speech commenting upon the ' extraordinary way ' in which the masters had behaved and suggesting the application of an Act like the Spitalfields Act to the cotton manufacture. ' That law might be extended to the cotton trade with much less difficulty, and in the silk trade there were above 1000 articles to become the object of the wages of workmen, whilst in the cotton trade there were not above 100.' [1]

The amending Arbitration Bill, as introduced in 1803, provided that the J.P. was to choose two arbitrators, one to be a master or manager or foreman, the other to be taken from a list drawn up by the workmen. The Act [2] in its final form empowered the magistrate to choose a panel (not less than four or more than six, half to be masters or their agents, the other half to be weavers) from which the two sides should each choose an arbitrator. Another provision in the Act sought to protect the workman from a common method of fraud by obliging the masters to give out tickets, if required, stating the quality, nature, and price of the work assigned to a workman. The new Act seems to have been practically inoperative. Richard Needham indeed declared later that it had answered its purpose to a great extent and that thousands of pounds had been recovered under it,[3] but Needham's views were not shared by his fellow weavers. From this time he became closely allied with the authorities and represented what they termed the ' loyal ' weavers, whilst the great mass of his fellow workers were gradually becoming convinced that application to an unreformed Parliament was useless. A

[1] *Parliamentary Register*, February 13, 1804.
[2] 44 George III. c. 87.
[3] Committee on Artisans and Machinery, 1824, p. 544; Committee on Hand-loom Weavers, 1834, p. 421.

petition from the cotton weavers at Bolton in 1813 described the Act as ' unavailing inasmuch as no one conviction before a Magistrate under this Law has ever been confirmed at any Quarter Sessions of the Peace ' ;[1] and in the Reform agitation of 1819 the uselessness of the Act was constantly mentioned as an illustration of the necessity for a radical reform of Parliament.[2]

The clause requiring the masters to give out tickets was evaded by giving tickets with ' no wages promised.' A witness before the Committee on the Cotton Weavers' Petitions in 1808 described how one master, who had suffered defeat in an arbitration, indemnified himself by a general reduction of wages. Arbitration, in fact, without the right and the power of combination was worthless from the moment the masters had set their faces against it. Moreover, apart from the Combination Laws, organised action amongst the weavers was particularly difficult, and every year the difficulty increased.

The Decline of the Weavers

Before describing the renewed and persistent applications of the weavers, and of many of their employers, for a regulation of wages, it will be well to discuss some of the peculiar circumstances of the weaving trade, and to glance ahead at that future of long-drawn-out misery which the victims were striving in vain to elude. From the prosperous men described by Radcliffe[3] who believe, in the depression of 1799, that Government has only to be told the truth to restore them to their former condition, the hand-loom weavers become by 1832 perhaps the most wretched and famished class in the community. The figures given in the Report of the Committee on Hand-loom Weavers in 1835 illustrate that decline graphically.[4] Assuming that the wage was spent in equal proportions on

[1] *House of Commons Journal*, February 25, 1813; cf. p. 87. Needham wanted the power of appeal to Quarter Sessions against the penalty taken away. See Committee on Artisans and Machinery, 1824, p. 544.

[2] *e.g.* In 1819 the Stockport weavers spoke of it as a law ' granted them after spending many thousands of pounds to obtain it ; which law professes to redress their grievances, and then to protect them from oppression in future. But the magistrates would not act upon it.' See *Manchester Observer* of July 3 in H.O., 42. 189. Cf. Broadhurst's speech at Blackburn Reform Meeting : see *Manchester Observer*, July 10, in H.O., 42. 189.

[3] See p. 58 above.

[4] *Parliamentary Papers*, 1835, xiii. p. 13, quoted by Chapman, *op. cit.*, p. 43.

flour, oatmeal, potatoes, and butcher's meat, the Committee
worked out the comparative wages as follows :

> 1797–1804—price 26s. 8d. amt. of provs. 281 lbs.
> 1804–1811   „   20s.   „   „   238 „
> 1811–1818   „   14s. 7d.   „   „   131 „
> 1818–1825   „   8s. 9d.   „   „   108 „
> 1825–1832   „   6s. 4d.   „   „   83 „

There were many causes at work to bring about this disastrous result. Weaving was easily learned,[1] and during its prosperous days it offered the attraction of high wages. In other
trades, the trade societies managed to restrict the flow of
incomers ; the weavers, disorganised and scattered, had no
such power. Ireland was pouring out her population from their
wretched homes into Lancashire ; peasants and cottagers, dis-
possessed by the agricultural revolution in England, were
leaving the land, and after 1815 discharged soldiers were
looking for employment. Hand-loom weaving became the
' refuge of the surplus numbers from nearly all other trades.' [2]
At the same time numbers of small masters sprang up,
because the cotton trade offered rapid profits and in the early
days comparatively little capital was needed. Competition
or the spirit of enterprise led them to vie with each other
in cheapening production by cutting wages. They took full
advantage of the weak and disorganised position of the
weavers, playing upon their necessities until they had reduced
them below subsistence level, and employers who would have
preferred to pay good wages thought themselves bound to
follow suit.

The Power-Loom

In the later years the extension of the use of the power-
loom was one element in the depression of the hand-loom
weavers. The process was slow, for though the power-loom
was invented in 1785, as late as 1835 the Select Committee that
reported on Hand-loom Weavers could report that while the
power-loom had been in operation for many years, it was only
of late that it had come into direct competition with hand-

---

[1] There were of course special kinds of weaving that required strength and
skill, and the Hand-loom Weavers' Commissioners pointed out that the men who
did this fine work suffered much less and were earning 20s. to 28s. a week in
1839 (Chapman, *op. cit.*, p. 43).

[2] Report from Hand-loom Weavers' Commissioners, 1841, p. 40.

looms. Its advance was actually retarded by the low rate at
which the hand labourers worked.[1]

The story of the original invention of the power-loom is a
curious one. The Rev. Edmund Cartwright, a country parson,
Fellow of Magdalene, Cambridge, and brother of Major Cartwright the reformer, was staying for a holiday at Matlock in
1784, and happened to fall into conversation with some Manchester men about the newly invented spinning machinery.
With the boldness of inexperience, for he had never even seen
a weaver at work, Cartwright advanced the proposition that
weaving no less than spinning should be done by machinery.
The experts derided him, advancing arguments which from
want of technical knowledge he could not even understand.
Cartwright went home, and from his theoretical knowledge of
the process of weaving invented the first power-loom which
he patented in 1785. This invention produced cloth indeed,
but it took ' two powerful men to work the machine at a slow
rate, and only for a short time. . . . This being done, I then
condescended to see how other people wove ; and you will
guess my astonishment, when I compared their easy mode of
operation with mine.' [2] He set himself to improve his power-
loom, and in 1787 took out a patent for an improved machine.
Cartwright, like Crompton, had little business ability, and his
attempts to profit by his invention were failures. A factory
for four hundred of his looms was indeed built by Messrs.
Grimshaw in Manchester, but it was burnt down in 1792 and
not rebuilt.

The power-loom was in fact still too clumsy a machine for
general use, but some of its defects were remedied by a dressing
machine, patented by William Radcliffe of Stockport in
1803-4.[3] Hitherto each power-loom had required a man to
dress the warp from time to time ; by this invention the warp
was dressed before it was put into the loom. In 1803 Mr.
H. Horrocks of Stockport patented power-looms of iron,
another important improvement. Yet in spite of these

---

[1] ' It is now found, for the first time in the history of mankind, so low are
wages fallen, so great is the pressure of distress, that manual labour is making
reprisals on machinery, standing a successful competition with it, beating it out
of the market, and precluding the use of an engine, far from costly in itself,
which saves three labourers in four. The farther introduction of the power loom
is actually stopped by the low rate of weavers' wages ! '—Brougham, Speech,
House of Commons, March 13, 1817 ; *Speeches*, 1838 edition, vol. i. p. 560.

[2] Cartwright's own statement (see Baines, *op. cit.*, p. 230).

[3] Baines, *op. cit.*, p. 231.

improvements power-looms were not universally adopted. The attempts of the workers to destroy them in 1812 are described in a later chapter.[1] In 1813 it was estimated that there were 2400 power-looms in the United Kingdom; in 1820 there were 14,150 (12,150 of them in England); in 1829 there were 55,500 (45,500 in England), and by 1833 they had reached a total of 100,000 (85,009 in England).[2]

In spite of this rapid growth in the number of power-looms, the number of hand-loom cotton weavers did not decrease during our period. All estimates, it is true, are more or less guesswork, but any marked diminution must have been noticed. Baines[3] accepts the estimates of the number of cotton hand-loom weavers in 1833 in England as 200,000, and thinks that they had probably increased rather than diminished during the previous years. It was only in the thirties that the power-looms were used for muslin goods.

The early power-loom weavers were all women or boys. In the case of spinning, when work left the cottage for the factory, men in factories with the help of children replaced the women domestic spinners : in weaving, when the change from domestic to factory industry took place, women and boys in factories replaced men who had worked at home.

The Agitation for a Minimum Wage

The weavers had desired a Bill for regulating wages, and had received instead from Parliament in 1804 the second Arbitration Act. They had not renounced their hopes, and Rose's speech in the debate on the Arbitration Act had given them some encouragement. The first move in the agitation, which culminated in the riots at Manchester on the rejection of the Minimum Wage Bill in 1808, seems to have come from the masters. The inner history of the movement is best told in Richard Needham's words : [4] ' In 1805 the master manufacturers, some of the most wealthy in Bolton, applied to me and others to desire the weavers to call a meeting and choose a committee, and they would go with us to Parliament to get a regulatory law on the principle of the Spitalfields Act, we were glad of it and we did do so : those gentlemen met us

[1] See Chapter x.
[2] Report from Assistant Hand-loom Weavers' Commissioners, 1840, quoted Chapman, *op. cit.*, p. 28.
[3] *Op. cit.*, p. 237.
[4] 1834 Report from Select Committee on Hand-loom Weavers, p. 421.

and a joint Committee was appointed.' It was in connection with this movement that Mr. Fletcher of Bolton noted the weavers' activity. The disaffected, he writes,[1] are ' under the mask of protecting the Weavers against their Employers, forming them into Societies, each consisting of any number of classes not exceeding eleven—these Classes by a manager corresponding with the Secretary of the Society and each Society sending a delegate to a general meeting.' They had printed rules ; the entrance fee was 4d. and the subscription 1d. a week. The growth of such a society, Mr. Fletcher points out, might become not only injurious to the ' manufacturing Interest,' but dangerous to Government, since the leaders would have at their disposal large sums of money, and most of the leaders are ' known to entertain Opinions adverse to our happy Constitution.' The same letter encloses a bill for £123, 3s. 6½d., being the payment for the services of four spies, B., C., T., and L. F. since the previous August.

The efforts of the weavers to obtain a minimum wage were connected by Mr. Fletcher with the further agitation also engineered by ' the disaffected ' against the Corn Law of 1804. This law, it will be remembered, practically prohibited the importation of foreign corn till the price of English corn had risen to 63s., instead of to the 50s. fixed in 1791. A petition against the law was extensively signed in Manchester and ' B.' was one of the Committee.[2]

The weavers meanwhile were very busy with their application. ' We applied to Parliament,' said Richard Needham,[3] ' in 1806, but a dissolution of Parliament took place in consequence of a disagreement between His Majesty and his Ministers.' The Whig Ministry of ' All the Talents ' then took office for a brief year, but they showed no favour to the application. ' At that time the present Earl Grey was Secretary of State for the Home Department,[4] and he would not suffer us to go into the question till we had had an interview with the Board of Trade. We had an interview with them and they opposed us.' [5] A monster petition was presented to Parliament on February 26, 1807,[6] signed (according to Needham) by no fewer than 130,000 cotton weavers from Lancashire,

[1] January 16, 1805, H.O., 42. 82.   [2] H.O., 42. 79, 42. 80, 42. 82.
[3] 1834 Report from Select Committee on Hand-loom Weavers, p. 421.
[4] This, of course, was a mistake. The Home Secretary was Lord Spencer.
[5] Lord Auckland was at the Board of Trade.
[6] *House of Commons Journal.*

Cheshire, and York. This petition pointed out 'that whenever the demand for goods becomes slack, many Master Manufacturers adopt the expedient of reducing wages, thereby
compelling the Petitioners, in order to obtain a livelihood, to
manufacture great quantities of goods at a time, when they
are absolutely not wanted, and that great quantities of goods
so manufactured are sacrificed in the market at low prices,
to the manifest injury of the fair dealer, and the great oppression of the Petitioners,' who could often only earn 9s. a week.
They asked for a Bill to regulate wages from time to time.

In March 1807 the Whig Ministry fell and Perceval became
Prime Minister, with Rose, the professed friend of the minimum
wage policy, at the Board of Trade. Hopes of Government
action ran high. Early in 1808 the Journeymen Cotton
Weavers again petitioned Parliament [1] asking that a minimum
price should be fixed, below which goods should not be manufactured, and drawing attention to their growing distress owing
to the bankruptcy of many masters. Their average earnings
were now six shillings a week. Several masters supported the
men's application. Richard Ainsworth, a manufacturer, sent
up a petition [2] stating that a meeting of masters at Bolton
had approved the action of the men,[3] and on March 9 an important petition from several Cotton Merchants, Manufacturers and others in Lancashire and Cheshire, was presented
to Parliament.[4] This petition stated that the petitioners had
suffered great injury from the fluctuation in wages, which
during the last three years had been more than 100 per cent.,
being at least 33 per cent. on the value of a great part of the
cotton goods in a finished state, ' and that this fluctuation of
wages gives no increase to the demand from foreign markets,
whilst its direct tendency is to ruin the fair Manufacturer by
reducing the value of his stock on hand ; and that capital,
ingenuity and industry cannot ensure success in the Cotton
Trade till some limits are fixed by the Legislative below which
the wages of workmen cannot be reduced.' The petitioners
appealed to the landlord interest in Parliament, pointing out
that it would ultimately be affected by the numbers of poor
thrown on to the parish for relief.

These petitions were referred to a Select Committee, who

[1] *House of Commons Journal,* February 19, 1808.
[2] *Ibid.,* March 7, 1808.
[3] Cf. Mr. Fletcher, December 27, 1807, in H.O., 42. 91.
[4] *House of Commons Journal.*

at first merely reported the evidence.[1]   The inner history of
negotiations has been told by Richard Needham and others.
The masters' petition, says Needham,[2] was 'signed by 101
master manufacturers, and most of them very wealthy, some
of them kept a thousand hands.'   They sent up six delegates
from Manchester, Chorley, Preston, Bolton, and Stockport.
The men also sent delegates whose expenses were largely paid
out of money loaned by different Friendly Societies.[3]   The
Bill favoured by the committee of men, which the delegates
went to London to promote, provided that fifteen towns or
districts were to send persons chosen by masters and men
to Manchester, where under the presidency of the presiding
magistrate they were to fix wages.[4]   The list of subscriptions
for the purpose, which has also been preserved, is interesting.[5]
£477, 1s. 6d. was raised, and the subscribers include

	£	S.	D.
By Mr. Ainsworth for masters . .	75	0	0
Mr. Horrocks, M.P. . . .	31	10	0
J. B. Spencer & Co. . . .	10	10	0
Sir Robert Peel, M.P. . . .	31	10	0

Even Mr. Fletcher of Bolton no longer saw disguised sedition
in the prayer for a minimum wage.   He wrote in February
1808 [6] to say that the weavers and some of the manufacturers had agreed to petition Parliament to regulate wages,
and that the committee for managing the application have
been detached from the agitators for peace.   'To secure these
Men by Attention to their Application—even though it should
not be deemed expedient to make the Law proposed—will
tend much to give a right Bias to the Weavers' Affections
both on this and future Occasions.'
   The London merchants joined forces with the applicants :[7]
' there was a meeting of merchants formed in London, and
the leaders of that meeting were Messrs. Helps, Lewis and
Ray, the two Goldschmidts, brothers, Messrs. Rowland and
Burrs, in fact the whole of the merchants of Cheapside were

[1] 1808 Report of Select Committee on Cotton Weavers' Petitions, printed
April 12.
[2] 1834 Report from Select Committee on Hand-loom Weavers, p. 421.
[3] See Mr. Fletcher, March 6, 1816, in H.O., 42. 149.
[4] See Philip Halliwell's evidence before Select Committee on Hand-loom
Weavers' Petitions, 1834, p. 447.
[5] *Ibid.*, p. 448.   [6] H.O., 42. 95.
[7] R. Needham, 1834 Committee on Hand-loom Weavers' Petitions. p. 422.

on the committee and joined with us, and they subscribed
money to support the application.' Needham gives an account
of a curious incident from which it seems that the policy of a
minimum wage was nearly adopted : '. . . Mr. Rose communicated to me when I arrived in London that the Privy
Council had had a meeting, and that the Ministers had agreed
to give us an Act for three years on condition we would submit
to that ; a meeting of the merchants of London took place
at Mr. Ainsworth's, Cheapside, and they were ready to receive
it ; however the following morning I was to have the ulti-
matum of Government ; and then they would only give it
for one year, and the merchants would not consent to take it
upon that principle.' An interview took place, between Perceval
and nineteen merchants and manufacturers at which Richard
Needham was also present. All urged Perceval to facilitate
the passing of the law. ' Mr. Perceval raised many objections,
and those objections were answered by many of the merchants,
large manufacturers and spinners, some of whom were employing 1400 persons ; Mr. Perceval proposed that there should
be a meeting called at Manchester of all the influential manufacturers, such as the Horrockses, Ainsworths, and others,
that they should meet and agree to this measure ; and if the
small manufacturers who afterwards competed with them
entered into a competition to run the prices down, he would
on the ensuing session of Parliament, pass those resolutions
into a law, but the manufacturers and merchants refused to
act upon that proposal.' [1]

How far were the manufacturers and merchants really
sincere in their advocacy of the minimum wage ? Whatever
their original sincerity it was clearly unable to stand the test
of opposition. Possibly some of the masters, in the spirit of
Mr. Fletcher of Bolton, thought it desirable to humour the
men by subscribing to their cause. Peel's conduct is a case
in point. Needham in his enthusiasm probably exaggerated
their zeal, for it is impossible to believe that had they been
truly in earnest the project would have been so friendless in
Parliament.

One manufacturer indeed, Thomas Ainsworth, a man paying
some £40,000 a year in wages, was unsparing in his advocacy.
Eleven years later he addressed to Sidmouth a long memorandum about the repeated vain applications to Government

---

[1] 1834 Committee on Hand-loom Weavers' Petitions, p. 425.

for a regulation of wages, a memorandum in which narrative is so mingled with rhetoric that there is some excuse for the flippant official endorsement ' A Rhapsody.' [1] ' I was . . . both pressed and led by inclination,' he writes, ' during Mr. Perceval's time, into the service of the distressed Manufacturers and Weavers, in order to state their case to Government, etc., and seek relief—To detail to your Lordship the support we had from the Country Manufacturers, and the Merchants in London, etc. The arguments then used, The causes of the distress assigned, The remedy proposed and the probable result of an unsuccessful application would fill a volume.' He then details a private interview he had with Mr. Perceval when Ainsworth warned him in vain of impending calamity.

The project had a very brief life in the House of Commons. Rose, Vice-President of the Board of Trade, moved apologetically for leave to bring in a Bill to regulate wages in cotton weaving.[2] The fate of the proposal was a foregone conclusion. Perceval explained naïvely ' that it was better that the cotton weavers should be disappointed after a discussion of the merits of their application in the House of Commons, than by a refusal of his honourable friend to submit it for consideration.' Sir Robert Peel expressed his disapproval of the measure and with regard to ' this application being countenanced by the masters, he was sure, if this was the case at all, it was only in a very limited degree ' : a curious commentary on his subscription of £31, 10s. No voice was raised on behalf of the Bill, whilst, in addition to Perceval and Peel, Davies Giddy, Horner, Lord Milton, Thomson, Tierney, Baring, and Lascelles all spoke against it. The arguments were of the usual kind : that abilities must be equalised before a minimum wage could be fixed ; that numbers of workmen would be discharged and left to destitution ; that the evil in the trade was not that wages were too low but that they had been too high and thereby attracted an abnormal supply of labour. Rose withdrew his proposal ; he had previously explained that he made it not from a conviction of the ' propriety ' of the measure, but from a desire to comply with the wishes of the cotton weavers ' backed with the consent of their employers.'

Unfortunately the reasoning that convinced the House of Commons seemed less conclusive to Manchester, and the

[1] H.O., 42. 197, October 21, 1819.
[2] *Parliamentary Register*, May 19, 1808.

refusal of Parliament to discuss the Bill was followed by
serious rioting. To appreciate the full extent of the distress
of the time we must bear in mind that a large number of the
weavers were Irishmen and therefore without a settlement
and not entitled to any parish relief.[1] The wages of the weavers
in employment were admittedly only 6s. a week. The workmen
started by holding orderly meetings on May 24 and 25, from
which they sent delegates to the principal manufacturers, and
to the borough-reeve and other town officers asking for a redress
of their grievances. A correspondent in the *Times* stated
that there were from 10,000 to 15,000 people present on the
second day. ' Loud indeed were the murmurs of the poor
wretches but not the least indication was there of a riot.
Many baskets of bread, with some ale, and several cans of
butter-milk were distributed among the multitude ; and their
sorrowful and piteous tales of distress quite unmanned me,
as also several other sympathetic spectators.' [2] As the assembly
failed to disperse when the borough - reeve advised them to
do so, the soldiers were called in and they killed one man,[3]
and wounded several others.

Having failed in their appeals to Parliament, to their employers, and to the local authorities, the men struck work,
demanding a 33⅓ per cent. advance in their wages. They
prevented any others from working by the simple expedient
of entering their houses and taking away the shuttles. The
policy spread over the cotton district : Stockport, Rochdale,
Wigan, and other places were affected. One gentleman who
went with a force of 100 volunteers to stop a party of strikers
near Manchester was much impressed by their reasonable-
ness, when he parleyed with them. ' The Language
they held forth to me was this, that for the last six months
their distress had been well known, and no prospect of being
relieved appeared, that driven to the miserable situation in
which they stood it was indifferent to them which way they
perish'd ; they acknowledged the Law was against their
present conduct, but extreme want was the cause.' [4]

The panacea suggested by one Lancashire magistrate,
Colonel Silvester, was to make the taking away of shuttles a

---

[1] *Times*, May 30, 1808 ; cf. H.O., 42. 95.   [2] *Times*, May 28, 1808.
[3] Prentice, *Historical Sketches of Manchester*, 1851, p. 31, says ' the officers
and soldiers of the 4th Dragoon Guard presented a day's pay to the widow of
the poor man who was killed.'
[4] H.O., 42. 95, May 30, 1808.

capital felony,[1] an expedient which also commended itself
to the energetic Mayor of Wigan who had arrested some
shuttle takers. 'This Case was considered by me to be barely
Felony—but I wished to give it that construction, conceiving
that such an interpretation of the Offence would have great
effect on the Minds of the People.'[2]

At Rochdale there was some disorder. The strikers
happened to leave unguarded two bags full of shuttles,
which the constables seized and deposited for safety in the
House of Correction. The strikers, after rescuing five or six
of their comrades who were being conveyed to prison, came
up and demanded the shuttles : their demand being refused
they broke into the prison and burnt it down. One ardent
spirit, Samuel Bayley, a book-keeper, was heard to hail this
event rather prematurely as a second fall of the Bastille, an
exclamation of which he afterwards repented at leisure in
prison.[3]

Early in June (1808) it was reported that 60,000 looms
were idle in the Manchester district. At the end of May the
masters—350 of them according to Needham [4]—held a meeting and agreed to give a 20 per cent. advance ; some person
signed this agreement for the weavers, but the main body of
weavers repudiated the agreement and held out for their
33⅓ per cent.[5] The men during the strike drew on the funds
of the Friendly Societies.[6]

The strike did not extend to Yorkshire, though the Lancashire woollen weavers joined the cotton weavers, and there
were some food riots on the borders of Yorkshire and Lancashire in the Clitheroe district.[7]

Curiously enough there is no record in the Home Office
Papers of the terms on which the strikers finally returned to
work ; apparently they gained their demands.[8] Richard
Needham, who dissociated himself from the extremists and

[1] H.O., 42. 95, May 31.   [2] H.O., 42. 95, June 15.
[3] H.O., 42. 95.
[4] Report from Select Committee on Hand-loom Weavers' Petitions, 1834.
[5] See H.O., 42. 95, Handbill enclosed in letter of June 2 ; also *Annual
Register*, 1808 ; *Chronicle*, p. 63.
[6] H.O., 42. 95, June 14 ; also H.O., 42. 149, March 16, 1816, where a
report from Adjt. Warr on Friendly Societies states that they gave 10s. a head
to be repaid in six or twelve months with interest.
[7] H.O., 42. 95, June 9.
[8] See H.O., 42. 95. Lord Ribblesdale, June 10, wrote that grain was
lowered and wages raised.

was willing to take the 20 per cent. advance offered by the masters, afterwards described the victory as lasting for about a month ' and then it all tumbled to ruins again.'[1] During that month the victorious weavers must have thought a strike a better method of gaining their ends than appeals to Parliament.

The weavers did not all return to work at once, and for some time spasmodic disorders continued, the malcontents occasionally syringing goods with vitriol. ' The women,' it was said, ' are, if possible, more turbulent and mischievous than the men. Their insolence to the soldiers and special constables is intolerable, and they seem to be confident of deriving impunity from their sex.'[2]

The movement for Parliamentary Reform was going on steadily all this time, but was quite unconnected with the strike ; indeed the politicians of Royton, that home of debating societies and disaffection, even issued a handbill to the weavers, urging them to return to work and to spend their energies on attacking the war, the root of evil.[3]

That public sympathy was on the side of the weavers is manifest from the trials of the rioters at the Lancaster Assizes on September 5. The Crown was clearly anxious not to press the charges, and the tone of the prosecution and the sentences are in marked contrast to those after the Luddite disturbances four years later. Six men were proved to have gone with other persons to Mr. Thomas Ashton's house at Heap near Manchester at night and to have forced him, after some rough handling, to sign a paper promising increased wages : '. . . from their violent conduct,' said Mr. Ashton, ' he was fearful that his life was in danger, and he signed the paper upon his knees in the public road.' Their counsel elicited from Mr. Ashton the admission that his wages were not above half as much as they used to be, and the Jury acquitted all the prisoners.[4] It is fair to add that Mr. Ashton had expressed his wish that the prosecution should be as lenient as possible.

Only one man was found guilty of firing the prison at Rochdale and his sentence was two years' imprisonment. The

---

[1] Report from Select Committee on Hand-loom Weavers, 1834.
[2] *Times*, June 25, 1808.
[3] H.O., 42. 95, Handbill enclosed in letter of June 2. For Royton see H.O., 42. 87, January 31, 1806; and H.O., 42. 99, October 30, 1809 ; and H.O., 42. 153, September 14, 1816; and H.O., 42. 163, April 7, 1817.
[4] *Times*, September 9, 1808.

offence was not capital because no one was dwelling in the prison. Seven other prisoners who had destroyed woollen machinery or broken into houses or extorted money escaped with sentences varying from one to twelve months; amongst them was a woman, Elizabeth Walmsley, who was sentenced for breaking three shopkeepers' windows in Blackburn with a big stick. Six strikers who had taken away shuttles or stopped persons from working were not proceeded against.[1]

The leniency shown to the riotous weavers was not extended to a man in a more prosperous condition of life, who was charged with having encouraged the strikers. Joseph Hanson, a colonel in the volunteers, who had stood as candidate for Preston and was popular with the weavers for his advocacy of the minimum wage Bill, rode on to the field during the monster meeting of May 25 and addressed the people in opposition to the wishes of the captain of Dragoons. His own witnesses, citizens of respectable character, swore that he merely urged the people to go home peaceably, but witnesses for the prosecution, a sergeant, two corporals, and two of Nadin's constables, swore that Hanson had used inciting expressions. ' My lads, your cause is good ; be firm and you will succeed.' ' I will support you as far as £3000 will go, and if that will not do, I will go farther.' ' Nadin and his faction shall not drive you from the field this day.' ' I am sorry your Bill is lost. My father was a weaver, and I am a weaver, and I am the weavers' friend.' [2]

The case was tried before Mr. Justice Grose in the King's Bench in May 1809, and Hanson, after a homily from the Judge, was sentenced to six months' imprisonment and to pay a fine of £100.[3] The treatment of Hanson seems to have made a profound impression on the minds of the Lancashire workers. Prentice dates from this event ' that bitter feeling of employed against employers' with which we shall meet later. In their generous indignation they wanted even to pay his fine by penny subscriptions, an offer which was declined ; but 39,600 subscribers presented him with a silver cup.[4]

Two months before Hanson's trial the Select Committee of the House of Commons, to whom the petition for a minimum wage had been referred, reported again.[5] This time they

[1] For account of trials see *Times*, September 9 and 10.
[2] Prentice, *op. cit.*, p. 32.   [3] See *State Trials*, vol. xxxi. pp. 1-99.
[4] Prentice, *op. cit.*, p. 33.
[5] Report from Select Committee on Cotton Weavers' Petitions, 1809.

declared a minimum wage to be 'wholly inadmissible in principle, incapable of being reduced to practice by any means which can possibly be devised, and, if practicable, would be productive of the most fatal consequences.'

Next year (1810) began well for the manufacturing districts, and a report to the Home Office from Manchester could even declare that ' the lower Classes in this populous district are perfectly happy, content and tranquil in their respective situations,' [1] a tranquillity that was destroyed by an extensive strike of the spinners.

The weavers' prosperity in 1810 was short-lived. By August trade was declining and their wages were seriously reduced. Their next effort as an organised body was to attempt to induce the masters to limit the quantity of work instead of lowering the price paid for it. Manifestoes were printed in various towns, signed by a committee of weavers and addressed to the manufacturers. The Blackburn Manifesto,[2] after enlarging on the identity of the interests of master and workman, submits a plan to meet the emergency of trade depression. 'It is simply this; Reduce the Quantity of Goods when the Market is overstock'd, and their value will undoubtedly increase with the scarcity.

' Gentlemen, the whole body of Weavers in this Town have come to a Determination not to submit to a Reduction of Prices, but will rather be limited in the Quantity of their Work, and will, in conjunction with their Masters, bear every privation for a few Weeks or Months, until a change takes place in the Markets.' This manifesto caused so much alarm to the Blackburn magistrates that they asked for troops to be sent there. The local militia, they pointed out, was mostly composed of weavers.

Trade went from bad to worse ; no mere restriction of output—even had the masters adopted the suggestion—could have tided over the evil days of the Orders in Council.[3]

The despair of the victims was voiced in an address to the

[1] H.O., 42. 106. A sidelight is thrown on a method by which the working classes tried to meet fluctuations by the complaint of a colonel of the Lancashire militia that it was a common practice for young men to be bound apprentice to their relatives, and to enlist when trade was bad only to be claimed back as soon as trade revived. See H.O., 42. 105, February 27.

[2] H.O., 42. 108, 1810.

[3] For an illuminating account of the vicissitudes of the cotton trade during this period, see G. W. Daniels, *The Cotton Trade during the Revolutionary and Napoleonic Wars.*

'Gentlemen, Landholders, Merchants, Manufacturers, and other respectable Inhabitants' of Great and Little Bolton from a committee of cotton weavers appealing for a public meeting to consider the distress.[1] 'It is true benevolent institutions have been established, and poor rates also are increased, but the temporary relief afforded by these establishments, is only to the most wretched, helpless, and worn-out children of indigence. We are well convinced anything of this nature can never be applied to the relief of many thousands mechanics, who are able and willing to labour hard to support their families honestly, and who of course disdain to become paupers, until forced by the arrogant lash of necessity.'

Petition followed petition to London; the Bolton and Stockport weavers urged the Prince Regent to intervene on their behalf.[2] One more effort was made to obtain relief from Parliament. A monster petition, signed by nearly 40,000 weavers from the Manchester district, was presented to the House of Commons on May 30, 1811;[3] and it was accompanied by petitions signed by 7000 Bolton weavers, and by 30,000 Scottish weavers.[4] These petitions described the miserable plight of the weavers and asked for measures of relief in general terms without mentioning the rating of wages. The Manchester petition indeed asked for the revocation of the Orders in Council, or if that were impossible a pecuniary grant; the Bolton petition suggested 'salutary laws,' but the delegate from Manchester and the three delegates from Scotland sent up to forward the business seem to have been more explicit in their demands and it was generally understood that the rating of wages was the weavers' ultimate object. The petitions were referred to a Select Committee on June 5, more from a sense of courtesy to the petitioners in their misery, than because any one thought that any relief could be afforded them. The consideration of the report of the Committee was put off time after time, till at last the question was dismissed and the petitioners were forced to be content with the many compliments lavished on their patience under suffering, and a suggestion that they should either 'work at lower prices or . . . employ their labour in some other manner.'[5]

According to Mr. Ainsworth[6] the delegates disappointed by Government 'applied to the opposition, to Mr. Whit-

[1] H.O., 42. 110, February 1811.   [2] See H.O., 42. 110, 42. 115.
[3] See Hansard.   [4] H.O., 42, 117, May 25, 1811.
[5] Hansard, June 24, 1811.   [6] See p. 76 above.

bread in particular, his answer as near as can be repeated was
as follows : " You have only to petition the King to dismiss
his Ministers, we can do nothing while they are in Office, etc."
The answer of the delegates was, " No, we will not make our
concern a party question, we only want the protection we
ought to have and we would sooner die than forward such
a petition." ' [1]

How the conduct of the House of Commons struck the
petitioners is told in a remarkable paper giving an account
of the proceedings, signed by Richard Taylor, secretary of
the committee for the petition, but said to be the composition of John Knight.[2] This paper may be said to mark a
definite date, from which the mass of the weavers, recognising
the uselessness of appeals to Parliament, as it was then constituted, were driven more and more to take up the cause of
reform.

The paper gives an account of the number of signatures and
delegates sent up and the reference of the question to a committee whose report was to be considered on the 19th June,
but as there was no House on the 19th or 20th the business did
not come on till the 21st, ' when, by a motion of the Chancellor
of the Exchequer, it was again put off till the 24th, when,
with a view, as it would appear, to get rid of so troublesome
a question, it was a second time put off to a period, at which
it was then expected the House would be prorogued, and the
Session ended.' The evidence produced by the delegates
gave ample proof of their sufferings, sufferings which the committee lamented without suggesting one solitary expedient
to remedy them. As for the expedients proposed by the
petitioners the committee found some of the measures too
big for the time they could give to them, and others likely to
interfere with individual liberty, and ' tending to circumscribe
matters which ought to be left to their own operation, and
which like water, would find their own level.' The suggestion
of pecuniary aid they dismissed as raising vain hopes and as
inadequate.

' We are only mechanics, of course ill acquainted with the
reason why the same measures are frequently opposed, at one
time, by the same arguments by which at other times they
are vindicated and suported.' But considering the number
of the petitioners and the extent of their sufferings ' was it

[1] H.O., 42. 197.
[2] Enclosed in a letter from Mr. Fletcher, November 21, 1811 (H.O., 42. 117).

possible that some reasonable portion of hope should not have been founded on these circumstances ?   But when we consider likewise, that the Legislature has already interfered in matters of apparently less moment—has enacted laws for regulating the price of *corn*, for fixing the assize of *bread*, for fixing the price of labour in the case of the Spitalfields Weavers, and Journeymen Tailors of London ; for augmenting the salaries of *Judges* and *Clergymen* ; for regulating commerce, and a multitude of other things, which time would fail to enumerate. To say nothing of the Act now pending, or just passed into a law, for fixing a minimum on bank paper ; and considering moreover, that every law by which society are (*sic*) bound together, are subject to the same objections as those brought forward against the prayer of our petition being granted ; namely that it is an infringement of individual liberty.   This Committee are utterly at a loss to conceive on what fair ground Legislative interference can be improper under circumstances so necessitous. If a large mound be projected from the one bank of a river, the stream must necessarily make inroads on the opposite shore ; and if laws be made to regulate the price of the necessaries of life, laws should also be enacted for regulating the wages by which such provisions must be purchased, especially when (*as in our case*) such wages have lost all reasonable balance and proportion.' The paper then enters into a statement of accounts showing the amount subscribed to have been £109, 6s. 11½d. and the expenses exclusive of this address £108, 12s. 4½d.

The most significant part of the paper follows. The moral to be drawn from these events is that the House of Commons (' as at present constituted or appointed ') is ' unfit to manage your affairs. . . . They, the Members of that House, can make arrangements which advance the price of provisions—increase your taxes—introduce such a state of things as diminishes your business and employment, and reduces your wages, but when you state to them that you cannot exist under these accumulated and accumulating evils, they then coolly tell you they *cannot* relieve you. Had you possessed 70,000 votes for the election of Members to sit in that House, would your application have been treated with such indifference, not to say inattention ? We believe not.' The petitioners are urged to exert themselves to recover the right of electing representatives and extending the franchise ' as far as taxation.'

The Luddite disturbances of 1812 are described fully else-where. It is in connection with these disturbances that we meet for the first time the complaint against the new rival, the power-loom.

As the wages for weaving sank lower and lower, the weavers grew more and more dependent on the earnings of their children. Weaving became in fact a parasitic trade.

Meanwhile the weavers tried one more expedient. Although the attempt to obtain a particular Act to regulate wages had failed, the Acts of Elizabeth and James empowering magistrates to fix wages were still unrepealed, and at this time the workers in various trades in London and elsewhere endeavoured to put them in force locally. The story of the cotton weavers in Scotland, who in 1811, at the expense of £3000, extorted a reasonable scale of rates from the magistrates, but failed to extort an order to enforce it, and were afterwards, when they struck, put into prison for their pains, has been told by Mr. and Mrs. Webb in their *History of Trade Unionism*.[1]

The cotton weavers in Carlisle also, after an inconclusive meeting with the magistrates and gentry in April 1812, ' waited on Mr. Christian with a petition, in which were abstracts from two Acts of Parliament, asserting the power of the magistrates to regulate the price of manufacturers' labour. Mr. Christian promised them that as soon as possible his father, Mr. Curwen, would hold a meeting of the magistrates, when their petition should be duly considered.' [2]

In Bolton, the magistrates themselves were favourable to this method of obtaining a minimum wage. In the very middle of the Luddite disturbances Mr. Fletcher wrote the following remarkable passage to the Home Office : [3] ' If the low Wages of Weavers (although they have been a little advanced) could be increased so as to meet the present high Price of Provisions ; it would doubtless tend to alleviate the distresses and to lessen the complaints of the poor ; but how to accomplish so desirable a Measure in regard to Provisions, is perhaps beyond the competence of Government ; with respect to Weavers' Wages, though it be very delicate to inter-fere—yet as it is acknowledged by almost all the Master Manu-facturers, that an advance of 5 per cent. on the value of the Goods, when sold, would not operate to lessen the demand

---

[1] P. 52. See Committee on Artisans and Machinery, 1824, pp. 60 ff.
[2] *Annual Register*, 1812 ; *Chronicle*, p. 63.
[3] H.O., 40. 1, April 11, 1812.

it would seem to follow that, if they *would agree* to advance
the Weavers' Wages 15 per cent. (equal to about 5 per cent.
on the Article) it would tend to the Benefit of the Weaver
without injury to his Employer. But this they cannot agree
to do amongst themselves to the Extent desired. There is
however a Statute 1st Jac. 1 which authorizes Magistrates
at their Easter Quarter Sessions to rate Wages not only of
Labourers but of all others—And lately in the Term Reports
July 1810 or 1811 the case came before the King's Bench in
an appeal from the Paper Manufacturers of Kent—The result
of which was that the *Power* of the Magistrates to rate Wages
was recognized—and that they had a right to exercise a discretion therein. It has been mentioned amongst the Magistrates and will be further agitated next Week (though perhaps
not formally) whether it will be prudent to provoke an application from the Weavers to this Effect—your opinion as to the
propriety of such a step would be very agreeable. . . .'

Unfortunately for the weavers' hopes, the opinion of the
Government was unfavourable to the propriety, so unfavourable indeed that they proceeded next year, 1813, to repeal
the laws which it was proposed to use. In moving the second
reading of the repealing Bill in the House of Lords,[1] Lord
Sidmouth remarked that at the time that recent petitions for
regulating wages had been discussed in the House of Commons
it was not known that there were Acts in existence for regulating the rate of wages ' but in the course of the last year,
it had been discovered that there were Acts both in England
and Scotland rendering it imperative on magistrates to fix
the rate of wages.' Sidmouth assumed—and rightly assumed
—that it was only necessary to mention the existence of this
legislation to secure its repeal. ' It did not require minds so
enlightened as those of their Lordships to be aware how pernicious such a state of things must be both to the employer
and the servant, but especially to the latter. They must all
be convinced therefore that it was expedient to repeal these
pernicious statutes.'

The disappointment of the weavers at the destruction of
their hopes is expressed in a petition from the cotton weavers
of Bolton presented to Parliament on February 25, 1813.[2]
After telling the old story of the failure of the Arbitration Act
and of their unavailing attempts to obtain an Act for regulating wages they continue ' that, about twelve months since,

[1] *Parliamentary Register*, April 6, 1813.   [2] *House of Commons Journal.*

it was found that the Statute of 5 Eliz. (if acted upon) was competent to afford the desired relief, and it was resorted to in certain cases, but the want of generality prevented its obtaining at that time, especially as it can be acted on only at the Easter Quarter Sessions, or six weeks thereafter; and that, as Petitions to the Magistrates were almost general at the Easter Quarter Sessions, and all graciously received at each different jurisdiction, much hope was entertained that at the next Easter Sessions the Magistrates would settle the wages of the Petitioners, and they obtain food by their industry, and that the present Bill to repeal the aforesaid Law has sunk the spirits of the Petitioners beyond description, having no hope left. . . .'

The spirits of the petitioners must have been raised in spite of the action of Parliament by the end of the year, for wheat fell and trade revived.[1] Even Mr. Fletcher could glean no tales of dark revolutionary plots from the reports of his ' confidants.' The Jacobins, he writes, can do little owing to the prosperous state of trade which enables industrious men to earn a comfortable subsistence for themselves and their families.[2] This prosperity continued through 1814,[3] which was looked back upon as a year of plenty by the starving weavers of 1816. A diligent weaver in 1814, they said, could earn an average of 16s. 6d. a week.[4] In spite of the prosperity there was an attempt to reduce the spinners' wages one-third (to 2d. instead of 3d. a pound), an attempt that was compromised by an agreement to work a shorter time at the old rate.

The end of the war next year, which was expected to bring the golden age, brought instead hordes of discharged soldiers and sailors to join the already overcrowded ranks of the weavers. Instead of work increasing, the demand for weavers' labour fell off.

[1] See Smart, *Economic Annals*, 1801-20, p. 364. Wheat which was 122s. 8d. in March fell to 73s. 6d. in December. The quartern loaf fell from 1s. 6½d. to less than 1s.

[2] H.O., 42. 136, December 16, 1813.

[3] Tooke, *History of Prices*, ii. 6, says that the manufacturing population were in a more satisfactory state than they had been for the last twenty years (quoted Smart, *op. cit.*, p. 397).

[4] Petition of Stockport Weavers, 1816; see H.O., 42. 150, May 21, 1816. Some sort of activity was going on amongst workmen's societies for Nadin early in 1814 reported that all trades, including the weavers, were meeting in different societies and forming combinations against their masters (H.O., 44. 138, March 26).

Not only was trade depressed but wheat rose steadily through the year 1816, till it reached the famine price of 103s. in December.[1] The iron and coal industries suffered perhaps most severely in 1816, but in the cotton districts of Lancashire too the misery was extreme. It was a year of soup and Reform agitation.

The Weavers turn to Reform

The most interesting feature of the year was the growth of a new spirit amongst the cotton operatives. The Reform agitation captured the district, and henceforth the disentangling of political and industrial movements is a hard task. The best minds amongst the weavers had followed the advice of the address of 1811. A spirit of hostility to employers and authorities is a marked feature of this new development. Soup might flow in streams from the kitchens of the charitable ; gentlemen of the old school might feel certain that ' such kind attentions at this juncture must have the happyest effect ' ; [2] the soup kettle became an object of ridicule.[3] Under the influence of the reformers the weavers looked rudely into the gift horse's mouth and began to talk of sinecures. The generous London subscription of £42,000 to relieve their distress was ungraciously defined as ' about £3000 more than Lord Arden receives for doing nothing,' [4] and inconvenient calculations were made of the extent to which the sinecures and pensions paid by the Government might relieve distress if diverted in that direction. ' What do the poor want ? ' ran one pamphlet. ' *Wages* not alms : *Work* not charity,' was the answer.[5]

At Bolton the weavers drew through the streets ' an effigy of an old worn-out Soldier, begging, in *vain*, for *Soup*, to relieve the Calls of Hunger.' [6] The procession ended by drowning the effigy. ' This was intended to ridicule the charitable Endeavours of the well-disposed to relieve by their contributions the necessities of the Poor,' and also, it is added, to show the unprofitable nature of a soldier's life and their hatred of

---

[1] Smart, *op. cit.*, p. 490.   [2] H.O., 42. 155, November 4, 1816.
[3] Cobbett issued a pamphlet representing the rich as offering the poor 'a Basin of Carrion Soup in the one hand and a Halter in the other' (H.O., 42. 156, December 6).   Cf. Bagguley in 1817 : 'We do not sell them pea Soup after taking from you tenpence out of every shilling, Gentlemen' (H.O., 42. 164).
[4] H.O., 42. 154, October 26, 1816.   [5] *Ibid.*
[6] H.O., 42. 153, September 14, 1816.

the profession.[1]   At Wigan the attitude of the poor was even more uncompromising: some declined to receive the local charitable subscription, ' using very impious language and observing they would have Reform not relief,[2] and they went to the length of stoning a charitable committee ' sitting to consider the distresses of and to administer relief to the Poor.' [3]

But though the Reform agitation was the leading movement, it would be a mistake to suppose that other movements were dead.   At Bolton, indeed, there was an anti-Reform party among the weavers calling themselves *loyal weavers* who sent Thomas Thorpe and Richard Needham to the magistrates as delegates to draw attention to the universal distress,[4] and the Stockport weavers again sent up a petition to the Prince Regent praying that Government should put a stop to the exportation of cotton yarn.[5] The question of the export of cotton yarn was hotly discussed, and the weavers were not the only persons in favour of prohibiting it.   Four Deputy Lieutenants of Lancashire sent up a memorial stating that whilst every other branch of the cotton trade was declining, the export of cotton twist was increasing the spinning trade to an unparalleled extent, and that unless some relief was afforded to the weavers it would be impossible to keep the peace.[6]   In Stockport, too, many ' respectable inhabitants ' signed a memorial to the Prince Regent against the exportation, without reflecting, as Mr. Lloyd, the magistrate's clerk, pointed out, that the spinning itself gave employment to nearly half the population.[7]

The regulation of wages was again advocated at this time by its consistent friend, Thomas Ainsworth.[8]   He recalled in a letter to Sidmouth later [9] the interview that he had with him in 1816 when he presented at Sidmouth's request ' a statement

---

[1] At Stockport when a proposal was made at a gathering of weavers to ask the Rector to call a general meeting on the subject of the distress, people called out ' Damn the Rector. . . . We may wait for ever if we wait for him.   He will order us soup ! ' (H.O., 42. 152, August 27).

[2] H.O., 42. 153 (Byng, October 15).   [3] H.O., 42. 154, October 29.

[4] They stated that the wages of those in work were 5s. a week and that half the weavers of the district (20,500 in all) would be out of work in three weeks (H.O., 42. 150, May 29).

[5] Lord Bulkeley (Lord Lieutenant), to whom the petition was sent for presentation, writes characteristically to Sidmouth saying that he had kept it back, 'as I did not like to be precipitate in sending your Lordship anything unpleasant' (H.O., 42. 152).

[6] H.O., 42. 151, June 19   [7] H.O., 42. 152, July 23.
[8] See p. 76 above.   [9] H.O., 42. 197.

of the fair average price of labour paid to Weavers,' adding his own suggestions for relief. At the time of the interview, ' a petition lay upon the Table signed by above 20,000 weavers to the Prince Regent. I hope your Lordship will pardon my being plain. I did feel most intensely the slight and cursory manner in which your Lordship overlooked the paper, and the few minutes you took to give a decisive answer to what concerned near a million of souls. Seeing their weekly earnings you said, " poor things ! but can nothing be done for them." I replied (feeling as I did, rather too warmly, for which I was afterwards very sorry), " It is as easy as for your Lordship to wind up your Watch." After a very few words, laying your hand upon the Weavers' Petition you said, " You may tell the Petitioners, I will present their Petition to the P. Regent at the Levee on Monday next." Then obeying your Lordship's motion, I bowed and left the Room. . . . Week after week I was enquired of, if any answer was received ? No, No, No, was as often repeated.'

Perhaps the most interesting instance of the blending of the old agitation with the new is afforded by the story of the Bolton meeting organised by the middle-class Reform party, with the object of considering the universal distress and pointing the moral that the only hope of relief lay in Parliamentary Reform. Amongst eighteen of the usual resolutions passed at meetings of the kind against war, taxation and sinecures,[1] and in favour of reform, is interposed a resolution not commonly found in the reports of such meetings : ' That until a general and effectual relief can be obtained for our National Distress, it is highly necessary as a Temporary Measure, that the export of Cotton Yarn should be prohibited, and that some Minimum of Wages should be fixed for the labour of the Manufacturing Artisan.' [2]

When the weavers were considering the question of striking for better wages at the end of the year, a strike that they carried out for a short time in one or two districts, the reformers seem to have dissuaded them from their purpose.[3]

The year 1817 brought a temporary check to the spread of the Reform movement in the suspension of the Habeas Corpus Act.

---

[1] Resolution 4 runs : ' That the Industrious Poor of this Town and neighbourhood would rather work than beg ; and have a particular aversion to receiving alms from those Placemen and Pensioners whose exorbitant and unmerited Incomes form one great cause of the public Distress.'

[2] H.O., 42. 153, October 7.   [3] H.O., 42. 156, December 6, 1816.

With the events of that year, including the Blanketeers' attempted march to London, we deal elsewhere.[1]

Trade revived at the end of 1817, and 1818 was a year of commercial prosperity.[2] Employment was brisk, but the wages which had been reduced avowedly under the stress of bad trade were not raised. The disastrous custom of supplementing the weavers' wages by parish relief had taken firm hold of the cotton district. An interesting paper sent up both by Mr. Lloyd and by Mr. Hay to the Home Office in 1818 touches on this development, and even Mr. Lloyd remarks, ' it is known that the Manufacturers do not pay their workpeople proper wages according to their present profits.' [3]

The paper is by a certain Mr. Smith, a gentleman of independent fortunes and principles, once a Jacobin now a friend to Government. He points out that the great increase of the cotton trade in 1817 over 1816 disposes of the argument that foreign competition makes it impossible to raise wages ; to the English manufacturers ' the price of the raw material is of no consideration if their workpeople can be paid out of the poor's rate—their capital in trade does not contribute to that fund but by the use of that fund their profits and their Capitals are gradually accumulating.' He narrates a story told him recently by the Rev. C. W. Ethelston of a workman earning 7s. a week who applied to his master, a man of the ' first respectability,' to raise his wages to 10s., to which the master replied ' that it would be of no service to him for that if he raised him to 10s. the Overseers of the Poor would *discontinue* their allowance of 3s. per week.' The practice of underselling by reducing wages, said Mr. Ethelston, began some thirty years before under the cry of foreign competition, and ' now the studied system is to *keep them* on the parish Books.' Mr. Smith adds that it would be to the advantage of the parish to support the weavers for a fortnight without their weaving a single piece, at the end of which time the masters would agree to pay half more than their present rates.[4]

The Spinners' Strike of 1810

The history of the cotton workers in the early years of the nineteenth century is mainly occupied with the melancholy

---

[1] See Chapter XII.   [2] Smart, *op. cit.*, pp. 610, 654.
[3] H.O., 42. 174, February 22 and 23, 1818 ; and H.O., 42. 179, August 1, 1818.
[4] Cf. the papers sent up by Mr. Hay (H.O., 42. 179, August 1, 1818): 'There is a *concurrence* of opinion among the English manufacturers that it serves their particular interests to have their workpeople at so low a price that they must be fed in part out of the Poors' rate which serves as a *bonus* to the Capital employed in manufacturing. The evil is growing into a system.'

fortunes of the weavers, but an important development must be noted among the spinners. They had formed themselves into Unions as soon as spinning became a separate industry for men.[1] As early as 1792 a friendly association of cotton spinners, whose members helped each other in times of distress or when resisting a reduction of wages, was founded in Stockport[2] and similar clubs were founded elsewhere under Friendly Society rules. Clubs would be broken up and restarted and broken up again. The first effort at amalgamation was made in 1810, when the different bodies in and round Manchester were organised as a 'General Union' whose affairs were conducted by a general congress of forty or fifty delegates. This General Union organised a strike, the object of which was to raise wages in the country up to the Manchester level.[3] The men at Preston and Stalybridge struck work and were supported by subscriptions from the spinners in Manchester and elsewhere who were still at work. Some interesting papers giving the amount of the contributions paid in by different shops and paid out to different towns were handed in to the Committee on Artisans and Machinery later; in one week the receipts at Manchester totalled £606, 16s. 9d., of which £363, 11s. was paid to 'Staley' and £62 to 'P' or Preston. Carlisle and Derbyshire contributed as well as the Lancashire towns. The answer of the masters to the men's action was to lock out the men in the whole district with the object of dissipating their funds, an object in which they succeeded. From 8000 to 10,000 persons were out of work for three or four months, most of these not themselves spinners, but children and persons involved with them in other branches. Only the spinners received relief from the funds, and when the funds were exhausted the men returned to work on the old terms. The Combination Laws were also used by the masters against the men at Stalybridge and there were a number of convictions at Stockport, most of which, however, on appeal were quashed at the next quarter sessions owing to technical informalities.[4]

[1] Chapman, *op. cit.*, p. 193.

[2] Committee on Artisans and Machinery, 1824, p. 409.

[3] For account of 1810 strike, see Committee on Artisans and Machinery, 1824, pp. 573-4 and 604-8.

[4] But Worsley, before Committee on Artisans and Machinery, 1824, p. 410, said that twenty-three men and one woman were committed to Manchester New Bailey for refusing to work under price and were sentenced to one month's imprisonment.

CHAPTER V

THE COTTON WORKERS

1818-1832

THE year 1818 was marked by the attempts of various sets of workers in Lancashire to improve their conditions. We have seen how from 1811 the weavers, disappointed by the results of their appeals to Parliament for a minimum wage, had taken up the cause of Parliamentary Reform. That slow movement had received a check from the events of 1817 and the imprisonment of its leaders, under the suspension of the Habeas Corpus Act, and the cotton workers turned once more to industrial action in the hope of gaining a share in the renewed commercial prosperity.[1]

There were four separate strikes amongst the cotton workers : (1) the jenny spinners at Stockport, (2) the power-loom weavers at Stockport, (3) the Manchester spinners, (4) the whole body of Lancashire and Yorkshire weavers.

The jenny spinners of Stockport who worked in factories on hand-jennies seem to have been an isolated body who acted apart from other spinners. From 1814-17 their wages had been gradually reduced from 3d. to 2d. a pound, with the result that the men were making only 15s. or 16s. a week for a fourteen-hour day instead of 24s. They asked to return to the 1814 rate of pay, offering to work fewer days, but were refused. About 800 of them then struck, and after remaining out for some six weeks, settled the dispute with their masters, by agreeing to take 2½d. a pound, a figure which worked out to a wage of 17s. 6d. to 19s. a week for a fourteen-hour day. There were no prosecutions, and they remained on 'agree-

---

[1] Cf. Knight's speech at Stockport : 'Some time ago you were tugging at the cable of Reform ; but Reform not coming, and your sufferings being deep, it is no wonder your patience became exhausted. In this state of things you were resolved to try another experiment and attempted to advance your wages . . .' (H.O., 42. 181, October 17, 1818).

able terms' with their masters for many years. They professed to have had no association or funds and to have lived during the six weeks' strike on credit from the shopkeepers.[1]

The second strike, that of the power-loom weavers of Stockport, is interesting as being the first instance of organised action by this new class of worker.[2] The power-looms, in contrast to the hand-looms, were massed together in factories and were worked, as we have said, by girls, women, boys, and young men. In Stockport there were many of these factories, and early in June the power-loom weavers struck for higher wages. According to Mr. Lloyd, at the time of the strike they were receiving 15s. a week ; they asked for an advance in rates which would come to an extra 5s. a week. Things went quietly till Mr. Garside, head of one of the chief factories, introduced some workpeople [3] from Burton-on-Trent to whom he was reported to be paying the wages which he refused his old workers.[4] Infuriated by this importation of blacklegs the Stockport mob rioted for three nights round Garside's factory and round the house where the imported workers were lodged, throwing stones and breaking windows. The Riot Act was read,[5] and the Yeomanry and some soldiers from Manchester called in before the mob would go home.[6] To the horror of the energetic Mr. Lloyd, many even of the ' respectable inhabitants,' including some of the constables themselves, were slow in rallying to Mr. Garside's defence, for they 'dared to dispute the policy of his conduct ' ; and they went so far

[1] See Committee on Artisans and Machinery, 1824, p. 412.

[2] For the documents from which the following account is drawn, see H.O., 42. 178, and H.O., 42. 179.

[3] Four or five according to Mr. Lloyd, sixteen men according to ' B.' (H.O., 42. 179).

[4] Mr. Lloyd denied this (H.O., 42. 179, August 1).

[5] The magistrate, Mr. Harrison, also harangued the populace with some strong language and accused Bagguley, Johnson, and Drummond of being at the bottom of the business, an accusation that produced some lively correspondence in the *Manchester Observer*. See *Manchester Observer* of August 8 (in H.O., 42. 179), where Drummond taunts Harrison with his ' propensity to become the rival of Oliver and the favourite of the sanctified Sidmouth . . .'

[6] One of the men wounded by the soldiers afterwards died. At the inquest he was decided to have ' died by the Visitation of God,' a verdict which caused some disorder, as the witnesses had sworn to the violence having been done by one of the Yeomanry, 'altho',' writes Mr. Lloyd, ' I knew it was one of the 13th whom I have seen and heard confess it at the Barracks this afternoon' (H.O., 42. 179, August 5).

later as to subscribe to the Turn Outs, from which it is perhaps fair to infer that the strikers had a good deal of justification.

But Mr. Lloyd was not the man to let the cause of law and order suffer ; the masters, indeed, he found lacking in energy and unanimity ; they asked for troops instead of using the Combination Act ; the strikers' numbers were small but they made it an unpleasant task to fill up their places, and did not hesitate to give young women who were prepared to work a warning by holding them under the pump. He determined to scotch the conspiracy by stopping their means of support. On August 8, about a month after the beginning of the strike, he raided a public-house where they were distributing strike pay and took various men and women into custody under the Combination Act. A few days later the magistrate sent four of the men who had been giving out the strike pay to Chester Castle for three months ; some young women who had been receiving it were merely bound over ; but, commented Mr. Lloyd, ' if the Workpeople continue refractory I have abundant Evidence to proceed farther.' The men arrested affected a strange lapse of memory with regard to the source and the destination of the money. ' I was counting some Coppers yesterday,' said one of them. ' I cannot pretend to say what for, I cannot pretend to say where it had been got—I cannot pretend to say the sum.' But Mr. Lloyd's policy had broken the strike and he rejoiced to see the beaten steam-loom weavers returning to work without an advance.

The Spinners' Strike of 1818

We must now turn to the most important strike of the year, that of the Manchester cotton spinners. This was one of a series of strikes in Manchester.[1] Early in June the bricksetters with their labourers, and next the joiners and carpenters, turned out for an advance in wages. The former gained all, the latter half their demand. Then followed the dyers, who paraded the streets for two or three weeks till they too gained their demands. A week after the dyers had returned to work, nearly all the spinners, after previous notice to their employers, turned out in one day, and with them of course came all the persons whose employment depended on

[1] H.O., 42. 178, July 29, 1818.

the spinners. The factories emptied their population into
the streets. By July 18 it was estimated that at least 20,000
persons were idle. The actual spinners seem to have numbered about 2200.[1]

Estimates of the spinners' wages before the strike were
given by their masters and transmitted by the magistrates
to the Home Office. Thirty or even thirty-one shillings a
week, clear of deductions, was the usual figure.[2] Their prosperous circumstances were contrasted with the lot of the
weavers whose wages were only a half or even a third of those
of the spinners. The advocates of the masters laid stress on
the ingratitude of the spinners. ' No class of people have
had such constant and uniform employment for the last twenty-
eight years, as they have had : and this advantage the spinner
enjoys at the risk and expense of his employer.'[3] It is
interesting to turn to the spinners' own account of the
dispute.

A first address ' to the Inhabitants of Manchester and its
Vicinity' merely asks for subscriptions :[4] ' We the distressed
Journeymen Cotton Spinners have been working a considerable Time for Prices very inadequate to procure even the
coarsest necessaries of Life for ourselves and Families, and
have been obliged by degrees to part with our Goods and
Clothing, and are now unable to pay the demands which
Justice requires from us ; but having solicited our Employers
for an advance of Prices (which has been refused) yet from
the present State of the Market, we have every Reason to
conclude that our reasonable Request ought to have been
complied with, and their Profits (had their humanity kept
Pace with their Avarice) would still have enabled them to
live in affluence.'

A second address to the public from the mule cotton spinners
of Manchester gives their case in moderate language.[5] They
wish to correct misstatements in newspapers. ' We are stated

[1] See H.O., 42. 179, August 7.

[2] e.g. Mr. Norris, July 29 (H.O., 42. 178) : 'The spinners averaging them
throughout the mills in Manchester gain 30s. per week each hand . . .' On
August 13 (H.O., 42. 179) he gives the average earnings as 31s. 10d. for adult
male spinners, and 18s. for women and boys of sixteen or eighteen. The
Manchester Chronicle of August 15, 1818, gives 31s. as the average wage clear
of deductions.

[3] Manchester Chronicle, August 15, 1818.

[4] H.O., 42. 178.

[5] H.O., 42, 179 ; also given in Annual Register, 1818 ; Chronicle, pp. 100-1,

in all the papers to have turned out for an advance of wages;
this we admit to be in part true, but not absolutely so.   Two
years ago, when our employers demanded a reduction of ten
hanks, they affirmed that the state of the market imperiously
called for such reduction ; but when the markets would admit
of an advance, they would willingly give it.   We depended
on their honour, and continued to labour for more than 12
months at the reduction proposed.   About 10 months since,
on comparing the price of cotton and yarn, we found that the
markets would allow our employers to fulfil their promise;
we therefore solicited them to that purpose, and only wished
to be reinstated in the same prices we worked at previously
to that reduction.   Some declared they could not give it;
others they would not ; but the greater part, that they would,
if others did, but they should not like to be the first.   Thus
we continued working and soliciting for the last eight months,
though the demand for yarn has been unprecedented, and the
consequent rise in twist great ; they have still refused our
just request ; and in order to cause a belief that trade was
in a declining state, gave notice, that their mills should only
work three days in the week, which appeared so extremely
ridiculous, that the very children employed in factories laughed
at it.

   ' It is asserted that our average wages amount to 30s. or
40s. per week—it is evident that this statement was made by
some individual either ignorant or interested.   In 1816, the
average clear wages of the spinners in Manchester was about
24s., they were then reduced from 20 to 25 per cent., and have
ever since laboured under that reduction.   And it is to be
remarked, that spinners relieve their own sick, as well as subscribe to other casualties ; therefore, when their hours of
labour, which are from 5 in the morning until 7 in the evening
(and in some mills longer) of unremitting toil, in rooms heated
from 70 to 90 degrees, are taken into consideratï‥, we believe
the public will say with us, that no body of workmen receive
so inadequate a compensation for their labour.'

   The discrepancy between the sum the masters professed
to give and the sum the men professed to receive is indeed
considerable.   The men accused some masters at any rate of
deliberate falsification : ' Our Master keeps a Book and takes
off 6d. the 1s. for Big Wheels and 4d. the 1s. for the little
wheels and I have gone home with 12s. and sometimes 10s. a
week.   It is a false statement of him [that we were getting 30s.

a week] and he said he could bring his Books before the Magistrates and shew that we got 35s. a week.'[1]

The spinners, as we have seen, were a well organised and compact body, and they imposed order and discipline on the large body of workers involved with them in the dispute. So quiet was their behaviour that it caused grave anxiety to General Byng: '. . . the peaceable demeanour of so many thousand unemployed Men is not natural.'[2] Their method of campaign was to assemble at 4 or 5 A.M., four hundred or five hundred or even a thousand strong, at any spinning factory where work was being carried on, 'and so carry off by force or intimidation though without any violent breach of the peace the hands who might be disposed to go to work.'[3] Another resource which gave an outlet to energies that might otherwise have caused disturbances was to parade the streets in great processions. The impression made on 'B.' alias Bent, the spy,[4] by these parades of the factory hands is perhaps worth notice.[5] 'The whole of the Spinners,' he writes, 'is out, Except about 500 . . .,' they march along twice a day, 'the[y] marched By piccadilly on Tuesday and was 23½ minets in going Bye if his Majests Minesters could see the people that day or ether of the days since the[y] would have

---

[1] Examination of John Hague, H.O., 42. 179, August 29.

A remarkable article in the *Gorgon* for September 12, 1818 (see H.O., 42. 180) gives the wages as follows:

		£	s.	d.
One operative spinner assisted by three children called piecers will spin 20 lbs. per week of 160 hanks to the lb. making	.	2	3	4
Out of this he pays:		£	s.	d.
1st piecer per week		0	9	2
2nd ,, ,, ...		0	7	2
3rd ,, ,, ...		0	5	8
Candles on average per week . . .		0	1	6
Sick and other incidental expenses . .		0	1	6
		1	5	0

Leaving per week for maintenance of himself and family, £0 18 4

The same article mentions that the number of spinners in different establishments varies from 14 to 150, and that there are 14 or 15 masters in Manchester who employ 150, and reckons that at the price at which cotton twist was selling when the men struck, the masters were making a profit of £4, 3s. 4d. a week on each spinner. The *Manchester Observer* (favourable to the men), August 8, 1818, says the wages vary: some make 25s., out of which they pay piecer 7s. 6d. and scavenger 2s., leaving 16s. net. Often there are other deductions too.

[2] H.O., 42. 178, July 26.   [3] H.O., 42. 178, July 29.
[4] See p. 67 above.   [5] H.O., 42. 178, July 11.

past Sir Robert peels Bill[1] those who should have apeared
as men was Like Boys of fifteen an sixteen and most of them
Cannot Mesure more than 5 feet 2 or 3 Inches, the plan the[y]
take is as follows, one man from Eich shop is chose by the
People and he commands them he forms them in Ranks
and atends them on the march and as the soal Command and
the[y] obey him as Strickley as the armey do their Colonel and
as Little Talking as in a Regiment.'

The spinners' strike spread on July 20 to Wigan, where the
strikers paraded the streets in much the same manner, headed
in this case by a delegate from Manchester or Stockport. The
Stockport spinners were accused of stirring up this strike for
fear that if Wigan wages were not advanced their own might
fall.

The connection between the Reform movement and the
strikes is a question of some interest. Even those who wished
to find the reformers at the root of all evil were unable to
credit the main body with an active part. If the Reform of
Parliament was a panacea for all the evils from which the
working classes was suffering, it was obviously a mistake to
expend energies on strikes. Added to this the middle-class
reformers, some of them employers, would hardly be enthusiastic on the strikers' side. Johnson, one of the more violent
section, was reported by one of Mr. Chippendale's 'confidants'[2]
to have declared that the reformers' party had considered the
question of taking an ostensible share in the discontents of
the different trades and had resolved against the policy,
and that the reformers who had individually joined in the
fray had annoyed the 'people of Property.'[3] The views of
the 'people of Property' are illustrated in the handbill circulated among the 'Discontented Manufacturers' which explained that wages could not rise without the trade passing
over to the foreigner, that the real evil was the high price of
provisions, that this was due to taxation, and that the remedy
was to lower taxation and abolish sinecures by reforming
the House of Commons.[4]

There was, however, an indirect way in which the Reform
movement had altered the atmosphere. Ogden, Knight, and
the other working-class reformers, undaunted by long months
of prison under the suspension of the Habeas Corpus Act,

---

[1] Peel's Eleven Hour Bill; see *Town Labourer*, p. 164.
[2] Mr. Chippendale kept a watch on the Oldham district for Mr. Fletcher.
[3] H.O., 42. 179.   [4] H.O., 42. 179, August 10.

were no sooner set free than they used their freedom to pour forth what Mr. Norris, the Stipendiary Magistrate of Manchester, termed 'the most poisonous and alarming sentiments' about the Government. These men said much that was foolish and extravagant; they sometimes gave themselves ridiculous airs; their speeches are tedious reading, and yet England owes them everlasting gratitude for their indomitable courage and for the spirit that refused to be silent though ruin faced them and their families. The effect of their conduct on the cotton operatives was thus described by Mr. Norris: 'I do not by any means think that the system of turning out in the different trades is connected with this idea' [reform] 'or that the sentiment itself has taken root in the minds of the mass of the population, yet I am disposed to think that this idea gains ground, and that in consequence the working classes have become not only more pertinacious but more insolent in their demands and demeanour. . . .'[1] This changed demeanour was also deplored by Mr. Gray, owner of one of the principal factories which were afterwards attacked. He advocated strong measures; 'Nothing in my opinion,' he writes, 'is more unwise in any case than to allow the lower orders to feel their strength, and to extend their communications with each other without restraint. Allow them to go on uninterrupted and they become daily more licentious. . . .'[2]

But though the main body of the Reformers held aloof from the strike, two men, Bagguley and Drummond, identified before with the disastrous Blanketeer movement,[3] threw themselves headlong into the battle. Closely associated with them was the Rev. Joseph Harrison, Methodist preacher of Stockport, who, to the disgust of Mr. Lloyd, ' preached for the turn outs in Manchester,' and called himself ' Chaplain to the poor and needy,' an offence only surpassed by that of Bagguley in calling Christ the greatest Reformer.[4] It is not unreasonable to trace the hand of the enthusiastic if indiscreet Bagguley in a handbill published early in July entitled 'The Mule Spinners' Address to the Public,'[5] an address which was afterwards repudiated by the spinners' committee.

During some weeks, except for a few unimportant riots, the strike continued its peaceful course without any check from the authorities. The magistrates and the masters did

[1] H.O., 42. 178, July 29.
[2] H.O., 42. 179, August 27.
[3] See Chapter XII.
[4] H.O., 42. 179, August 11.
[5] See text of address in *Town Labourer*, pp. 301 f.

not see eye to eye, and the strikers reaped the benefit. The
magistrates blamed the masters for their inactivity. ' My
impression,' wrote the Rev. Mr. Hay, ' is that they are collec-
tively and individually frightened. . . . Some of the masters
have cases of combination, but they decline, in fact refuse,
to bring the cases forward.' [1] The masters, or at any rate
some of them, on the other hand, found the magistrates supine.
Mr. Gray arranged for a number of mills to send their over-
lookers to identify the men who were standing about in the
streets ; armed with a list of names he and another big master
spinner then waited on the magistrates and asked for warrants
under the Combination Act ; the magistrates, with curious
caution, refused to grant the warrants, explaining that they
did not think standing round the mill without using threats
or gestures was sufficient evidence of intimidation under the
Combination Act. The magistrates were in fact acting under
advice from the Law Officers. Mr. Norris and the borough-
reeve had both written to the Home Office to ask whether it
would be prudent or indeed legal to drive away those troublesome persons who stood about ' in clusters ' in the streets
and declared their right to stand in the highway. The answer
of the Solicitor-General (R. Gifford) is remarkable : ' If the
persons assembled about the Mills, or on Kersall Moor conduct
themselves peaceably and quietly, and there are no circumstances attending these meetings of actual force or violence,
or having an apparent tendency thereto, I do not think the
Magistrates will be justified in interfering to disperse them.' [2]

In a few instances men were tried under the Combination
Act.[3] However much employers and magistrates differed
in their opinions of each other's activity, they agreed in thinking that the Combination Law should be strengthened. ' It
is very much to be regretted,' wrote Mr. Gray, ' that the Laws
applicable to Combinations do not grant greater latitude to
the powers vested in Magistrates. If they had Authority to

[1] H.O., 42. 178, July 30.   [2] H.O., 42. 179, August 19.
[3] e.g. On August 4 Mr. Hay reports that a man has been sent to Lancaster
Castle for two months, and on August 13 two spinners were tried for obstructing
and ill-treating others at Mr. Houldsworth's mill and were sentenced by the
magistrates to three months of Lancaster Castle : whereupon they gave notice
of appeal, ' thus rendering, wrote Mr. Norris on August 13, ' all that has been
done a perfect nullity, and it does appear from this case that the Combination
Act is of very little if of any use. The case could not be made out against them
as for a conspiracy. The power of appeal should in my humble opinion be taken
away' (H.O., 42. 179).

disperse the assemblages above described and to grant stationary protection during the existence of combinations, such
remedies applied to the present case would in a very short
time terminate the whole matter.'[1]

How were the spinners, and the workers involved with them,
supported during the strike ?   As we have seen, they appealed
to the public for subscriptions, but there is nothing to show
that they met with any large response.   In addition to their
own funds some other trades certainly sent contributions ;
the hatters at Newcastle, Staffordshire, sent £5, and money was
collected in the Potteries ; the Fustian Cutters, the Weavers,
the Millwrights, the Calico Printers, the Tailors, and the
London Shoemakers all sent subscriptions.[2]   'The money,'
said one of the Committee, 'is a gift to us from all Trades.
They see that the Masters are determined to starve us out
and they give us a trifle to keep us as well as they can.'[3]   The
sums sent were not very considerable, except in the spy Samuel
Fleming's reports.[4]   The London Boot and Shoe makers, for
example sent £20, the Hatters £10.   At the end of July after
four weeks' unemployment the funds ran low, and the spinners
were reported to have received only 1s. 4d. per head on pay
day, of which 6d. went to the piecers ; whilst next week the
sum fell to 9d. a head to *male* spinners and nothing to any
one else.[5]   The misery 'amongst those connected with the
factories (women and children) but who are not really turnout
Spinners' soon became acute, and appeals for Poor Relief
were generally refused.[6]   As usual in such cases the strikers
lived chiefly on credit from the small shops ; one small huckster
was said to have given the men credit for £250.[7]

It was clear that the strike must soon collapse for want of
funds, and early in August a desperate effort was made to
form a General Union of Trades.   This short-lived scheme
we describe in detail elsewhere.[8]

An intercepted letter which fell into Mr. Lloyd's hands, a
copy of which he sent up to the Home Office, gives an account
of the position of the Spinners.   It is from Spinners to Colliers,

[1] H.O., 42. 179, August 24.   [2] H.O., 42. 179, August 12, 24, 28, 29.
[3] H.O., 42. 179, August 29.
[4] See H.O., 42. 179, August 24, where he says the London delegate brought
back £300.   Mr. Hobhouse of the Home Office endorses this, 'Probably
untrue or at least exaggerated.'   For Fleming, see Chapter x.
[5] H.O., 42. 178, July 28; H.O., 42. 179, August 1.
[6] H.O., 42. 179, August 5.   [7] H.O., 42. 179, August 11 and 12.
[8] *Town Labourer*, pp. 306 ff.

asking them to join the new General Union; it is dated August
7, 1818, from Staley Bridge, and runs as follows : [1]

'Sir,—The Spinners of Manchester have authorized me to
solicit you to join in their union of trade, as all trades in England
are uniting in one body for Trade and Reform, and you are desired
to send a delegate to all Meetings to consult matters over and
to inform you that you will be supported in your Trade in turn ;
A letter was received from London this day from the Silk Weavers
wishing to join them and offering their support, they have taken
all the big piecers in pay lest they should do mischief and their
numbers is 800, they have no less now on pay than 3000 in the
whole, we must try our Friends in every corner of the Land
wherever they can be found and which every exertion is now
making to accomplish and hope it will contribute to carry them
into ultimate success they seem quite determined not to return to
their Egyptian Slavery and haughty language and cruel usage for
the same terms they quited it for, and indeed nothing less than a
serious determination will ever bring their employers to any reason
for if Manchester is obliged to give way at last the Work People
in this and every other Town may bid an everlasting farewell to
having any comfort or above one half of the Wages that will
supply the common necessaries of Life.
  'I am for the Staley Bridge Spinners and by their Order,
Gentlemen, Your obedient Servant,   James Fielding.
  'To all Colliers in
      Newton Duckenfield Hyde
          and Staley Bridge.'

Before the actual formation of the General Union two delegates from the spinners, Henry Swindells and William Jones,
had been sent to London to enlist support. Swindells in his
absence was appointed 'Grand Secretary for the United
Trades of England.' [2]
Unfortunately for the Manchester strikers the support that
the delegates found in London was moral rather than financial.
Trades might join the General Union but it was another thing
to subscribe. The delegates scraped together some £30 and
sent it off to Manchester, but when they were collecting a few
pounds more at a meeting a reformer named Preston rather
brutally reminded them that what they were doing was illegal,
as there was an Act of Parliament called the Combination
Act to forbid it. [3]
Meantime in Manchester things were going badly for the

[1] H.O., 42. 179.   [2] H.O., 42. 179, August 8 and 14.
[3] H.O., 42. 179, August 24.

strikers; one master, Mr. Naylor, had yielded to the men's
demand about August 19, but he had never joined the body
of masters and was described by the borough-reeve as con-
sulting ' his own immediate Interests rather than the general
Welfare.' [1] His example was not followed, and the strikers'
funds got low; hunger sharpened their anger, and as workers
gradually dribbled into the mills the anger broke out into
riots. At the end of August there were various riots at Mr.
Birley's and at Messrs. Houldsworth's, whilst at Mr. Gray's mill
the Riot Act was read and some of the regular soldiers brought
in. On one occasion Nadin, the Deputy Constable, was
imprisoned in a mill and had to be rescued by soldiers, on
other occasions the mob bruised the beadles and carried off
some blacklegs in triumph. It was in vain that the magistrates took fifty constables into pay on August 26 instead of
the usual ten; the millowners asked for a horse patrol in
Oxford Road and Ancoats during the hours of going in and
coming out. The women and children gave great trouble.
' The women,' wrote Mr. Norris, ' (who are infinitely the
worst) and children are always put in front of the mobs, the
men keeping aloof.' [2]

The weavers were also about to strike, and the magistrates
became alarmed and determined to deal a decisive blow at
the spinners' organisation. On August 29 the constables
seized five of the committee of the cotton spinners with their
papers, and the magistrates committed them for conspiracy.
Warrants were issued against five others. The examination,
wrote Mr. Norris, shows that the system has not yet gone to
extreme length, but that the ultimate object is ' of the most
serious nature in a commercial point of view, though nothing
of a *political* nature *seems* mixed with it.' The men ordered
to watch the mills, he notes, were called ' Pickets.' There
seems to have been little secrecy and much organisation about
the proceedings of these pickets. They were ordered out in
the mornings, to the number of 40 or 50, or even one day 100.
The committee sat from 7.30 A.M. to 8 P.M. at the Rifleman
in the New Market.[3]

The committee were crippled also by the absconding of their
treasurer, John Medcalf, with £150, and it was thought advisable to recall Jones, his brother-in-law, the delegate in London,
lest he too should prove untrustworthy.[4] A new committee

[1] H.O., 42. 179, August 19 and 21.   [2] H.O., 42. 179, August 26 and 28.
[3] H.O., 42. 179, August 29.   [4] H.O., 42. 179, August 26, 29, and 31.

was appointed and delegates sent to Norwich, Carlisle, and elsewhere, but the spinners were fighting a losing battle. The turn-out of the weavers and colliers did them no good, and a second and more serious riot at Gray's mill on September 2 brought matters to a head. At this mill about 150 hands out of five or six hundred were working at the old rates. The superintendent, James Frost, was a person peculiarly obnoxious to the strikers, because he had himself formerly been a prominent member of the cotton spinners' Union and had played a part in the 1810 strike, and was hence regarded as a renegade. On September 2 the mob about midday attacked the mill with stones; the persons within the mill fired on the mob killing one man, Thomas Brookes, a spinner of twenty-two, and wounding six or seven before the military arrived. The evidence at the inquest on Thomas Brookes, who was found to have been ' justifiably and of necessity shot and killed,' was, as is usual in such cases, conflicting. Of the witnesses from outside the mill most declared that stones were thrown first from the mill, and the inside witnesses were certain that the attack began from outside. The impression left by the evidence is that an attempt was made to force the mill door from outside in pursuit of the unpopular Frost, that stones were thereupon thrown down, and that the main body of the crowd, thinking that stones were being thrown without provocation, retorted by attacking the mill.[1]

Not much harm was done but panic seized the magistrates. ' Two or three pieces of artillery here would have considerable effect,' wrote Mr. Norris, announcing at the same time that Government itself will soon have ' to attend to this insurrectionary and turbulent spirit.' [2] General Byng, in command at Manchester, kept a cooler head. He had for some time been resisting demands for military protection. Mr. Houldsworth, he wrote on August 28,[3] ' said it was necessary that some soldiers should be stationed at every Mill, and that others should constantly parade the Town. I asked Him in reply, who would order the soldiers to fire, or who would justify them for doing so, as I did not apprehend a Magistrate would be

---

[1] See Coroner's Report, H.O., 42. 180, September 9. ' B.' wrote : ' the knobsticks was prepared for the Turnouts an ever the Turnouts came along side the[y] stoned them the[y] in the street Returned the salute ' (H.O., 42. 180, September 4). For Frost's own account of what happened, see his evidence before the Committee on Artisans and Machinery, 1824, pp. 575 ff.

[2] H.O., 42. 180, September 2.   [3] H.O., 42. 179.

present with each, and whether it was not necessary for soldiers
and their Horses to have some rest as well as others. . . .
Will they,' he adds pertinently, ' submit the cause of the
dispute, which occasions their alarm, to the Government, will
they give the increase of wages upon the decision of its justice,
an opinion which is very prevalent among those well informed.'
General Byng was indeed very critical of the conduct of the
masters who expected the soldiers to do everything for them.
' I found,' he wrote on August 30,[1] ' a guard of Infantry at
Mr. Gray's Factory which had been there two or three days,
and had been promised to remain for some days longer, but
Mr. Gray himself had gone into the country to pass Saturday
and Sunday—thus leaving the soldiers to defend His property
while He took His ease. . . .' The withdrawal of the guard
was followed by the attack on the mill. General Byng still
thought the alarm unreasonable and the magistrates and
masters less active than they might be, but he marched two
additional companies of the 95th into the town, and on
September 5 he reports : ' They are fitting up places where I
can station Troops, near to the principal Factorys, which will
give confidence to the Masters and protection to those who
will work.' [2]

The spinners' strike was in fact at an end now, the men
were beaten, ' their spirit though not their obstinacy appears
broken,' wrote Mr. Norris. The activity of the magistrates, the
employment of troops, and last but not least hunger, ' all co-
operated to produce this happy and satisfactory state of things.' [3]
By the exertions of Mr. Lloyd, Bagguley, Drummond, and
Johnson had been arrested on September 7 for their speeches
at Stockport on September 3, clapped into prison and ordered
to find an impossible bail. They needed in all twelve sureties
of £200 each. When the Rev. J. Harrison, who had been
chairman at the meeting, began to make himself ' busy about
Bail,' Mr. Lloyd made short work of him. ' I have summoned
him before the Justices, to find bail also to answer for being
in an unlawful Assembly.' [4] By September 8, Mr. Houldsworth, the new M.P. for Pontefract, had filled his mill, ' and
so much at ease does he feel now that he immediately set out
for Pontefract to attend the races which commence to-day.' [5]

[1] H.O., 42. 179.　　[2] H.O., 42. 180, September 3 and 5.
[3] H.O., 42. 180, September 5 and 8.
[4] H.O., 42. 180, September 3, 10, and 12.
[5] H.O., 42. 180, September 8.

The men went back on the old terms, and in many instances had to sign declarations abjuring all combinations for the future. Delegates from Birmingham and Nottingham were reported by Mr. Norris to have arrived in Manchester with funds, but it was too late to help the strike.[1]

The masters had gained a complete victory, but no magnanimity was shown to the vanquished. The men's combination was broken up; the masters' combination remained in force,[2] far removed from any fears of legal proceedings. It was decided to proscribe ' the *worst people* amongst the turnouts.' ' There are about 100 hands of this description,' wrote Mr. Norris, ' who will never be received again into any mill.'[3] The support of these proscribed men was a constant drain on the resources of the spinners who had returned to work, and if Mr. Norris is to be believed, there were ugly quarrels and recriminations in the beaten ranks.[4] The General Union or Philanthropic Society that had started with such high hopes dwindled away after Bagguley's imprisonment and the spinners' submission.

Broken though they were, the spinners still sent delegates to and fro to London ; some of these delegates were reported to be at Norwich. Their object no doubt was to collect money for the forthcoming trials of the committee. Two of them, one of them a committee man out on bail, sent to London in November, were told that their expenses were not to exceed £2 per week each on any account whatever.[5] It seemed a very formidable proceeding to Mr. Norris.

' The System of delegation is in every point of view so pregnant with danger and mischief that so long as it is unchecked by the *strong* arm of the Law the system of general turnouts will be kept alive and may by such means become more formidable and extensive than they have hitherto been. Perhaps if being a delegate were to be made a felony or to subject the party to a long imprisonment the evil might be subdued.'[6]

Meanwhile the cotton spinners' committee arrested on August 29 had removed their trial by writ of certiorari to the King's Bench. The issue of other trials, however, showed them that they had little good to expect, and by February

---

[1] H.O., 42. 180, September 10 and 11.
[2] For the masters' attitude towards the proposals for Factory Legislation at this time, see *Town Labourer*, p. 167.
[3] H.O., 42. 180, September 12.   [4] H.O., 42. 181, October 11.
[5] H.O., 42. 182, November 24.   [6] H.O., 42. 182, November 18.

they offered to plead guilty and offer proper submission, a course to which the prosecution, now that quiet was restored, offered no objection. On March 8 they entered into recognisances of £100 each to attend at Westminster and receive sentence on their plea of guilty when called upon. They expressed themselves ' *extremely thankful* for the lenity which had been shewn to them and *appeared* very penitent, promising never to offend in like manner again.' [1] So ended the attempt of a compact well-organised body of men to obtain some fuller share of the increased commercial prosperity. For eight weeks they kept up the struggle. In the end they were utterly defeated.

The Weavers' Strike of 1818

We must now turn to the scattered ill-organised body of weavers who in their turn were struggling to escape from a standard of wages that meant poverty and degradation. All persons outside the trade agreed that the weavers' wages were too low, however much they disapproved of all attempts made by the weavers to raise them.

The weavers indeed, so long as they remained passive, received sympathy in abundance; their sufferings and their patience were contrasted with the impatience and the prosperity of the spinners. Long years of privation had purged them of the bad effects of the old evil days of luxury when they ' spent a great portion of their time and money in ale houses; and at home had their tea tables twice a day, provided with a rum bottle and the finest wheaten bread and butter.' [2] The old spirit that could not brook the indignity of the pauper position had been killed by hunger, and they had shown themselves in 1816 and 1817 ' always thankful for a very moderate pittance of parochial relief.' [3] So long as they merely asked their employers in a respectful manner to ncrease their pay, éven Mr. Chippendale himself could find nothing sinister in their action; [4] but when they took more active steps it was a different matter.

In describing what happened in 1818, it is best to give the weavers' thoughts and hopes in their own words. The most moderate and respectful statement comes in two manifestoes from the Oldham weavers. The first, dated July 15, addressed

[1] H.O., 42. 183, January 21, February 3, March 8.
[2] H.O., 42. 179, August 17 (Mr. Marriott, J.P.).
[3] *Ibid.*   [4] H.O., 41. 178, July 26,

to the manufacturers of Oldham and signed 'The Poor Weavers,' runs : [1]

'We the Weavers of this Town and Neighbourhood respectfully request your attention to the wretched situation to which we have a long time been exposed, owing to the extreme depression of our Wages, and request you to call a Meeting among yourselves, and try if there cannot be some alleviation made to our Sufferings, by an advance thereof, as you well know they are not adequate to purchase the common Necessaries of Life. We are of opinion that if you would exert yourselves as a body, the thing might be accomplished without affecting your profits, which we are far from wishing to injure.'

They then asked for 1d. per hank advance.

The second handbill, dated July 20, is addressed 'To the Gentlemen, Landholders and Leypayers of this Town and Neighbourhood,' before whom the weavers presume to lay their situation after addressing the manufacturers : [2]

'After the peace of Amiens, during the years 1802 and 3 our Wages were from 3/3 to 3/6 per Pound for 24 Hanks Weft and a pound being considered a reasonable day's work for a man, after deducting 3d. per shilling for Bobbin winding, House room and other Incidental charges, which is the customary price, the wages of a Journeyman Weaver would then amount to 2/7½ per Day or 15/9 per Week, and this was pretty near upon a par with other Mechanicks and we maintained our rank in Society : We will now contrast our present situation with the past, and it will demonstrate pretty clearly the degraded state to which we have been reduced.

'During the last two years our wages have been reduced to so low an Ebb, that for the greatest part of that time we have received no more than from 12d. to 15d. per Pound which after deducting as before stated would bring the Journeyman's Wages to the shameful price of 9d. or 10d. a day, or from 4/6 to 5/- per Week, and we appeal to your candour and good sense, whether such a paltry sum be sufficient to keep the soul and Body together, as we have our provisions to purchase from the same Market and at the same price with other people, who have been earning three times the Money. . . .'

They explain that they ask for an advance of 1d. a hank, which will bring wages up to 9s. a week, and refer to 'the late increased and increasing demand for Goods' as a reason why their very moderate demands should be granted.[3]

---

[1] H.O., 42. 178, July 26.   [2] *Ibid.*

[3] It is worth noting that the Oldham masters agreed to the advance of 1d. per hank on certain goods provided other masters would pay the same, and even

Meanwhile the weavers from all over the cotton district were stirring, and on July 27 a meeting was held at Bury of delegates from a number of places including Manchester, Bolton, Bury, Blackburn, Burnley, Padiham, Higher Darwen, Lower Darwen, Heywood, Haslingden, Todmorden, Walshawlane, Tottington, Cockeymoor, Prestwich, Pilkington, Stockport, Ashton-under-Lyne, Chadderton, and Middleton. This meeting issued a handbill, signed by John Hibbert, president, and Robert Ellison, secretary, and addressed to the cotton manufacturers of Lancashire, Yorkshire, Cheshire, Derbyshire, etc. : [1]

'GENTLEMEN. It is from a gulph that absorbs all the faculties of body and mind we address you, supposing you capable of ameliorating the sufferings of an immense body of useful Artizans; in this you must admit that we have suspended our exertions in calling upon you, until our vitals are affected, proved by indications in our visage, of an untimely approach of nature's messenger, surely there is not a man in civilized society so devoid of humanity, so devoid of everything that dignifies the mind, as to have the least desire to perpetuate sufferings of such magnitude;—yet we must confess it is with pain we have witnessed the perpetuation of them to an extent unparalleled in the annals of any Country, at a time too, when Peace overspreads all Europe, when Commerce, retarded by the operations of a protracted War, is presumed to have regained her wonted vigour, and to be heightening the prosperity of Nations—Gentlemen, we hope your minds are not become so callous, nor yet so indifferent to our situation, as to rejoice over our misfortunes, thereby increasing your triumph in proportion to our calamity, or suffer a degree of unconcern to our case, to take possession of your minds, when you must be sensible at the same time of the justice of our cause, and the injustice of the cause which protracts such misery.

'Gentlemen, we have been given to understand for some time, that prosperity pervaded our Country, 'tis true, we see the Land overspread with *Houses* and *Manufactories* of immense value, and we hear our *Manufacturers* boasting our pre-eminence in the Commercial world.[2] That we stand pre-eminent in Commerce is a fact which cannot be denied, as the changes in *South America* has given us the command of Commerce in that part of the World, which is the most material part as those States contain near

---

subscribed £41, 15s. towards sending delegates to induce other manufacturers of the same kind of goods to join in granting it (H.O., 42. 184, February 2).

[1] H.O., 42. 178.

[2] Smart, *Economic Annals*, 1801-20, p. 652, points out that the return of prosperity was shown in the figures of foreign trade. There was an increase of about six millions in imports, three millions in exports, half a million in re-exports.

twenty millions of Souls, furnished with Manufactories from Europe; and as the Government of *Venezuela* has thought proper to favour this country on account of our Government maintaining strict neutrality by only subjecting our goods to an impost of *seven and a half per cent.*, while the goods of every other Nation in Europe are subject to an impost of from *twenty to thirty per cent.*, yet while this is our envied situation as a Nation with respect to Commerce, with unexampled industry we find ourselves incompetent to procure what will meet the exigencies of our families.

‘Adam Smith in his Treatise on the Wealth of Nations says "that if the labour of one man would not provide the comforts of life for himself, a Wife, and three Children, such a Nation was on the decline, and would by emigration or ceasing to propagate, sink into insignificance, as importance must always fall with numbers." Smith says "a Labourer or Artizan should be able to maintain five," good God, but how must they exist on SIX SHILLINGS per week, which is the sum the greatest part of Weavers must work early and late to procure ; not more than one-half the sum that is received by every other branch of the Trade, and not more than one-fourth of the wages of some. Therefore, if such a vast body of ingenious, useful and laborious men must remain in such a degraded state, it must ultimately militate against the State.

‘Gentlemen, we ask you for an advance of *seven shillings on the pound*, in this you must admit we have confined ourselves within the boundaries of moderation, as several other branches of the trade have called for a greater advance than the whole of our income, but we trust you will not look on us with contumacy, on account of our pacific dispositions, proved by our moderate demand.’

The delegates went home to their various districts and attempted to induce their employers to grant the 7s. advance. Some employers gave it, some refused, many promised to grant it provided all other masters came into line.[1] Some offered a smaller advance.[2] Public feeling, according to Mr. Norris of Manchester, was in favour of the men.[3]

In some places the weavers called meetings to give publicity to their demands ; at Bolton the authorities twice refused to call a meeting at their request, but the borough-reeve called a private meeting of the manufacturers, who resolved that they would not ‘enter into any combination to advance the

[1] *e.g.* The Oldham and Leigh manufacturers agreed provided the same was done in other places. The Ashton masters not only agreed to give if secured elsewhere but gave a donation towards helping the cause (H.O., 42. 179; 42. 180).

[2] *e.g.* At Bolton they offered 3s. in the pound (H.O., 42. 160, September 4).

[3] H.O., 42. 179, August 2.

Wages, that the Weavers were too numerous, and that trade should find its own level,'[1] an act which caused the Bolton weavers, including even the loyalist Richard Needham,[2] to protest in a manifesto that they had been 'neglected, degraded and insulted.' These weavers called a meeting on their own account on August 13, at which they passed resolutions about the 7s. advance, and gave it as the opinion of the meeting 'that the causes of our Low Wages are of such a nature that they can be removed,' *i.e.* by raising the price of cotton goods ; they also declared that the fear of foreign rivalry was groundless, being merely a pretext to blindfold the weaver invented by those who wish to fill their own Coffers at the expense of the Sweat and Blood of the poor Industrious Weaver.'[3]

The weavers as a body, in marked contrast to the spinners, were non-political. They refused to hear political speakers[4] and kept themselves distinct from all the spinners' doings. Perhaps the most striking instance of this detachment from the spinners was shown later at the time of the big riot at Gray's Mill on September 2, when the weavers from various districts to the number of some fifteen thousand were holding a peaceful meeting in St. George's Fields at the time of the disturbance. There were of course politicians amongst them, notably Robert Pilkington of Bury, who had been imprisoned under the suspension of the Habeas Corpus Act, and sometimes this political section voiced their grievances, as in a weavers' handbill issued about this time in Stockport addressed to the weavers of Stockport, which is as unrestrained in its language as any production of the spinners.[5] It begins with a sort of outburst headed 'Motto' :

'They say, by them our Mouths are filled with Plenty, though thousands now are starving in our streets ;

[1] H.O., 42. 179.
[2] There is a curious irony in the fact that Richard Needham, who had acted as a 'loyal' informant to Mr. Fletcher in 1812 (see H.O., 42. 124), was now being informed about by A. B. *alias* R. Waddington, one of the disaffected in 1812. A. B. on August 7 says that Richard Needham is angry because the fact that a delegate from Prestwich had been round to see the Bolton Committee had reached Mr. Fletcher's ears (H.O., 42. 179). For A. B., see Chapter x.
[3] H.O., 42. 179.
[4] *e.g.* On August 3 Mr. Hay writes that when some speakers introduced politics at an Ashton Moss meeting the weavers refused to have anything to do with it, and Mr. Lloyd on August 24 writes that the Stockport weavers refused to allow Bagguley to speak (H.O., 42. 179).
[5] H.O., 42. 179, August 15.

' They say, they treat us as a free born People, yet drive us roughly down the stream of power;

' They say, our misery always finds a friend, yet no hold is left to save us from destruction ;

' They say, our Earnings more than fit our Wants, yet a hundred pence is all that we can earn for six days' labour :

' All that bear this, are cowards, not to rise up at the great call of nature, and check the growth of these domestic spoilers, who made them slaves, and tell them 'tis their charter.'

After urging the weavers to procure an advance in the price of labour, and assuring them that the people are the masters of the Government, the address ends with fierce threats of hell fire to the employers :

' And you, ye Oppressors of the Poor ! be cautious of your Actions ; for if you meet not your merited punishment in this World, it is certain in that where the Wicked cease from troubling and where the righteous are everlastingly at rest. Remember Him who hath said, it is easier for a Camel to go through the Eye of a Needle than for a rich Man to enter the Kingdom of Heaven.'

The connection of the weavers with the General Union or Philanthropic Society [1] founded by the spinners is obscure. Some weavers were certainly present at the meeting on August 19 at Manchester, and at the last meeting on September 21, but according to Mr. Fletcher the meeting of deputies at Bury on August 22 refused to join the Union.[2] It seems probable that isolated bodies of weavers joined, but not the whole organisation.

As the position was so unsatisfactory, it was decided by the delegates towards the end of August to try the policy of refusing to work for masters who would not give the 7s. advance. This policy was agreed to first at Stockport on August 19, and afterwards more formally at another meeting of deputies at Bury on August 22. The policy, it may be noted, was urged by various masters who were willing enough to give the advance provided they were not undersold by others.[3] The Bury meeting issued yet another handbill addressed this time to the weavers themselves.[4]

' Gentlemen,' it begins, ' 'Tis with incessant toil you have struggled against penury. . . .

---

[1] See *Town Labourer*, p. 309.   [2] H.O., 42. 179, August 24.
[3] Committee on Artisans and Machinery, 1824, p. 394 (Ellison's evidence).
[4] H.O., 42. 179.

' Gentlemen, Mr. Locke, who has been justly denominated the greatest Logician that ever England produced, said that " every man, that possesses his natural powers, has a property in himself, viz. in the work of his hands and the labour of his body "; if so, we argue that they who by fraud or violence deprive the labourer of the fruits arising from his own property are Peculators, and if these are Peculators, those are Tyrants that would prevent him from taking the only commodity he has to the best Market, and as labour is the only property you have, you alone have the right of appreciating its value.'

It was resolved at this meeting that after September 1 nobody was to weave for any manufacturer who did not pay the advance of 7s. in the pound. Another resolution recorded the ' abhorrence and contempt of the meeting at the appearance of that ' notorious Villain,' Samuel Fleming the spy, his dismissal from the meeting and the formal application to the Constable of the Township to attend the proceedings as a protection against such ' perjured Villains.' The strike was duly carried out a day before the appointed date, on August 31. At Bolton it was estimated that four or five thousand out of nine thousand inhabitants were idle. At Manchester thousands came in from the surrounding country, in groups, to ask for the advance from their employers, from whom they received various answers. The behaviour of the strikers was perfectly quiet and orderly, but their action caused grave anxiety ; it was sinning against the laws of political economy. '. . . This species of restraint or coercion,' wrote Mr. Norris,[1] might ' be ultimately a great evil as nothing can be more clear than that commerce in every respect should be allowed to be entirely unshakled and free.' The practice of meeting together he describes as very dangerous : ' It consolidates their power as a body and points out to them a system of co-operation which on future occasions if not in the present may occasion the almost destruction of our Commerce. . . . '

For the next few days processions of weavers not only marched about their own towns but went in turns with banners flying to swell the ranks at meetings in other towns. A shuttle draped with crape was often carried aloft. Women too took their share in the display ; 1222 men and 355 women paraded the streets of Stockport on September 3 with two fifes, and they were joined afterwards by many thousands.[2] On the

---

[1] H.O., 42. 179, August 31.   [2] H.O., 42. 180.

same day, it may be noted, there was a Reform meeting at
Stockport addressed by Bagguley, Drummond, and Johnson,
to which 500 spinners came from Manchester, but the
weavers had no more to do with this than with the riot at
Gray's factory the day before.   One of Mr. Chippendale's informants from Ashton-under-Lyne, who went by the name
of ' Brother to No. 2,' noted that the Ashton Moss weavers
were ' proceeded bv about 100 women who all say old and
young the will go forward to Stockport and from the women
being there in the heat and hiritation they now appear in I
Auger no good.' [1]

The Manchester magistrates also augured no good from this
system of processions, and on September 4, when the weavers
had planned to meet at Ashton Moss, a placard was issued,
signed by the Justices Wright, Marriott, Ethelston, and Norris,
forbidding such assemblies and processions of ' voluntarily
unemployed Labourers,' and declaring them illegal and dangerous to the Public Peace.[2]   Mr. Wright and the borough-reeve,
accompanied by General Byng with a posse of soldiers, followed
the Manchester weavers who were making for Ashton Moss,
and coming up with them about three miles from Ashton
succeeded in dispersing them by explaining to them the dangers
they ran.   The people, wrote General Byng afterwards, were
I think ' pleased and grateful at the kind manner they
were spoken to.' [3]   The method of keeping up enthusiasm
and concerted action by means of meetings was thus abruptly
brought to an end.   Even without this prohibition concerted
action was difficult enough, for the masters' promises varied,
as we have said, and in some places a gradual advance was
agreed to, in others a smaller rise was offered.

Even the smallest advance was looked at askance by Lord
Sidmouth.   A 2s. and 3s. advance, wrote Mr. Norris on September 5,[4] ' has certainly been offered by many masters a
little perhaps through fear, and on this subject I perfectly
coincide with your Lordship in opinion, most unfortunately
for the general interests of commerce and the community, but
as the weavers have been working hard for small wages for
some few years, if any description of laborer in this district
be entitled to indulgence in this respect it is the weaver.'

The difference in the offers of the different masters led
to a modification of the original strike decision, and at a

[1] H.O., 42. 180.   [2] Ibid.
[3] Ibid., September 5.   [4] Ibid.

meeting of forty of the deputies on September 5 at Bury, it was decided to take the advance in two instalments, namely 4s. on September 7, and 3s. on October 1. In hopes no doubt of keeping free from the meshes of the law, the deputies passed the following resolution :

'That as it is in the power of the manufacturer to compel the weaver to weave out his work in the loom, or on hand, he is advised, in such case, to obey the dictates of the law ; yet no injunction is hereby laid upon him by this meeting, and he is left entirely to his own discretion ; but he is not to bring any more work from any manufacturer under the proposed advance mentioned in the first resolution.' [1]   At this meeting the deputy constable of Bury was paid for his time as a protection.

The weavers after September 5 settled down to enforce their demands in the different districts. They were now faced with the problem of supporting those men whose masters refused to grant the advance. In Stockport they adopted the system of billeting out the workless weavers amongst those in work, a system which Mr. Lloyd viewed with much suspicion.   At Bolton, where a large proportion of the masters were favourable to their demands, they appealed to the public for subscriptions, a policy adopted also in Manchester where the Manchester Branch of Associated Weavers issued an address ' To the Generous Public ' headed with the weavers' arms : [2]

' We the Operative Weavers of Manchester and its Vicinity,' runs the address, ' are happy to state the willingness of some of the Principal Manufacturers both in Town and Country, to meet us in respect to our Advance of Wages, agreeably to Resolutions agreed upon at Bury the 5th instant. But in consequence of others making objections, we find ourselves under the necessity of soliciting the aid of those who may be friendly to our cause, in order that such as are out of employ may receive a support from such contributions as are collected by subscription.

' It has often been suggested that every Trade ought to afford such Wages as would be a reasonable support without the assistance of Ley Payers ; and as it is well known to the Public, the various privations that Cotton Weavers have laboured under, the manner in which we have stood in need

[1] H.O., 42. 180 ; and Committee on Artisans and Machinery, 1824, pp. 394-5.   [2] H.O., 42. 180.

of the above support both in times past, and even at the present ;
and as we feel an inclination to extricate ourselves from this
state, we trust we shall meet with universal countenance.'

The weavers were not to be allowed to extricate themselves.
In spite of the isolation of their lives they were showing unexpected powers of organisation and co-operation. They had
been allowed to act unchecked too long, and it was time to
set the law in motion. The Manchester magistrates issued a
placard explaining that the Combination Act made the collec-
tion of subscriptions illegal ; the merchants met to consider
how to ' subdue the confederacy.' It was not after all a very
difficult matter, and it needed no Flemings to compass it,
for all their doings had been open and had rendered them
subject to penalties if the employers chose to exact them.
Robert Ellison, Richard Kay, and Robert Pilkington on September 16 were committed for conspiracy for their share in
the Bury meeting of September 5.[1] All three had signed the
handbill, the first as president, the two latter as secretaries
of the meeting. The death blow was struck at concerted
action amongst the weavers. In most places some small
advance was granted for a time,[2] but in Manchester, at any
rate, even in October, before the committed men had been
brought to trial, prices were again being reduced.[3] By February
1819 there was a general reduction for all lighter fabrics.[4]
Complaint was useless, for the magistrates were now on the
alert to check all ' insubordination.' When the bleachers,
undeterred by the fate of the weavers and spinners, began to
turn out in October, their masters complained to the magistrates, who immediately sent five of the men to prison for
neglect of work, a policy, wrote Mr. Fletcher, which will
' crush in its Bud this dangerous Spirit amongst the Workmen
in that Branch.'[5]

The weavers, as we have seen, had behaved throughout the
dispute in an absolutely orderly and, as they thought, law-
abiding manner. There was, however, one exception. In
the Blackburn and Burnley district, the centre of the weaving
of plain cotton fabrics, the weavers were ill content with the
advance offered them, and at Burnley on September 15 they
sent the bellman round to give notice of a meeting to enforce

[1] H.O., 42. 180; Committee on Artisans and Machinery, 1824, p. 395.
[2] The advances granted by many masters on condition that others came into
line were of course withdrawn.   [3] H.O., 42. 181, October 20.
[4] H.O., 42. 184, February 11.   [5] H.O., 42. 181, October 20.

their demands. The bellman, as 'the active agent of the combination,' was at once seized by the civil authorities and thrown into the lock-up ; the weavers then forced open the lock-up, freed the bellman, and held possession of the streets till the arrival of a troop of yeomanry cavalry from Manchester released the powers of law and order from their humiliating position, when seven of the liberators of the bellman were in their turn safely lodged in prison, this time in Blackburn gaol.[1]

The trial of the three conspirators from the Bury meeting did not take place till the Quarter Sessions early in February next year. The result was 'such as the Friends of Order wished,' and showed that the freeholders of Lancashire were not contaminated with the 'London disease.'[2] Ellison, whose fourteen witnesses included his master and Mr. White, a prominent manufacturer of Manchester, who had recommended the policy adopted at the Bury meeting of September 5, was sentenced to one year in prison, Kay and Pilkington were both sentenced to two years.[3]

This was the last occasion on which the weavers made any considerable attempt to extricate themselves by organised action from their miserable conditions. The masters had subdued their confederacy with such effect that it never raised its head again.

The weavers now divided themselves into two parties, the one sought salvation through Reform, the other which called itself 'loyal' made further efforts to secure a minimum wage at home, or failing that, asked for assistance towards emigration.

[1] H.O., 42. 180, September 17 ; *Annual Register*, 1818 ; *Chronicle*, pp. 128 ff.

[2] H.O., 42. 184, February 4. The London juries were famous for their independence.

[3] Committee on Artisans and Machinery, 1824, p. 395. An outspoken letter in the *Manchester Observer* for February 6 asked how the Chairman of Quarter Sessions could condemn men to two years' imprisonment for trying to get 12s. a week whilst he was receiving £50 a week for attending the Sessions (H.O., 42. 184). Pilkington had already spent seven months of the previous year in solitary confinement, under the suspension of the Habeas Corpus Act, 'without being permitted to walk in the open air for a single hour,' and his wife and six small children had been reduced to the workhouse. His crime apparently was that he was secretary of the Bury Auxiliary Hampden Club. He seems to have been a man much given to theological discussion judging from the papers found on him, which include 'an antidote to modern socinianism.' See Petition to the House of Commons, Hansard, February 27, 1818, and H.O., 40. 9.

The prosecutions in 1818 had made a deep impression, and it is clear that much of the driving force in the Reform agitation of 1819 came from denunciations of the Combination Law.[1] The weavers, wrote Parson Harrison to Bagguley in prison, ' are the best givers, but, alas ! they have nothing to give now.' [2] The story of Peterloo we have told elsewhere.[3] It overshadows the year 1819, but we must not forget that during that same year constant appeals were still being made for a minimum wage.   Bolton and Stockport were the strongholds of the movement.   A Bolton petition to the magistrates, signed on behalf of the committee by Thomas Thorpe, Richard Needham, and Thomas Kenyon, pointed out that the weavers had foretold the evils that would come, but their applications for a minimum were refused ; '. . . dear bought experience demonstrates that there is a method of conducting our trade which for the moment appears to be advantageous to the individual, but which undoubtedly bears within itself a germ of ruin to the workman and eventually to the speculator himself.' [4]

[1] See speeches at Reform meetings at Manchester, Ashton, and Blackburn (H.O., 42. 183, January 23; H.O., 42. 188, June 19; H.O., 42. 189, July 10); also Placard in Manchester *re* Police Association : ' The oppressors have got possession of a great part of the property of the Nation, through the operation of Corn Bills and Combination Acts, which are directly calculated to make Provisions DEAR and wages low' (H.O., 42. 189, July 14).

[2] H.O., 42. 189, July 15.   [3] See *Town Labourer*, pp. 89 ff.

[4] H.O., 42. 187, May 4.   This same petition gives an interesting estimate of a weaver's earnings corroborated by two magistrates.   The family are taken to consist of father, mother, and six children, three of whom are capable of weaving. The four looms belong to the father.

						£	s	d
The father makes	.	.	.	.	.	0	9	0
Eldest child	.	.	.	.	.	0	7	6
Next child	.	.	.	.	.	0	6	0
Youngest child	.	.	.	.	.	0	4	6
						£1	7	0

Added to this 'the Mother must be fully employed in winding, washing, etc. Indeed her employment is toil incessant.'

The expenses are put as follows :

						£	s	d
Rent per week	.	.	.	.	.	0	3	9
Fire	.	.	.	.	.	0	1	6
Candles	.	.	.	.	.	0	1	8
Soap and Looming	.	.	.	.	.	0	1	6
Sizeing and Sowing	.	.	.	.	.	0	2	0
Gaiting, wear and tear	.	.	.	.	.	0	1	0
						£0	11	5

Leaving 15s. 7d. for food, clothing, etc. for eight persons.

The Stockport weavers in their address to the magistrates and gentlemen, reviewed the history of their failures to procure help from Parliament.[1] This document, remarks Mr. Lloyd on sending it up, 'smells strong of the North.' Mr. Lloyd himself during this year was busily engaged in attempts to seize the Cap of Liberty at the various Reform meetings in the neighbourhood, and these scuffles and preparations for scuffles left him little time for other pursuits. The weavers were told in answer to their request for a minimum that they had the arbitration law:[2] the offer of this cold comfort convinced them that Reform was their only hope.

The weavers in the Carlisle district had struck work and were also demanding a minimum. This they hoped to obtain by direct dealing with their employers. In politicians they put little trust: 'We have no peculiar affection for one denomination of public men more than another. Both Whigs and Tories have, in their turn, cajoled the people, and profited by their credulity.'[3] In an interview with their masters they explained that if there were a regular or fixed price for their work ' the market would be kept from those fluctuations that deterred the shopkeeper from keeping any large stock; for if there was a minimum of wages, then the price of goods in the market would not fall below the ratio of that minimum, and a security being given the shopkeeper so far, he would not, on every reduction of weavers' wages, hurry a sale, not knowing how far a reduction might descend.' When the masters refused the men's demands the latter were open in their condemnation: '. . . your ambition and maddened views of aggrandisement have blinded and perverted your understandings to such a degree, that you no more understand your own interests than you regard ours.'[4]

The Masters' Plans for a Minimum Wage

This same year (1819) a movement for a minimum wage was taking place amongst the master manufacturers of calicoes and cambrics in the district embracing Burnley, Bury, Blackburn, and Preston. These manufacturers who were supported by nearly all the calico-printing firms began by issuing in June a declaration signed by fourteen firms of calico manu-

[1] See *Town Labourer*, p. 296.   [2] H.O., 42. 189, July 3.
[3] H.O., 42. 188, June 5,
[4] H.O., 42. 188, June 10. The Carlisle weavers seem to have returned to work after a compromise (*ibid.*, June 17).

facturers and approved in a further declaration by twenty-seven
firms of calico printers, regretting the low rates of pay to
weavers.[1] Next, thirty-five firms of manufacturers signed a
summons to other manufacturers to meet in Manchester on
August 24 ' to take into consideration the propriety of applying to Parliament to fix a Minimum of Wages or to adopt
such other measures as may appear most advisable for regulating the Wages of the Weavers.' [2] This meeting, owing to
the Peterloo disturbances, was postponed, and postponed
indefinitely, for before fixing a fresh date, James Hutchinson
of Bury, one of the movers, wrote a long letter to Sidmouth
asking ' whether His Majesty's Ministers, if it should appear
to be the wish of a majority of the Manufacturers, would
countenance or listen to a Minimum of wages.' The minimum,
he explains, was to be a low and variable one, fixed by commissioners chosen from the principal manufacturers, and it
was suggested that a temporary and experimental Act for the
purpose should be passed.[3] The reply or the absence of reply
successfully damped down the agitation. Hutchinson himself was a recent convert to belief in Government regulation
of wages. ' I have till lately been of opinion jointly with my
fellow manufacturers, that a minimum of wages was an evil
to be avoided ; but the unequal and low wages that have
been paid for the last three years, added to the extreme and
unnecessary oppression to which the weavers have consequently been subject, has affected a change in our sentiments.'
The decline in wages he attributes to the ' number of people
of little capital and less feeling ' who obtain credit, embark in
business and ' attempt to realise a profit by underselling their
more respectable competitors ' who pay higher wages.

A gloomy picture of the cotton trade at this time was
given by Thomas Ainsworth,[4] himself a ruined man :

' I have thought a great deal upon the subject of Trade as
relates to Master and workmen, having been embarked in it
above 40 years. For 25 years past I have paid on an average
£40,000 a year to Workpeople, and I believe maintained a
Character for industry, honesty, and ability, to this day, though
unfortunate, but those qualities have for some years ceased to be
of use, nay ruinous. It is now a Trade of oppression, *demi-*
swindling, and deception. A Master cannot live by the honest
pursuit of Trade, nor can a Weaver by hard labour. The Capital

[1] H.O., 42. 194, September 8.   [2] *Ibid.*   [3] *Ibid.*
[4] H.O., 42. 197.

is gone (I mean the Manufacturing Capital) we cannot hold Stocks
of Goods; there is not 3 months Stock of Manufactured Goods on
Sale in the whole Trade, yet 100,000 Weavers do the work of
150,000 for half wages. I have cloth on hand I paid 24s. to 28s. a
piece weaving I could now get done for 8s. and 9s. a piece. Those
who could hold Stocks are ruined. I have lost £50,000 by
holding Stocks in the last 6 years, and £30,000 by bad
debts. Our Merchants at home and abroad are ruined in same
way. Goods at *half price* have found their way into parts where
immense Depots were laying through the whole world.

'A great many men of Capital that could, have given up the
Cotton Trade except Spinning to supply foreign Weavers (Manufacturers). The active Capital is gone, we have only buildings
and machinery (comparatively) left. Our Wages have varied
100 p.c. within the course of two months. The Wages of Woollens
have not altered 5 p.c. the last 25 years, there are 2 years con-
sumption of Woollen Goods on hand on a fair calculation, and
a capital to hold them, there is not a 3 Months Stock of Cotton
Goods on hand, nor do I think there is any capital to hold more.
Did Dr. A. Smith ever contemplate such a state of things? it is
in vain to read his book to find a remedy for a complaint which
he could not conceive existed, viz. 100,000 weavers doing the
work of 150,000 when there was no demand (as 'tis said) and that
for half meat, and the rest paid by Poor Rates, could he conceive
that the profits of a Manufacture should be what one Master
could wring from the hard earnings of the poor, more than
another? That deception in the article was the only way to get
money. That a town like Manchester which when Trade was
not ⅓d what it now is, could boast 30 or 40 respectable Merchants who supplied Europe with Goods ready for wear, and yet
it cannot now find four. . . .'

This multiplication of small manufacturers owing to the
ease with which credit could be obtained is noted several
times during this and the succeeding years.[1] Curiously enough
it comes at the very time when the power-loom was beginning
to threaten the position of the small man, for the coming of the
power-loom meant of course that more capital was required
for starting a weaving business. This introduction of power-
looms and preparations for their introduction overshadow
the years 1822-25. In answer to queries from the Home

---

[1] *e.g.* Mr. Chippendale of Oldham writes in 1822: 'Weavers and mechanics
are daily springing up into Manufacturers commencing Business with their
accumulated Savings' (H.O., 40. 17); and Major Eckersley writes in 1827: 'A
very great evil about Blackburn and Burnley is the number of weavers who
(owing to the late facility of obtaining credit and County Bank paper) have
become small manufacturers . . .' (H.O., 40. 22).

Office on the state of trade in 1822, a correspondent from Manchester described the general feeling of alarm that the power-looms would destroy ' the ratio of product and demand.' [1]

What the position looked like to the weavers is told in the striking letter from a committee of Manchester weavers in 1823, urging the old remedy of a minimum wage and the new one of a tax on power-looms.[2] Next year the Combination Laws were repealed, but the weavers were now too weak to take advantage of such opportunities as the new law offered, consequently repeal helped them little.

Two years later (1826) another movement was started by several employers for the establishment of a voluntary minimum of wages.[3] These employers drew up a list of prices and bound themselves not to give less than these prices, provided the Poor Law authorities would ' pledge themselves to provide other employment, or subsistence, for such as are unable to obtain employment at the said list prices.' The leader of this movement was John Fielden, the great cotton spinner of Todmorden ; it began with a meeting of the principal calico manufacturers of Burnley, Colne, Blackburn, Todmorden, and the neighbourhood, held at Burnley on April 14, 1826, and an adjourned meeting was held in Manchester on April 18. Forty-eight firms [4] signed the agreement, and fifty-three ' printers and purchasers of calicoes ' signed the statement to show their approval. A letter was drawn up to explain the policy addressed ' to the Church wardens and Overseers of the Poor of the Township of —— ' :

'. . . On every stagnation in trade, for many years past, the prices of weaving have generally been reduced lower than were paid previously to each stagnation ; and on a revival of demand, prices have not got up to where they were when the reduction commenced.

---

[1] H.O., 40. 17, May 17. Ure, *Cotton Manufacture of Great Britain*, ii. pp. 429-30, points out the injurious effects at first of power-looms on the spinners. Owing to the competition with power-looms, hand-loom weavers could no longer afford to pay the old prices for the yarn, and the prices they could afford to give were insufficient to pay the cost of production. Hence for a time the demand for yarn, and consequently the prices, fell so low as almost to annihilate the spinners' profits ; many went bankrupt and those alone prospered who had added power-looms to their spinning establishment.

[2] See *Town Labourer*, p. 298.

[3] For account of this movement, see Report from Select Committee on Hand-loom Weavers' Petitions, 1834, pp. 598 ff.

[4] Ten had signed the 1819 manifesto.

'Should the townships reject the measure proposed for fixing a minimum of prices for weaving, then, prices as low, or lower than the lowest now paid, will become general; a further reduction in the value of goods will consequently be submitted to, and established in the market, and the restoration of confidence thereby longer protracted; and, if the experience of the past be any guide for the future, there are the strongest reasons for believing, that for a very long period (even after a revival of demand) no advance in prices can be obtained by the manufacturer, that will enable him to pay to the weaver what may be necessary to keep him from the parish. But if, on the other hand, the measure be adopted, it will probably inspire confidence in the prices at which goods are sold; at present, the demand may be improved, and full work given sooner to the weaver, who, as soon as this is the case, will cease to be a burthen to the parish.

'The townships, by adopting the measure proposed, may possibly, for a short period, be subjected to higher rates for the relief of the poor, than they would be for the same period, should they refuse to adopt it; but the permanent advantages are so manifest, that any increased exertions they may be required to make, in the first instance, will be amply repaid by the good that will follow; it is therefore hoped that no other suggestion will be needed to induce those who are the possessors of property, and who are deeply interested in the prosperity of the townships, promptly and manfully to come forward to protect the value of their property, by voluntary subscriptions, in aid of the poor's-rate, or else to afford supplies of food to such weavers as cannot obtain work at remunerating prices, until such work can be obtained. By so doing, they will greatly contribute to put a stop to the oppressive and detestable practice of reducing the value of the poor man's labour, below the standard that will afford him subsistence.

'The townships will find their interests much more effectually secured by coinciding in what is here recommended, than in continuing a practice, it is said, some townships have lately resorted to, of giving a bonus of 3d., or more, per piece to manufacturers, to employ their poor. It is lamentable that there should be any manufacturers so destitute of good feeling as to accept such an offer; and still more lamentable that such townships should not foresee that such a practice is only calculated to aggravate the evil it is intended to avoid, viz. that of increased poor's-rates, for the want of employment for the poor. The most humane and respectable part of the manufacturers must quit the trade if this practice be persevered in; for what manufacturer in his senses will go on making goods on his own account, whilst he is compelled to contribute his proportion to a rate that is expended in paying another to undersell him in the market?'

The manufacturers agreed to meet again on the 28th of

April in Burnley and receive the answers of the townships;
but before that date the starving weavers had taken matters
into their own hands and directed their blind anger against
the power-looms, which belonged in several cases to the very
firms who had signed the statement of prices.   These disturbances put an end to the project of a minimum wage, though
it is more than doubtful whether the Poor Law authorities
would have consented to take on themselves the burden of
supporting men who refused to work below the scheduled
prices.

The Destruction of Power-Looms in 1826

The year 1826 was a year of unprecedented financial panic
and disorder with an epidemic of bankruptcies.   The weavers
suffered acutely in the general distress, and by this time they
were very sensible of the competition of the power-loom.   In
the misery of starvation the populace in April vented its anger
on the new machinery, destroying in three days over one
thousand power-looms, and doing more than £16,000 worth of
damage in the districts round Blackburn and Bury.   How far
the attack was arranged beforehand is doubtful ; Mr. Fletcher's
informant ' Alpha ' sent him news of meetings where delegates
discussed the repeal of the Corn Laws, the destruction of public
granaries, the destruction of power-looms, and the destruction
of yarn packed for export : it was further recommended at one
of these meetings ' that those who had relatives serving in the
Army should sound their Inclination, as to injuring the People,
in case of any Tumult.' [1]

The actual outburst seems to have been unexpected, for
the poor appeared to be bearing the prospects of starvation
with laudable equanimity.   ' . . . It is certainly very different
now (for the better),' wrote Major Eckersley from Manchester,[2]
' from 1819 and 1820, when Politics were mixed up with the
distresses of the People.'   The increase in Poor Rates, he
mentions, is 50 per cent., and in addition some thousand pounds
a week were distributed in voluntary contributions.   At Blackburn, fourteen thousand persons out of a population of twenty-
six thousand were kept from sheer starvation by provisions
bought out of public subscriptions,[3] but from the inadequacy

[1] H.O., 40. 19, March 21, April 9, April 20.
[2] H.O., 40. 19, March 5.   In Manchester there are, he says later, some
thirty or forty thousand Irish, ' all needy.'
[3] H.O., 40. 19, April 18.

of the relief grave fears of dysentery were entertained. 'The demeanour of the afflicted poor,' wrote the Vicar of Blackburn in an appeal published in the *Blackburn Mail*, April 5,[1] 'at this time of unparalleled distress has been such as to recommend them effectually to our respectful consideration, and continued bounty. With very few exceptions none of them have transgressed the bounds of propriety, or shewn a spirit of insubordination to the laws of their country. To their praise be it spoken, there have been no symptoms of discontent, disaffection, or sedition. . . . They have trusted in Providence; and God's servants will not desert them.' Their trust in Providence gave way before the end of the month and, as we shall see, they transgressed the bounds of propriety in a serious fashion.

On Monday, April 24, a mob met at Henfield at the crossroads to Blackburn, Burnley, Whalley, and Haslingden.[2] They first destroyed the power-looms at the different factories round Accrington and then went on to Blackburn. By the evening not a single power-loom was left standing within six miles of Blackburn. In conflicts with small bodies of soldiers sent to protect the mills two or three men were killed and several seriously wounded.

On Tuesday little was done beyond an attack on some power-looms at Haslingden. On Wednesday, April 26, the work of destruction spread along the banks of the Irwell down to Bury. At Rawtenstall, Long Holme, Edenfield, Chadderton, Summerseat, mills were entered and power-looms destroyed. At Chadderton in an affray with the soldiers seven rioters were killed and many wounded.[3] With the destruction of Mr. Hutchinson's factory in Bury the activities of the rioters in this part ceased. The excitement, however, had spread to Manchester, and on Thursday, April 27, a mob, after attacking several power-loom factories which were successfully defended, managed to set fire to Mr. Beaver's factory in Jersey Street and refused to allow the firemen to extinguish the fire. On Friday Manchester was the scene of a carnival of disorder

[1] H.O., 40. 19.

[2] For accounts of the disturbances, see H.O., 40. 19, and 44. 16; and the *Annual Register* for 1826; *Chronicle*, pp. 63 ff.

[3] Complaints were afterwards made of the conduct of the 'riflemen' (not the dragoons). Mr. Aiken, the proprietor of the mill, seems to have implored the military not to fire but to go away. In the inquest over the seven victims, a verdict of accidental death was brought in in one case, of justifiable homicide in four others, and in one case a verdict of murder against a rifleman unknown (H.O., 40. 19).

in which shops were sacked ' and the number of street robberies committed was such, as, in broad day, and in the centre of a great town, was never before heard of.'

It was not surprising that Sir John Byng wrote to say that the alarm among the owners of factories was greater than any he had ever known ; arms were distributed to them for self-defence, and an attack on Messrs. Johnson and Brooke's factory in Manchester on May 3 was successfully repelled.

Things quieted down, not because trade improved—on July 9 Sir J. Byng reported that the two last Tuesdays had been the worst markets since the Exchange was built [1]—but because the appetite for disorder in an English crowd is soon sated.

The punishments appointed by law for the offences committed in April were inflicted at the August Assizes at Lancaster. Compared with the punishments inflicted on the Luddites they were mild. Sixty-six persons were charged with offences varying from rioting to the destruction of machinery. Ten persons received the death sentence but none were executed, all being transported for life instead. Thirty-three others were imprisoned for terms varying from three to eighteen months.[2]

The cotton weavers never recovered. Those who wish to follow the melancholy history of the evening of their trade can find the conditions described in the Poor Law Commission Report of 1834, where it is pointed out that whereas under the Speenhamland system of parish allowances the agricultural labourer, knowing existence at any rate assured, fails to exert himself, the weaver whose parish relief is calculated on what he could earn by piece-work, if industrious, is stimulated beyond his powers, and hence is noted for his ' lean and hungry look.' [3] In the Reports of the Select Committee on the Hand-loom Weavers' Petitions in 1834 and 1835 can be read the account of their last dying efforts, aided by Fielden, to obtain from Parliament a minimum wage. Their miserable plight in 1840 is described by the Commission on Hand-loom Weavers.

The Spinners' Strikes of 1829 and 1830

During the closing years of this period the chief part in the industrial struggle in the cotton trade is taken by the spinners.

[1] H.O., 40. 20.   [2] *Leeds Mercury*, August 12 and 19, October 14, 1826.
[3] See Mr. Henderson's Report from Lancashire, in *Extracts from Information received on Poor Laws*, 1833.

Again, as in 1818, a project of a General Union for all trades comes from their body.

The separate Cotton Spinners' Associations had for some years been growing in strength and importance, and since the repeal of the Combination Law in 1824, their proceedings had of course been more open.[1] In 1829 the spinners at Stockport and at Manchester, after refusing to accept reductions of wages, entered upon a long and disastrous conflict with their employers, in which John Doherty (secretary of the Manchester Union) played a leading part.

The turn-out at Stockport, which involved some ten thousand workers, began in January 1829 and lasted till June, when, in spite of help from other societies, the men were beaten and forced to return to work.[2] The struggle in Manchester began in April. The fine-cotton master spinners wanted to reduce wages—the reduction was said by the masters to amount to an eighth, by the men to amount to a third of their earnings—and the men objected. The men's leaders, who were less eager for a strike than the rank and file, made efforts to compromise. 'We appointed a deputation,' said Doherty afterwards,[3] ' to see the masters, to induce them, if possible, either to give up the proposed reduction, or to give us time to ascertain whether it was practicable to get the other masters in the surrounding districts to pay the same prices they were paying, and proposing in the event of not getting their consent to that, we should consent to their terms ; they would not hear of it, and the consequence was the strike.' By May 9 at least ten thousand hands were out.

The prolonged dispute proved a severe strain on the funds of the Union, although the men only received 2s. 2¼d. a week,[4] and the situation became more serious in July, when the coarse master spinners joined with the fine master spinners in a deliberate attempt to crush the men's combination. It was resolved that the fine master spinners should open their mills and offer work at a reduction to the turn-outs and then to any others, whilst, on a certain day, ' notice being given, the

---

[1] Doherty (Committee on Combinations of Workmen, 1838, p. 250) stated that since the repeal of the Act there had been no oath in the Spinners' Association.

[2] It was claimed on behalf of the masters that wages were previously 7½ to 15 per cent. higher in Stockport than elsewhere, and that the masters were compelled to assimilate ' their price to the majority of the trade ' by the continually decreasing value of yarns and cloths (H.O., 40. 23, May 25).

[3] Committee on Combinations of Workmen, 1838, p. 264.   [4] *Ibid.*, p. 251.

coarse numbers masters will make a reduction in the wages
of all their spinners who are members of or subscribe to the
Spinners' Union and that they will repeat this reduction from
time to time until the Fine Spinners return to work and further
that until they do return no work shall be given to any new
hands amongst the coarse spinners who are thus connected
with the Spinners Union.'[1] The coarse spinners refused to
renounce the Union and came out.

At the end of August the men appealed to the magistrates
in an address signed by John Doherty,[2] to arbitrate in the case.
' We are not aware,' ran the appeal, ' that any body of workmen have ever, under similar circumstances, offered to entrust
their case to the magistrates. . . . We only wish you, as we
know you will, to administer justice with an equal as well as a
firm hand, and when you furnish forces to protect the inanimate
property of the masters, the machines and cotton, the bricks
and mortar of their mills, you will equally respect *animate*
property, and afford the same protection to the blood and
bones of a large portion of his majesty's subjects.'   The appeal
was fruitless, and so was a similar appeal in September to the
Manchester churchwardens, asking them to arrange a meeting
between masters and workmen.[3] In October, after twenty-
seven weeks of struggle, the men were forced to return to
work at the reduced rates.

Such a defeat might well have made the men despair, but
under Doherty's guidance they decided immediately that what
was needed was an organisation more efficient and extensive.
On December 5, 1829, a meeting was held at Ramsey in
the Isle of Man of fifteen delegates from different Spinners'
Societies in England, Scotland, and Ireland, who resolved to
form ' a Grand General Union of all the Operative Spinners in
the United Kingdom, for the mutual support and protection
of all.'[4] Each member was to pay 1d. a week to the general

---

[1] H.O., 40. 24 (Report of July 16). The terms of the undertaking which
the coarse masters tried to make their men sign were as follows: ' I do hereby
agree to work for so and so and to give him satisfactory evidence that I do not
contribute to the fine mule spinners who have turned out, and to suffer an abate-
ment from my wages every fortnight until I have given such proof that I do not
contribute to the Union.' See Doherty's evidence, Committee on Combinations of Workmen, 1838, p. 265. For another version, see William Arrowsmith's evidence, *ibid.*, p. 279.   [2] H.O., 40. 24.

[3] Committee on Combinations of Workmen, 1838, p. 266.

[4] See H.O., 40. 27, May 10 and June 7. Webb's *History of Trade Unionism*,
pp. 104 f., gives an account of this Union.

fund in addition to local levies, and each member on strike against a reduction of wages was to receive 10s. a week. The same payments and allowances applied to ' all male piecers capable of spinning,' but strict rules were laid down that no piecers were to be allowed to spin ' on any account whatever ' unless these piecers were near relations of spinners or ' poor relations of the proprietors of the Mill,' and then the spinning was only allowed during the absence of the spinners in the wheel houses. Female spinners were not admitted members of the Union, but were urged to form a separate Association and assured of the ' aid of the whole Confederation in supporting them to obtain men's prices, or such remuneration as may be deemed sufficient under general and particular circumstances.' The consent of the whole district had to be obtained before any strike took place, and it was decreed ' that no more be allowed to come out at any time than what can be supported with the stipulated sums on any consideration whatsoever.' New Factory Legislation was to be pressed for by the different districts.

No sooner was the Grand General Union of Operative Spinners launched on its career than Doherty set about an even more ambitious project, the formation of a General Union embracing different trades. The organ of this new body, called the *United Trades' Co-operative Journal* was started, under Doherty's editorship, in March 1830, but the body itself was not formally constituted till July 1830, when it received the name of ' the National Association for the Protection of Labour.' Doherty was succeeded as secretary of the Manchester Spinners' Union by Peter Maddocks who still continued work as a spinner,[1] whilst Thomas Foster took his place on the General Union of Spinners.

The year 1830, whilst this further movement for union amongst different trades was developing, was a year of strain for the newly formed General Union of Spinners. Various minor strikes took place during the year, notably at Bolton and Ashton in May and at Manchester in October. A strike was threatened in August in the whole of the Stalybridge and Ashton-under-Lyne district, for the masters announced that instead of paying prices varying from 3s. 5d. to 4s. 2d. they wished to pay a uniform rate of 3s. 9d., a rate, which, so they declared, would be an increase on the wages the men were actually receiving.[2] The men thought otherwise, and declined the new rate, asking for 4s. 2d. instead. Colonel Shaw at

[1] H.O., 40. 26, December 22.   [2] H.O., 40. 26, August 29.

Manchester became seriously alarmed at the prospect of the masters introducing blackleg labour in the midst of the excitement caused by the Revolution in France ; [1] the working classes, he writes on August 26,[2] 'talk a great deal of their power of putting down the military and constables, and until a few weeks have passed over, so as to allow these fumes and follies to evaporate, it would be well to avoid all extreme measures.' The extreme measures he deprecated were in fact avoided, and a compromise reached at the beginning of September by which the masters agreed to pay a uniform rate of 3s. 11d.[3]

In Manchester, in October 1830, the spinners organised a series of strikes in different mills for the restoration of their former wages. 'Their system,' wrote General Bouverie,[4] 'is to order the Hands in only a limited number of Mills to turn out at a time in order that, until these shall have gained their point, they may be supported by the Funds of the Union. When they have got their wages increased to the extent of their demands, another set of Mills are turned out, and so on, so that a constant state of irritation is kept up.'[5] The same plan was pursued in Cheshire. The policy of striking at different mills in succession proved too successful. The millowners grew seriously alarmed. The General Union had expressly deprecated any interference with the management of any mill, but the masters felt that their rights were being invaded. Colonel Shaw, putting the views of the masters, wrote in August [6] that the men 'insist not only on the masters giving them such wages as they demand, but that they regulate the whole work in the Factories, in all its details, in the manner which the Union prescribes ; and the men refuse to communicate with the Masters, referring them for terms to the leaders of the Union.'

In November the masters of factories at Stalybridge, Ashton, and Dukinfield resolved upon a serious step with the object of crushing the men's Union.[7] It was the men's policy

---

[1] For the effect on England of the 1830 Revolution in France, see Butler, *The Passing of the Great Reform Bill*, pp. 85-88.   [2] H.O., 40. 26, August 26.

[3] *Ibid.*, December 2.   [4] *Ibid.*, October 30.

[5] One of the mills selected for a strike at Manchester was Mr. Gray's. Mr. Gray, who had been prominent in the 1818 strike, wrote on this occasion to the Home Office deploring 'the improvident measure of repealing the Combination Laws' (H.O., 40. 27, December 22).   [6] H.O., 40. 26, August 29.

[7] General Bouverie wrote: The masters think that if the men are reduced to accept their terms 'the power of the Union and the Union itself will be at an end' (H.O., 40. 26, December 8, 1830). The account that follows of the lock-

to avoid the drain on their Union funds involved in a big strike; the masters determined to precipitate the crisis. They bound themselves, under a penalty of £500, to reduce wages from the 3s. 11d. agreed on in September to the 3s. 9d. rejected at that time. Fifty-two firms signed the agreement, which was to come into effect on December 4 (altered subsequently to December 11), and it was estimated that the firms involved spun one-eighth of the cotton produced in England. If the men refused to accept the reduction the mills would be closed. ' What effect,' wrote General Bouverie on November 14, ' this measure will have upon the Public Peace it is impossible to say, but it is equally impossible to contemplate the possibility of so large a number of Persons being thrown out of employment in the middle of winter without great anxiety—at the same time it is certainly possible that the great numbers which must be thrown upon the Funds of the Trades Union for support will tend very materially to diminish those Funds and thereby to weaken the hold which the Union has upon the Working Classes.'

The men, as was expected, refused to accept the reduced terms and the mills were closed. It was estimated that twenty-three thousand men were thus thrown out of employment. A mass meeting was held (December 4), addressed by Doherty and Betts, and there was some talk of arresting these leaders, but nobody would come forward to give evidence. Nor could special constables be induced to act. Strikers paraded the streets with pistols and bludgeons, broke windows, and forced those still at work to come out. The workpeople at Hyde, who had hitherto worked at lower wages than elsewhere, and had refused to join the Union, were visited and compelled to come out. Sir Henry Bouverie was anxious not to billet soldiers ' among a population in so excited a state as that of these towns is at present.' The masters he considered had brought this state of things upon themselves, '. . . and it is a question whether the Troops are to be employed to prevent the ill consequences to the Masters of this their own measure at the risk of much greater evils than the destruction of all the Property which they possess (however serious it may be).' Melbourne, on the other hand, who was now Home Secretary, thought that ' illegal meetings '—a comprehensive term in his own construction of it—must be stopped at all costs.

out and attempt at a general strike is based on documents scattered about in H.O., 40. 25, 40. 26, 40. 27, 52. 12.

The Spinners' Union, however, had no wish to quarrel with the authorities, and set itself against any disturbances. It even ordered all processions to be given up, and so rigid was the discipline imposed that by December 24 not a stick was to be seen in Ashton or Stalybridge. The drain on the men's funds was serious, and it was resolved to risk a desperate throw. A meeting of the General Union of Spinners of the United Kingdom was held in Manchester on December 16 and 17, and a resolution passed calling a General Strike on December 27 of all spinners ' receiving less than 4s. 2d. per thousand hanks of No. 40's (and other Nos. in proportion).'[1] The Scottish and Irish delegates however did not wish to be drawn in till they saw how Manchester affairs turned out, and in England itself Preston, Stockport, Bolton, and Lancaster held back, either refusing to join the Union or refusing to obey. The finances of the Union were in a desperate state in spite of help from the National Association for the Protection of Labour. The payment of 10s. a week to spinners was reduced to 5s., or in some places to 2s. 6d., and the piecers and labourers were given nothing.[2]

The attempt to enforce a General Strike was a failure. A few mills turned out in Glossop and in Manchester, but most remained quietly at work. ' Although the result,' wrote Mr. Foster, the Manchester magistrate,[3] ' will very much weaken the Union and create much division amongst its members, it also lessens the security we had for their peaceable conduct whilst they were strong and united and under the control of leaders who had sufficient sense to know, that nothing was so likely to defeat their object as the attempt to attain it by open and violent disturbances of the Peace.' Mr. Foster's words seemed justified a few days later, on January 3, by the lamentable murder of Mr. Thomas Ashton, son of one of the chief cotton spinners at Hyde. Thomas Ashton himself seems to have had no special cause of quarrel with the men, but his

---

[1] The resolution pointed out that 'the system of every Master paying such prices as he may think proper, enables the worst and most unprincipled of them to take advantage of the weakness and defencelessness of the men by reducing them to such prices as the fair and honourable masters would scorn to offer to their men, were they not forced in self-defence to do so by the unfair competition of those who do.'

[2] Money was saved by stopping the allowance of 7s. a week per head to the women spinners at Mr. M'Connell's mills on the ground that they did not come out when first ordered (H.O., 40. 25, December 25).

[3] H.O., 40. 26, December 27.

brother, to whose mill he was going when he was murdered, had recently dismissed some men for belonging to the Union.[1]

The strikers in the Ashton and Stalybridge district were being starved back to work, and feeling was said to be very 'savage' against the fifty-two masters who had brought such misery on the population, a feeling not improved by some Oldham employers who took the opportunity of telling the men they intended to imitate the Ashton masters if the latter were successful. Report said that the Union tried to induce the colliers to refuse to supply with coal all mills that paid below the stipulated price ; but this policy had no result. By March the spinners were all at work again.

Thus at the time of the Reform Bill the new power was most firmly established in the industry in which machinery had made the most sweeping revolution. The cotton weavers supplied the standing misery which was the chief permanent cause of the degradation of Lancashire life. The cotton spinners, far more advantageously placed for combination, had tried ambitious projects which had failed. Their wisest leaders had grasped the moral that the workers could only combat the new power by organising and developing their forces on larger lines. For this purpose they were cruelly crippled by the state of education, and by the success with which the class in possession had guided and controlled all the changes of the last two centuries. John Doherty, a man of vision, knowledge, and great public spirit, saw what was needed, but to educate and unite the workers' forces rapidly and effectively, under existing conditions, was beyond his power or that of any one else.

---

[1] See *Annual Register*, 1831 ; *Chronicle*, p. 7. It is sometimes asserted that the Trade Union officials instigated this murder (see Chapman, *op. cit.*, p. 199 *n*), but there seems very little basis for this charge. Lieut.-Col. Shaw, in his official report on January 4, wrote : 'The Turn Outs have lately been behaving peaceably and in a very subdued manner, nor is there the least proof that the murder was perpetrated by them.' He also mentions that Thomas Ashton's father had 'been in no difficulty with his workpeople and that he was not even visited by the procession when the workpeople went from Hyde to Staleybridge and Ashton' (H.O., 40. 29). The charge against the Union rests on statements in the confessions of the murderers themselves, and in view of the circumstances under which they were obtained it is difficult to attach any value to these confessions. See account of trial in the *Annual Register*, 1834, pp. 290 ff.

CHAPTER VI

THE WOOLLEN AND WORSTED WORKERS

I.—INTRODUCTION

IN the eighteenth century the woollen manufacture enjoyed the prestige and the dignity of an old-established national institution.[1] During the Industrial Revolution it was deposed from its proud position of the first trade in the realm by its new rival, the cotton trade, whose sudden growth and dependence on foreign products were often contrasted with the stability of an indigenous industry that used for its material the fleeces of British sheep. The vain efforts of wool to stifle its new rival are described elsewhere. Though unsuccessful in that struggle, the woollen industry retained so much of its old influence and importance that till 1824 it was able to thwart the efforts of the powerful agricultural interest to obtain permission to export British wool.

The story of the long struggle between the wool growers and the wool manufacturers can only be sketched here very briefly.[2] For centuries the export of British wool had been prohibited. In 1780 the wool growers, finding the home market overstocked, agitated for the repeal of the enactments against exportation. But the manufacturers were too strong for them; so strong indeed that they induced Parliament in 1788 to impose still more stringent penalties on the exporters of wool.[3] Innumerable pamphlets were written on both sides, and the manufacturers were severely handled by Arthur Young in some acrid pages of the *Annals of Agriculture*. At last in 1819 the wool growers gained an important point in the

[1] For the regulations dating from the time of the Tudors to which the industry was still subject, see below.

[2] See James, *History of the Worsted Manufacture*, 1857, pp. 304, 305, 393 ff.

[3] 28 George III. c. 38. Any person concerned in exporting wool was liable to a fine of £3 per lb. or £50 on the whole, together with three months' imprisonment for the first, and six months for the second offence. Ships were forfeited as well. See James, *History of the Worsted Manufacture*, 1857, p. 305 *n*.

struggle, for in that year Parliament agreed to the imposition of a duty of 6d. a lb. on foreign wool.   The imposition of this duty led later to the establishment of free trade in wool, for the Government could now bargain with the manufacturing interest, promising to repeal this tax on foreign wool, provided the export of British wool was allowed.   Thanks to divisions in the ranks of the manufacturers (the woollen trade agreeing to the proposals, whilst the worsted trade still held out) an Act was passed in 1824 which allowed the export of British and the import of foreign wool for a duty of 1d. a lb. in each case : a measure which ended the long conflict, and, contrary to expectations, had no evil effects on the worsted trade.

During the Industrial Revolution the centre of gravity of the woollen trade shifted from the South of England to the North, that is from the clothing districts in the South-West, Gloucestershire, Wiltshire, and Somerset,[1] and from the worsted districts of the South-East, Norfolk, Suffolk, and Essex, to the West Riding of Yorkshire.   Yorkshire increased whilst the South-West and the South-East decreased.

To understand the different classes of workers and the problems with which they were confronted it will be necessary to give a brief sketch of the history of the trade during the time with which we deal.   First we must note that though there were certain special centres, the making of woollens and worsteds was also spread to some extent all over the kingdom, and there were few counties in which the manufacture of wool was not carried on in some form.   Before the days of rapid intercommunication and exchange of goods, it would seem as necessary for a neighbourhood to produce its own clothes as to produce its own food, and in spite of the gradual concentration of the trade into special neighbourhoods, the old state of things lingered on.

First of all we must distinguish between the two branches of the trade, (1) the cloth trade, usually called the woollen trade, and (2) the worsted trade, sometimes called the woollen stuff trade.[2]   For the cloth or woollen trade the wool used was short wool, prepared for the process of spinning by carding : for the worsted trade long wool was used, and this was prepared for spinning by the process of combing.   Both

[1] Devonshire was also a centre for light woollens which lost much work to the North (see Clapham, *Woollen and Worsted Industries*, 1907, p. 15).

[2] For the best account of the differences between woollen and worsted, see Clapham, *The Woollen and Worsted Industries*.

woollens and worsteds were spun and then woven, but after woollen cloth was woven, it passed through additional processes, unnecessary in the case of worsted goods. First it was felted (milling or fulling were the terms generally used), that is to say, by pressure and moisture the fibres of the cloth were interlocked and the cloth made thick and opaque. After the felting was done, the fibres were raised, till a nap was formed on the surface and this nap was then shorn off. These last processes were called 'finishing.' The distinction between the two classes of goods has been thus described: 'The worsted fabric is not homogeneous like the fulled cloth, but is reticulated like linen and cotton fabrics.'[1] Into the various products of the worsted branch, the camblets, shalloons, calimancoes, tammies, and others, it is impossible to enter here; roughly they all come under the head of what we call woollen stuffs as opposed to cloth.

The two branches, as we have seen, were distinct and their interests sometimes differed. We will deal first with the woollen branch.

Woollen or Cloth Trade

Although the South-West district remained and still remains an important centre for the production of the highest quality of cloth, much of its trade passed to the West Riding of Yorkshire, and Leeds and Huddersfield became the chief woollen centres.

The woollen industry in the South-West counties had early become a highly developed and capitalised industry, with big master manufacturers on the one side, and more or less organised bodies of operatives on the other. The former were called 'Gentlemen Clothiers.' They bought the wool and employed various classes of persons to work it up for them. As trade increased in the early years of the nineteenth century many of these gentlemen clothiers turned merchants as well.[2]

The high-water mark of the prosperity in the South-West is usually put at 1816 or 1817. After that the decline began. The coarser trade went up to Yorkshire, where attention was early paid to the middle and lower qualities of woollens. The migration to the North of the woollen industry was not

[1] Bischoff, *History of the Woollen and Worsted Manufactures*, 1842, ii. p. 402.
[2] See Report of Committee on South-West Woollen Clothiers' Petition, 1802-3 (Ed. Sheppard).

affected so much by the introduction of the earlier kinds of
machinery in the North as by the later developments of steam
power.

Yorkshire had had a flourishing woollen industry for centuries. Unlike the gentleman clothier of the South-West, the
typical Yorkshire cloth manufacturer was a small master
manufacturer, much like the men described by Defoe, living
on a few acres of ground, working up the wool himself and
carrying it into market. In spite of the introduction of
machinery and the growth of the factory system, these small
domestic manufacturers increased in number. Round the
clothing towns the land was cut up into small holdings, and
there was an increase of this system after 1795.[1] Arthur
Young described in 1793 the ' mixture of pasturage and manufacture ' near Leeds. At Pudsey, he says, ' the common size
holding, rather than farm, is from two to five acres, which let
at 30s. to 50s. an acre. . . . Yet the same land, twenty-five
years ago, let, though grass, at only 10s. an acre ; the vast
rise being occasioned entirely by the manufacture. . . . These
little grass farmers buy the wool they work, and go through
the whole operation of converting it into cloth, going to market
twice a week to sell it.' [2] ' I viewed the Cloth Hall on a market
day, and the scene was animated ; but I could not help being
struck with the reflection, that such an immense number of
men were idle, twice a week, to come from all parts of the
clothing country, in order for half a dozen to execute business
which might as well be performed by one woman ; or, if these
men inhabited towns, who would, instead of a day, lose not
more than an hour : one-third of the productive time of such
multitudes thus lost, to say the least, is a disadvantage attending this mode of spreading a manufacture.' [3]

This domestic system, in spite of Arthur Young's strictures,
lived long in Yorkshire, and was only finally extinguished in
the nineteenth century, by the coming of the power-looms.
It adapted itself successfully to new conditions, for the factory
system and the domestic system went on side by side, various
processes, such as carding, slubbing, and spinning, being done
in factories, and the rest at home. Small manufacturers survived the rise of the big manufacturers represented by Mr.
Gott of Leeds. As late as 1858, Baines, speaking of the Leeds
district, describes it much as Arthur Young did : '. . . the

[1] Report of Committee on State of Woollen Manufacture, 1806, p. 444.
[2] *Annals of Agriculture*, vol. xxvii. p. 309.   [3] *Ibid.*, p. 311.

Manufacturers of the outlying districts bring the cloth made
in their looms, twice in the week, to be sold to the merchants in
the two great cloth halls of this town.' [1] The great factories, he
says, with ' the power of capital, the power of machinery and
the saving of time,' have not materially affected the system
of domestic and village manufacture. 'They [the small
manufacturers] combined to establish joint-stock mills, where
each shareholder takes his own wool, and has it cleaned, dyed,
carded and spun : then, taking the warp or weft to his own
house or workshop, he has it woven by the hand-loom, often
by members of his own family. The cloth is afterwards fulled
at the mill, washed and tentered.' [2]

Yorkshire, in fact, with its number of small manufacturers
who combined a semi-domestic system with the use of steam
for various processes, outstripped the South-West with its
capitalised system and its water power.

Worsted Trade

Norwich had long been the centre of the worsted industry,
' the chief seat of the chief manufacture of the realm ' as
Macaulay called her, but it was in the middle of the eighteenth
century that she ' attained the greatest prosperity.' She was
famous not only for the making but for the dyeing of worsted
fabrics. The years from 1743 to 1763 are counted her happiest
days.[3] The trade was conducted by merchant manufacturers,
' the acknowledged aristocracy of the city, opulent men and
generally surrounded by their dependents, they had something of a lordly bearing. . . . To improve their carriage they
were sometimes accustomed to learn the use of the small sword.
. . . From this probably they derived their peculiar air on
entering a drawing room. What with shouting, scraping, stamp-
ing and bowing, a well-bred gentleman made as much bustle
at the door as if an ambassador had just returned from a
foreign court.' [4] They were men of remarkable resource,
and what they lost by the competition of cotton goods at
home, they gained by increasing their foreign trade. ' Their
travellers penetrated through Europe, and their pattern-
cards were exhibited in every principal town, from the frozen

---

[1] Baines, *Yorkshire Past and Present*, p. 655.   [2] *Ibid.*, p. 656.
[3] James, *op. cit.*, p. 259.
[4] James, *op. cit.*, p. 261, quoting from *Senex*, East Anglian newspaper,
February 7, 1832.

plains of Moscow to the milder climes of Lisbon, Seville, and
Naples.' [1] The yarn for the manufacture was for the most
part spun in the neighbouring counties, but, in spite of the
difficulties of transit, some of the wool was sent to be spun in
Yorkshire, and even as far north as Westmoreland.[2]

In the middle years of the eighteenth century the worsted
trade in the West Riding of Yorkshire began to increase very
rapidly. It was no new importation, for the industry had
been there before 1700, but between 1750-60, whilst Norwich
was flourishing, Yorkshire too greatly increased her trade,
and many men who had formerly made cloth now turned to
the worsted branch. The structure of the industry differed
from that at Norwich. 'Merchants had in abundance sprung
up, who rode from town to town, and valley to valley, to
purchase those goods which were mostly shipped to the continent of Europe. A new road to wealth had been opened—
the farmer either forsook the tilling of the ground to follow
altogether the stuff business, or else carried it on as a domestic
employment along with the cultivation of the land, and with
thrifty habits, was often in an incredibly short time, enabled
to purchase his homestead and farm. The art spread into the
most remote dells, as well as in the towns and villages of the
south-western portion of the Riding.' [3]

After 1763 the Norwich trade began to decline. This was
partly due to the growth of trade in Yorkshire, partly to the
quarrels with the American colonies, which, even before the
outbreak of war, hit Norwich hard. When Arthur Young
visited and described Norwich in 1771, it was still considered
the most important centre of the worsted trade, with about
12,000 looms which gave employment to some 72,000 persons
in and near the town. The value of the trade in Norfolk and
the adjoining districts he estimated at £1,200,000.[4] A year
later (1772) the value of the worsted trade in the West Riding
was estimated for Parliament as some £1,404,000. James
calculates that by 1774 no fewer than 84,000 persons were
employed in the trade in Yorkshire.[5]

The American war, with its continental complications, caused
great depression in the whole industry ; when peace came and
trade revived Norwich never recovered her position, whereas
the Yorkshire trade throve and prospered. It must not,

[1] James, *op. cit.*, p. 308, quoting *Old Monthly Magazine* for 1798.
[2] James, *op. cit.*, p. 253.   [3] James, *op. cit.*, p. 267.
[4] Quoted James, *op. cit.*, pp. 271, 272.   [5] *Op. cit.*, pp. 284, 285.

however, be supposed that the Norwich trade decayed away
at once. In the twelve years after the American war it was
still great, though not growing. Its final ruin is often attributed to the French war, but it must be remembered that till
1818 Norwich retained the monopoly of fine stuffs, and still
employed about ten thousand looms.[1]

Norwich was losing her trade to Yorkshire long before there
was any question of the introduction of machinery, but her
downfall was, no doubt, hastened by her inability to adapt
herself to new conditions. The south-west of Yorkshire had
overwhelming natural advantages. The streams of numerous
small valleys supplied water power for machinery, and, when
the age of the steam engine came, coal and iron were close at
hand. The rivers and streams helped also the creation of a
canal system for the transit of goods. Hence it is more than
doubtful whether Norfolk could have held her own, however
eagerly she had adopted every new invention. As it was,
her merchant manufacturers would not take the risk of introducing machinery among a hostile population who feared
that their livelihood would be taken from them. Their enterprise and inventive gifts spent themselves on devising new
stuffs, many of them mixtures of silk and wool, such as Norwich
crape, poplin, or ‘ Challis,’ some of which suited the whims of
fashion and gave Norwich from time to time a gleam of her
old prosperity. But no sooner had a new fabric become
popular than Yorkshire began to make it, and to make it
cheaper,[2] and the Norwich manufacturers had to turn their
minds to new fields. The gleams of prosperity were transient,
and by 1838 there were only about five thousand looms in
Norwich, and of these about a fifth were idle.[3]

In Yorkshire on the other hand, although the worsted trade
did not increase during the first years of the French war,
progress was made in utilising new inventions. Also, before
the end of the eighteenth century Yorkshire began to dye
her own goods instead of sending them south to be dyed.[4]
Hitherto Norwich, London, and Coventry had been the chief
dyeing centres, and goods were shipped from London for the
Continent. As soon as Yorkshire took to dyeing her own
goods, Yorkshire merchants began to ship the goods from

---

[1] James, *op. cit.*, p. 306.

[2] Yorkshire early devoted herself to the manufacture of cheap goods (see
Baines, *Yorkshire Past and Present*, p. 644).

[3] James, *op. cit.*, p. 483.   [4] James, *op. cit.*, p. 314.

Liverpool and Hull to other countries. Unlike the merchant manufacturers of Norwich, the merchants in the West Riding were, as a rule, a separate class from the manufacturers.[1] The manufacturers might be quite small men, buying the wool and working it up themselves, or they might be big men buying the wool and distributing it through agents to spinners and weavers, from whom they received it back, ready for delivery to the merchants in the Piece Hall at Halifax or Bradford.[2] The big manufacturers drove out the small men more quickly in Yorkshire worsteds than in Yorkshire woollens where power-looms were introduced later.

Like all other trades dependent on foreign markets the worsted trade had considerable fluctuations during the early years of the nineteenth century, but it suffered less than the other textiles, though the rosy picture given by the stuff manu-facturers in 1823 was perhaps overdrawn. 'During the last eventful thirty years, the manufacture of long wool had never languished ; the operative hands had been fully employed ; and the master manufacturer had been enabled to give a rate of wages sufficient to afford to the labourer the means of sub-sistence, even in times of scarcity.'[3] We may take as a sober estimate the calculation of James that the trade in the West Riding doubled between 1810-20, increased by two-thirds between 1820-25, and by a seventh between 1825-30.[4]

II.—THE SPINNERS

No process changed its character more completely during the Industrial Revolution than the process of spinning. It begins as a cottage art carried on by women and children plying their distaff or spinning wheel ; it ends as a factory industry carried on by machine worked by power with men and children to minister to the wants of the machine. The spinning of wool or worsted—and it will be convenient for this purpose to comprise worsted under the head of wool—was an old-estab-lished and widespread art. The typical family would prepare its own wool and send it to the village weaver to be woven. Such a system remained in vogue in some districts till the end

[1] There were of course some who were both merchants and manufacturers.

[2] Bradford after 1800 grew more important than Halifax, becoming the undisputed capital of the worsted trade.

[3] James, *op. cit.*, p. 397.   [4] James, *op. cit.*, pp. 388, 408, 429-30.

of the eighteenth century.[1] Eden's thrifty and frugal Cumberland woman in 1796 ' who spins wool for her neighbours about 15 weeks a year, and earns 4d. a day and victuals ' [2] was a survival of this old system. By 1760 spinning was a specialised industry, carried on by the women and even more by the children in the counties round the big centres of trade, for wool staplers who brought the wool and took away the yarn when spun.

The system by which the work was given out differed in the different districts. With the great difficulties of transit before the improvements in roads and the making of canals, it must have been no easy business to convey the wool to and fro. ' The wool after being combed was sent out by travellers in tilted carts, who left it with the spinners in one journey, and took back the yarn, paying the amount of spinning, at the next.' [3] The spinners near at hand, such as the relatives of the weaver, would naturally have the preference, but so great was the demand for yarn that the Norwich trade gave employment to spinners beyond the boundaries of Norfolk and Suffolk,[4] in Essex, Cambridgeshire, and Bedford, and in early days wool was even sent up to Yorkshire to be turned into yarn and then brought back.[5] The growth of the worsted trade in Yorkshire from 1750 to 1760 gave a great stimulus to the learning of spinning, and numerous spinning schools were set up for the instruction of the young. The trade pushed into the Colne and Burnley districts of Lancashire, but was overpowered by the competition of the growing cotton trade. Peel and other manufacturers were spreading their factories through the valleys of North and East Lancashire and attracting away the worsted spinners by higher wages.[6]

What were the conditions under which spinning was done ?

---

[1] e.g. Anglesey. *Annals of Agriculture*, 14. 408 (1790): 'Almost every farmer combs, cards and spins his own wool, and sends it to the weaver, who charges from 1½d. to 3d. per yard, according to the fineness and breadth of the web. There is none exported, either wool or woollen cloth.'

[2] Eden, *The State of the Poor*, vol. ii. p. 75.

[3] James, *History of the Worsted Manufacture*, p. 272.

[4] Of Suffolk, Prof. Unwin says (*Victoria County History of Suffolk*, vol. ii. p. 253) 'the chief occupation of the county, so far as the textile manufactures was concerned, was the combing of wool and the spinning of yarn for the worsted weavers of Norwich.' A moderate estimate of the numbers employed in spinning in the middle of the eighteenth century he gives as 36,000 women and children.

[5] James, *op. cit.*, pp. 252 f.   [6] James, *op. cit.*, p. 633.

It is clear that they varied greatly, even as the homes of the spinners varied.   One advantage was that it could sometimes be carried on out of doors.   ' On fine days,' we read of Bradford, ' the women and children might be found in the streets and lanes fully employed with the labour of spinning upon the one-thread wheel, in which they greatly excelled ' : [1]   and many a traveller through a village would see ' Contentment spinning at the cottage door.'   Possibly the children whose hands were being thus closely kept from the mischief with which Satan would otherwise have provided them, might have had a different tale to tell, and Arthur Young, who thanks to the Woollen Bill [2] was under no illusions as to the benevolence of the woollen manufacturers, gave lurid pictures of the state to which the spinners had been reduced, even before the competition with machinery had seriously begun.   In an attack on the Norwich master manufacturers in 1788 he talks of ' the sufferings of thousands of wretched individuals, willing to work, but starving from their ill-requited labour : of whole families of honest, industrious children offering their little hands to the wheel, and asking bread of the helpless mother, unable through this *well-regulated* manufacture, to give it them.' [3]

But whatever the hardships of the hand-spinner's lot, there is no doubt that the introduction of machinery caused widespread suffering to those for whom the developments in the industry brought no work in its place.   Machinery for spinning and for the previous processes in the woollen and worsted industry was adopted much later than in the cotton industry, nor was this entirely due to want of enterprise in the trade which Arthur Young taunted with being ' sluggish, inactive, dead.' [4]   It arose partly from the weakness of the material which broke more readily than cotton when subjected to any strain.

It will be convenient to deal with the introduction of machinery into the different districts in turn.

Introduction of Machinery into the South-West

The use of the jenny was introduced into the South-West clothing district first in 1776 at Shepton Mallet, where it caused

---

[1] James, *op. cit.*, p. 589.
[2] See note 3 on p. 136.
[3] *Annals of Agriculture*, vol. ix. p. 269.
[4] *Ibid.*, vol. vii. p. 164.

considerable riots.[1] In a petition to the House of Commons we are given the spinners' point of view :

'A Petition of the Wire-drawers, Card-board-makers, Card-makers, Scribblers, Spinners, Twisters, Weavers, and others, employed in the Woollen Manufactory, in *Fromeselwood, Shepton Mallett,* and other Cloth-working Towns in the County of *Somerset ;* Setting forth, That a machine called *The Spinning Jenny,* for carding and spinning of Wool into Yarn, had been lately introduced and put in practice in the Town of *Shepton Mallett,* in the said County; and that the Petitioners were apprehensive that the same would be established in every Cloth-working Town throughout the Counties of *Somerset, Gloucester,* and *Wilts,* and would thereby tend greatly to the Damage and Ruin of many Thousands of the industrious Poor employed in that Manufacture : And therefore praying the House to take the Premises into Consideration, and abolish the Use of the said Spinning Machine in the said County, being offered to be presented to the House ;
And a Motion being made, and the Question being put, That the said Petition be brought up ;
It passed in the Negative.' [2]

The introduction was by no means universal all over the district. A note on the proposed Shearmen's Bill of 1804-5, a Bill which if carried would have limited the number of jennies one person might possess and the number of spindles on each jenny, mentions 1784 as the date of its introduction.[3] Of Trowbridge in Wilts we read in 1795 : ' The machines have been introduced chiefly within the last six or seven years, and as the people are much averse to them, they are brought into use by degrees.' [4] The writers of the Surveys of the Agriculture of Wilts and Somerset, for the Board of Agriculture in 1794, discuss the probable effects of the newly introduced machinery. By 1803 the transformation was practically complete.[5] The clothiers had one by one introduced the system of having ' spinning houses ' on their own premises, and the weavers were filled with apprehension lest they too should be forced to work under their employer's roof.
At the same time the employers began to use machinery

---

[1] Evidence on Woollen Trade Bill, 1802-3, p. 68.

[2] *House of Commons Journal,* November 1, 1776.

[3] H.O., 42. 83.

[4] Eden, *op. cit.,* vol. iii. p. 802.

[5] Hand-spinning still survived in some places (see Minutes of Evidence on Woollen Trade Bill, 1802-3, p. 14).

for the preliminary processes of carding, slubbing and scribbling necessary to make the wool fit for spinning.[1]

The introduction of machinery for these preliminary processes and for spinning took place whilst the industry was in a flourishing condition and able to absorb a great deal of the labour so displaced.[2] But, without doubt, the more distant districts suffered by the concentration of work. ' The earnings by spinning,' wrote a correspondent from North-East Cornwall in 1795,[3] ' have, for the last year, been much curtailed, owing to the wool-staplers using spinning engines, near their place of residence, in preference to sending their wool into the country to be spun by hand. And whereas a poor woman and two small children (which is the average household of a labourer) could heretofore earn fourteen pence per day, they cannot now earn more than ten pence. . . .'

Eden draws in 1796 a melancholy picture of what the introduction of machinery elsewhere meant to a village that had hitherto largely subsisted on hand-spinning. The place is Seend in Wiltshire, not far from the clothing centre of Melksham.[4] ' As the chapelry consists almost entirely of dairy farms, and consequently affords very little employment in husbandry, except during the hay-harvest, the labouring poor are very dependent on the neighbouring towns, where the cloth manufacture is carried on ; but, unfortunately, since the introduction of machinery, which lately took place, hand-spinning has fallen into disuse, and for these two reasons, the clothier no longer depends on the Poor for the yarn which they formerly spun for him at their own homes, as he finds that 50 persons (to speak within compass), with the help of machines, will do as much work as 500 without them ; and the Poor, from the

---

[1] Scribbling by hand took a man 96 hours, by machine a child performed the same amount in 14 hours (Reports from Assistant Hand-loom Weavers' Commissioners, 1840, part ii. pp. 439 f.).

[2] Cf., e.g., Annals of Agriculture, vol. ix. pp. 298-9. A correspondent from Pucklechurch, Gloucestershire, wrote: 'I know that a very considerable Wiltshire clothier from a great distance, lately wished to put out spinning in this place, where the hands were before full of work, that the same person has opened a spinning house, at a still greater distance from his residence, and that he wants to introduce the spinning machines.'

N.B.—In some copies of vol. ix. of the Annals of Agriculture the full answers of correspondents to questions about the woollen industry, from which the above is taken, are not given.

[3] Annals of Agriculture, vol. xxvi. p. 19.

[4] Eden, op. cit., vol. iii. p. 796.

great reduction in the price of spinning, scarcely have the heart to earn the little that is obtained by it.'[1]

But although the introduction of machinery brought disaster to some villages, to others it brought life and prosperity. Water power was used for working the jennies and the other machinery, and this caused a migration from the towns to those villages where streams were available. Just when steam engines were beginning to be used in the North, the use of water power became common in the South-West. This tendency to move from towns to villages is noted by most of the witnesses before the Committee on the Woollen Trade Bill in 1802-3. ' In consequence of the introduction of Machinery Manufacturers are now looking out for Mill Scites to work by Water which cannot be obtained in Market Towns, and those Places where the Manufacture has been formerly carried on,' said one Wiltshire clothier;[2] and a Gloucestershire clothier stated categorically, ' since the Introduction of Machinery there is much more work for the Women and Children in the Villages than formerly,'[3] a statement which is hard to reconcile with the loss of hand-spinning, until we realise that village differed from village in its fate.[4] The migration of the weavers to the villages we have mentioned elsewhere. Owing to the competition of the spinning factories it was complained that the services of children as ' Quillers ' to help the weavers were difficult to obtain. ' A Child then, through the Introduction of Machinery, can be useful from five or six Years old ? Yes.'[5]

It must not, however, be supposed that in consequence of the migration from towns to the villages, the towns languished. The cloth trade itself was increasing and with it the population of the manufacturing towns as well. A Frome

[1] At Pewsey in Wiltshire, where the women and children were suddenly deprived of their work by the competition of spinning mills and the poor rates rose to 15s. in the pound, ' the Rector applied to the manufacturer for a continuance of employment, offering to do it at the same rate as the wool was spun at the mills, or even at less, he was answered that the work was supplied with more ease and certainty from the mills, and therefore they could not employ the poor on any terms ' (Reports of Society for Bettering the Condition of the Poor, vol. iv. p. 82).

[2] Minutes of Evidence on Woollen Trade Bill, 1802-3, p. 335.

[3] Report of Committee on South-West Clothiers' Petition, 1802-3 (Henry Dyer).

[4] Compare also another witness : ' Women who used to go out to Leasing and Harvest are now employed about Spinning ' (Evidence on Woollen Trade Bill, 1802-3, p. 303).   [5] Ibid., p. 300.

manufacturer declared in 1803 [1] 'That he is so necessitated, from the Want of Workwomen, as to have applied to the Overseers of his Parish, for some Months past, to send him such as apply for Relief to be employed in the Woollen Manufacture; and that he also sends Wool into different Parishes to be picked, from the want of Hands.'

The change from hand work to machine work did not take place without some disturbances. A scribbling mill at Bradford, Wilts, was burnt down about 1790, whereupon the owner moved his works to Malmesbury,[2] and threats of attacks on other establishments where machinery is used are reported from time to time. Thus a magistrate in Somersetshire describes in 1790 [3] how he was called in by two of the principal manufacturers of Keynsham to protect their property ' from the Depredations of a lawless Banditti of Colliers and their Wives.' The wives had no doubt lost their work by the erection of 'spinning engines.' ' They advanced at first with much Insolence, avowing their Intention of cutting to Pieces the Machines lately introduced in the Woollen Manufacture; which they suppose, if generally adopted, will lessen the Demand for manual Labour. The Women became clamorous. The Men were more open to conviction and after some Expostulations were induced to desist from their Purpose and return peaceably home.'

A later change in spinning in the South-West clothing trade was made about 1828 by the introduction of the mule; this time there was no increase in general employment to compensate for the decrease of work in a particular process; by two mules worked by one man and a child the whole spinning of warp and weft for a piece of cloth could be done in twelve hours. With the spinning-jenny a woman could spin the warp in thirty-eight hours, a man with two children could spin the weft in thirty-four hours. Six hundred and twelve hours was the time originally required for a woman with one or two children's help to do the same amount.[4]

Introduction of Machinery into Yorkshire.—(1) *Wool*

The introduction of spinning-jennies into Yorkshire for wool seems to have taken place about 1780, and though for

[1] Committee on South-West Clothiers' Petition, 1802-3 (William Sheppard).
[2] Evidence on Woollen Trade Bill, 1802-3, p. 84.   [3] H.O., 42. 16, March 17.
[4] Report from Assistant Hand-loom Weavers' Commissioners, 1840, part ii. pp. 439 f.

various reasons it caused less suffering than in the south, it was not entirely free from disturbance. At Hunslet, for example, there are said to have been riots when spinning-jennies were introduced.[1] But the increase in the trade soon dispelled the prejudices against their introduction. ' At the first and for some time after the introduction of spinning-jennies, pulling out and twisting from forty to sixty threads at once in the place of one, and of carding, slubbing and scribbling billies, performing with one man the work of twenty, etc., all seemed in the woollen trade to go on well ; and instead of men being thrown idle as they apprehended, webs were prepared so much more quickly than before, that they all found themselves called upon to the looms, and the women and children only were left without work in their own houses.' So wrote the author of *Observations on Woollen Machinery*[2] in 1803.

One feature of this development of the industry that throws an ominous shadow over the new prosperity is mentioned by a correspondent from Gloucester to the *Annals of Agriculture* in 1791 :[3]

' A Gentleman from York passed through this city a few days ago, who gave us a new confirmation of the flourishing state of the woollen trade in that county. He says, that although so many machines have been erected, yet the trade has thereby been encreased to that degree, that at this time no less than seventy additional machines are now setting up in the neighbourhood of Leeds, Bradford, and Huddersfield. One manufacturer assured this gentleman, that he was in such want of hands as to be driven to the expedient of procuring from the workhouses in London, 500 poor children to be employed in his workshops.'

This introduction of machinery into the clothing trade for spinning and the preliminary processes seemed, to many observers, to involve as a necessary consequence the extinction of the small manufacturers. Men put capital into the industry on a large scale, and steam was applied as early as 1793. ' The application of steam engines,' wrote Arthur Young in that year,[4] ' to move the machinery of manufactures, is nowhere carried further than at Leeds ; there are six or

[1] Report of Committee on Woollen Manufacture, 1806, p. 81.
[2] Page 12.
[3] *Annals of Agriculture*, vol. xvi. p. 422.
[4] *Ibid.*, vol. xxvii. p. 310.

seven for mills, etc., and a dying house has also one. . . .
Viewed with great pleasure the machines for unclothing and
puffing out wool, if I may use the expression, also for spinning,
and various other operations. The inventions that have done
so much in cotton, are here fast introducing for wool.' The
change that seemed imminent is clearly described by the
writer of the *Observations on Woollen Machinery* in 1803 : [1]
' Formerly the mode of making cloth in this large cloathing
district was as follows : A class of men with tolerable capitals
called woolstaplers, rode over the country about cliptime, to
buy up the wool from the growers. They then have the
fleece carefully broke into its various qualities, and afterwards sell it out in small quantities thus assorted, to innumerable master manufacturers of little or no capitals, spread
around in the adjacent villages. These master-makers super-
intend all the remaining operations ; have many performed
in their own houses and hire out the rest to their neighbouring families : the whole of which husbands, wives, and children,
were employed together in their own dwellings, some in weaving, others scribbling, carding, or spinning.

' Since the introduction of machinery a new class of men, as
machinery, or mill-owners, are concerned ; and many of the
master-makers have their own mills. The effect of which is,
that wool is very much faster made into cloth, considerably
more weavers are employed, and no home work left for women
and children. Now after the wool is dyed by the master, it is
sent to a mill, where, with the help of a man or two and a few
children, it is most expeditiously scribbled, milled, slubbed,
spun and made ready for the loom.'

The writer underestimated the powers and tenacity of the
' innumerable master manufacturers of little or no capitals,'
for, as we have said elsewhere, they adapted themselves to
the new circumstances, and set up their own mills where the
preliminary processes could be carried out. The women and
children either followed the work into the mills or were employed in weaving or in helping to weave.

Mules for spinning wool seem to have been introduced into
Yorkshire about the same time that they were introduced
into the South-West, in 1826.[2]

[1] Page 14.
[2] Baines, *Yorkshire Past and Present*, p. 650.

(2) *Worsted*

The story of the introduction of machinery for spinning
worsted in Yorkshire differs in some respects from the story
of its introduction for wool. ' Spinning engines ' were introduced earlier for wool than for worsted, and it is clear that
any women and children displaced by the use of the jenny for
wool could find employment at the wheel for worsted. The
jenny indeed seems to have been used very little for worsted,[1]
and the one-thread wheel remained the common implement
till the end of the eighteenth century and indeed later.[2]

The real competitor with the one-thread wheel was the
worsted mill or factory, where Arkwright's water frame or
developments of it were used,[3] worked by either water power
or steam.

The first worsted mill with water frames was built in 1784
in Lancashire, at Dolphin Holme on the river Wyre, but for
some time it was not a success.[4] Others followed towards
the end of the century. By 1800 there were about ten, including one worked by steam built that year in Bradford.[5] An
attempt to build one in Bradford in 1793 had been stopped
by the remonstrances of a number of ' respectable residents,'
who, fearing ' such a smoky nuisance as a steam engine,' had
threatened the proprietor with legal proceedings for nuisance.[6]

The building of worsted mills was hastened by the shortage
of yarn, for owing no doubt partly to the growing competition
of the cotton industry,[7] and partly to the great growth of
trade, Yorkshire towards the end of the century could not
even supply enough yarn for its own worsted trade, and
Norwich and the surrounding districts were now spinning
yarn for use in the north.[8] Early next century, with the
coming of the mill-spun yarn, the tables were reversed, and
the north supplied the south, for after 1807 fine yarn spun

[1] Arthur Young, however, notes its use for worsted at Leeds in 1793 (*Annals
of Agriculture*, xxvii. p. 312).

[2] James, *op. cit.*, pp. 335, 355, 358.

[3] There were also a few mules worked by hand or a gin horse introduced
into Bradford about 1794 (see James, *op. cit.*, pp. 328-9).

[4] James, *op. cit.*, p. 327.   [5] James, *op. cit.*, pp. 355 and 592.

[6] James, *op. cit.*, p. 592.

[7] Cf. *Annals of Agriculture*, vol. xvi. p. 423: Halifax manufacturers
complain of scarcity of hands owing to rapid progress of the cotton trade.

[8] James, *op. cit.*, p. 306. In earlier days wool had been sent from Norwich
to be spun in Yorkshire.

by water frames in Yorkshire was despatched south to Norwich with its decaying trade, and by 1818 most of the Norwich yarn was coming from the northern mills. [1]

It must not be supposed that the worsted mills killed hand spinning at once ; long after 1800 the two methods of production went on side by side. Mill-spun yarn was rougher than that spun by hand, but the invention of the false reed or slay about 1800, a device which helped to guide the shuttle and made the use of rougher yarn less troublesome, together with improvements in the mill-spun yarn itself, made the extinction of hand spinning a question of time. [2]

Machinery and the South-East

Whilst in the north worsted mills were being built and machines worked by steam were taking the place of human hands, in the south-east districts the processes remained unchanged though the work constantly diminished in volume. [3] As the cheap mill-spun yarn from the north flooded the markets, the demand for the hand-spun yarn of the south decreased, the rates of payment fell, and the southern yarn was only used for particular sorts of stuffs, such as the finer kinds of poplins. Not only was the spinning done by machinery instead of by hand, but it was done elsewhere. Some attempts to introduce the spinning-jenny must have been made, for in 1816 its introduction was assigned as one of the causes of the misery that brought about the rising of the labourers in the eastern counties. [4] No serious attempt was made to compete with the worsted mills of the north, though after 1832 one or two mills were started in Norwich. [5]

It was the south-eastern counties of Norfolk, Suffolk, and Essex that suffered most severely from the loss of domestic spinning, and employment was further decreased by the scarcity and dearness of wool from 1785 to 1795, and again from 1798 to 1809, which pressed hardest on the districts where trade was failing. [6] There was no temporary increase in other branches of the trade to help the workers in these counties

[1] James, op. cit., pp. 366 and 386.   [2] James, op. cit., pp. 355 f.
[3] The primitive distaff and spindle was still used in Norfolk for the finest yarn (James, op. cit., p. 334).   [4] H.O., 42. 151, June 7.
[5] Report from Assistant Hand-loom Weavers' Commissioners, 1840, part ii. p. 335.
[6] Cunningham, Growth of English Industry and Commerce, ii. p. 452.

to tide over the evil time, and no other trades came at once to those districts to sweep in the hands left idle by the decay of the worsted industry.[1] The overseers sometimes adopted the disastrous practice of giving bounties to spinners, in other words making the manufacturer's wage up to a living wage. ' In some parishes a happy practice has obtained, of stepping in to the aid of the industrious spinner, by supplying the deficiency of the manufacturers' prices of labour, and paying her earnings at a stated price ; thus, by a small addition in money, preventing the vicissitudes ever attendant on commercial concerns.—Admirable device ! at once leading to the employment of the poor, and to the incitement of their industry.' [2]

By 1830 the spinning of wool or worsted as a domestic industry for commercial purposes was obsolete.

After spinning had passed into the factories the spinners in the woollen factories seem to have been in much the same position as the spinners in the cotton factories : they were a small class of skilled men superintending the work of women and children. They do not figure so prominently as the cotton spinners in the records from which the material for this history has been drawn : they were of course fewer in number and their organisation was weaker. We have some account of their conditions from a witness before the Committee on Artisans and Machinery in 1824.[3] The witness was himself a woollen cloth maker, by name Joseph Oates, of Leeds, representing ' the body of labouring manufacturers in Leeds, Holbeck, Armley, and Wortley.' Oates described the establishment of a Union in Dewsbury in 1822 which embraced both spinners and weavers, with the object of ' equalising wages,' *i.e.* of bringing the bad employers to the standard of the good. From Oates' answers it is possible to piece together some information about the spinners in the heavy woollen district. The wages of spinners and weavers seem to have been much the same in Leeds, they were higher in Leeds than in Stanningley and the surrounding villages, higher also than in Dewsbury. The hours were fourteen to fifteen

---

[1] For the use made by other trades of the ' large fund of cheap technical skill seeking occupation' in Suffolk, see *Victoria County History of Suffolk*, vol. ii. p. 253..

[2] *Annals of Agriculture*, vol. xxvi. p. 253 (of Essex), 1796.

[3] Report of Select Committee on Artisans and Machinery, 1824, p. 533.

including two hours for meals. Spinners were making about twenty to twenty-five shillings a week in Leeds in 1819,[1] but that year the larger employers forced a reduction of five shillings in the pound : the workers, spinners and weavers, struck, and they received considerable support from the general public, but after holding out for six months they were compelled to submit. The Dewsbury workers struck at the same time with rather better result : it is interesting to note that they had the support of a large number of employers. The General Union of Weavers and Spinners there had five thousand members.

In the worsted mills, on the other hand, the spinners were chiefly 'children or young persons,'[2] for there Arkwright's water frame was in use. The conditions were very bad and cripples were very common.[3] We have an account of her life in one of these mills from a girl of eighteen who started work when about nine years old :[4] 'I was put to learn to spin. . . . I was put to the one spindle frame. I was put at first with another to learn me, and in two or three weeks I was able to mind it myself. My next sister went with me ; she was put to spin too, at the one spindle frame. . . . I got 3s. at first and then 3s. 6d. When I first went, we worked from six to seven . . . we had three-quarters of an hour for dinner and afterwards only half an hour and no time for breakfast or drinking.' When she was 'turned ten' and her sister was nine the mill changed hands, and the new master picked out these two girls and one or two others to work long hours. 'We went from five to nine. We had over-money for that : it made a week of seven days. My standing wage then was 5s. 6d., we reckoned that from six to seven. We gave over at five on Saturdays. I had 6s. odd when we worked this time. I forget the coppers. . . . I had my health very well till I worked from five to nine . . . I worked on till better than a year ago. I worked those hours all the time. We sometimes worked from six to seven but it was mostly from five to nine. . . . I went from there to the Infirmary. My lameness has been coming on nearly six years. . . . It

[1] Baines gives the following figures taken from 'an old and eminent firm' in the Leeds district : 1795, 16s. 9d. ; 1805, 24s. 8d. ; 1815, 31s. 8d. ; 1825, 20s. 4d. After introduction of mule spinning in 1826 workmen earned 40s. less 12s. paid to two piecers : in 1835 this figure was 37s. 1d. (Baines, *Yorkshire Past and Present*, p. 650).

[2] James, *op. cit.*, p. 549.   [3] *Ibid.*, p. 550.
[4] 1833 Factory Commission First Report, p. 72, c. 1.

was having to crook my knee to stop the spindle that lamed me as much as anything else.'

It will be remembered that the earlier Factory Acts,[1] such as they were, applied only to cotton factories, and that there was no protection at all for the children in the woollen and worsted mills at this time.   It was stated in the *Leeds Mercury* in 1830 [2] that the children were employed in the worsted mills thirteen hours with an interval of half an hour, and in the woollen mills fifteen hours with an interval of two hours. John Wood, the famous worsted spinner of Bradford, who was one of the earliest champions of the children, declared to Oastler, when urging him to embark on the crusade with which his name is so gloriously associated, that the factory children were worse off than the slaves in the West Indies.   Sadler made great play with this comparison when moving the second reading of the Factories Regulation Bill in March 1832. He showed that the Orders in Council of November 1831 had limited the work of adult slaves to nine hours a day and that of children under the age of fourteen to six hours a day.   ' You have limited the labour of the robust negro to nine hours : but when I propose that the labour of the young white slave shall not exceed ten, the proposition is deemed extravagant.'

Thus the decay of the old system of domestic spinning did not bring more misery on the villages that suffered from its loss than the birth of the new system brought to the towns for which it found employment.

III.—THE WOOLLEN WEAVERS

The woollen weavers of the south-west, like the worsted weavers of the Norwich district, were early an organised body of men, whose interests were often in sharp opposition to those of their masters. ' Discontent,' it has been said, ' was the prevalent attitude of the operatives engaged in the wool in- dustries for centuries,' [3] a discontent expressed in the old ballad of the *Clothier's Delight*, written in the seventeenth century, which describes the methods by which the clothiers oppressed their various classes of workers.   One verse runs :

[1] Except the 1802 Act which applied to cotton and woollen mills but dealt with apprentices only.

[2] October 30, 1830.

[3] Burnley, *History of Wool and Woolcombing*, 1889, p. 160.

' We'll make the poor Weavers work at a low rate;
We'll find fault where there's no fault, and so we will bate;
If trading grows dead, we will presently show it:
But if it grows good, they shall never know it:
We'll tell them that cloth beyond sea will not go,
We care not whether we keep clothing or no.
    Chorus.—And this is the way for to fill up our purse,
            Although we do get it with many a curse.'[1]

The woollen weavers had been the objects of Parliamentary
attention long before the time with which we deal. Their
combinations had been forbidden, their masters had been
ordered to pay them in money and not in goods, and the
magistrates had been instructed to fix their rates of wages.
But men, masters, and magistrates paid very little regard to
the directions of the legislature. In the middle of the
eighteenth century, we find the men trying to obtain the
enforcement of the regulation of wages. It is worth while to
give a brief account of this attempt.

In 1756 the workers employed in the woollen weaving trade
in Gloucestershire petitioned Parliament, asking that the
Parliamentary regulations for paying their wages should be
better observed.[2] In 1726 and 1727 two Acts had been passed
to regulate the woollen trade, which forbade combinations
of workmen, prohibited truck, and also arranged for the fixing
of wages by the magistrates. In 1728 at the Michaelmas
Quarter Sessions an order for a rate of wages was made, but
this order was never complied with. The petition stated that
the men had no redress, for there was no summary way of
dealing with offenders. The evidence before the committee
to whom the petition was referred showed that the ' Clothiers
entered into an Association not to pay by that Order,' and that
when complaint was made to Quarter Sessions ' the Clothiers
have removed the Tryals into Westminster Hall and the
Expence of carrying on such Prosecutions have been too heavy
for the Workmen to carry on.'[3]

Parliament granted the men's request, and a fresh Act was
passed in 1756,[4] empowering the justices to fix wages. The
men, accordingly, petitioned the justices at the October Quarter
Sessions at Gloucester to use their powers; the masters sent

[1] Burnley, *History of Wool and Woolcombing*, 1889, p. 162.
[2] *House of Commons Journal*, February 24, 1756.
[3] *Ibid.*, March 9, 1756 (Report of Committee).
[4] 29 George II. c. 33.

a contrary petition ; the justices decided against action.[1]
Then the men resorted to another kind of pressure, they
' appeared in a very tumultuous manner . . . committed great
Outrages,' and kept the countryside in disorder for six or
seven weeks. At last for the sake of the peace of the county
the justices held an adjourned Quarter Sessions, at which
some of the masters who were favourable to the men, or
else wished for quiet, drew up a scale which the justices
fixed as the rate.[2] In Somerset the men were not successful
in obtaining a rate. They petitioned the Quarter Sessions,
but the justices ' upon a full hearing of the matter did
openly declare that they could not adjust and settle the
said Wages.' [3]

The men's triumph in Gloucestershire was short-lived, for
many of the masters refused obedience to the rate, and, to
prevent disturbances, soldiers were quartered in the district.[4]
On February 7, 1757, petitions from the masters in Gloucestershire and Somerset were read in Parliament, asking that the
sections in various Acts, beginning with the 5th Elizabeth,
which empowered justices to rate wages, should be repealed.
A few days later some Wiltshire masters also petitioned in
the same sense.[5] The matter was referred to a committee
which heard the evidence of a master clothier from Stroud
and four workmen, two of them master weavers with looms
of their own, and two journeymen weavers, who had clearly
been selected with great care. One of the master weavers
declared his opinion ' that if a Rate should be made agreeable
to the Weavers it would certainly transfer the Work to other
Counties ' ; the other stated that the journeymen weavers,
if in work, could earn 1s. in a day of fourteen hours including
meals, ' which he thinks Money enough,' and ' that the Master
Weavers allow them Privilege, which is Small Beer, Lodging
and Firing, which is reckoned at 1s. a week more,' and the
two journeymen weavers were living examples of this scale of
pay, one remarking that if he worked close he could make 1d.
an hour, the other stating that for thirty years he had
earned 6s. a week with an extra shilling for ' privilege.' His
hours were fourteen a day. The committee reported that

[1] For an account of the petitions to the justices, see Hewins, *English Trade
and Finance*, pp. 118 ff.
[2] *House of Commons Journal*, February 24, 1757.
[3] *Ibid.*, February 7, 1757.   [4] *Ibid.*, February 22, 1757.
[5] *Ibid.*, February 12, 1757.

the masters had made out their case, and recommended that the Acts in question should be amended.[1]

A new Act was, accordingly, passed (30 George II. c. 12) which repealed the wage-rating clause in the Act of the previous year, declaring it to have proved mischievous and inconvenient. No attention was paid to the petition of ' several poor and distressed Broad Cloth Weavers of Stroud, Minchin Hampton, Bisley, and thereabouts,' who urged that whatever the House thought fit to do, there might be ' some Power lodged in the said Justices of the Peace, or elsewhere . . . to ascertain and settle the said Wages, that the Petitioners may not be subject to the arbitrary Will and Power of the said Clothiers,' [2] nor to the further petition from the Gentlemen and Landholders of the same district who asked that the powers of the justices might not be taken away.[3]

The history of the persistent efforts of the South-West weavers to bring about the enforcement of semi-obsolete laws in the early years of the nineteenth century shows that they were effectively organised at this time. Of these efforts we give an account elsewhere.[4] The Gloucestershire weavers seem to have had a closer and more efficient organisation than the weavers of the other South-Western counties.

A measure of some importance in the history of the weavers was the adoption of Kay's flying shuttle, invented in 1733. The introduction of this flying shuttle, or ' spring loom ' as it was frequently called, into the South-West clothing district is one of the few instances where mechanical improvements benefited the workers immediately and directly. The story illustrates the difficulty of making any generalisations covering whole districts, for though the flying shuttle was used at some places in Gloucestershire by 1757,[5] and was in common use in Gloucestershire and parts of Wiltshire [6] by 1803, yet in Somerset its introduction caused disturbances as late as 1822. An attempt had indeed been made to introduce it in 1801, but a riotous mob had intervened.[7] In Yorkshire the spring

---

[1] *House of Commons Journal*, February 24, 1757.   [2] *Ibid.*, March 1, 1757.
[3] *Ibid.*, March 7, 1757.   [4] See p. 168.
[5] Hewins, *English Trade and Finance*, p. 122.

[6] In the parts round Bradford it was not yet used. See Report of Committee on South-West Woollen Clothiers' Petition, 1802-3 (John Jones); and Minutes of Evidence on Woollen Trade Bill, 1802-3, p. 81.

[7] Report of Committee on South-West Clothiers' Petition, 1802-3 (Thomas Joyce).

shuttle was used for woollens after about 1782.[1] The story
of its introduction at Stroud in Gloucestershire as told by a
weaver, John Clayfield, in 1803,[2] shows the master clothiers
in a sympathetic temper. A certain Mr. Nathaniel Watts
introduced the new invention about 1793 or 1795 : ' it caused
Uneasiness in the Minds of the Weavers, and they went to
Mr. Nathaniel Watts ; there was a public Meeting at which I
have heard People say Twenty Thousand People met ; and
the Gentlemen Clothiers met and formed a Committee, and
sent to the Weavers to know their Grievance ; and they formed
a Committee of Seven, who met them at the Fleece at Rodbury.
They asked what was their Grievance ; they replied, they
were afraid themselves and their Families should be ruined by
Spring Looms. The Committee said, if that is your Grievance,
they shall be given up. They said, we are afraid the Introduction of them will reduce our Wages. To which the Committee replied, that they would not reduce their Wages.' The
upshot of the conference was that Mr. Watts gave up the use
of the spring looms himself, but sold them to the weavers
who adopted them on their own account. Another witness
from Gloucestershire in 1803 described it as ' a Measure of
the Weavers own Adoption : they are paid the same per Piece
as before the Introduction of Spring Shuttles.' [3]

The writer of the Report on the South-West clothing district
in 1840 estimated that before the introduction of the spring
shuttle the persons engaged in weaving a piece of cloth were a
master weaver who received about 12s. 3d. a week, out of
which he had to pay house rent and wear and tear of loom
and tackle, a journeyman weaver making 3s. 6d. a week, and
a child receiving 2s. ; after the spring shuttle came in (he gives
1796 as the date) the workers were a child receiving 2s. and
one man receiving £1, 2s. 6d., out of which, of course, deductions had to be made.[4] A weaver witness in 1803 put the
clear earnings before and after the spring shuttle came in as
6s. to 7s. and 9s. to 11s. respectively. A master clothier in
the same year estimated them as 10s. to 12s. and 18s. to 21s.
respectively.[5]

---

[1] Evidence on Woollen Trade Bill, 1802-3, p. 232.   [2] *Ibid.*, pp. 15 f.
[3] Committee on South-West Clothiers' Petition (Edward Sheppard).
[4] Report from Assistant Hand-loom Weavers' Commissioners, 1840, part ii.
pp. 439 f.
[5] Evidence on Woollen Trade Bill, 1802-3, p. 10 ; and Committee on South-
West Clothiers' Petition, 1802-3 (Daniel Lloyd).

In Gloucestershire and Wiltshire increased trade absorbed the weavers whom the use of the spring shuttle would have thrown out of work had trade remained stationary. In Somerset, as we have mentioned, the flying shuttle was not introduced till many years later. It is curious to read in 1822 a request that cavalry should be stationed at Frome ' in order to prevent any disturbances during the introduction of spring Looms, which will now be generally used here, as they have long been in Yorkshire, Gloucestershire and Wiltshire.' [1] This introduction of the spring shuttle at Frome meant, not that the masters had looms of their own, but that they refused to give out work to the old double looms and paid 1s. a yard instead of the previous 1s. 3d. a yard. However mistaken their policy, it is a remarkable instance of the solidarity of the Frome weavers that they had resisted so long the introduction of an invention which would fill the pockets of those who adopted it even though it might be at the expense of loss of work to their fellows. Its tardy introduction into Frome fulfilled their worst anticipations ; it came when trade was decaying and caused much suffering. Eighteen months later, in 1823, the Frome weavers struck, demanding the old wages paid before the introduction of the spring shuttle and the abolition of truck. They were unsuccessful in their objects, and after eighteen had been sent to gaol with hard labour, the rest were starved into submission. The magistrates, it must be noticed, did their best for the weavers on the question of truck, by convicting one employer in £20 and announcing that they were ready to convict in other cases where it was proved. [2]

The stability of the prices paid for weaving in the clothing trade of the south-west is in remarkable contrast to the feverish oscillations in the cotton trade during the same period. The spring shuttle doubled earnings, women entered the trade, and still the price paid remained unaltered. In 1825 the weavers in a petition to their masters could claim that ' for ninety-six years their wages had remained unaltered,' [3] a statement referring of course not to their earnings but to their piece rate. If we may believe the writer of the Report on Gloucestershire in 1840, it was a settled policy of the large clothiers to help the men in their struggles with masters who paid lower rates. [4]

[1] H.O., 40. 17, January 27.   [2] For above see H.O., 40. 18.
[3] Report from Assistant Hand-loom Weavers' Commissioners, 1840, part ii. p. 441.   [4] Ibid., part v. p. 448.

Women had become weavers in considerable numbers before 1802, as we learn from the various committees on the woollen trade in 1802-3. During the French war in the years 1797-9 there was a great scarcity of Spanish wool, employment was consequently bad and many men enlisted. Probably it was to take their places, when large supplies of Spanish wool arrived afterwards, that women went to the looms. One employer from Freshford in Somerset had as many women working for him as men, and at Bradford, Wilts, there were said to be ' Two parts female weavers out of five.' Little is heard of them later, and there is nothing to show that they were paid at a different rate from men. Perhaps the weaving of the cloth proved too hard for them, for by 1840 women seem to have been working mostly in the lighter branches, for low rates of pay, such as the Exeter serges, which still employed over 3000 looms scattered about in Devonshire, and nearly 600 at Wellington, in Somerset. This work was done almost entirely by women, ' those who do the work being the wives or daughters of agricultural labourers, of mechanics or others.' There was one curious exception in the case of this trade, at Cullompton, where the men had bound themselves not to allow any woman to learn the trade. This prohibition lasted for nearly a century, till 1825, when the advantages of obtaining help from their own wives and daughters broke down resistance. Nearly fifteen years later there were still 250 men to 62 women, and the prices paid were higher than in other parts of the district.[1]

In 1825, among the outburst of strikes after the repeal of the Combination Act, the Gloucestershire weavers struck for an advance of rates, claiming that more work was now required owing to a change in the makes of the fabrics. In this strike they were successful. The manufacturers in the Uley district, headed by Mr. Sheppard, agreed to the advance at once, and ' after agreeing to the price were as strenuous as the weavers themselves that the other manufacturers should be brought up to the same mark,' but the Stroud clothiers held out some five weeks. There were considerable riots, and the masons, carpenters, and millwrights struck in sympathy.[2]

A private letter from a Gloucestershire magistrate in

[1] See Report from Assistant Hand-loom Weavers' Commissioners, 1840, part ii. pp. 410 and 442.

[2] Report from Assistant Hand-loom Weavers' Commissioners, 1840, part v. pp. 451 f.

1826 [1] shows that the close combination among the weavers caused some alarm to the authorities. The Union, he writes, embraces all parishes in Stroud, Dursley, Wotton, and Kingswood, and its delegates correspond with Wiltshire and Yorkshire. They declare, too, that they can communicate with every combination of every trade in Great Britain. The writer makes various suggestions for meeting the evil, amongst them the payment from public funds of the expenses of the apprehension and prosecution of offenders. He has sometimes had to defray them himself, and he considers it undesirable that he should act both as judge and prosecutor.

A strike in 1828-9, although unsuccessful, showed that the weavers and other woollen workers were very highly organised. ' Nine out of ten,' wrote Mr. Sheppard of Uley,[2] ' of the whole body of operatives in every department of the woollen trade are sworn and entered, and a very considerable number of shopkeepers, tradesmen, artificers, etc.—in all full 20,000 persons in this country.' The strikers chose their first ground of conflict well, refusing to work for two masters notorious for their payments in truck. The gentlemen clothiers on January 20, 1829, held a meeting at Stroud at which, whilst deprecating the formation of secret societies and clubs, they passed a strong resolution against payment in truck ' as oppressive to the workmen and injurious to the respectable manufacturer.' [3] But the workmen combined other demands with those for the abolition of truck, notably the abolition of ' shop,' or home looms as they were called, *i.e.* looms belonging to the master clothiers and worked on premises owned by them. Mr. Sheppard calculated that by this time about half the weaving in Gloucestershire was done on these shop looms,[4] and the men failed to carry their point.

The Government early in 1829 sent down a certain Francis Fagan from Bow Street to conduct an inquiry into the workmen's clubs, and to obtain evidence of their illegality. He described their ceremonies with all the paraphernalia of swords, masks, scarves, and turbans.

' The original object of these Union Lodges,' he wrote,[5] ' was professedly to suppress the practice of paying wages in what is termed truck, which had become prevalent with the manufacturers in this neighbourhood, but at length from the great

[1] H.O., 40. 19.
[3] H.O., 44. 19, January 30.
[5] H.O., 40. 23, February 24.
[2] H.O., 44. 19.
[4] H.O., 44. 19, January 24.

increase in the funds and numbers of members, lodges began to assume greater powers and importance, and endeavour to contest and regulate the price of wages and to prevent the adoption and use of Power looms in the Clothing manufacturies, and the practice of Clothiers having their weaving performed in their own manufacturies.   The members of the Lodges,' he says later, ' consist of all sorts of people, tradesmen, pensioners, and even attornies and surgeons, so that it is almost impossible to conjecture how far or to what extent the object of these regulations may be carried.'

Organisation among the weavers in Yorkshire begins much later than among the weavers in the south-west, a difference due to the difference in the two types of industry.   There was indeed a striking contrast between the two sets of workers, for whereas the normal Yorkshire weaver was a smallholder, it was said of the Gloucestershire weavers in 1806, ' There is not one family in twenty who have as much land as this room.' [1] In the south-west the weavers were organised bodies of workmen weaving in their homes or shops for capitalist employers who were chiefly concerned how to retain their markets by the excellence of their products, and were not unwilling to keep up the level of wages in order to prevent the competition of men with smaller capital.[2]   In Yorkshire we find, side by side, the small men who sold their pieces in Leeds or Halifax, and capitalists who carried on different processes in the manufacture of shawls or carpets or one or other form of woollen goods in factories, but gave out the weaving to bodies of workmen.   In this way a manufacturer might employ as many as three or four hundred men.

There were successful examples of organisation among these weavers in Yorkshire and Lancashire, as we know from the evidence of witnesses before the Committee on Artisans and Machinery (1824) and the Committee on the Combination Laws (1825).   There was a general Union in Dewsbury, embracing both weavers and spinners, established in 1822, reported two years later to be five thousand strong.   This Union arose out of a long struggle beginning in 1819, in the course of which the larger Leeds employers succeeded in reducing wages (at that time twenty to twenty-five shillings a week) by five shil-

[1] Report from Committee on State of Woollen Manufacture, 1806, p. 340.
[2] Report from Assistant Hand-loom Weavers' Commissioners, 1840, part ii, p. 450.

lings in the pound.[1]   In Rochdale there was an Association of
Journeymen Weavers, Men Spinners, and others in the Woollen
Trade reported to have from two to three thousand members
in 1825 with a curious and interesting history.[2]

The principal flannel manufacturers had been alarmed by
the growing poverty of the weavers and the burden of the
poor rates, and they decided in 1819 to try to arrest this
ominous tendency.   They consequently agreed on a table of
wages and induced all the chief employers to undertake not
to pay less.   Their declaration on the subject is worth notice,
as it is in striking contrast to most of the utterances of the
time :

'The present low price of labour in the manufacture of
flannels in this district, is become a subject of vital importance
to the property of this parish, as well as to the character and
morals of the community.   An effort to check the evils arising
from this source, is surely worth the assistance and support
of every well-wisher to his country.

'The first necessary step to the attainment of this desirable
end, is to endeavour to equalise the present price of work, by
bringing up those who, from ignorance or any other motive,
have been giving less than the long standing prices of others.
We, the undersigned manufacturers, are of opinion, that the
annexed list of wages, if generally adopted, could be no way
prejudicial to trade, but would greatly ameliorate the condition of the working classes, and we have therefore agreed not
to give less.'

The men's Union worked in co-operation with the best
employers to force this scale on the small minority that either
did not consent to it or broke away from it.   No less than
twelve employers subscribed to the support of workmen on
strike until the refractory employers yielded.   The Committee
on the Combination Laws were scandalised by this conduct.
'Of a course, so reprehensible and inconsistent with every
principle of fair dealing and justice, either towards the individual or the public, Your Committee cannot too strongly
express their reprobation.'[3]

The men's witness before the committee said that the

---

[1] Evidence of Joseph Oates, Report of Select Committee on Artisans and
Machinery, 1824, p. 535.

[2] Evidence of J. F. Taylor before Committee on Combination Laws, 1825,
p. 154.

[3] Report of Committee on Combination Laws, 1825, p. 6.

average wage of the journeyman weaver was 11s. to 12s. a
week. It is interesting to remark the note struck by the
committee when appealing to weavers to join the Union :
' In order that you may become men and consider your own
importance in the trade, the government in its wisdom has
repealed the combination and conspiracy laws : you cannot
be prosecuted by statute or common law for combining to
support or even to raise your wages.' [1] These workmen unfortunately did more than justice to the spirit in which their
rulers had consented to repeal the Combination Laws, as they
discovered next year. but that expression ' in order that you
may become men ' was the best and simplest statement of
the aims of the workers that the age produced.

The state of goodwill between employers and workmen in
Rochdale which had been carried to lengths that shocked the
committee does not seem to have lasted very long, for a
magistrate wrote to the Home Office in 1827 to say that the
manufacturers were reducing wages though they could well
afford to advance them : ' they scruple not to tell the weavers
that if their wages are insufficient for their support, they must
make application to the overseers of the poor of their respective Townships to obtain relief to supply deficiencies.' A few
days later he writes : ' The weavers are perfectly peaceable
at present but not a loom in motion.' Some of the manufacturers asked the magistrates for special protection but
without giving any sufficient reason, and the officer commanding in the district had a troop of carabiniers in readiness if
required, though he evidently agreed with the view of the
magistrate about the conduct of the manufacturers. Ultimately the dispute was settled by the mediation of a local
parson, Mr. Dodds, whose help was requested by the Weavers'
Committee, but the terms are not given. [2]

There was at the same time a flourishing Union at Huddersfield covering a district about thirty miles in circumference
with five thousand members. A member paid 3d. a week
until he had paid a pound in all and then he was a life member,
paying no further subscriptions except in case of a strike.
This Union appears for a time to have been tolerably powerful,
for it was able to compel one employer to pay a fine of £100 in
compensation for the wages the men had lost while on strike.
One of the employers, a manufacturer of waistcoat pieces and

[1] Report of Committee on Combination Laws, 1825, p. 37.
[2] For above see H.O., 40. 22.

other fancy goods near Huddersfield, invited his men to dinner, and told them that they must choose between the Union and himself. According to his account twenty-four stood by the Union and forty stayed with him : a workman witness said that the forty-five men out of seventy who belonged to the Union were all discharged. The most significant fact in the story is that the employer found himself obliged to swallow his scruples and to ask his men to come back.[1]

It is difficult to get any exact idea of the wages the woollen weavers were receiving in 1830. It is clear from the evidence given before the committees already quoted that wages were higher in Leeds than in Dewsbury. Employers and work-men often differed in their estimates. One employer from Huddersfield told the committee in 1825 that his weavers were making thirty shillings a week : a workman witness said that these same weavers were making seventeen. But it is clear that the woollen weavers had not sunk into anything like the pitiable poverty of the cotton or worsted weavers.[2] A happy accident had saved them for the present from their common enemy, the power-loom. The thread used for woollen fabrics was feebler, looser, less twisted than the thread for other stuffs, and for this reason it was more liable to break and less suited to the swift motions of the power-loom.[3] Woollen weaving thus remained a domestic industry for many years after the disappearance of the hand-loom weaver in cotton or worsted.[4]

IV.—THE SHEARMEN OR CROPPERS

The weavers and the shearmen were quite separate classes, for both weaving and shearing were largely hereditary industries

[1] Committee on Combination Laws, 1825, pp. 120-48.

[2] James Kay, a cotton and woollen manufacturer near Bury, gave some particulars of the wages he paid to his cotton weavers to the Committee on Trade in 1812 (p. 217). These wages dropped from 7s. in March 1810 to 4s. in May 1811. In November 1811 they had risen to 4s. 6d. Asked to account for this last rise he answered, 'On account of the disposition of the people to riot and the Committee of Masters recommending it.' He was then asked about his woollen weavers, and he answered that woollen weavers' wages did not vary much.   [3] Baines, *Yorkshire Past and Present*, p. 361.

[4] See Report from Hand-loom Weavers' Commissioners, 1841, p. 24 : 'Nearly twenty years have passed since the application of the power-loom to wool, and though constantly extending it is still much less employed for that purpose than the hand-loom. So much less that its use does not seem to have as yet affected wages in the woollen trade.' Even as late as 1858 Baines states that the shuttle of a power-loom can only fly at the rate of a hand-loom for broadcloth (*op. cit.*, p. 631).

and they were never carried on under the same roof. It is therefore specially interesting to notice that they joined forces at the beginning of the nineteenth century in a campaign that was to last for many years. The story falls into this section, because, though the weavers took an active part in the struggle, and the programme presented to Parliament included special demands of their own, it was the shearmen whose fate was finally determined by the issue. The workers hoped to persuade Parliament that certain semi-obsolete regulations should be put into practice, and in this effort they had the help at one time of the small master manufacturers who had reasons of their own for disliking the development of the factory system.

For many centuries the woollen trade had been subject to various regulations. They seemed indeed an integral part of the industry, and the industry itself had a traditional character as a national institution, a fact which, no doubt, accounts for the serious consideration paid by Parliament to the men's proposals.[1]

The main laws dealing with the manufacture on the Statute-book were briefly these :

1. A statute of Edward vi.'s time (5 & 6 Edw. vi. c. 22) which prohibited the use of gig mills.
2. The famous statute (5 Eliz. c. 4) which enforced a seven years' apprenticeship on workers in the woollen trade.
3. A statute (2 & 3 Philip and Mary, c. 11) which limited the number of looms any clothier could possess to one, and any weaver to two, outside a ' city, borough, ' market town or town corporate.' [2]

---

[1] The peculiar position of the woollen trade as regards the introduction of machinery is clearly set out in the little pamphlet issued at Leeds in 1803 called *Observations on Woollen Machinery*. In this it is argued that since the raw material for the trade is a monopoly and limited in quantity, the reasons that recommend the introduction of machinery for cotton and flax do not apply to wool.

[2] This Act, however, did not apply to Yorkshire. There was also a labyrinth of statutes regulating minutely the processes of manufacture and arranging for inspection, but these seem to have fallen into disuse. Mr. Sheppard, the big clothier of Uley, declared that he had never known of an inspector in Gloucestershire, whilst a Somerset clothier described the functions of the inspector, a shoemaker by trade, with whom he had dealings in Somerset, as merely nominal, consisting of the receipt of 2d. per piece of cloth and an annual visit to the Quarter Sessions to swear he had done his duty (Report of Committee on South-West Woollen Clothiers' Petition, 1802-3). About these laws the workmen did not concern themselves.

1. *Gig Mills.*—A Gig Mill was the name given to the machinery used for raising the fibres in the cloth in order to form a nap on the surface, a nap which was afterwards shorn off. These two processes of raising and shearing together were called ' finishing,' and the men who worked them were called cloth workers, or shearmen, or, in Yorkshire, croppers.[1] Originally the raising of the nap was done by hand, with teazles. A gig mill was ' a machine containing a cylinder about a yard in diameter, covered with teazles, and revolving with great rapidity between two upright posts. Above and below this cylinder are two others, round which the cloth is gradually wound. . . .'[2] The saving of a gig mill in time and labour was very great. By hand work it took a man eighty-eight hours to raise the nap on a given piece of cloth : by a gig mill, worked by one man and a boy, the same process was done in twelve hours. The process of shearing off the nap after it was raised either by hand or by a gig mill was performed by shearmen, working heavy hand shears which weighed thirty to forty pounds. Their work in this second process of finishing was also threatened by the introduction of shearing frames, a device by which several pairs of shears were fixed in a frame ' which travelled over the cloth.' By this device, so it was estimated, the time required for shearing a piece of cloth was reduced from eighty-eight hours to eighteen.[3] Although gig mills were illegal, there was no law on the Statute-book prohibiting shearing frames.

By 1802 gig mills had been used in a few places for a great number of years. There had been some gig mills in Gloucestershire and Yorkshire for sixty years, and round Halifax several had been set up twenty years previously.[4] Great discontent had been roused by the use of these mills, and a curious letter amongst the Chatham MSS.[5] addressed to Pitt by a certain

[1] These processes are described by Baines (*Yorkshire Past and Present,* p. 630):

    (1) ' raising up all the fibres of the wool which can be detached by violent and long continued brushing of the cloth with teazles, so as to make a nap on the surface ' ;

    (2) ' shearing off that nap . . . so clean and smooth as to give a soft and almost velvety appearance and feel to the cloth.'

[2] Report from Assistant Hand-loom Weavers' Commissioners, part v. p. 373.

[3] For above figures see Tables in Reports from Assistant Hand-loom Weavers' Commissioners, 1840, part ii. pp. 439 f.

[4] Minutes of Evidence on Woollen Trade Bill, 1802-3, pp. 249 and 372 ; H.O., 42. 66.   [5] Chatham MSS., 146.

Mr. Thomas Phipps Howard in 1795, contains a suggestion (whether authorised or not by the gentlemen clothiers does not appear) that the ' turbulent spirits ' amongst the workers in the South-West should be the objects of the Press Gang's attention. The master clothiers, says the writer, desire to get rid of the men, and ' they think they might be made useful to their Country in the Army and Navy ; their present Masters would provide for their Families.' He estimates the possible numbers as between three thousand and four thousand.

Both in Yorkshire and in the south-west actions had been instituted before 1795 by the shearmen against users of gig mills under the old law of Edward vi., but as they had failed to prove that the gig mills were the same as those prohibited by the statute, the question was still open.[1] The adoption of gig mills in Wiltshire was the cause of the renewed agitation of 1802.

2. *Apprenticeship.*—The practice of enforcing a seven years' apprenticeship for weavers and cloth workers had fallen into disuse by 1802. A big Gloucester master manufacturer asserted in 1803 that out of 158 weavers employed by him only twenty-one had served a regular apprenticeship, whilst no one of his cloth workers had been apprenticed.[2] In Wiltshire apprenticeship seems to have been more common.[3] In Yorkshire only about one in twenty of the men had been regularly apprenticed.[4]

3. *Limitation of Looms.*—Neither of the two former questions, gig mills or apprenticeship, affected the small master manufacturers in Yorkshire with their domestic system. It was the regulations with regard to the limitation of looms that they wished to use against the big masters, and hence they joined forces with the workmen who desired to enforce not only this but the other restrictions as well.[5] These Yorkshire

[1] Evidence on Woollen Trade Bill, 1802-3, p. 372 ; and H.O., 42. 83 (Mr. Read's report).

[2] Committee on South-West Woollen Clothiers' Petition, 1802-3 (Edward Sheppard).

[3] See *ibid.* Two manufacturers gave the proportion of apprenticed to unapprenticed as two to one. There had also been of recent years a considerable influx of unapprenticed women weavers both in Yorkshire and the South-West.

[4] Report of Committee on Yorkshire Woollen Petitions, 1802-3.

[5] Committee on State of Woollen Manufacture, 1806, p. 9. As a matter of fact the statute of Philip and Mary did not apply to Yorkshire, but no doubt they hoped for the substitution of a new statute limiting looms everywhere (see Report of Committee on Petition of Manufacturers of Woollen Cloth in Yorkshire, 1803-4).

small masters with their two or three journeymen saw themselves in danger of extinction at the hands of the big masters who were concentrating numbers of looms in one building : whilst the weavers in the south-west dreaded that weaving like spinning might in future be carried on in the master manufacturers' own premises, instead of, as hitherto, in their own homes. All this time in the south-west clothing district a migration was going on from the towns to the villages, where there was water power to work machinery. An enforcement of the Act of Philip and Mary would stop the concentration of looms in these villages. In Wiltshire, it may be noted, there was already one factory where the employer had gathered the looms working for him together into one building,[1] but as a rule the weavers worked in their own homes at looms belonging to themselves.

The chief advantage claimed by those few masters who had the weaving, like the spinning, done on their own premises, was the prevention of embezzlement which was said to be rife when weaving was done at home ; [2] most master clothiers, however, preferred the risk to the trouble of providing large premises and the difficulties of inducing workers to enter them.

The serious campaign against gig mills began with their introduction into Wiltshire, in the towns of Warminster and Bradford in the spring of 1802.[3] The shearmen refused to finish cloth previously put in a gig mill, and a series of outrages ensued in the course of which the men not only destroyed property but fired into the windows of the owners or workers of the unpopular machinery. Public sympathy was on the side of the shearmen.[4] In addition to the disputes about gig mills the shearmen at Trowbridge, where there were no gig mills, had a difference with the master clothiers on the subject of wages early in July, but after a week's strike five clothiers met a deputation of five shearmen and acceded to their terms. But the dissatisfaction with the use of gig mills

---

[1] Committee on South-West Clothiers' Petition, 1802-3 (John Jones).
[2] *Ibid.* (Edward Sheppard).
[3] Committee on South-West Clothiers' Petition, 1802-3. For what follows see H.O., 42. 65, and 42. 66.
[4] The High Constable of Warminster complained that the inhabitants were apathetic or sympathetic owing to ' disgust at the introduction of machinery,' and Mr. John Jones wrote that many persons refused to act as special constables.

still remained and showed itself in violent forms. On July 21,
1802, a cottage fulling and spinning mill at Littleton was burnt
down ; another mill at Steeple Ashton was also fired a few
days later, and by the end of July it was estimated that no
less than £8000 of damage had been done.

The headquarters of the shearmen's organisation in the south-
west was at Trowbridge, and their affairs were managed by
a committee of thirteen. Members had a printed ticket
with the motto, ' May Industry and Freedom unite us in
Friendship,' and without this ticket no shearman was allowed
to work. The ticket held good in Yorkshire also where similar
tickets were in use.[1]

The most remarkable feature of the proceedings was a
regular and intimate correspondence between the south-west
and Yorkshire. Shearmen's clubs must have been in existence a considerable time, but possibly the communication
between them had been less close. Mr. Read, a London
magistrate sent down by Government to inquire into the
outrages, wrote : [2] ' these Clubs are certainly not of many
months' standing, and I think their Government is at Leeds, a
letter has been seen as coming from thence, directing the formation of Clubs and Committees of Correspondence and to write
as sensible a Letter as they could and direct it and any other
Letters to George Palmer . . . Leeds, the person who communicated this to me is a respectable clothier at Warminster,
and as he did not come by his knowledge of the Contents in an
honourable manner I at present can give your Lordship no
further information about it.'

The leading spirits among the shearmen were men who had
been discharged from the Army and Navy during the Peace
of Amiens and had come home to find themselves without
employment. As one of the masters put it, it is ' not an
assembly of a common Mob but a body of armed, regulated,
and systematical people composed principally of Militia Men
and Marines.' [3] Their point of view is given in an anonymous
letter to Mr. Benjamin Hobhouse, M.P. for Hindon : [4]

' MOST WORTHY SIR,—Called by the general voice at Bradford to
one of whom We hope have a natural feeling for his Brother
Mortals to whom We hope will intercede for us so that We may

---

[1] H.O., 42. 65, and 42. 66.   [2] H.O., 42. 66, August 10.
[3] H.O., 42. 65, July 26.
[4] H.O., 42. 65. We have inserted punctuation.

have labour to earn our Daily Bread. Some of us may perhaps
more or less served in His Majesty's Service some Six, Eight
or ten years in Defence of him and his Country. Now the Contending Nations are at Peace with each other we are send home
to starve. Will our Masters that have discharged us hold with
this? We know that it have been mentioned to our great men
and Ministers in Parliament by them that have Factorys how
many poor they employ, forgetting at the same time how many
more they would employ were they to have it done by hand as
they used to do. The Poor house we find full of great lurking
Boys who could earn a Shilling a day on the Scribling horse.
The last granting of Poors Rates is not collected by 300 Pounds
or the Parish is that behind. Five grantings of Poors Rates
granted last year, and our Gentlemens time is so took up with
skeming Inventions to take away Poors Labour that if a Vestry
is called there is hardly any Person to Attend, so we find them
grantings is not settled, that People is determined not to pay such
a number of Rates, and so often I am informed by many that
there will be a Revolution and that there is in Yorkshire about
30 thousand in a Correspondent Society. The fresh assessment
of Taxes and poors Rates Through so many being put out
of employ will soon bring it to an Issue, if Government do not
take it in hand Quickly for the Poor to have Plenty of Work.
The Lord will sooner or later Punish those that wants to Abate
the hireling in his wages. The burning of Factorys or setting fire
to the property of People we know is not right, but Starvation
forces Nature to do that which he would not, nor would it reach
his Thoughts had he sufficient Employ. We have tried every
Effort to live by Pawning our Cloaths and Chattles, so we are
now on the brink for the last struggle. Do with us and for us as
you would wish to be done unto that We may before we give up
the Ghost Clasp our hands and say Hobhouse for ever.

from a Souldier
Returned to his Wife and weeping Orphans.'

A deputation of seven shearmen waited on July 26 on Mr.
Jones of Bradford, one of the masters who had lately set up a
gig mill. Mr. Hobhouse was also present at the deputation.
Mr. Jones made the fair offer not only to give work to all at
present unemployed in the parish of Bradford (stated by them
to be thirty in number), but ' always to give a preference to
the employment of Men of the said Parish rather than use
Frames for the cutting or Sheering of Cloth whilst any such
men should want work ' ; he further promised not to do gigging
or shearing for hire. These liberal terms did not satisfy the
deputation ; they rejected them on behalf of the body of shearmen ' and declared it was the resolution of the Shearmen

throughout England, Scotland, and Ireland not to work after Machinery.' [1]

The master clothiers of the south-west seem on the whole to have adopted a conciliatory and reasonable attitude. On August 16, 1802, they held a meeting at Bath, at which, after dealing with the question of granting rewards for the discovery of outrages, they passed the following important resolution : [2]

'That for the Preservation of the Trade of this Part of the Country, it is the Determination of this Meeting to defend the Machinery already introduced, and any which, from its Utility, may be judged adviseable hereafter to introduce into the Woollen Manufactures, against the Attacks of any Person or Persons whomsoever; the Manufacturers engaging to find Employ for all Persons in their respective Employment in some other Branch of the Manufacture, of which such Person shall be capable, at ample and sufficient Wages, in case by the Introduction of Machinery the Services of any such Persons shall be rendered unnecessary in the particular Branch of the Manufacture, in which they are now or have lately been employed ; so long as such Persons shall demean themselves with Propriety.'

These negotiations were poisoned like all negotiations of the kind by the existence of the Combination Act. On the face of it the offer seemed a fair one, and the workers would have been wise to accept it. But there was no security that the promise would be kept, and if the workmen wished at any time to discuss an apparent breach of the agreement or the meaning of such terms as ' ample and sufficient,' the employers could effectually restrain them by the use of the Combination Act. Already, indeed, proceedings had begun against them under that Act and the Conspiracy Law. It is, therefore, not surprising that they were unwilling to surrender what they considered their trump card, the claim that gig mills were illegal, without some more definite guarantee than a promise of this kind. Arrests had already begun. The Law Officers had wished to proceed against the deputation who waited on Mr. Jones.

'We are of opinion' [they wrote] [3] 'that the Conduct of the Individuals who came to Mr. Jones' House will support an Indictment for a Conspiracy—and we should recommend an Indictment

---

[1] H.O., 42. 65, July 26 ; and Committee on South-West Clothiers' Petition, 1802-3.
[2] H.O., 42. 66, September 6.   [3] H.O., 42. 65, July 28.

to be prepared and sent down to the assizes for Wiltshire charging these seven men with such Conspiracy and that Mr. Hobhouse and the other persons present with Mr. Jones should attend at the Assizes to go before the Grand Jury with the Bill.

SPENCER PERCEVAL,
THOMAS MANNERS SUTTON.'

Mr. Jones, however, had a more delicate sense of honour and he demurred to this ; the seven delegates, he wrote,[1] had been promised that no advantage should be taken of their attendance, and hence however desirable it might be to make examples, ' I shall personally become reprobated for an apparent deception towards these Men.' He asked that proceedings should at any rate be suspended. Apparently no further action was taken in the case of this deputation ; attention was directed instead to the question of arresting the committee at Trowbridge. Mr. Jones had urged the necessity of this step and of examining all letters to and from Yorkshire—' the effects of such Combinations,' he wrote, ' are more to be dreaded than even open Attacks.' [2]

The Government early in August sent down Mr. Read from London to help the justices on the spot and to find out if the militia were implicated.[3] Before his arrival, Mr. Jones, who seems to have played the double part of manufacturer and magistrate, had arrested Thomas Elleker or Hilleker on the charge of burning the mill at Littleton, and wrote : [4] ' I have also secured three other Men on suspicion, hoping one of them, after a little Confinement, may be induced to come forward as an Evidence.' He added that he did not intend to discharge the men for some days, ' believing their apprehension will produce a general dismay amongst these offenders.'

Mr. Jones' plan was not very successful ; ' the working Clothiers,' wrote Lord Pembroke, the Lord Lieutenant, ' when once so deeply engaged as these are, are unfortunately true to each other.' [5] Mr. Read, when he reached the district about August 9, urged the magistrates to arrest the committee and to search their houses for papers ; ' although I have not yet discovered that they have any other object in View than that of making better Terms with their Employers and of getting rid of the Gig Mills, yet it appears to me that the Club is likely to become a dangerous Engine, upon the present extensive

[1] H.O., 42. 65, July 30.   [2] H.O., 42. 65, July 27.
[3] H.O., 42. 66, August 3.   [4] Ibid.   [5] H.O., 42. 66, August 7.

Plan.'[1] Five of the committee were secured by August 13 and were charged under the Act of 37 Geo. III. c. 123,[2] with administering an illegal oath. Their trial was fixed for the March Assizes.

The Combination Act with its more summary methods was also called into play; temptations held out to accomplices, wrote Mr. Read on September 1,[3] have hitherto been useless, but six shearmen were sent to gaol last week under the Combination Act, four for offences, the other two for refusing to give testimony, ' and we have had one pecuniary conviction for paying a Shearman to keep him out of Work. I am bringing forward as many Cases as I can under the Combination Act, and by forcing some to give Evidence against others, I hope to provoke some quarrels amongst them, and by that means to be able to bring some of their Deeds to light.' Twelve days later he wrote : [4] ' Two or more Justices meet daily at one or other of the Manufacturing Towns and as the Combination Act affords a very convenient pretext for summoning and examining upon Oath any suspected Persons I have continually some before them. It answers the double purpose of keeping the Magistrates at their Post and of alarming the disaffected, we have six in confinement for Offences against the Act and three for refusing to give testimony.' He adds a sentence which illustrates the alternative before workmen against whom active magistrates chose to enforce the law ; two men had come with money from Leeds, and he regrets that he did not hear about them in time for he had intended to have ' summoned them before Two justices in Somerset and to have made them either perjure themselves or disclose their Secrets.'

Meantime in Yorkshire the shearmen, or the croppers as they were called in that district, were gaining their object. Mr. Jones of Bradford in Wilts, it may be noticed, had not ceased using his gig mill, but seeing that the shearmen refused to cut his cloth for him after the nap had been raised in the mill, he introduced shearing frames, superintended by persons not shearmen.[5] In Yorkshire, on the other hand, the croppers not only succeeded in preventing the erection of new gig mills, but even stopped those already in use.

[1] H.O., 42. 66, August 9.
[2] An Act passed at the time of the Mutiny of the Nore.
[3] H.O., 42. 66.   [4] Ibid., September 13.
[5] Ibid., September 5.

Mr. Cookson, the Mayor of Leeds, wrote on August 21, 1802 : [1] 'The whole system upon which the Shearmen in the West act, was, I am afraid engendered here, being perfectly congenial to the threats and tone of language they use on any occasion attracting their hostility.' Knowing the dangers of their threats, he continues, 'I have, within these last nine months by my own personal influence privately prevailed upon one or two Houses who meditated the adding a Gig mill, or a shearing Machine to their Works to desist for the present, or I am firmly convinced we should have had such horrid outrages to deplore here, as have been practised in the West. . . . Every Class of Workmen,' he adds, 'make a common Cause with that of the Cloth workers and every turn out for advance of Wages, is supported by general contributions from almost every other Class.' Later on he writes [2] that the Yorkshire croppers are alarmed about the Bath meeting of August 16, for they know that the use of machinery in the south-west will lead to its use in Yorkshire, [3] or else carry away much trade. Within the last three weeks by threatening a strike the shearmen had succeeded in stopping all the gig mills at Huddersfield, some of which had worked for twenty years. The masters yielded rather than lose the shipping season, 'and the Law here against Gig mills is now as complete in affect, nay more so, than if enacted by Parliament.'

The situation was complicated in Yorkshire by a strike of croppers against Mr. Gott, the well-known woollen manufacturer of Leeds, for apprenticing two boys who were over fourteen. The eighty croppers working for Mr. Gott refused to do any more work unless he dismissed the boys. This Mr. Gott refused to do, and the eighty croppers struck work, involving some nine hundred other workers with them. [4] The quarrel extended to other houses too. The croppers were in a strong position. 'They are the Tyrants of the Country,' wrote Lord Fitzwilliam, [5] 'their power and influence has grown out of their high wages, which enable them to make deposits,

[1] H.O., 42. 66.   [2] H.O., 40. 66.

[3] At the bottom of a printed advertisement for shearmen wanted at Leeds circulated in the west is a note in writing explaining 'how well things went in Yorkshire where there were no gig mills or Shearing Frames and the poor Man's Labour not abridged, and that if Things were to become so here everything would be peace and Harmony' (H.O., 42. 66, October 3).

[4] H.O., 42. 66, September 27 and October 3 ; and Committee on Woollen Manufacture, 1806, p. 24.

[5] H.O., 42. 66, September 27.

that puts them beyond all fear of inconvenience from mis-
conduct.' The croppers' funds, in fact, enabled them to hold
out till the masters yielded early next year. Lord Fitzwilliam's
comments on the position of the small skilled body of workmen who acted as missionaries to other trades are interesting,
and are written as if there were no such law as the Combination Act.[1]

'By the reports I receive, it does not appear that the Croppers
commit any acts of violence, nor do I know upon what principle
the measures they adopt, and which render them so powerful can
be restricted or even reprobated. What is objectionable in bodies
of Men laying up in the days of prosperity against those of
adversity? Within these few years Parliament has sanctioned
and encouraged the principle to the full extent of anything these
People appear to do.[2] However, I fear it will be productive of
serious evil hereafter. The advantage these People derive from
their system of combination becomes an example to every other
branch of trade and manufacture, and the pains they take to
disseminate their system amongst other trades, gives just cause
for apprehension that the trouble they take in this cause, will not
be without its consequences. Others will do as they have done.
Wages will increase universally, and of consequence the prices of
manufacture. The question that arises, is, How far can the
foreign Market bear increase of price? It is an alarming incitement to the industry of other Nations,—there is the evil—I see
little else to be uneasy about.'

The masters' panacea in Yorkshire was to attempt to make
the Combination Laws more stringent, though they do not
seem to have tried to enforce the existing laws. Lord Fitzwilliam, the Lord Lieutenant, it must be noticed, though
lamenting the tyranny of the croppers deprecated this policy.[3]

Communications between Yorkshire and the south-west continued through the year 1802 partly by means of delegates,
partly by letters. Copies of a few of the letters which were
intercepted in the post by the authorities, survive amongst the
Home Office Papers. The originals were sent on in order to
prevent suspicion. It is interesting to know what the shearmen were thinking. 'Gentlemen,' writes James Griffon from
Trowbridge to George Palmer at Leeds on September 5.[4]
'The two friends that you sent amongst us gave every information and council that we could desire.' The obstacles, he goes

[1] H.O., 42. 70, January 30, 1803.
[2] He refers, no doubt, to the Friendly Society Acts of 1793 (33 Geo. III.
c. 54) and 1795 (35 Geo. III. c. 111).
[3] H.O., 42. 66, September 27.   [4] H.O., 42. 66.

on, are many, ' but we hope by the blessing of God and your help to surmount them all, we think that we may say that excepting one or two places which is but very little consequence that the whole country will be harmonized.'   The writer urges his friends to accept information only from Trowbridge.   ' We are informed that something have turned up in our favour, but for the truth of it we cannot say, and we hope that some of our friends will be at home soon,[1] and those that do remain will not be so cruel used as they have been, but, if it is possible we shall bail them out, and if so we shall give you information. . . . By Order of the Community,   Jas. Griffon C.'

Another packet of letters directed to George Palmer at Leeds [2] was intended for a certain Joseph Warren, a shearman, nephew of the James May who had been arrested as a leading member of the committee.   Warren in fear for his own safety had made off to Yorkshire.   ' I know that you cannot come to me yet,' writes Ann Waller his sweetheart, ' unless you do mean to involve yourself in trouble and put it out of your Power to do any good to your Friend.'   ' Your Uncle James,' writes his mother, Phœbe Warren, ' has been used very bad since he have been in Gaol.   I hope, my Son,' she adds cautiously, ' that you will think on this that a Friend in the Pocket is better than to trust to another.'

Another letter comes from Charles Thomas, the president of some trade or other at Bristol, and is also directed to George Palmer at Leeds : [3] ' Gentlemen,' it runs, ' we received your kind Letter the 5th Instant and am sorry to hear that you have so many Enemies to contend with, as it must be very expensive to you when so many men is out of employ, hope you have had liberal supplies from most Towns in the Kingdom ; if you should be in want we have no objection of making you a small remittance.   Hope you will in a short time be able to give us an account of your having met with good success, and be able to let the Merchants and Manufacturers know they are in the wrong, and be ashamed of their nasty mean conduct. We shall always be happy to hear from our Brethren the Cloth Dressers of Leeds, as they are a set of men which ought to be esteemed, and I hope is by all Trades.   Gentlemen, wishing you health and Respect, I remain your most obedient,

CHARLES THOMAS, *President*.'

[1] Clearly the men in prison.   [2] H.O., 42. 66, October 3.
[3] H.O., 42. 70, March 17.

William May, brother of James May, went up to Leeds late
in the year 1802, and wrote on December 16 that he was doing
much business with the committee; [1] that he had visited
Huddersfield, Saddleworth, and Manchester; that it had been
decided to pay £50 to Mr. W.[2] before he left Leeds, and to send
another £100 to Trowbridge by December 28.   He, William
May, had promised that £50 should be raised in the west
by that time ' in order that a Petition may be immediately
carried into Parliament.   Mr. W.,' he adds, ' have received
positive instructions to retain the first Counsel for the Trial.'

To understand William May's references to a petition to
Parliament it is necessary to go back a little.   The activities
of the men in the woollen industry that summer were not
confined to violence against gig mills.   In Gloucestershire
the weavers formed or revived an association, with Mr. Walter
Hilton Jessop, an attorney, as President, and started a campaign against unapprenticed weavers.[3]   Mr. Jessop issued
notices of actions against some 150 weavers for illegally exercising their trade ; the action was only proceeded with in one
case against a Mr. Webb, a master clothier, for employing a
non-apprenticed man, and this case which came up at the
August Assizes, 1802, was dropped on the understanding that
Mr. Webb would no longer employ unapprenticed weavers.
Of the other weavers about a hundred were said to have stopped
weaving.

Prosecutions were threatened as well under the statute
of Philip and Mary for using more than the prescribed
number of looms.   The shearmen of Wilts and Somerset
also threatened actions against unapprenticed men, and
solemnly presented some gig mills as a nuisance to the Grand
Jury at the Salisbury Assizes in August.[4]   The Grand Jury
took no action, and it was of course very doubtful whether
the gig mills were the same as those prohibited by Edward VI.
But the masters felt themselves placed in an awkward position,
and in order to put an end to the various actions hanging over
them, applied to Parliament in the autumn of 1802 for a Bill
to suspend the woollen statutes till July 1803.   The statutes
which they wished to have suspended were twenty-four in

[1] H.O., 42. 66.

[2] Mr. W. = Mr. Wilmot, an attorney at Bradford who acted for the men.

[3] Evidence on Woollen Trade Bill, 1802-3 (Mr. Jessop's evidence), pp. 44 ff.;
and Committee on Woollen Manufacture, 1806, p. 351.

[4] H.O., 42. 66, September 6.

all, including various Acts regulating the manufacture. It was to promote a petition against this Bill, which would of course have been fatal to the men's cause, that William May was seeking help in the north. The shearmen all this while were receiving support from a number of different trades. From the books that fell into the hands of the House of Commons Committee of 1806 it appeared ' that contributions have been received from all descriptions of persons in 1802, clothiers, colliers, bricklayers, wool-sorters, from the clothiers' community, joiners, sawyers, flax-dressers, shoemakers, turnpike-men, cabinet-makers receipts from Manchester, patten-ring makers and paper-makers.' [1]

The masters' Bill for suspending the operation of the woollen statutes crept through the House of Commons,[2] but its career was checked at the second reading in the Lords on February 8, 1803, when Lord Pelham (Home Secretary) asked the House to defer the second reading a month in order that the question of repeal could be discussed.[3] This rather doubtful victory was hailed with more joy than the occasion warranted by the weavers and shearmen. ' Barton the weaver,' runs a letter of February 10, 1803, sent up by Mr. Jones,[4] ' has written to his Comrades at Bradford that their Enemies are defeated, that praise was due to Mr. Jessop (their attorney) and that they had obtained a complete victory. . . .' Again on February 11, ' Some few Weavers paraded the streets of Bradford yesterday with blue Cockades, and the Bells at Trowbridge have been ringing most part of this morning. Barton came home with others in Post Chaises.'

Early in March at the Salisbury Assizes, Thomas Elleker or Hilleker was capitally convicted of arson for the burning of Littleton mill and paid the penalty with his life. James May and the four other men charged with administering an illegal oath were acquitted. The witness, an accomplice, broke down. ' The execution of Hilliker will, I hope,' wrote Mr. Read, ' answer all the Ends of Public Justice.' [5] The disturb-

---

[1] Committee on Woollen Manufacture, 1806, p. 355.

[2] ' The country at large not knowing anything of its nature,' said the shearmen afterwards (H.O., 42. 83).

[3] See *Parliamentary Register*, February 8, 1803. That the question caused some anxiety to the Government is shown by a draft letter to the Lords Lieutenant of the clothing counties asking for their opinions on the subject, a letter which was not sent lest there should seem a difference of opinion amongst the ministers (H.O., 42. 70, January 3).

[4] H.O., 42. 70.
[5] H.O., 42. 70, March 9.

ances, indeed, had ceased many months previously and the men were busy with their legal and Parliamentary campaign, though the master clothiers were seriously alarmed at ' the more than common respect' shown by the multitude of workmen at Hilleker's funeral.[1] No breach of the peace occurred.

The master manufacturers of the three south-western clothing counties petitioned in March 1803 for a Bill to repeal parts of thirteen Acts of Parliament, including the Acts about apprenticeship, gig mills, and limitation of looms.[2] The merchants and manufacturers from Yorkshire also petitioned on the same side, whilst the weavers, the shearmen, the occupiers of houses and tenements in clothing towns in Wilts, Somerset, and Gloucestershire, and the shearmen from the West Riding petitioned against the Bill. The Bill went through the Commons after some discussion,[3] but was changed in the Lords into a Bill suspending the statutes for a year. There was an understanding that the whole question of the woollen laws should come up for final revision the next year.[4]

The evidence given by the different sides in support of petitions for and against the Bill is voluminous and interesting.[5] Much of it is technical. The one side says that gig mills strain and damage the cloth ; the other side claims that they produce a better result than hand work ; one side declares it takes seven years to learn weaving—as one witness puts it, a weaver is not ' compus mentis ' under seven years—the other puts the length of time required as under a year. The witnesses on the men's side include, besides weavers and shearmen, some small master clothiers. All are closely questioned on the subject of the man's associations, and exhibit the dogged secretiveness engendered by the Combination Act. They

[1] *Parliamentary Register*, April 1, 1803. The Shearmen's Union evidently gave his widow a small allowance (see Report on Woollen Manufacture, 1806, p. 355).

[2] *Parliamentary Register*, April 6, 1803.

[3] See *Parliamentary Register*, March 28, April 1, April 6, April 7, April 27, July 1, 1803.

[4] See H.O., 42. 83 : undated petition of shearmen in which they say that the master clothiers only obtained the suspending Act in August 1803 'under as your Petitioners were informed and believe a solemn pledge and assurance that they would come forward early in the ensuing sessions with a Bill for a general revision and regulation of the said Laws.' Cf. letter from Nath. Edwards and John Tate, *ibid.*

[5] See Report on South-West Woollen Clothiers' Petition, 1802-3 ; Report of Committee on Yorkshire Woollen Petitions, 1802-3 ; Minutes of Evidence on Woollen Trade Bill, 1802-3.

must in truth ' either perjure themselves or disclose their secrets,' and they choose the former.   Nothing could exceed their obstinacy in maintaining both the truth of their assertions about apprenticeship and gig mills, and their ignorance about recent events in Wiltshire and Gloucestershire.   The news of rioting or of correspondence between the men in the south-west and in Yorkshire comes to them as new and interesting information.   The only club they have ever heard of is an innocent Benefit Club.   One, when hard pressed, admits that he belongs to ' An Association, to subscribe our Mites to bring this before the Honourable House of Commons. To bring what ?   Our Case that we might not be sent to the Factories.' [1]

In 1804 there was a change of Ministry, and Parliament was too busy to pay much attention to the subject of the woollen laws.   The weavers of Gloucestershire tried without success to come to an arrangement for a revising Bill with the master clothiers.   They declared, ' We the Weavers of the said County do solemnly declare that we have been and ever will be unconnected with the workmen in every other branch of the Woollen Manufacture.'   They proposed that villages should be treated as towns, that those at present working should be unmolested, but that apprenticeship should be enforced in future, except in the case of the weavers' own children ; that there should be no factories, but that the number of looms one man might have should be three broad, or six narrow, or one broad and four narrow, or two broad and two narrow ; the other statutes to remain unchanged.[2]   A Bill of some sort or other was indeed introduced on the subject but was shelved on the second reading, and a fresh suspending Bill brought in and carried instead, Pitt observing that ' at this late period of the session it was impossible that the House could attend to the regulation of a subject of such magnitude.' [3]   According to the shearmen he ' pledged his word to the House that Ministers would take up the Business ' early next session.[4]

In 1805 the shearmen made a determined effort to obtain a settlement in their favour.   This year the small clothiers of Yorkshire took an active part as well as the weavers of the west.[5]   A Bill favouring their cause was prepared by Mr.

[1] Evidence on Woollen Trade Bill, 1802-3, p. 26.
[2] Committee on Woollen Manufacture, 1806, pp. 336 f.
[3] *Parliamentary Register*, June 13, 1804.   [4] H.O., 42. 83.
[5] Report of Committee on Cloth-workers and others' Petitions, 1805.

Brooke, long their champion, by Wilberforce and Sir William Young.[1] This Bill, whilst repealing some of the statutes objected to, proposed : [2]

(1) To reinforce restrictions about apprenticeship with exemptions for those already at work :

(2) To set a limit to the number of looms in a clothier's or a weaver's house :

(3) To limit the number of spinning jennies to be used by a clothier on his premises, and to limit the number of spindles on each jenny :

(4) To prevent truck more efficiently.

(5) To regulate the duties of inspectors.

(6) To declare that the Act of Edw. VI. about gig mills applied to the present gig mills.

The Yorkshire clothiers backed the Bill vigorously, 39,000 of them petitioning in its favour.[3] This Bill, which would certainly, as its opponents pointed out, have proved a serious check to machinery, was withdrawn on its second reading (June 19) on the understanding that the matter would be dealt with finally in a similar Bill next year. Pitt, ' though he could give no pledge that such a Bill should be brought forward, yet assured the hon. gentleman that the attention of parliament should certainly be drawn to the subject as early as possible in the next session.' [4] Meanwhile another suspending Bill was rushed through both Houses. There were numbers of hostile petitions. Mr. Peter Moore, who opposed the suspending Bill, estimated that whilst there were only the signatures of 83 manufacturers on behalf of the Bill, its opponents numbered 200,000.[5] Counsel was not heard against the Bill either in the Commons or the Lords, for the question of time was urgent ; the previous suspending Bill expired on July 1, and this only received its second reading in the Lords on June 28, and the royal assent on July 2. Had there been any gap between the two Acts many of the woollen manufacturers would have been liable to considerable penalties. The new suspending Bill instead of lasting a year was to expire on May

[1] *Parliamentary Register*, May 24, 1805.

[2] In H.O., 42. 83, there is an undated memorandum on the Shearmen's Bill from which the following is taken.

[3] *Parliamentary Register*, June 6, 1805.

[4] *Ibid.*, June 19, 1805.

[5] *Ibid.*, June 20, 1805.

1, 1806, a provision meant to ensure that the question would be finally settled early next year.

That the Government were by no means unfriendly to the men's side is proved by the memoranda on the business in the Home Office Papers ; indeed unless one bears in mind that the woollen trade seemed to be on a different basis to any other trade and that, as Mr. Read put it, the experience of five hundred years showed that some regulations were necessary,[1] it is difficult to reconcile their attitude with their dislike of restrictions in other trades.

One memorandum of 1805, in what looks like the hand-writing of the Under Secretary,[2] advises that instead of repeal-ing the Act about gig mills the shearmen should be allowed to try the case at law, and then if the gig mills are the same—and the writer thinks they are not—the men should have their remedies. Apprenticeship the writer declares to be a difficult question ; if 5 Eliz. c. 4 continues to be sus-pended ' mischief may arise to our manufactures, from a too general use of Labourers not properly instructed.' The question had better be reported on by the Committee of the Privy Council for Trade. The attitude of the writer on the question of the limitation of looms and the factory as opposed to the domestic system is interesting ; the case of the weavers, he writes, ' merits attention, and if the principles upon which the use of looms is restricted to private Houses, is set aside, this great branch of business will as far as the *Persons* of those Individuals are concerned, be carried on upon the same prin-ciple with Machinery—that is they will be collected in Work-houses, and become the hired Servants of the Manufacturer instead of being Housekeepers and heads of Families. But there seems no objection to allowing the Weavers, in their present state, to have as many looms in their Houses as their Families can work.' Another memorandum [3] points out that the question bristles with difficulties, and the writer sees ' great objections to Government taking the Measure up in the first Instance and making what is to be done *their own Act*. The Shearmen therefore should have an Interview first with one of the Secretaries of the Treasury and afterwards with Mr. Pitt and Mr. Rose and endeavour to settle with them the best mode of putting the Business in a course of Investiga-tion and of bringing it to a speedy conclusion by a Decision of Parliament.'

[1] H.O., 42. 83.　　　　　[2] *Ibid.*　　　　　[3] *Ibid.*

But Mr. Pitt had other things to think about, for in those short months the Third Coalition against Napoleon—his last unhappy creation—was constructed and shattered, and the shearmen's hopes and fears counted for little in the great march of events that winter. Their persistence, however, was unabated. No sooner was Pitt dead and the Ministry of ' All the Talents ' installed, than they began their applications again, this time to Lord Spencer the new Home Secretary.[1] Again in 1806 the matter was shelved and a suspending Bill brought in. ' The two last Ministries,' wrote Lord Auckland,[2] ' having been unable to form any practicable opinion on this subject during a period of four years, we may, without taking shame to ourselves, recommend a further suspension to the next session. . . .' Again the suspending Bill was passed, and again a promise given that the question should be settled finally the next year, 1807.

In addition to this a Committee of the House of Commons was appointed to inquire into the state of the woollen manu-facture in England, and their Report, drawn up by Wilber-force,[3] and the Minutes of Evidence taken before them give a most valuable picture of the industry.[4] The Report recom-mended the repeal of the statutes to which the masters objected. Wilberforce had long been a firm ally of the small clothiers in Yorkshire, but he had come to the conclusion that their posi-tion was not seriously threatened, and that they would con-tinue to exist side by side with the factories, a forecast in which he was justified by events. ' If the factory system,' said one member of the committee, James Graham, a landowner near Leeds, in giving evidence,[5] ' if the factory system were to exclude from the country the domestic system, it would be dreadful indeed, for it is very pleasing in Yorkshire to see the domestic Clothiers living in a field, with their homestead, rather than shut up in a street.' Towards the shearmen the committee adopted a very different tone. Their Society with its com-munications between different districts was credited with almost unlimited power, and Wilberforce's old horror of work-men's combinations was given full rein.

' The least of the evils to be apprehended (though an evil

[1] H.O., 42. 83, February 10.
[2] Ibid., February 22.   Lord Auckland was President of the Board of Trade.
[3] Smart, Economic Annals, i. p. 128.
[4] The Report was printed July 4, 1806.
[5] Committee on Woollen Manufacture, 1806, p. 445.

in itself abundantly sufficient to accomplish the ruin, not only of any particular branch of Trade, but even of the whole commercial greatness of our Country) is, the progressive rise of Wages which among all classes of Workmen must be the inevitable, though gradual result of such a Society's operations : —an evil, the fatal though more distant, and in each particular increase, more doubtful consequence of which it cannot be expected that the Workmen themselves should foresee so plainly, or feel so forcibly, as not to incur them, under the powerful temptation of a strong and immediate interest.'[1] Dark hints are further thrown out of the political dangers of such societies.

The Report of the Committee of 1806 was a death-blow to any hopes that the shearmen might still cherish of the prohibition of gig mills. Close behind the gig mills came the shearing frames which if generally used would, as Mr. Read had pointed out in 1802,[2] 'entirely cut off the Artists in that branch of the Trade.' The domestic weavers and the small Yorkshire clothiers who had built hopes on the limitation of looms were also disappointed, but the Report prophesied correctly in their case so far at any rate as the immediate future was concerned.[3]

Although the Report of the 1806 Committee showed that the attempt to resuscitate the old statutes was doomed to failure, the actual question of the woollen laws was not definitely settled by Parliament till 1809. In 1807 another suspending Bill was passed, and there were fresh petitions against it. In 1808 yet another suspending Bill was passed. It must be noticed that though each suspending Act only exempted existing gig mills from prosecution, new ones were set up, which were indemnified by the next Act. This device of shelving the question by passing one suspending Bill after another was very unfair to the shearmen. A rather despairing set of resolutions from the cloth-workers and shearmen of the West Riding of Yorkshire and Lancashire sent up to the Home Office in 1808 [4] sets out ' That the great question respecting the use of that Machine in the Woollen Manufacture, having

[1] Committee on Woollen Manufacture, 1806, p. 17.
[2] H.O., 42. 66, September 5.
[3] The 'shoploom' system, i.e. of masters having their own looms on their own premises, was only introduced into Gloucestershire after the 1828 strike and was not universal in 1840 (see Reports from Assistant Hand-loom Weavers Commissoners, 1840, part v. p. 448).   [4] H.O., 42. 92, January 27.

been brought in so many Sessions of Parliament, the Expenses have greatly distressed them.' Indeed the amount of money spent by the woollen workers on the whole business must have been considerable; Mr. Jessop, the attorney, who had been President of the Gloucestershire Weavers' Association in 1803, said afterwards that he had spent about £1500 of the weavers' money in Parliamentary expenses that year without counting his own charges.[1] In the summer of 1808, riots were feared in the Bradford (Wilts) district, and an employer wrote to the Home Office asking for troops; '. . . in the improvements of the Factorys,' he explains, 'the misguided and evil disposed Shearmen erroneously fear their Interests are suffering.'[2] In 1809 the disputed question was at last settled by the Act 49 Geo. III. c. 109, which definitely repealed the Acts and clauses of Acts on which the workers had built so many hopes.[3]

The subsequent history of the shearmen or cloth-workers is a melancholy tale. Gig mills and shearing frames came into general use earlier in the south-west than in Yorkshire;[4] and if we may believe the writer of the Report on the South-West in 1840, owing to the briskness of trade, most of the men displaced by machinery found other work.[5] In 1816, however, when many extra hands returned from the war there was the old complaint of 1802; the journeymen cloth-workers of the West of England petitioned the Prince Regent for help;[6] they had hoped when peace came to return home to a trade, but find nothing to do, ' and it is Distressing to see so many out of work and are now at this Present moment lying on the streets of Bradford and Trowbridge and its Neighbourhood and in time of War there was no giggs nor Frames at Trowbridge but sad to relate it is now Increasin Every Day.' The petitioners, they declare, are compelled to wish for another war.

[1] Committee on Woollen Manufacture, 1806, p. 350.

[2] H.O., 42. 95.

[3] By this Act woollen workers were allowed to exercise any trade in any place.

[4] In 1806 John Tate was sent down from the Yorkshire Central Committee of Shearmen to find out the disposition of the people in the west about Parliamentary proceedings, 'the principal [object] was to know, as machinery was more general there than in any other county, whether it had the same injurious effects, and whether they felt it a grievance or not' (Committee on Woollen Manufacture, 1806, p. 353).

[5] Report from Assistant Hand-loom Weavers' Commissioners, 1840, part ii. p. 440.   [6] H.O., 42. 171, June 30.

In Yorkshire the Luddite disturbances of 1812, of which we give a description elsewhere, were connected with the introduction of shearing frames, still more or less of a novelty in Yorkshire. Gig mills had indeed come into use in spite of the croppers' protests, violent or pacific, except in Leeds, where, as late as 1814, it was said that the manufacturers dared not introduce them.[1] By 1817 the condition of the Yorkshire cloth-workers was pitiable in the extreme. A petition to Parliament presented by Lord Lascelles [2] stated that the number of gig mills had increased in Yorkshire since 1806 from five to seventy-two ; that the number of shears worked by machinery had increased from 100 to 1462, and that among the shearmen only 763 were fully employed, 1445 partly employed and 1170 entirely out of work. The shearmen renewed their old prayers for the prohibition of the machinery that was injuring them. The petition by its respectful tone and ' proper manner ' drew encomiums from both Castlereagh and Brougham, the latter remarking that ' the people were still sound at heart; that they still looked up to that House as their constitutional safeguard, and the grand source from which they were to expect relief.'

The petition was ordered to lie on the table, and finding that this did them no good the shearmen, under Lord Lascelles' advice, turned their minds to an attempt to get help for emigration to North America. The existing laws, as they pointed out, debarred them as artificers in the woollen trade from seeking employment in other lands, even though their trade had deserted them at home.[3] Lord Lascelles, writing to Lord Sidmouth,[4] urged that the Government should help those who wished to go to North America.[5] ' The restraints imposed by the Laws,' he wrote, ' do not appear to be as necessary now as at the time they were made, because not only in Europe, but in other parts of the world, improvements in manufactures are no longer unknown.' Even were they allowed to go, they could not pay their own expenses, so that Government aid was necessary. Sidmouth, however, would do nothing to help them. He answered curtly that both Lord Liverpool and he agreed that machinery could not be stopped in the woollen

[1] H.O., 42. 137, January 24.

[2] See Hansard, House of Commons, February 11, 1817.

[3] By 5 Geo. I. c. 27 (1719) artificers in the woollen and other trades were forbidden to emigrate. This Act and the successive Acts that strengthened it were far from being a dead letter.

[4] H.O., 42. 170, September 28.

[5] Brougham had suggested that they should be allowed to emigrate.

trade, and that no special terms could be made for the displaced men who wished to emigrate to the colonies.[1]   The shearmen, in fact, were left to starve as best they might.

An improvement in the machinery for cutting cloth, invented about 1820 by Mr. Lewis of Brinscomb, enabled the masters to substitute boys for the few men still employed.[2] The ' Tyrants of the Country ' had indeed met with the fate foretold by Lord Fitzwilliam in 1802. They should be superseded by machinery, he wrote,[3] for then ' their consequence would be lost, their Banks would waste, their combinations would fall to the ground, and we should hear no more of meetings of any sort of description.' The shearmen thus pass out of the pages of history.

V.—THE WORSTED WEAVERS

Early in the history of the Yorkshire worsted trade the interests of masters and men were displayed in striking contrast in the passing of the curious enactments called the Worsted Acts. With the growth of the industry the masters complained of an increase of frauds among the workpeople ; the woolcombers, it was said, embezzled, and the spinners reeled falsely.   Severe penalties for these offences existed on the Statute-book,[4] but the masters complained that they found it impossible to enforce them.   Accordingly the worsted manufacturers of Yorkshire, acting in concert with those in Lancashire and Cheshire, succeeded in inducing Parliament in 1777 to pass two Acts, commonly called the Worsted Acts (17 Geo. III. c. 11, and 17 Geo. III. c. 56). By these Acts the previous penalties were increased, and the manufacturers were now authorised to appoint a committee of twenty-seven (eighteen for Yorkshire, nine for Lancashire and Cheshire), and this committee was to appoint inspectors whose salaries were to be paid out

---

[1] H.O., 79. 3, October 12.

[2] Report from Assistant Hand-loom Weavers' Commissioners, part ii. p. 441.

[3] H.O., 42. 66, September 27.

[4] These penalties for embezzlement were : first offence, fourteen days' hard labour and a public whipping ; second offence, one to three months' hard labour and a public whipping.   For false spinning the penalties were : first offence, a fine of from 5s. to 20s.; second offence, a fine of from 40s. to £5 ; third offence, a month's hard labour and a public whipping (see 22 Geo. II. c. 27, and 14 Geo. III. c. 44).   It is worth noticing that the penalties for false spinning had been made less severe, because offenders went unpunished and many honest industrious persons were deterred from spinning by their severity.

of the drawback on soap employed in the manufacture of
wool.   Seven inspectors were appointed, each in charge of a
district, at a salary of £50 each.   Prosecutions were under the
direction of the committee ; offenders could be convicted on
the oath of the owner of the wool, of an inspector, or of one
or more credible witness.

The most drastic clause in the Acts was one in direct contradiction to the maxim that in English law a man is deemed
innocent until guilt is proved against him.   This clause gave
two justices of the peace the right to grant a search warrant
for embezzled material, before conviction, and enacted that
if materials were found the person on whose premises they
were found was to be deemed guilty unless he could prove
his innocence.   Constables could apprehend any person
' reasonably suspected ' of carrying embezzled stuff, and here
again, unless the person apprehended could prove his innocence,
he was deemed guilty.   An appeal in both cases was allowed
to Quarter Sessions.   These subversive clauses were applied by
the Act (17 Geo. III. c. 56) to the other textile trades, as
well as to hats, iron, leather, and fur, but the worsted trade in
Yorkshire was distinguished by its machinery for enforcing
them.[1]   In spite of this machinery, it was at first difficult to
put the Act in force.   ' Justices of the Peace,' we read, ' especially in agricultural districts, until compelled by mandamus,
refused to entertain charges against or convict upon proper
evidence, embezzlers or false reelers.' [2]

Apologists of the Acts maintained that prosecutions were
carried out ' prudently and without vindictiveness.' [3]   It seems
difficult to believe that injustice can have been avoided.[4]

The most important body of worsted weavers in the eighteenth century were the weavers of Norwich and the neighbourhood ; in spite of the gradual decay of trade and in
spite of long periods of unemployment, they were remarkably
successful in keeping up their rates of wages.   In the prosperous days of Norwich they were a well-organised body like
the woolcombers and like the woollen weavers of the south-
west, attracting the attention of Parliament by their combinations, and maintaining a certain standard of living, described

[1] James, *History of the Worsted Manufacture*, p. 299, says the manufacturers
of some Midland Counties followed their example soon after.
[2] James, *op. cit.*, p. 298.
[3] James, *op. cit.*, p. 295 ; cf. Baines, *Yorkshire Past and Present*, p. 677.
[4] The Act is still in force.   See *The Wool Year Book*, 1817, p. 505.

in the report ' that every weaver of any character made a
point of having a goose, or some equivalent, for his Sunday
dinner.' [1] They worked hard for their goose. ' One remarkable feature of the city noticed by all observers, was the still-
ness of the streets by day and night. The weavers and their
families kept at home, and when drawn forth by a fine Sunday
or holiday, the chairing of a member, or some *Mousehold* hoax,
people wondered where they all came from.' [2]   This busy
silence was a marked characteristic of Norwich.

It is impossible to trace the fortunes of the Norwich weavers
in all their vicissitudes. We hear little, for example, of the
introduction of the flying shuttle. In Essex it was said to
have been introduced about 1750, and Arthur Young mentions
it as in use for Colchester baize in 1784.[3] In Yorkshire, on
the other hand, the fly shuttle was very little used by worsted
weavers till after 1800, when the invention of the false reed or
slay, added to an improvement in the quality of mill-spun yarn
which was no longer so liable to break, overcame the prejudices against it.[4] The use of the fly shuttle in Yorkshire clearly
increased the earnings of worsted weavers. ' The Spring
Shuttle was the Weavers' Invention,' said a witness in 1803,
and he explained that as the prices had not been lowered the
weavers received all the advantage. A witness in 1838 stated
that whereas before 1800 he had made about 5s. a week, after
that time he earned from 12s. 9d. to 17s.[5]

It is sometimes asserted that the worsted trade was originally
introduced into Yorkshire from the south because wages were
lower in the north and the weavers could live on oatmeal.[6]
But as James points out,[7] by the time Arthur Young took his six
months' tour through the North of England in 1768, wages
in Leeds were higher than those in Norwich, and Eden in 1796
even suggests that the low wages in Norwich are one of the
causes of the decline of the trade.[8] But though the wages
were low, it was only by organisation that the weavers
prevented them from falling lower. Their general policy in
the Norwich district was to refuse reductions of prices even

[1] James, *op. cit.*, p. 261.   [2] James, *op. cit.*, p. 262.
[3] *Annals of Agriculture*, ii. p. 108, and xv. p. 261.
[4] James, *op. cit.*, p. 356.
[5] See Report of Committee on Yorkshire Woollen Petitions, 1802-3
(Nathaniel Murgatroyd) ; and James, *op. cit.*, p. 480.
[6] James, *op. cit.*, p. 586. James, however, on p. 200 doubts it.
[7] James, *op. cit.*, p. 291.
[8] Eden, *State of the Poor*, 1797, vol. ii. p. 478.

when work was slack, preferring no work to work at reduced rates. During the French war the scale of pay was raised and this scale was maintained till 1829.[1] One of the Norwich masters, before the Commission on Hand-loom Weavers in 1840, lamented this policy as handicapping the Norwich trade. It would be better, he suggested, if the masters were free to reduce wages in slack times rather than be forced to keep up the rates and so turn workmen off when trade was bad.[2] The example of the cotton trade, it might be remarked, was not an argument in favour of this change of policy.

Of the position held by the weavers in Norwich one illustration will suffice. In 1822 the manufacturers agreed on and announced a reduction of wages. The weavers at once took concerted action and asked for a deputation to be received by the manufacturers at the Guildhall. It was agreed to receive a deputation of twelve, and whilst these twelve were conferring with the masters, the crowd behaved in a very violent manner, attacking an unpopular master, and beating and kicking him. The military were called in, but all disturbances were ended by a declaration from the Guildhall balcony that the masters had consented to the old prices, a declaration received with ' thundering shouts of joy and exultation.' The masters had not been an unanimous body, for the men's hero, Mr. Arthur Beloe, himself a manufacturer who had lately established a factory, was strongly against the reduction and ridiculed the fear of competition with Yorkshire. ' I do not feel afraid of competing with the Yorkshireman, though he may be paying a penny or two per dozen less than we are.'[3]

Individual workmen or bodies of workmen were no doubt prevented from accepting work at lower rates by the knowledge that their fellow workmen were strong enough to show their sharp displeasure. Wymondham came to attack Ashwellthorpe in 1827 because Ashwellthorpe was taking work at reduced rates.[4] In protesting against new machinery they were not less violent, and the power-loom was not introduced into Norwich till after our period. How little the system of ' shop looms ' had been introduced into Norwich is shown by the remarkable figures in the Hand-loom Weavers' Commission

[1] Reports from Assistant Hand-loom Weavers' Commissioners, 1840, part ii. p. 311.
[2] Report from Hand-loom Weavers' Commissioners, 1841, p. 35.
[3] See *Annual Register*, 1822; *Chronicle*, pp. 122-4; and H.O., 52. 3, July 23.　　　　　　　　　　　　　　　　　　[4] H.O., 40. 22.

Report of 1840.   Out of the 4054 looms at work in Norwich, 3398 were in the weavers' own homes, and of these, 2890 were in houses where there were either one or two looms only.[1]

James, after commenting on the lack of enterprise shown by the Norwich manufacturers in the introduction of machinery, adds : ' Again, there existed a strong party spirit in the city, and neither party durst introduce machinery in dread of offending the bulk of the citizens, who with a short sightedness which has been extremely injurious to their interest, were violently opposed to the use of spinning and weaving machines, and as before seen, this opposition sometimes occasioned dangerous riots in the city. . . . In truth for any one at this period to attempt to set up machinery in Norwich, was to venture his life.' [2]

It must not be supposed that the introduction of power-looms into the West Riding was an easy matter.   There also the weavers fought against this menace to their livelihood. The earliest power-loom for worsteds was sent secretly by a manufacturer in 1822 from Bradford to Shipley, where he hoped that it might be worked without attracting notice. But no sooner had it arrived and begun to work, than the bell-man was sent round to the neighbouring villages, whence the weavers issued in force, surrounded the mill, destroyed the loom, and carried its remains round in triumph.[3]   Their triumph only lasted two years, for in 1824 Messrs. Horsfall and other firms established power-looms in Bradford and elsewhere.   In 1826, when the fury against power-looms spread from the starving cotton weavers in Lancashire to the starving worsted weavers of Bradford, Horsfall's mill with its power-looms was the object of a bitter attack.   This attack followed a meeting at Fairweather Green on May 3, called by some woolcombers and stuff weavers.   The terms of the notice are curious :

' At the suggestion of some of our employers, we, the Wool-combers and Stuff-weavers of Bradford and its vicinity, hereby convene a meeting . . . to take into consideration the present unparalleled distress and famishing state of the operatives, and if possible, to devise some prompt and effectual means to afford them relief.

' A numerous attendance is particularly requested.' [4]

[1] Report from Assistant Hand-loom Weavers' Commissioners, 1840, part ii. p. 309.   [2] James, *op. cit.*, p. 437.
[3] James, *op. cit.*, p. 414.   [4] *Annual Register*, 1826 ; *Chronicle*, p. 72.

There were no speakers or leaders at the meeting, and the mob marched to attack Messrs. Horsfall's mill. The mill was garrisoned by ten of Horsfall's men and thirty soldiers, ten of them dragoons and the other twenty members of the recruiting staff at Leeds. The mob attacked the windows with stones and tried to force an entrance, but failed to do so, owing to the iron bars fixed in front. The garrison, however, thought that they were making their way in and fired, killing a youth of eighteen and a boy of thirteen. A magistrate came up afterwards and read the Riot Act, and finally two troops of the Yorkshire Hussars were called in to restore order. Two rioters were afterwards tried at the York Assizes. One was acquitted, the other, John Holdsworth, who had demanded of the magistrate, Colonel Temple, ' What are we to do ? Are we to starve ? ' was found guilty but his life was spared.[1]

The coming of the power-loom meant that the hand-loom weaver must starve or seek other work ; year after year more work was done by power, less by hand, till in 1838 the 14,000 hand-loom worsted weavers left in the Bradford district were making on an average only 6s. or 7s. a week. [2]

VI.—THE WOOLCOMBERS

The woolcombers may be called the aristocracy of the worsted workers. An ancient, skilled, select, and well-organised body whose insubordinate conduct gave much trouble to their employers, they form an example of a trade that was long able by combination to keep up its wages, but was ultimately destroyed by the coming of machinery. Before worsted can be spun the fibres of the wool must be laid in a parallel direction, and this work used to be performed by the woolcombers, whose stock in trade was two hand-combs with two or three rows of teeth apiece, a stove at which to heat the combs, and a post on which to fix one of them. The work was hard and skilled, the atmosphere in which it was done was generally vitiated by the fumes of the stove. The woolcombers themselves have been described as ' a well-informed class . . . memorable for strikes and general improvidence, and strongly impregnated with political doctrines of the democratic school.' [3]

---

[1] For an account of the attack see *Annual Register*, 1826 ; *Chronicle*, pp. 72 f., and Appendix to *Chronicle*, pp. 31 f. ; James, *op. cit.*, p. 599 ; also *Leeds Mercury*, July 15, 1826.

[2] James, *op. cit.*, p. 482.   [3] James, *op. cit.*, p. 559.

It was the action of the woolcombers, this formidable class
of workmen, and the worsted weavers that led the Norwich
masters and merchants to take measures to obtain the Act
of Parliament in 1726 ' to prevent unlawful Combinations of
workmen employed in Woollen Manufactures, and for better
Payment of their Wages.' [1]   But the laws had little effect on
their actions, and in a notable strike at Norwich in August
1752 they quarrelled with their masters on the subject of the
employment of one Trye, whom they declared to be not only
a ' colt ' [2] but a thief.   They left work until he was discharged
and sent agents to different parts of the kingdom to prevent
other woolcombers from taking their places.   They themselves
' retired from the city to a heath about three miles off called
Rackheath, where they erected booths, and about three
hundred of them being supported by purse clubs lived without
any irregularities.'   After several weeks of camping out they
won their point and returned to work.[3]

With the growth of the worsted industry in the West Riding
the number of woolcombers increased, and like their fellows
in Norwich, some of whom had no doubt come up to Yorkshire, they proved themselves in their employers' eyes ' a
turbulent, ill-ordered class,' organised in clubs with strict
rules for all who followed their craft.[4]

The first blow at their independence was struck when Cartwright, the inventor of the power-loom, devised a machine for
combing wool.   His first two patents were taken out in 1790,
his third in 1792.   His machine, which was called ' Big Ben '
after a prize-fighter of the day, caused great consternation
amongst the combers, a consternation that was premature,
for the invention, ingenious though it was, required, like the
power-loom, improvements from many other minds before it
superseded hand labour.   Employers however, here and there,
began to set up ' Big Bens,' and the worsted manufacturers
in the south-west seem to have set the example.   Some other
new inventions for woolcombing were patented just after
Cartwright's, including one by William Toplis of Cuckney,
Nottingham.   In April 1793 a meeting of woolcombers was held
at Bradninch, near Cullompton, to take into consideration this
new and serious evil that threatened annihilation to the woolcombers, 70,000 of whom, they declared, would be reduced to

---

[1] 12 Geo. I. c. 34.
[2] A ' colt ' was a man who had not served a regular apprenticeship.
[3] James, *op. cit.*, pp. 262 f.   [4] *Ibid.*, p. 322.

poverty. It was resolved that land holders and others be requested to petition Parliament for the abolition of this machinery.[1]

In the early months of 1794 the woolcombers marshalled their forces to oppose the introduction of machinery. Petitions poured into Parliament against the new machinery from Barnstaple, from New Sarum and Exeter, from Somerset, from Plymouth, from Tiverton, from Devonshire, from London, from Honiton, from Wilton, from Ashburton, from Tavistock, from Southwark, from Kidderminster and Bromsgrove, from Coventry and Atherstone, from Cornwall, from Warwick, from the North Riding of Yorkshire, from the County and City of Durham, from Ripon, and from Leicester.[2]

The Barnstable petitioners [3]

'beg leave to state to the House that by the Invention and Practice of a Machine for the combing of Wool which diminishes Labour to an alarming Degree, the Petitioners entertain serious and just fears that themselves and Families will speedily become a useless and heavy Burthen to the State ; That it appears to the Petitioners that One Machine only, with the assistance of One Person and Four or Five Children, will perform as much Labour as Thirty Men in the customary Manual Manner. . . . That the Machines, of which the Petitioners complain, are rapidly multiplying throughout the Kingdom, the pernicious Effects of which have already been sensibly felt by the Petitioners, numbers of whom thereby are in want of Occupation and Food ; and that it is with the most heartfelt sorrow and anguish the Petitioners anticipate that fast approaching period of Consummate Wretchedness and Poverty, when Fifty Thousand of the Petitioners, together with their distressed families, by a lucrative Monopoly of the Means of earning their Bread, will be inevitably compelled to seek Relief from their several Parishes.'

Several of the petitions draw attention to the difference between the introduction of machinery into trades capable of expansion and into the woollen trade where the raw material is limited ; for example the Leicester woolcombers state : [4]

'. . . In other departments of Trade, wherein Machines have conduced to the Extension of the Wealth and Commerce of the Nation, the Raw Material has been capable of indefinite Increase, whereas the Growth of Wool is definite, and never equals the

[1] H.O., 42. 25.
[2] *House of Commons Journal*, 1794, January, February, and March.
[3] *Ibid.*, 1794, January 24.
[4] *Ibid.*, 1794, March 31.

Ability of the Woolcombers to manufacture, and therefore any sudden and unexplored Diminution of the Quantity of Manual Labour will reduce the Petitioners to a state of the most wretched Poverty, and be attended with the most calamitous Consequences to their Wives, Children and numerous Apprentices.'

In contrast to these appeals from men alarmed lest their property in a skilled and well-paid trade should be taken from them, it is interesting to read the petition of William Toplis, the worsted manufacturer of Cuckney in Nottingham, with its complaints of the clubs or societies of the woolcombers and its fears of foreign competition.[1] He states :

'That, for several Years past, the Petitioner has employed from 100 to 150 Woolcombers in combing Wool, which he has spun into Worsted Yarn by Machinery, and that, experiencing great Inconveniences from the Inadequate Number of Woolcombers for the Purposes of Trade, when the same is extensive and flourishing, and from their irregular and improper Conduct in forming themselves into Societies and Combinations, the Petitioner, after great Labour and Study, invented a Machine for combing wool, to be worked by Water, and for the Exclusive Use and Exercise of which the Petitioner on the 8th day of June 1793, obtained His Majesty's Letters Patent for a Term of Fourteen Years, and by the Machines invented by the Petitioner Wool can be combed as well as by Hand, and with a great Saving of Manual Labour and Expence, whereby the Worsted Yarn, and the Goods manufactured from it are produced both better in Quality and cheaper: That in the Year 1792, when the Worsted Manufactory was carried on to a greater Extent than at present, the Wool-combers in some Parts of the Kingdom were found insufficient to comb the Wool wanted, and they are formed into Clubs or Societies in different Parts, and governed by Laws or Rules of their own, by which they are restrained from taking Apprentices (except their Eldest Sons) or extending their Number by instruct-ing the Apprentices or Servants of their Employers; that many of them are single Men, and lead Itinerant Lives, travelling from One Part of the Kingdom to another, and seldom work half their Time ; that the Woolcombers employed by the Petitioner can, upon an Average, earn from Twenty-five to Twenty-eight Shillings *per* Week, when they chuse to work every Day, whereas the Average Wages paid to them seldom exceed Ten Shillings *per* Week, and this Difference arises solely from their refusing to do more Work, and not from its being withheld from them: That by Means of the Societies or Clubs formed by the Woolcombers in all the Manufacturing Parts of the Country, the Manufacturers are entirely at the Mercy of their Combers, and must pay them what-

[1] *House of Commons Journal*, 1794, March 31.

ever Wages they demand, particularly when Trade is in a flourishing State, insomuch that if a Manufacturer displeases one Woolcomber all the others either quit his Service entirely, or until he
appeases the offended Member, and no other Woolcomber will
work for him so long as he continues under the Displeasure of any
of the Members of their Society : That there are various Societies
independent of, and who refuse to mix or work with each other,
so that a *Yorkshire* or *Lancashire* Woolcomber could not obtain
Employment amongst the Midland Woolcombers, whose Chief
Society or Club is held in *Leicestershire*; and that the Use of
Machines for combing Wool will reduce the Quantity of Manual
Labour consumed in the Fabrication of Worsted Goods, and consequently enable the Manufacturer to bring them to Market at a
lower Price, and to undersell the Manufacturers of other Countries,
and the Petitioner submits to the House, that the Principle upon
which the Woolcombers oppose the Use of Machines in combing
Wool would equally apply to restrain or prohibit every other
Species of Manufacturing Machinery, as the Object of all such
Machinery is the reduction of Manual Labour, and without it
the Manufacturers of *Great Britain* could not support a successful
Competition with those of other Countries, and the Objection
made by the Woolcombers to the Use of combing Machines would
equally apply to all the Machinery used in the preparing and
spinning of Cotton, Worsted, and Woollen Yarn, and Silk, and in
weaving, printing, and dressing, many of the most valuable
Manufactures in this Country ; and that, in addition to these
Considerations, the House will recollect that all the Inventions
and Improvements in the Manufactures of *Great Britain* are
adopted and imitated in other Countries, and, if the House should
in any Degree restrain the Use of Manufacturing Machinery, it
would enable Foreigners by the Use of them to undersell the
British Manufacturers: And therefore praying, That in Case the
House shall proceed to take the Petitions of the Woolcombers
into Consideration, it will, at the same Time, also take the
Petitioner's Case into Consideration, and that (if Occasion should
require) the Petitioner may be heard, by himself, or by his Counsel,
at the Bar of the House, and may be permitted to adduce Evidence in support of the Allegations contained in this Petition.'

In spite of Mr. Toplis the woolcombers were strong enough
to get a Bill introduced into Parliament in 1794 to protect
them 'from being injured in their manufacture by the use
of certain machines.' [1] Woolcombers from all districts joined
to defray the expenses, which were very heavy. The Yorkshire Worsted Committee was active on the other side, and
a petition against the Bill was presented by the worsted
manufacturers of Yorkshire, Lancashire, and Cheshire. The

---

[1] *House of Commons Journal*, 1794, April 8.

Bill was defeated on its second reading on May 9 by 67 votes to 24.[1] Next year (1795) the woolcombers were given a certain relief by an Act which relaxed 5 Eliz. c. 4 in their favour, allowing them to exercise any 'Trade or Business which they are apt and able for, in any Town or Place within this Kingdom.' [2]

In the west of England the woolcombers were said to turn their thoughts to the destruction of machinery, darkly hinting that these machines should share the fate of the Albion mills.[3] 'The Miners,' we read,[4] ' who work on Mendip in Somerset-shire have already offered their services to destroy the Machine that is at Twarton near Bath.' These friendly services, how-ever, do not seem to have been accepted ; perhaps the combers were beginning to realise the fact that the superiority of their work would protect them against the machines already in-troduced. For may years indeed the woolcombers main-tained their aristocratic position amongst the working classes, a position described by Lieut.-General Simcoe in his re-ports to the Home Office on the food riots in the Exeter and Tiverton district in 1801 [5]—' they both were certainly directed by inferior Tradesmen, Wool-combers and Dis-senters, who keep aloof, but by their language and immediate influence, govern the lower classes. . . . The numerous association of Wool-combers (who as they boast consist of sixty thousand persons in different parts of the Kingdom) being for the most part Dissenters are the just objects of attention to Government, and to those who support the constitution of Great Britain against Republican machina-tions.'

So well organised were the woolcombers that they seem to have been no more troubled by the Combination Act than by the previous Act to put down combination in their own trade. In 1812 a document was sent up to the Home Office,[6] respecting a Congress of Woolcombers to be held in August in Coventry, at which it was hoped that divisions in the ranks would be closed up, by the adoption of some forty-four articles. It is interesting to note that one of the

---

[1] *House of Commons Journal*, 1794, May 9.

[2] 35 Geo. III. c. 124. An exception was made in the case of Oxford and Cambridge, where they were not to set up as vintners or sell wine or liquors without the leave of the Vice-Chancellors.

[3] The Albion mills in Southwark were burnt down in 1791.

[4] H.O., 42. 30, May 18.   [5] H.O., 42. 61, March 27.

[6] H.O., 42. 130, December 12.

articles pledged the Union to help any master in a remote district to procure a regular supply of labour. The Law Officers when appealed to on the question of prosecuting the woolcombers were not encouraging: ' These combinations are mischievous and dangerous, but it is very difficult to know how to deal with them.' [1]

Luck turned against the woolcombers in 1825. The year began with rejoicings and ended in calamity. Every seven years it was the custom to hold woolcombers' celebrations, called Bishop Blaize Festivals in honour of their patron saint, whose flesh had been torn from him by iron combs in the second century A.D. In 1825 the festival in Bradford (Yorks), now the recognised centre of the worsted industry,[2] was of a specially imposing character. Jason, Medea, the King, the Queen, and Bishop Blaize, with their numerous retinue, went in solemn procession through the streets, and the whole town gave itself up to celebrating its prosperity. A few months later began a deadly struggle between the woolcombers and weavers on one side and their employers on the other. The woolcombers not only wanted certain anomalies in payment abolished, but demanded a share in the increased prosperity of trade in the shape of higher wages. In the previous autumn they had persuaded the weavers to join with them in a Union, an interesting instance of combination between workers receiving different rates of pay. Estimates of combers' earnings varied very much. Tester, the secretary of the Union, put them at 14s. to 16s. a week for working from 4 A.M. to 10 P.M. In reply to this it was alleged that comb shops opened at 5 A.M. and shut at 8 P.M., and that Tester himself had earned about 23s. a week.[3] No doubt the payment for different kinds of work varied very much and this was one of the grievances. The weavers admittedly made only 10s. to 12s. The weavers like the combers demanded an increase in pay.

A conference between masters and men early in June was fruitless. The men then struck against three firms in Bradford. Next day, June 8, fifty masters met and pledged them-

[1] H.O., 42. 130, December 21.

[2] It was calculated that in and round Bradford within a radius of six miles there were seven or eight thousand hand-combers and twenty-one or twenty-four thousand weavers (James, *op. cit.*, p. 401).

[3] Burnley, *History of Wool and Woolcombing*, p. 172. James instances one man who was making 30s. a week for ten hours a day (*op. cit.*, p. 402).

selves not to employ any comber or weaver belonging to
the Union. The masters further dismissed children employed
in their mills whose parents were in the Union or refused
to repudiate it.[1] For twenty-two weeks the struggle went
on ; it was estimated that quite twenty thousand workers
were unemployed.

The strikers all this time were being supported by contributions from outside. The repeal of the Combination Act
had of course made this possible. From all over the country
money was subscribed. The masters did their best to cut off
supplies by inducing the employers in other worsted towns
to dismiss their Union combers and weavers. The Halifax
worsted weavers declared that they would not submit to such
'unprincipled oppression' from their masters ; 'they were
resolved not to be their absolute slaves, or to suffer themselves,
their wives and children, to remain in the abject and degraded
condition of irrational animals, but to enjoy that share of
happiness and mental improvement designed for them by that
gracious Providence which had placed them here as proba-
tioners for another and a better world.'[2] The committees
for raising subscriptions in other towns redoubled their efforts ;
thus the Committee of Trades in Newcastle urged 'every
Mechanic, Artisan and others interested in the common Weal,'
to help their fellow workmen at Bradford. 'We view with
the utmost Degree of Contempt,' so ran their manifesto,[3]
'the unmanly conduct of the Master Worsted Manufacturers
of Bradford, Keighley, Halifax and Darlington, in expelling
the Workmen from their employ who belonged to or supported any Union, which had for its Object the Protection
of Wages.

'That as a Combination exists amongst the Employers
of almost every Branch of Business, for the Purpose of regulating the Wages of the labouring Classes agreeable to their
own Wishes, we, therefore, recommend GOOD FELLOWSHIP
amongst every Class of Workmen, as the only safe guard
to protect our undoubted and natural Rights.'

Good fellowship all over the country responded through
the strike to the extent of subscribing some £20,000,[4] a tan-
gible proof of the outburst of enthusiasm and hope amongst
the working classes in 1825. But even £20,000 does not

[1] Burnley, *History of Wool and Woolcombing*, p. 167.
[2] Burnley, *op. cit.*, p. 172.   [3] H.O., 40. 18, October 29.
[4] James, *op. cit.*, p. 406.

go far when many thousands of workers are without wages week after week. The Union funds were further drained by the necessity of supporting the woolcombers from the neighbourhood who had been locked out for belonging to the Union. As the strike went on the conditions of trade altered; depression succeeded activity ; the masters were less eager to begin work again and demanded unconditional surrender. Finally, early in November, the men crept back to work as best they could, on the masters' terms, but when all the hands needed by the masters were supplied there were 1700 left without work.

In spite of the sufferings during the strike there had been no violence or outrage of any kind.

The dogged resistance of the woolcombers turned the masters' thoughts towards machinery. Although ' for the first forty years of this century the hand-comber held the position of being able to produce better combings than any machine that had been invented,' [1] yet he never recovered his position, and by 1882 his condition was so miserable that it was considered a mockery to hold the Bishop Blaize celebrations. Another strike, that same year, at the Dolphin Holme Mill near Lancaster, ended in disaster.[2] The combers lingered for many years competing with machinery, and as the machines improved their wages decreased. Their extinction it is said was practically accomplished by the display of woolcombing machinery at the Great Exhibition of 1851.[3] The lament of a dying industry is contained in the address to the Bradford Masters in 1840 : [4] ' Our homes, which were not many years ago the abodes of comfort and domestic enjoyment have now in consequence of the frequent reductions in our wages and other alterations in the sorts, become the dwelling places of misery and receptacles of wretchedness. . . . We are compelled to work from fourteen to sixteen hours per day, and with all this sweat and toil we are not able to procure sufficient of the necessaries of life wherewith to subsist on. When we leave off work at night our sensorial power is worn out with fatigue ; we have no energy left to exert in any useful object or domestic duty ; we are only fit for sleep or sensual indulgence, the only alternations our leisure knows ; we have no moral elasticity to enable us to resist the seductions of appetite or sloth ; no heart for

[1] Burnley, *op. cit.*, p. 144.   [2] James, *op. cit.*, p. 435.
[3] Burnley, *op. cit.*, p. 185.   [4] Burnley, *op. cit.*, pp. 176 f.

regulating our households, superintending our family concerns, or enforcing economy in our domestic arrangements ; no power or capability to rise above our circumstances or better our condition ; we have no time to be wise, no leisure to be good : we are sunken, debilitated, depressed, emasculated, unnerved for effort ; incapable of virtue, unfit for anything which is calculated to be of any benefit to us at present or any future period.'

CHAPTER VII

THE SPITALFIELDS SILKWEAVERS

THE silk industry in England, unlike the other textile industries, was an ' exotic trade.' [1] It was strictly protected, and although there was a good deal of smuggling of foreign silks [2] the main bulk of the silks used in England were of home manufacture. The chief centre of the industry in the middle of the eighteenth century was Spitalfields, and the Spitalfields silk weavers alone amongst textile workers obtained an Act for regulating their wages. Before the Spitalfields Act, as it was called, was passed in 1773, Spitalfields was the scene of constant rioting and confusion. The passing of the Act brought peace and there were no more damaged looms or spoilt pieces of silk. The journeymen weavers were bold, determined, and strongly organised. [3] In 1763, their masters petitioned the Government for military aid, stating that the men wished ' to increase the Prices of their Labour, according to certain sums inserted in a Book, which they have caused to be printed and delivered to each Master.' [4] The increase was refused and the weavers took to violence ; ' masked and disguised in Sailors Habits and otherwise, and armed with Cutlasses and other Dangerous Weapons,' they proceeded to cut and destroy the silk in looms, and the looms themselves, to illtreat the journeymen who refused to join them, and to parade the streets with the effigy of an unpopular master in a cart, ' with a halter about his neck, an executioner on one side, and a coffin on the other.' The effigy was solemnly hung and burnt before they dispersed. [5] A detachment of

[1] See Cunningham, *Growth of English Industry and Commerce*, ii. p. 636.

[2] So strong was the fashionable prejudice in favour of foreign articles that English manufacturers would even send their goods down to the coast to be sold as French smuggled products (see *Annual Register*, 1824, p. 77).

[3] In 1769, the Committee of Silk Weavers were corresponding with the journeymen silk weavers in Dublin. The latter reported the hearts of their masters to be ' like adamant' (H.O. Dom. E.B., 142).

[4] H.O. Dom. E.B., 194.   [5] *Annual Register*, 1763, p. 105.

guards was sent to Spitalfields and overawed the weavers for the time.

In 1765 the journeymen weavers gave another exhibition of their strength ; ' conceiving themselves greatly injured by the too free use of French and other wrought silks,' they induced Parliament to pass a Bill totally prohibiting their import.[1] The weavers with their wives and children assembled in their thousands in Spitalfields and Moorfields,[2] accompanied by drums and ' arrayed under such colours as might not only contribute to keep them together, but remind themselves and acquaint the public with the supposed causes of that distress, which their pallid looks and emaciated carcases made sufficiently evident,' and they marched to St. James and Westminster Hall, which they surrounded. ' They even stopt several of the members in their chairs and coaches ; and though it was only to beseech them in the humblest terms to pity their wretched condition, so unusual a step, considering the reports spread of the weavers of the inland towns and their dependents in trade coming up to join their distressed brethren in London, could not fail of creating the most alarming apprehensions for the public tranquillity. For had this once happened, or had these afflicted members, instead of seeking redress from the head, taken upon them to redress themselves, there is no telling how far the flame might have spread, or what ravages it might have made before it could be extinguished. But, providentially, their rage, which was prevented from breaking out into greater outrages by a mild yet steady exertion of the civil power, assisted by the military ' spent itself in besetting the house of a nobleman, suspected of favouring French silks, and in breaking a few windows, and was appeased by a subscription for their relief, a promise from the silk mercers to countermand their orders for foreign goods, and finally by the passing of the Protective Act.

In 1769 serious riots broke out in August and lasted till October.[3] The handkerchief weavers were the leaders in this outbreak, and they instituted a subscription of 6d. or 4d. a loom. In cases where the rate of payment was unsatisfactory, or where the masters would not allow their men to pay the subscription, the work in the looms was cut. The master weavers published a notice announcing ' that

---

[1] 5 Geo. III. c. 48.   [2] *Annual Register*, 1765, p. 41.
[3] For papers quoted see S.P. Dom., Geo. III. vol. vii.

we will support the journeymen in all their just rights, and will pay them their full prices, it being our unanimous determination to give an equal attention to their interest as to our own,' and Sir John Fielding, the blind magistrate, Henry Fielding's half-brother, issued notices of rewards for the apprehension of fourteen miscreants,[1] but neither notice produced any result.

Sir John Fielding played a prominent part in the attempt to check these disturbances. On September 28 he urged the Government to send two companies of the Guards with some 'sensible discreet officers,' to be quartered in public houses. Nothing but vigorous action 'can check the present Outrages,' and, he added, 'nothing can prevent them for the future but an Act of Parliament, giving a clearer Authority to the Magistrates to settle the Wages between these Manufacturers and their Journeymen.' He had himself attempted to set the Elizabethan Act in motion ; masters and men had agreed on prices and had on his advice petitioned ' the Session at Hicks Hall to establish the Prices so mutually agreed to by Law, but the Magistrates then differing in Opinion relative to the Act of Parliament this matter was unfortunately defeated.' Soldiers were sent to Spitalfields. One of the masters had handed to the Magistrates a paper he had received which ran as follows : ' Mr. Hill, You are desired to send the full Donation of all your Loombs to the Dolphin in Cock Lane. This from the Conquering and bold Defiance to be levied 4d.[2] per Loomb.' Instead of Mr. Hill's donation a party of soldiers was sent to the Dolphin Ale House, where the men's committee were sitting, with the result that in the affray that ensued, one soldier and two weavers or ' cutters ' as they were called, were killed and four weavers were taken prisoners. This was not the last affray between the soldiers and the cutters that year, for on October 7, five of the latter were killed and many wounded,[3] but soon after this the disturbances stopped.

---

[1] It is noticeable that with the exception of Gossett all the fourteen names are English. The descriptions are minute and vivid, *e.g.* 'John Smith, a very short man, much pitted with the small pox, remarkable bow legs, did live in Artillery-lane, Spitalfields, now supposed to lurk about the Borough': or 'Joseph Coleman abt. 5 ft. 8 ins. high, rather thin, remarkable carbuncles in his face, well-made, has a strong Irish accent, & goes by the name of Jolly Dog.

[2] It is not clear in the original whether this is 4d. or 4s., but as the subscription mentioned in the *Annual Register*, 1769, p. 126 is 6d., 4d. is the more probable reading.

[3] *Annual Register*, 1769, p. 138.

The use of troops in this dispute between masters and men received a good deal of criticism from a party headed by the sheriffs Messrs. Townsend and Sawbridge. 'They mean,' suggested Sir John Fielding, 'to make the Publick believe, that the Master Weavers, under the Protection of the Troops, are oppressing the Poor Workmen.' The sheriffs had a further dispute with the higher authorities.[1] On October 21 two of the 'cutters' John Doyle and John Valline, were sentenced to death at the Old Bailey. For the sake of example the Government decided to execute them near the scene of the disturbances. To this the sheriffs took exception. The sentence, they said, had ordered the prisoners to be taken to 'the usual place of execution,' and the neighbourhood of Bethnal Green Church was not the usual place. Their business was merely to carry out the sentence of the court, and they were not justified in any deviation from it. The King, they urged, had the prerogative of mercy, but could not add to the rigour of the sentence. 'Now, my lord, it will not be said, that the present alteration is, or is intended as, a mitigation of the judgment pronounced. To force, in a manner, the wives and children of the unhappy sufferers to be spectators of the infamous death of their husbands and fathers, by executing them as near as conveniently may be to their own houses, cannot be intended, nor will it be esteemed, a matter of royal grace ; nor is it granted at the prayer of the parties or their friends. . . .' The point at issue was finally submitted to twelve judges, who decided against the sheriffs, and the sheriffs then carried out the sentence in Bethnal Green unaided by the military. The *Annual Register* gives the whole correspondence with comments. 'Thus ended this affair ; from the proceedings in which, this writer thinks it is evident, that there is a settled plan, a wicked conspiracy, to expose and set aside the civil power of this country.'

Three more 'cutters' were executed at Tyburn in December, and various sentences of imprisonment were imposed on rioters, including a sentence of one year on a weaver who shot a woman through the hand 'for refusing to deliver up her husband, in order that he might be placed on a jack-ass for a misdemeanour.'[2]

For the next few years Spitalfields was comparatively quiet. Prices were fixed between masters and men, but there was

[1] See *Annual Register*, 1769, pp. 181-7.
[2] *Annual Register*, 1769, p. 162.

nothing to force the masters to adhere to them, and in 1773 discontent was again rife. This time it took a more orderly form. The authorities it is true were much alarmed in April by certain handbills distributed in the East End of London, addressed not only to the weavers, but to the coal heavers, to the watermen, porters and carmen, urging them to ' Rise up as one Man, and wait humbly upon the King at St. James every Day, that His Majesty may see our Misery ; he will then be convinced of our Distress, and his Royal Heart will bleed to behold us.' [1] The weavers met for this purpose at Moorfields on April 26. ' Suffer yourselves no longer,' ran the handbill that summoned them, ' to be prevented by a set of Miscreants, whose way to Riches and Power lays through your Families, by every attempt to Starve and enslave you, in a Land where Freedom and Plenty is the native Product ; exert yourselves like Britons, nor let the latent spark be quench'd that glows in every manly Breast.' [2] They were persuaded however to change their plans and to confer with the magistrates rather than petition the King. To the magistrates accordingly they submitted proposals regarding apprenticeship, and asked ' That some means may be devis'd to compel the Masters to abide by the prices of their work, as settled between them and the Journeymen by certain printed Articles, to which the Masters exact a punctual obedience in the workman ; but have themselves broke through in many respects particularly in sending work to be done in the Country at under prices by men sent down by themselves for that purpose.' [3] The weavers had a friend not only in Sir John Fielding but in the Lord Mayor (James Townsend, one of the sheriffs of 1769), who sent the City Marshal down to inquire into the weavers' grievances.[4] The result of the discussions was the famous Spitalfields Act (13 Geo. III. c. 68), which received the royal assent at the beginning of July.

By this Act the wages for silk weavers were to be fixed in London by the Lord Mayor, Recorder and aldermen, in Middlesex and Westminster by the magistrates, and masters who paid higher or lower wages than those fixed were liable to a fine of £50. In 1792 by 32 Geo. III. c. 44, the provisions of the Act were extended to manufactures of silk mixed with other materials, and in 1811 by 51 Geo. III. c. 7, the Act was extended to include journeywomen.

[1] Dom. Geo. III., vol. x. [2] Ibid.
[3] Ibid. [4] Ibid.

Sir John Fielding's letter to Lord Suffolk describing the first working of the Act is interesting.[1] It is dated July 9, 1773, ' . . . he had the Pleasure Yesterday of assisting at the General Quarter Sessions for the County of Middlesex, to carry into Execution the late act of parliament for the regulating the Wages of Journeymen Weavers in Spitalfields, &c., and the Wages were then settled by a Numerous and unanimous Bench to the entire satisfaction of those Masters and Journeymen Weavers who appeared there in behalf of their respective bodies, and I sincerely hope that this step will prove a radical cure for all tumultuous Assemblies from that Quarter so disrespectful to the King and so disagreeable to Government, as it will amply reward your Lordship's Judicious attention to a Matter so conducive to Peace and good Order, for by this Statute your Lordship has conveyed contentment to the minds of thousands of his Majesty's Subjects.'

What was the effect of the Spitalfields Act, which remained in force for over fifty years ? It was a commonplace amongst opponents of regulation in other trades that the effects of the Act were bad,[2] and lurid pictures were drawn of the disastrous state of Spitalfields. ' In consequence of this [Act],' wrote a correspondent to the *Annals of Agriculture* in 1788,[3] ' some principal employers removed with some of the most respectable families, into distant countries and into Scotland, where they have the work done cheaper. Hence, the trade of Spitalfields is, in a great measure, ruined ; many of the houses going to rack as may be plainly seen. Abundance of people are out of employment, being deterred by their associates from working lower than the rates fixed :—they have no alternative but to rob or starve ! although they might otherwise have work enough, and the trade would again revive.' And yet the persons mainly affected and presumably ruined by the Act clung to it with a passionate attachment.[4] Fowell Buxton in 1819 summed up the position : ' An honourable friend of his had said, that bad consequences had resulted from the Spitalfields Act. He could only say, that the people of Spitalfields were ignorant of such evil consequences.' [5]

---

[1] Dom. Geo. III., vol. x.

[2] Cf. Hume in Debate on Frame-work Knitters' Bill, Hansard, July 21, 1812.

[3] Vol. x. p. 453.

[4] See Evidence before 1818 Committee on Ribbon Weavers' Petitions, and the striking declaration in favour of the Act by eighty-eight employers, pp. 196-8.

[5] Hansard, May 13, 1819.

The truth seems to be that though some trade left London [1] —in 1818 it was said that the crape, gauze, bandana and bombazine trades had all gone into the country—a large proportion remained,[2] and masters and men alike preferred a limited business done under the conditions imposed by the Act, to a large business in which masters devoted their energies to undercutting each other, and men, as at Coventry,[3] brought tickets from their masters to the parish officers in order that they might have their wages made up to the lowest figure at which human life could be sustained. The state of Coventry, where the work was largely done by half pay apprentices, mostly girls, who were partly supported by the rates, was indeed an object lesson to those who believed that Spitalfields would benefit by the repeal of the Act. Nor can the migration of silk manfacture from Spitalfields to the eastern counties be attributed solely to the Spitalfields Act. The worsted manufacture was moving from Essex, Norfolk, and Suffolk up to Yorkshire, and silk weaving was introduced to replace it.[4]

Opponents of the Act laid great stress on the hardships inflicted on weavers during the depressions of trade—' the law saying, " You shall rather starve than take less than your full wages," is a barbarous infringement of a man's plainest right ' — nor could the demoralising effects of the inequality in treatment be ignored, for in a time of restricted work ' many amongst them were getting their usual com-

[1] The Act provided a penalty of £50 for a manufacturer who sent work to be done at cheaper rates out of London, but of course this did not apply to persons who moved from London. At Sudbury, in Suffolk, it was reported in 1797 that there was a small silk manufactory established by the London mercers about twenty years before, on account of the dearness of labour in Spitalfields (*Agriculture of Suffolk*, p. 209). Arthur Young, however, writing in 1784, stated that the silk manufactory at Sudbury was established in 1769 or 1770, that is, before the Spitalfields Act (see *Annals of Agriculture*, ii. 106). Silk weaving from Spitalfields was sent to various places in Essex, Suffolk, Berks, and Hants, and in all the price paid was regularly two-thirds of the Spitalfields' ' book ' (see Reports from Assistant Hand-loom Weavers' Commissioners, 1840, part ii. p. 285).

[2] Cf. Mr. Wm. Hale, 1818, Committee on Ribbon Weavers, p. 47. ' Has the Spitalfields trade increased or diminished since the passing of the Act ?—Increased ; there have been more silks manufactured within the last seven years, I should think, in Spitalfields, than were manufactured in the same given time at any former period. At the same time I ought, I think, in candour to those who differ with me on the subject of these Acts to state that the manufactories have also increased in Macclesfield and other places.' Cf. also Mr. Hale's evidence before 1834 Committee on Hand-loom Weavers' Petitions.

[3] 1818 Committee on Ribbon Weavers, p. 61.

[4] See Cunningham, *Growth of English Industry and Commerce*, ii. p. 637.

fortable living, whilst their less fortunate neighbours were
totally destitute.' [1] Upholders of the Act on the other hand,
pointed to its effect during times of distress as a proof of its
benefits ; ' it prevents,' said one employer afterwards, ' the
cupidity of selfish men from taking every advantage of the
temporary depressions of trade to reduce the price of wages ' ; [2]
it prevented in fact that glutting of the market with goods
made at famine rates, which was so common a feature in the
cotton industry. The temporary distress might be great—
that could not be avoided—but when trade revived the
benefits were felt at once. An argument in favour of the Act
that weighed strongly with those responsible for law and
order was the change in the character of the district. Turbulence and rioting had become a thing of the past. A magistrate writing up to the Home Office in 1795, estimated that
owing to the recent raising of the wages by the justices, an
additional £150,000 a year in this time of scarcity would
circulate among the weavers, and pointed with pride to the
fact that no weavers had taken part in the recent riots.[3]

An interesting picture of the varied interests of the Spitalfields weavers was given in 1840 by Mr. Edward Church, a
solicitor, who had lived for thirty years among them in Spital
Square.[4] He described their numerous societies for amuse-
ment and instruction.[5] ' The Spitalfields Mathematical
Society is second in point of time to the Royal Society, and
still exists. There was an Historical Society, which was
merged in the Mathematical Society. There was a Flori-
cultural Society, very numerously attended, but now extinct.
The weavers were almost the only botanists of their day in
the metropolis. They passed their leisure hours, and generally the whole family dined on Sundays, at the little gardens
in the environs of London, now mostly built upon, in small
rooms, about the size of modern omnibuses, with a fireplace
at the end. There was an Entomological Society, and they
were the first entomologists in the kingdom. The Society is

[1] Mr. Ambrose Moore before 1818 Committee on Ribbon Weavers, p. 159.
[2] Report of Committee on Hand-loom Weavers, 1834, p. 9.
[3] H.O., 42. 35, July 1795.
[4] Reports from Assistant Hand-loom Weavers' Commissioners, 1840, part ii.
pp. 216 f.
[5] For the various Trade Societies see Sholl, *Short Historical Account of the
Silk Manufacture*, London, 1811. He complains that the weavers failed to
support them.

gone. They had a Recitation Society for Shakespearean readings, as well as reading other authors, which is now almost forgotten. They had a Musical Society, but this is also gone. There was a Columbarian Society, which gave a silver medal as a prize for the best pigeon of a fancy breed. . . . They were great bird fanciers, and breeders of canaries, many of whom now cheer their quiet hours while at the loom.

'Their breed of spaniels, called Splashers, are now much reduced in size, and from being bred small, were of the best sporting blood. . . .

'Many of the weavers were freemasons, but there are now very few left, and these old men. Many of the houses in Spitalfields had porticos, with seats at their door, where the weavers might be seen on summer evenings enjoying their pipes. The porticos have given way to improvements of the pavements.'

The Spitalfields weavers in fact became an aristocracy amongst wage earners. It cannot be said that the price paid for their orderly behaviour was very high ; in 1818 for instance, a large number of masters agreed that the average wage after deductions were made was not higher than 12s. 6d. a week,[1] but compared with the starvation rates of 6s. or 7s. paid elsewhere this was riches, and it was the earnest desire of the silk weavers in other parts of the country [2] that the Act should be extended to them. This extension would of course have abolished any unfairness inflicted by the Act on the Spitalfields masters. In 1799 the ribbon workers

---

[1] 1818 Committee on Ribbon Weavers, pp. 180-2.
The common idea that the Spitalfields weavers earned very large wages came from the fact that their fat weeks received more attention from their employers than their lean weeks. Mr. Hale, a large manufacturer of great experience, put the matter clearly : 'I know some, who I have a very great respect for and who would say nothing but what they conscientiously believe is true, that will tell you their weavers can earn two guineas a week a single hand. . . . I have for many years endeavoured to ascertain the aggregate amount of the most industrious of my hands, and though I can produce many instances of journeymen, steady men who work for me, who have frequently earned two guineas a week for weeks together, yet the aggregate amount of their earnings throughout the year, though they were equally industrious throughout the year, and though I make use of every means to keep them constantly employed, never exceeded 24s. a week and seldom more than a pound' (1818 Committee, pp. 45-6). The average earnings of all his weavers he put at 13s. a week, p. 141.

[2] In Dublin there were Acts regulating wages (see 1818 Committee on Ribbon Weavers, pp. 86-7).

of the county of Warwick and the city and county of Coventry,
asked Parliament that they should be brought under regulations similar to those in Spitalfields, declaring that they
laboured under great difficulties and inconveniences, because
there was 'no power of properly fixing, settling, and regulating the Wages, Pay, and Price of Labour of the Journeymen and Work people.'[1] A Bill that met their wishes actually
passed through the House of Commons but was held up in
the Lords. When Lord Carrington presented a petition in
its favour signed by twelve thousand ribbon weavers from
Coventry, and moved its third reading, the Lord Chancellor,
Lord Loughborough, talked of the mischievous tendency of
the Spitalfields Act and the Bill was lost.[2]

In 1818 a determined effort was made for the extension
of the Act, not only by the ribbon weavers of Coventry, but
by the ribbon weavers of Leek and the silk weavers of Macclesfield and Reading.[3] Voluntary attempts, favoured by many
masters, to avoid the ruinous system of undercutting in wages
had failed both in Coventry and Macclesfield. In 1816 the
principal employers in Coventry, Nuneaton and Bedworth
nominated 'three respectable persons' to join with 'three
respectable undertakers'[4] in order to draw up a list of rates.
This list was drawn up but was not adhered to uniformly
for a single week, and after a year all the employers had
ignored it.[5] In Macclesfield the system of voluntary regulation had a much longer life. Regulations about wages
and apprenticeship of one sort or another were in force there
from 1796 to 1815.[6] In 1815 the masters suddenly tore
them up. To the men it seemed that 'the masters' idea
upon that subject, was to break us up entirely, and to have a

[1] *House of Commons Journal*, February 25, 1799.
[2] *Parliamentary Register*, July 8, 1799 and *True Briton*, July 9, 1799.
[3] Estimates of numbers of looms and of numbers employed from 1818
Committee on Ribbon Weavers:

  Coventry and neighbourhood.—Male weavers, 5056; female weavers,
      4365; warpers and winders, 3905; looms, 8491.
  Macclesfield.—Silk weavers, 1300 to 1400; looms, 1200.
  Leek.—Ribbon weavers, 300; broad silk weavers, 50 or 60.
  Reading.—Ribbon looms, 100; broad silk looms, 100.

[4] The undertaker was a middleman who for his services received a third of
the earnings. It was said in 1818 that the masters were beginning to dispense
with undertakers but that the journeymen were not benefited (Committee on
Ribbon Weavers, p. 8).
[5] 1818 Committee on Ribbon Weavers, pp. 9 and 11.   [6] *Ibid.*, p. 106.

predominant power over us, and give us what they thought proper, and do as they liked with us.'[1] The masters affirmed that the system of regulations had to be abolished because work was going to Manchester, where the masters had freed themselves from a similar system of regulations in 1812.[2]

Voluntary arrangements between masters and men having failed, efforts were made, as we have said, to obtain an extension of the Spitalfields Act. A Committee of the House of Commons was appointed to consider the various petitions and ' proceeded ' as they themselves stated ' at great length ' to investigate the petitions and to examine witnesses.[3] It is worthy of note that though the Macclesfield masters who were silkweavers were opposed to the extension, the Committee reported that ' the whole of the Masters and Weavers in the Ribbon Trade concur in the propriety of an extension of the Spitalfields Act.'[4] The Committee recommended the extension of this Act, at any rate for a few years, by way of experiment, but when Mr. Peter Moore, member for Coventry, next year introduced a bill founded on the Committee's report the reception it met with in the House of Commons was so hostile that he felt forced to withdraw it.[5]

In Coventry in 1819 a striking example was given of the helpless position of the workmen, even when many masters and public opinion were on their side. A list of prices, as has been mentioned, had been drawn up in 1816, and a committee of workmen was appointed at the request of the masters to ' protect the minimum of wages then laid down.' The masters subscribed to the Committee, and ' respectable gentlemen ' acted as treasurer and secretary. The list of prices, as we have said, was soon disregarded by the masters, but the Committee continued to exist and so did the Combination Act, a weapon ready for the hand of any master who chose to use it. Two years after the formation of the Committee the secretary and the treasurer were

---

[1] 1818 Committee on Ribbon Weavers, p. 92.

[2] *Ibid.*, pp. 63 and 152. The Macclesfield masters were not content with half measures but made all the weavers sign a document: ' I do hereby solemnly declare, that I do not belong to any committee or associated body of weavers, and that no committee or associated body has any power or control over me whatsoever ' (*ibid.*, p. 93).

[3] Committee on Ribbon Weavers' Petitions, 1818.

[4] The Mayor and Corporation of Coventry were strongly in favour of the extension (*ibid.*, p. 130).

[5] See Hansard, May 13, 1819, for debate on subject.

proceeded against at Warwick, and damages of £50 were assessed against them, and ' at the next quarter sessions for Coventry, the treasurer and seven poor men were indicted criminally for a conspiracy for the same offence ; the very same thing. . . . The treasurer being a very respectable man, other respectable persons endeavoured to effect a compromise. The whole of the fund was given up, and the poor men acknowledged their offence by a public advertisement, and the prosecutor dropped it.' [1]

The special Act fixing wages for silkweavers in Spitalfields still survived, and it survived until 1824. In May of the previous year [2] a petition for the repeal of the Act was presented from employers in London and Westminster who complained that the Act prohibited machinery, because the magistrates had one and the same rate for hand-made and machine-made work, that the cost of production was from 50 to 66 per cent. cheaper elsewhere, and that consequently many manufacturers had transferred their works to Norwich, Macclesfield, Manchester, Taunton or Reading. When a Bill to repeal the Act was introduced there were petitions against repeal from the silkweavers of Sudbury, the silkweavers of London and Middlesex, the inhabitants of Spitalfields, the overseers and inhabitants of St. Matthews, Bethnal Green, and the overseers and inhabitants of Mile End New Town.[3] A resolution from the journeymen silkweavers of Spitalfields asked Huskisson to withdraw the Bill 'to repeal those Acts which we humbly conceive to be our greatest Blessing.' [4]

It is clear that repeal was very unpopular in Spitalfields : eleven thousand signatures were attached in three days to a petition, although as it was explained, ' Females had not been permitted to sign, nor any person under the age of twenty,' [5] and Palace Yard was crowded on the day of the third reading of the Bill with agitated silkweavers. This fact that repeal was unpopular was recognised by the repealers, Huskisson declaring that ' some prejudice and indeed a good deal still existed among the workmen ; but the House really ought to act for them without reference to those prejudices,' [6] while Baring discounted the petitions

[1] Committee on Artisans and Machinery, 1824, p. 603.
[2] See Hansard, May 9, 1823.   [3] Ibid., May 21, 1823.
[4] H.O., 40. 18.   [5] Hansard, May 9, 1823.
[6] Ibid.

against repeal on the ground that they ' came from a set of persons who were either labourers in the trade, or tradesmen and shopkeepers with whom those labourers dealt and who would, of course, join in the prayer of their customers.' [1]

There were considerable debates in the House of Commons on the subject. The chief champion of the men was Fowell Buxton (1786-1845), generally known as the Emancipator, from his exertions in the crusade against negro slavery. He lived at his brewery in Spitalfields, and therefore spoke with a good deal of local knowledge.[2] Repeal was demanded in the name of political economy by Ricardo, Huskisson, and Hume. Ricardo said that if the Acts were repealed, the number of labourers would be increased. ' They might not indeed receive such high wages ; but it was improper that those wages should be artificially kept up by the interference of a magistrate. If a manufacturer was obliged to use a certain quantity of labour, he ought to obtain it at a fair price.' [3]

Hume argued that the petitioners who attributed the comparative prosperity of Spitalfields to this system were really mistaken. The trade was in point of fact migrating to Sudbury where the Acts did not apply. Some who were repealers on principle were in favour of delay. These included Brougham, who thought that the petitioners against repeal might be given a fair hearing, seeing that the Acts had been in force for half a century, and Ellice, who argued that the repeal of these Acts ought to follow, and not to precede the Repeal of the Combination Laws.

Fowell Buxton had some stinging sarcasms for Ricardo's abstractions. He said his clients did not pretend to understand political economy, which appeared to change its principles every two or three years, and that, considering that their subsistence depended on these Acts, it was not unnatural that they should be impatient of the authority of this mysterious science. He reminded the House that the silkweavers of Coventry had asked for similar legislation. In Coventry the poor rates were 19s. in the £1, and in Spitalfields 6s., and in Coventry wages ranged from 5s. 6d. to 10s. a week, in Spitalfields from 14s. to 15s. The

---

[1] Hansard, May 21, 1823.
[2] Ibid., May 9 and 21 ; June 9.
[3] Ibid., June 9, 1823.

weavers who saw that these wages were just double the wages
of the Coventry weavers, could not understand how a Bill
which was to reduce their wages to the Coventry scale was
going to benefit them. A speaker on the other side used an
argument which was scarcely calculated to reassure the
weavers on this point. ' It was a remarkable circumstance
that since that bill had been passed the rate of the weavers'
wages had risen, but had never fallen. No instance of a fall
had occurred although the wages in other branches of the
trade had been reduced.' The Bill, though it passed the
Commons in 1823, was so amended in the Lords that the
Government, to the weavers' joy, dropped it.

So confident were the weavers of their strength that early
next year they refused to join in the agitation conducted
by Place for the repeal of the Combination Laws, answering
that ' protected as we have been for years under the salutary
laws and wisdom of the Legislature, and being completely
unapprehensive of any sort of combination on our part, we
cannot therefore take any sort of notice of the invitation
held out by Mr. Place.' ' The law, cling to the law, it will
protect us,' was the cry of the meeting that passed this resolution.[1] But the protection of the law was soon to fail them.
In the very same year, 1824, in which they expressed their
satisfaction with the existing state of things, the position of
the silk trade was altered by Huskisson's measure which
substituted an import duty of 30 per cent. for the prohibition of foreign goods, and lowered the duties on the raw
material. The trade was now faced with foreign competition, and when a fresh bill for repealing the Spitalfields
Act was introduced by Lauderdale in the Lords, it passed
by a majority of three, and was let through by the Commons
without discussion. The petitions of the weavers to Parliament against repeal were disregarded ; their request to the
King to withhold his assent was answered by a statement
of the Royal belief ' that under all circumstances they will
remain steady in their attachment to his person, and will
continue to set that example of industry and good order for
which they have always been conspicuous.'[2] The scene
outside the House of Commons was vividly described by
the *Times*.[3]

[1] Place MSS. 27,800-52 ; *Morning Chronicle*, February 9, 1824, quoted by
Webb, *History of Trade Unionism*, p. 87 *n*.

[2] *Times*, April 13, 1824.   [3] June 12, 1824.

'The great interest excited by the third reading of the Silk-manufacturers' Bill (or more properly speaking the Bill for the repeal of the Spitalfields regulations) brought down yesterday nearly the whole of the poor persons employed in the silk trade to the neighbourhood of the House of Commons. Palace-yard was thronged with them in every part, as was every avenue of the house from the outer door to the members' lobby. Some had paid half-a-crown for the luxury of a squeeze in the gallery to hear the debate on the measure. Many members, and strangers who were mistaken for members, were earnestly solicited by various groups, as they passed in, to oppose the bill. At seven o'clock the crowd about the house was immense. The interest excited among the crowd was intense, when it was communicated to them that the House was dividing on the third reading. As soon as the division was over, a person who came from the House informed those nearest the door that the bill was lost. This pleasing news spread instantly amongst the crowd, and was received with loud shouts and waving of hats. The exultation was, however, but short-lived. The real state of the case was soon made known—that the bill was passed by a majority of thirteen. The disappointment seemed to be deeply felt by all, but we never saw so large an assemblage bear a disappointment better. There was not the slightest disposition to disorder of any kind. The crowd separated into small groups, by whom the merits of the bill were again discussed, and after a time the whole had peacably retired.'

The later history of the Spitalfields weavers is melancholy reading. Under the stress of foreign competition the trade which hitherto had been sheltered declined. Wages, no longer kept up by regulations, were reduced to starvation level or below it. Public subscriptions were started to relieve the distress, but the weavers no longer continued to set that 'example of . . . good order for which they had always been conspicuous.' Strikes, window breaking and the cutting of silk on the looms began again.[1] And in spite of the repeal of the Spitalfields Act much of the trade that survived the competition of the Continent passed from Spitalfields to Macclesfield.

In 1834, ten years after the repeal of the Act, two Spitalfields masters gave evidence before the Select Committee on Hand-loom Weavers' Petitions. They regretted the repeal, for 'the Spitalfields Act at the time saved us from much greater distress than if it had not been in existence,' and they favoured the policy advocated by the petitioners of setting up a board

[1] See H.O., 42. 22 ; 42. 23 ; 42. 24.

or boards of masters and workmen, to regulate wages and fix a minimum.[1]   In 1840 it was reported that all the silk-weavers in every district wished for a board of trade to regulate wages.[2] But such a policy was contrary to the spirit of the nine-teenth century, and labour continued to find its own level of starvation.

[1] See Evidence of Mr. Ballance and Mr. Hale before Committee, p. 9 and pp. 320 ff.
[2] Report from Assistant Hand-loom Weavers' Commissioners, 1840, part ii. p. 395.

CHAPTER VIII

THE FRAME-WORK KNITTERS

THE ancient art or mystery of frame-work knitting was an important industry long before our period. It dates back to the year 1589, when the Rev. William Lee, a graduate of Cambridge and curate of Calverton, completed his invention of the stocking frame. The stocking frame, or stocking loom, as it is sometimes called, was a small machine at which the workman sat—as it might be at a piano or a typewriter—working it both with hands and feet. In hand knitting the needle deals with one stitch after another all down the row : in the stocking frame each stitch had a needle to itself, and all the needles worked simultaneously. The material produced by a stocking frame, like the product of hand-knitting and unlike woven stuff, was composed of one continuous thread formed into a series of loops and hence easily unravelled. Lee himself profited little by his invention and died in France where he had tried to acclimatise it. His brother brought the trade back to England, and London was its centre.[1] The employment of parish apprentices early became an abuse in the frame-work knitting trade, and as far back as 1710 the London journeymen, in protest against the large scale on which apprentices were employed, broke one hundred frames, threw them out of window, and beat master and apprentices into the bargain.[2]

The London frame-work knitters had obtained from Charles II. a charter by which they became a close corporation. The heavy fines levied by this company encouraged the transference of the trade from London to the Midlands, where the frame-work knitters contrived to escape from their jurisdiction.[3] The company attempted to assert their authority

[1] In the middle of the seventeenth century out of the 650 frames in England 400 were in London.

[2] Felkin, *History of Machine-wrought Hosiery and Lace Manufactures*, 1867, p. 227.

[3] By 1727 there were 2,500 frames in London and 5500 in the provinces ; by 1782 there were 500 in London, 200 in Surrey, 17,350 in the Midlands, and

in the Midlands, but after various efforts the question was settled against them in 1753 by the decision of a Committee of the House of Commons that their regulations were injurious, vexatious, hurtful to the trade, and contrary to the liberty of the subject. The company were supported by the journeymen, and opposed by a combination of the masters and the country gentlemen. Henceforth the Midlands were the chief seat of the trade which grew steadily more important, and was an early instance of a capitalised industry. Strutt, who patented an important improvement in the stocking frame by which ribbed hose could be made (known as ' Derby ribs '), was able to provide the capital for Arkwright's early ventures, and the growth of the cotton trade in its turn reacted on the frame-work knitting trade, by cheapening the yarn for stockings. Nottingham became the centre for cotton, Leicester for woollen, and Derby for silk hose.

In 1788 an attempt was made in Leicester to apply Arkwright's cotton spinning invention to the spinning of woollen yarn for stockings, but a mob destroyed both machinery and houses, with the result that the industry moved elsewhere, and Leicester made woollen stockings from yarn produced in other districts.[1]

Of the condition of the workers during these early years accounts vary. An idyllic picture of Leicestershire in the middle of the eighteenth century, quoted by Felkin,[2] describes how ' every village had its wake ; the lower orders lived in comparative ease and plenty, having right of common for pig and poultry, and sometimes for a cow. The stocking-makers each had a garden, a barrel of home-brewed ale, a week-day suit of clothes and one for Sundays, and plenty of leisure, seldom working more than three days a week. Moreover music was much cultivated by them.' On the other hand, a gloomy picture is given in the evidence before House of Commons Committees in 1778 and 1779 of pauper children enslaved to long hours at work which destroyed the nerves and the bodily strength of grown men and women,[3] toiling

950 elsewhere in England.   There were also 1000 in Ireland.   Felkin, *op. cit.*, pp. 72 and 117.

[1] Felkin, *op. cit.*, p. 229.

[2] Felkin, *op. cit.* p. 118, quoting from Gardiner, *Music and Friends*, vol. ii. p. 810.

[3] Women in the frame-work knitting trade seem always to have obtained the same rate as men.

from 5 A.M. to 10 P.M., day after day, for a pittance of 4s. 6d. a week.

Grievances on the subject of frame rents, a perpetual sore in the trade, were already acute. Frames were not worked on the employers' premises, but were scattered about in workmen's cottages in the various centres of the trade and in the neighbouring villages. They belonged sometimes to the workman himself, sometimes to persons unconnected with the trade who had invested money as a speculation in frames,[1] more often to the employer himself, who charged the workman a fixed rent. Sometimes a workman would hire one frame only; in other cases he would hire four or five, and employ other workmen or apprentices, or members of his own family, to work them. Sometimes he would have frames of his own side by side with hired frames. 'The Bulk of the Hosiers,' it was stated later,[2] ' possess very considerable property in Frames and through them contrive to acquire the entire Control over their Workmen.' In 1779 the men complained that the masters refused to employ men who possessed frames of their own and charged rents for frames even when the frames were idle.[3]

The truth about the general condition of the workers towards the end of the eighteenth century seems to be that, although in some branches of the trade there was undoubtedly sweating, in others, notably in the many new fancy articles that came into fashion during this period, the workers could obtain a fair living, though they did not obtain their due share of the growing profits of the industry. The industry itself depended largely on the whims of fashion, so that a flourishing branch one year might find that its market had entirely disappeared the following year.

In 1778-9 the men in the trade made a determined effort to secure a minimum wage. On January 28, 1778,[4] the

---

[1] These were called 'Independent Frames.' Felkin, *op. cit.*, p. 435, says of a later date that many frames belonged to clubs in which workmen invested their savings; cf. 'Butchers, bakers, publicans, gentlemen's servants, women of various classes, and persons engaged in almost every trade, are found to be the owners of frames.' Report from Commissioner on Frame-Work Knitters, 1845, p. 56.

[2] H.O., 42. 139, June 29, 1814.

[3] Frame rents at that time seem to have varied from 9d. to 2s. a week. The frames themselves cost £7 or £8. See Reports on Frame-Work Knitters' Petitions, *House of Commons Journal*, February 25, 1778, and May 5, 1779.

[4] *House of Commons Journal.*

frame-work knitters of London, Nottinghamshire, Middlesex, Surrey, Leicester, Derby, Northampton and Gloucestershire petitioned for a Bill to settle and regulate their wages. Their petition was referred to a committee. The hosiers of Nottinghamshire and Derby [1] petitioned against the proposals, declaring that owing to the intricacy of trade and the 'Mutability of Fashions' it was impossible to fix wages, and that 'if an Advance of Wages should be established upon Parliamentary Authority' it would be prejudicial to all sides. The committee reported on February 25,[2] and its report consisted entirely of the evidence given before it. Wages, which were paid by piece-work, varied from 6s. a week (after deductions for frame, materials, etc., were paid) in the silk branch, to 4s. 6d. in the coarse worsted branch. The men asked for an increase of wages which would represent 1s. 6d. to 2s. a week. The proposal that leave should be given to bring in a Bill was defeated by 52 to 27 votes.[3]

Next year (1779) the men made another attempt, on this occasion petitioning more generally for a Bill 'to regulate the Art and Mystery of Frame-Work Knitting.' [4] Petitions came from many places, Nottingham, Leicester, Derby, Godalming, London and West Middlesex, Tewkesbury and Northampton.[5] A Committee of the House considered these petitions and heard evidence in the course of which it came out that there had been disputes between masters and men about the application to Parliament the previous year, and that some men had been turned off in consequence.[6] This time a Bill to regulate frame-work knitting was brought in,[7] and, in spite of petitions from the masters against it,[8] the Bill reached the Committee stage, only to be dropped on Report.[9]

Disappointment at Nottingham showed itself in characteristic fashion. From all the villages round, the country stockingers flocked in. Three hundred frames belonging to Mr. Need, the chief opponent of the Bill, and others, were broken and thrown out into the streets, and finally a house was burnt down. Troops were sent to Nottingham,[10] but in spite of their arrival 'such was the effect upon

---

[1] *House of Commons Journal*, February 23, 1778.   [2] *Ibid.*
[3] *Ibid.*, February 25, 1778.   [4] *Ibid.*, February 2, 1779.
[5] *Ibid.*, March 29 and 30, 1779.   [6] *Ibid.*, May 5, 1779.
[7] May 10, 1779.   [8] May 13.
[9] June 9.   [10] See S.P. Dom., Geo. III., vol. xiii.

the minds of the authorities as well as the hosiers, that at the instance of the former, the latter, on 19th June, declared themselves unanimously determined as a body, "provided an immediate cessation of violence took place, to remove every oppression from their workmen, and to bring all the manufacturers up to a fair price, not the highest rate, but the best generally given." Upon this peace was restored. A man, Mephringham, was tried at the Assizes for aiding in burning the house, but was acquitted ; upon which this sad conflict was allowed to come to an end.'[1] Rioting in fact had proved more successful than applications to Parliament. In 1787 a fresh list of prices was drawn up and agreed to by masters and men. This list was observed in the main for the next twenty years or so :[2] after which the frame-work knitters entered upon their long period of misery.

The twenty years before 1810 were regarded afterwards as the halcyon days of the frame-work knitters. The witnesses before the 1819 Committee on the Frame-Work Knitters' Petition all agree, whether masters or men, that the wages earned during this prosperous time were 14s. or 15s. a week for some twelve or thirteen hours a day. 'The workmen,' said one witness, 'were enabled to maintain themselves and families by their labour.' A lurid picture of the disastrous effects of these wages was given in 1812 by the Rev. J. T. Becker, an active magistrate at Southwell. 'Abundance thus rapidly acquired by those who were ignorant of its proper application hastened the progress of luxury and licentiousness, and the lower orders were almost universally corrupted by profusion and depravity scarcely to be credited by those who are strangers to our district. Among the men the discussion of politics, the destruction of game, or the dissipation of the ale houses was substituted for the duties of their occupation during the former part of the week, and in the remaining three or four days a sufficiency was earned for defraying the current expenses.'[3]

The latter part of the eighteenth century, when the leg was considered worthy of ornament, was the great era for fancy hosiery. In 1800 there were still seventeen or eighteen kinds of hose worn, differing in shape, colour, and texture,[4] and numerous fancy articles were made on stocking frames. The

---

[1] Felkin, *op. cit.*, p. 229.
[2] Felkin, *op. cit.*, p. 230.
[3] H.O., 42. 120.
[4] Felkin, *op. cit.*, p. 434.

warp machine, a mixture of the weaving loom and the stocking frame, constructed about 1775, produced not only attractive novelties for the world of fashion, such as silk hose with blue and white zig-zag stripes, but also heavy woollen articles, and during the Napoleonic wars our sailors fought in woollen jackets and trousers of Nottingham manufacture.[1] With the nineteenth century dress grew more sombre and fancy hose passed out of fashion,[2] together with such productions as 'silk tickler mitts' and 'silk elastic mitts and gloves' for which 600 or 700 frames had been used, or 'cotton spider net for ladies' habit shirts,' which employed 1500 frames.[3] Frames and workmen alike were by 1810 thrown back into the plain hose branch, always the worst paid branch, and a period of hopeless over-production began, during which the masters' only remedy was the policy of forcing a demand for goods by lowering prices.[4]

About this time were introduced wide frames with their inferior 'cut-up' goods. As the term 'cut-ups' occurs frequently in connection with the Luddite riots, and with the efforts of the men to obtain Parliamentary regulations, it is necessary to explain its meaning. In addition to the ordinary stocking frames, which were narrow machines, there had been for a considerable time a number of wide frames constructed to make (1) pantaloons, and (2) fancy stockings called 'twills.'[5] Now the demand for both these articles had fallen off; pantaloons were no longer required for the Continent: 'twills,' in common with other fancy stockings, had gone out of fashion. The owners of these frames, instead of discarding them as useless, employed them in a manner best described in the words of a well-informed writer in the *Nottingham Review* for December 6, 1811.[6] The wide frames 'are employed by some of the hosiers in making pieces, which are cut up into gloves, socks, sandals, or stockings, according as they want these respective articles; which articles, through their being thus cut and shaped with scissors, are deprived of proper loop selvages, and of the means of being stitched with a lacy seam, and instead thereof are stitched together in the same manner as a tailor stitches

---

[1] Felkin, *op. cit.*, p. 145.

[2] The fashion of wearing boots and gaiters was also a factor (see Committee on Frame-Work Knitters' Petition, 1819, p. 18).

[3] Felkin, *op. cit.*, p. 435.   [4] H.O., 42. 118.

[5] H.O., 42. 131.   [6] H.O., 42. 118.

a garment.' In consequence of 'the loopy nature of the stocking-frame manufacture,' these cut selvedges give way, goods become useless, and well-made stockings come into disrepute. The immediate results of this new system of manufacture are that the market is stocked with these worth-less goods and that those who continue to make hose 'in a tradesmanlike manner,' must either make them cheaper or starve.[1] 'If cut-up stockings are to be tolerated,' adds the writer with indignation, ' we may as well proclaim a new era in the trade, and let tailors and milliners take measure of our legs.' [2]

These cheap cut-up goods, which were spoiling the market for the better class of hosiery, were as much disliked by those hosiers who refused to make them, as by the men, and attempts were made to stop their production. In 1809 various hosiers of standing agreed together to reduce wages 3s. a dozen, unless the workmen could obtain a reduc-tion of frame rents and a cessation of 'cut-up' work.[3] But the workmen were too ill-organised and too hard pressed by starvation to achieve this. Instead, they turned first, as in 1778, to Parliament in hopes of obtaining an Act to regulate wages, but were advised to apply to the old London Company instead. This company, supposed to be defunct long before, was resuscitated for the occasion, and many workmen became freemen of it on payment of £1, 13s. 4d. each. An action was brought before Lord Mansfield against Mr. Payne of Burbage, Leicester, for 'colting,' that is having too many apprentices contrary to the bye-laws of the company. The jury found for the plaintiff, but awarded 1s. damage only, and though Mr. Payne was ruined by the heavy ex-penses he had incurred, the result brought little advantage

[1] A still inferior cut-up article was produced later, for when the raw material grew more costly, instead of shaping the articles with the scissors it was stretched to the shape required, but, of course, lost its shape the first time it was washed. See 1819 Committee on Frame-Work Knitters' Petition, p. 8.

[2] In connection with the perennial agitation of the workmen against 'cut-ups' it is interesting to notice the Report on the Frame-Work Knitters in 1845 as summarised by Dr. Cunningham : '. . . there was a class of hosiery known as *cut work*, and purchasers were not able to distinguish it readily from sound work. Under these circumstances, the demand for sound work had greatly fallen off, and some steps were necessary in order to give the public confidence in the goods offered for sale' (Cunningham, *English Industry and Commerce*, ii. p. 617).

[3] Felkin, *op. cit.*, p. 230.

to the men, and did not deter other employers with longer
purses from taking the risk of a lawsuit.[1]

The depression in the stocking trade during the early years
of the nineteenth century was in part relieved by the growth
of the lace trade, which started as an offshoot of the frame-
work knitters' industry, and was developing upon different
and more prosperous lines. From 1760 onwards, the more
ingenious minds in the stocking trade had exercised themselves over the problem of adapting the stocking frame to
the making of lace net. A point net machine by which
cushion lace with its six equal sides could be imitated, was
finally patented (not by its original inventor) in 1778 ; little
use, however, was made of it till it fell into the hands of the
Messrs. Haynes, keen business men, who towards the end of
the century introduced certain modifications, and made a
great commercial success of their point net lace. The point
net lace trade had risen to considerable prosperity by 1810,
and it was estimated that there were over 1500 point net
frames in Nottingham.[2]

After 1810 the demand fell off, and hard hit by the competition of other methods of making lace, the manufacturers,
to cheapen production, resorted to the original form of point
net, called ' single press,' an inferior article which unravelled
easily, and which held a position analogous to that of ' cut-
ups ' in the hosiery trade. According to Mr. Haynes, the
chief manufacturer of point net, the lace hands objected to
the single press point, not on account of the price, but because
of its inferior quality.[3] It was against ' cut-ups ' and ' single-
press lace,' as well as against low wages and the evils of the
truck system, that the Luddite campaign was directed. As
this campaign is described in a separate chapter, it is unnecessary to discuss it here, further than to say that the
main results were that one thousand frames were broken, and
wages raised, for a short period, 2s. a week.

At the end of the Luddite disturbances the energy of the
frame-work knitters was concentrated on the effort to
obtain Parliamentary regulation for the programme which

[1] Felkin, *op. cit.*, pp. 435, 436.   [2] Felkin, *op. cit.*, pp. 138, 139.
[3] H.O., 42. 131. Felkin evidently thought the objection justified. ' In consequence of the falling off of demand and to cheapen the article, it was made
again of single press in 1811 ; and still further to lessen the cost of cotton point
net, single yarn was used. This completed the ruin of the manufacture in England. By 1815 the demand had entirely ceased here ' (Felkin, *op. cit.*, p. 140).

they had partially enforced by their campaign of frame breaking.   Mr. Coldham, the Town Clerk of Nottingham, drew a
sad picture of the terror-stricken state of the masters, afraid
to lay their views before the House of Commons.[1]   He might
well have spared his pity, for the masters were to find firm
advocates in the Lords.   The Bill, which was termed a Bill
' For preventing Frauds and Abuses in the Frame-Work
Knitting Manufacture, and in the payment of persons employed
therein,' in its first form prohibited the making of obnoxious
cheap goods (notably ' cut-ups ') both in hosiery and lace
work, ordered the masters to fix schedules of prices for
different classes of goods, and forbade the payment of wages in
truck.   By the end of its career in the Commons the references
to hosiery had dropped out except in so far as truck was concerned.   The Bill passed the Commons in spite of a long
speech against all interference with trade by Hume,[2] but in
the Lords its life was short, and it was rejected on July 24,
after speeches against it by Lauderdale, Liverpool, Holland
and Sidmouth.[3]   No voice was raised in its favour, and Sidmouth ' trusted in God that no such principle would be
again attempted to be introduced in any Bill brought up to
that House.'

The disappointment amongst the frame-work knitters
was keen.   Delegates from Leicester and Nottingham had
been up in London to support the Bill,[4] and there was a
general movement towards united action, as we learn from an
intercepted letter from a frame-work knitter in London to
a friend in Glasgow, announcing that Godalming, Dublin,
London, and Derby had formed societies for the maintenance
of their trade, and hoping that Glasgow would ' follow the
noble example.' [5]

Their hopes defeated, their funds exhausted by the Parliamentary campaign, the frame-work knitters might not
unnaturally have resorted again to frame breaking.   Instead
of this, largely under the influence of Gravener Henson,[6]

[1] H.O., 42. 123.   [2] Hansard, July 21, 1812.   [3] *Ibid.*, July 24, 1812.
[4] H.O., 40. 1.   [5] H.O., 42. 124.
[6] Gravener Henson was a bobbin-net maker of Nottingham and leader of
Frame-Work Knitters' Combinations.   He prepared an elaborate Bill in concert
with George White, a clerk of Committees of the House of Commons, repealing
Combination Acts, with some constructive industrial proposals.   His Bill was
introduced by Peter Moore, M.P. for Coventry (see Webb, *History of Trade
Unionism*, p. 89.)

who, after witnessing the defeat of the Bill, had been urged
by the members for Nottingham, ' to soothe and moderate
the public mind,' [1] they set themselves to form a closer and
more efficient combination than any they had yet achieved.
The Articles and General Regulations were framed with the
utmost care in 1813.   Report said that the plan of association had been drawn up by counsel of great eminence, namely
Sir S. Romilly and Mr. Samuel Marryatt, so that it should
be kept within the bounds of the law.[2]   It was called by the
unobjectionable name of a society ' for obtaining parliamentary
relief and the encouragement of Mechanics in the improvement of Mechanism.' [3]

The combination was a federation of societies, each consisting of not less than thirty and not more than one hundred
members, and a hierarchy of committees was established
for the different districts with an executive committee in
Nottingham at their head.   The districts which it was proposed to cover comprised not only the Midlands, but London,
Godalming, Tewkesbury, Scotland and Ireland.   A General
Conference for representatives from Central Committees
in Nottinghamshire, Derby and Leicester was to be held
annually, and a General National Conference attended by
a deputy from every ' Central Committee in the Empire '
was to be held every three years.   The rules were mainly
occupied with the constitution of the Society, and the relations of the different committees to one another.   The coat
of arms of the Society represented the different districts
concerned, with the device of a loom and an arm holding
a hammer with the motto, ' Taisez vous.'   These arms were
omitted from the second set of tickets issued to members
since they were supposed to arouse suspicion.[4]

A good many wild ideas were current about this new organisation which started on its career in January 1813.   It is agreed
by certain individuals at Nottingham, wrote one enthusiastic
informant, ' that the Constitution of this Club is founded
upon the Methodist system of Wesley, and this particularly
struck one of my friends as a convincing proof that Latham
who is a Methodist was one.' [5]   The Union was also credited
with instigating the spasmodic attempts at frame breaking
which still occurred from time to time, and which were as

[1] H.O., 42. 166.   [2] H.O., 42. 139.
[3] For constitution of Society see H.O., 42. 137, and 42. 139.
[4] H.O., 42. 135.   [5] H.O., 42. 138.

a matter of fact contrary to its policy. The Minutes of the first Central Conference of the Society, held some time in 1813, are among the Home Office Papers.[1] Deputies from the three Midland hosiery counties were present, and the figures given show that the total membership in these districts and in London (27 members) and Godalming (70 members) was 2390, whilst the funds in hand were £195 in all, including £126 in Nottingham, and £1 in London. Ten out of the fifteen resolutions passed deal with the establishment of Houses of Call in each place where a Society exists, 'for the better convenience and information of the taking and letting of Frames, and for the obtaining more certain employ for Members.' Each House of Call in fact was to act as a sort of employment bureau, keeping a list of frames, of work and of workers.

The Society embarked on a striking and novel plan of action. In November 1813, 'The Societies hire all the un-employed frames and engage all the work they can which they let out to their members but to no other person, if a member has employment elsewhere with which he is dissatisfied, the Society make him a weekly allowance until he finds better Employment either from the Society or other persons.'[2] 'The main prop of their Exchequer,' wrote Mr. Coldham in July 1814, after examining the papers and accounts of the Society, ' has been borrowing Money for the purpose of being applied to Manufacturing, and by this means they have pro-duced a great many Silk Hose which are now sent to London to be sold.'[3]

The Societies of course only acted incidentally as pro-ducers, their main object was to keep up the standard of wages, and for eighteen months they met with consider-able success. First one and then another branch pressed for an advance. Lace hands, we read, are not to make a claim on the funds, ' till the grievances of the Plain Trade is redressed '; again the plain two needle branch are to have their grievances redressed before those of the plain three needle branch are taken in hand.[4] Amongst the Home Office Papers is the copy of a letter, dated June 16, 1814, from a Nottingham frame-work knitter to a frame-work knitter in Dumfries.[5] This letter came into the hands of the Pro-

[1] H.O., 42. 139. [2] Mr. Woodcock, H.O., 42. 135.
[3] H.O., 42. 140. [4] Ibid.
[5] Ibid.

curator-Fiscal of Dumfries, who sent it to the Town Clerk of Nottingham. It runs as follows :

'NOTTINGHAM, *June* 16, 1814.

'SIR,—Having seen a letter you have sent to your Brother Timothy explaining the Disposition of the Trade of Dumfries to join their Friends in England in uniting themselves under the Union, I feel it my Duty to give you every Information on the Subject. You will see by the Articles that the intent of the Institution is to unite every branch for the support of each other in times of Distress. The Institution has been found to be very beneficial to every branch, as we have all received a small advance on our work except the Plain Silk Hands, which we are now contending for; We have had 300 hands out of employ for more than six weeks because the Hosiers have not the honour to give a reasonable advance. The Hosiers have formed a powerful Combination against us, but this we have not cared for, we have persevered, and resolved to persevere until we accomplish the object in view which we hope is not far distant.

'The Union is well-established in Nottingham, Derby and their Counties, and is making very rapid progress throughout Leicestershire, London, Godalming, Tewkesbury and Northamptonshire have all formed themselves, and we have long wished to form an Interest in North Britain in order that the principle may be diffused throughout the North; and we are happy to find that Dumfries is anctious to set the example, and hope when you have formed yourselves you will disseminate the principle through all Scotland, for depend upon it if the Trade are united and true to their own Interest, we shall be able to make our Trade as respectable as any other in the Kingdom and no longer be designated by the application of " Stracking Stockingers."   According to request I have sent four Articles and sixty Diplomas that you may form yourselves as soon as possible. . . . I hope you will excuse us not writing sooner as we are now so throng, we have scarcely time to attend to anything but the Turn Out.   S. SIMPSON.

'*N.B.*—Direct for me Newtons Head, Glasshouse Lane, Nottingham.'

It was the conflict in the plain silk branch mentioned in this letter that proved the ruin of the men's Union.[1]   In April 1814 the men demanded an advance in the wages for plain silk hose. On April 21 a 'large and respectable meeting of Hosiers' in London, composed no doubt of representatives of houses in Nottingham and elsewhere, decided to refuse any such advance, and to form a Society for prosecuting frame breakers instead. Now Messrs. Ray, the chief makers of plain silk

---

[1] For the account of the collapse of the men's Union that follows, see the papers in H.O., 42. 139, and 42. 140.

hose in Nottingham, found themselves in what Mr. Coldham called ' an unpleasant Predicament,' for they ' had proposed, in consequence of an Engagement as I believe with their Workmen to do so, the very Advance which the Combination demanded, and which the great body of the trade had refused to grant to the Frame-Work Knitters.' Under pressure from their fellow employers they went back on their word, and refused the increase. Unlike most hosiers they owned few frames themselves, the bulk of their work being done on ' independent' frames. The Union on April 24 called out Messrs. Ray's men, amounting to two hundred or three hundred, and proceeded to give them strike pay, or else to employ them on making silk hose to be sold by the Union. Messrs. Ray suffered a heavy blow by this desertion of their men, and even wished to give in and keep their word, but after many negotiations and ' clashing opinions' were persuaded to throw in their lot with their fellow employers.

The hosiers at Nottingham had previously founded a Secret Committee of which Mr. Coldham, the town clerk, acted as secretary. It was decided by this masters' combination to pursue all legal means to break up the men's combination, and to refuse employment to any workmen who had struck for an advance in wages, ' or who are otherwise engaged in this illegal combination.' The Law Officers had given it as their opinion that the men's society was illegal, but had added that it was useless to prosecute until persons could be found to become members of the different societies in order to give information.[1] The committees set themselves to obtain such information, but, wrote Mr. Coldham, it is ' inconceivable the difficulty there is in getting amongst Frame-Work Knitters upon whom you can depend to obtain information for you, and no other person can be of the smallest use.' A more hopeful plan of crushing the men's resistance was suggested by the Secret Committee of Hosiers on May 23, after the turn out had lasted a month, namely, that the Leicester, Nottingham and Derby Regiments of Militia should be disbanded. This, as Mr. Coldham pointed out, would largely increase the number of hands wanting work. If these new hands worked for the masters at the old rates it would become more difficult for the manufacturing committee

[1] H.O., 42. 137. By the mere fact of having different branches the Society was illegal according to 39 Geo. III. c. 79, ' An Act for the Suppression of Seditious and Treasonable Societies.'

of men to dispose of their own goods ; if, on the other hand, the new hands joined the Combination, the Society must either find them work or support them. This suggestion was evidently acted on.

The long struggle was exhausting the men's resources ; their own funds were insufficient to support them, and collections were organised through the district. A copy of the men's accounts in the Home Office Papers shows that between April 25 and July 4, 1814, no less than £1302 passed through their hands, mostly collections and subscriptions. In addition there is a mention of a book containing an account of the money lent for carrying on the manufacturing of silk hose. The masters waited to deal their blow till the process of exhaustion was sufficiently advanced, and early in July they judged the moment propitious. Action was taken nominally by Mr. Ray, in reality by the Secret Committee. Mr. Ray's master hands, summoned to answer the charge of neglecting their work, proved a disappointment, almost all being ' devoted to the Combination.' Some of the journeymen, however, were taken up on secret information, and from one of these information was obtained against three of the leading members of the men's committee. One of the three, Samuel Simpson, writer of the letter quoted above, escaped from the district, the other two, George Gibson and Thomas Judd, were convicted of collecting money for illegal purposes. ' As this,' wrote Mr. Coldham, on July 7, 1814, ' was the first prosecution under the Combinations Act, it was not thought politic to push the conviction up to the full extent,' either by prosecutors or magistrates, and one month's hard labour was the sentence imposed. The books and papers of the combination had all been seized.

The sentence though blamed by some as too lenient did its work. The Union, unable to stand against the opposing forces, broke up, and its collapse was followed by a recrudescence of frame breaking. A letter written by Mr. Coldham on August 12, whether in his capacity as town clerk or as secretary of the Secret Committee is not stated, is a significant commentary on the situation. ' I have the pleasure to assure you that I regard the resumption of the Practice of Frame breaking as a strong and decisive Evidence of the Disorganisation of the System of Combination as applied for the purpose of accomplishing an Increase of Wages. I consider that this has been effected by the joint aid of a depressed Trade, of an increasing supply of Labourers in the Manufactory from the Discharge of the Militia Regiments of the Manufacturing Districts, and of the Confusion and Dismay occasioned by the Seizure of the Books and Papers of the Committee of the Combination.' [1]

The collapse of the ' Society for obtaining Parliamentary Relief' made the men despair of obtaining redress by orderly methods. Gravener Henson, with his policy of clubs and combinations and his hostility to violence was discredited,[2] and a small section of frame breakers, who did not scruple to use personal violence when any of their body got into trouble, revived the policy of 1811, and continued it till the bloodstained retribution which followed the destruction of lace machines in Heathcoat's Loughborough factory closed the epoch of Luddism. ' The branch who broke the frames,' said Gravener Henson afterwards in 1824,[3] ' never contemplated any such thing as the combining ; they broke them merely because it was the only means that presented itself of rescuing themselves, as they conceived, from the combinations of their masters.'

It would be a mistake however to think that the whole body of frame-work knitters now turned to frame breaking. A spy was at last found by Mr. Coldham in March 1815, who, for the wages of £2, 2s. a week,[4] was willing to send in descriptions of the inconsequent and irresponsible talk at public-houses, in which projects of revolution and reform, proposals for frame breaking and for prosecutions of masters under the Truck Act, and petty personal quarrels are wound together in inextricable confusion. In one of these reports the secret agent writes of the would-be Revolutionaries, ' there is somebody concerting a plan and will make it known in proper time, but I cannot learn who these persons are, and I think they

[1] H.O., 42. 152. This letter has by mistake been placed amongst the papers of 1816.

[2] See Gravener Henson's evidence before Committee on Artisans and Machinery, 1824, p. 282 : ' In order to prevent the breaking machinery, which generally ended in some other cause of vengence, I advised them to form clubs and combinations ' ; and his letter to Sidmouth, June 10, 1817 (H.O., 42. 166) : ' I have offended the more desperate Luddites whom I have been informed have repeatedly threatened to shoot me for counteracting their designs, and for the freedom of language I have used at various times against their practices.'

[3] Committee on Artisans and Machinery, 1824, p. 281.

[4] H.O., 42. 143.

don't know.' [1]   When Mr. Coldham died early in 1816 Mr.
Enfield, who like his predecessor combined the offices of
town clerk and secretary to the Secret Committee of Employers,
continued to send up reports from time to time to the Home
Office.

Gravener Henson himself now devoted his untiring energies
to organising prosecutions of the masters under the Truck
Act.   In two test cases against ' two very respectable
tradesmen ' in 1816, the men were successful, and much
alarm was created among the masters, whose contention, as
stated by an apologist in a letter to the Home Office,[2] was
that when overstocked with their own goods ' they barter
with other tradesmen for such goods as they know their men
will be wanting,' and that if informations were laid on a big
scale, and the system stopped, thousands of men would be
thrown out of work.   In the two cases tried, it may be remarked, the goods in which the men were paid happened
to be frames which the men certainly did not want.   Henson
afterwards attributed his own arrest [3] largely to the unpopularity he had thus incurred among ' the unprincipled mali-
cious part of the manufacturers.' [4]

In the year 1816 there was an organised renewal of frame
breaking.   As in 1811 the attacks were confined to frames
working under price.   ' It is not a war against any particular
description of loom,' wrote General Fane, who was in command of the Midlands, ' but against all looms let for work
below certain fixed rates of wages.' [5]   Scrupulous care was
usually taken not to damage other articles.   Whereas in
1811 the attacks were made on stocking frames, they were
now chiefly directed against the lace frames, and in order
to explain the most famous of these attacks it is necessary
here to give some brief account of the new developments
in the lace trade.[6]

The point net trade by 1816 was a dying industry, but
two new trades had grown up :

(1) The trade in warp lace, a lace that went by the name
of Mechlin lace, and was made upon the warp machine, a
mixture of the weaving loom and the stocking frame.   This
trade grew considerably after 1807, when rotary power was
introduced.

[1] H.O., 42. 144.   [2] September 21, 1816, H.O., 42. 153.
[3] See p. 241.   [4] H.O., 42. 166.
[5] October 24, 1816, H.O., 42. 154.   [6] See Felkin, *op. cit.*

(2) The bobbin-net trade, the most important branch of
the lace business, associated with the name of Heathcoat,
who patented the first bobbin-net machine in 1808, and the
second in 1809.

How far Heathcoat was himself an inventor is a much disputed point. Many men had spent themselves over the attempt
to produce by machinery a more exact imitation of twisted
and traversed cushion lace. 'Some of these,' says Felkin,
'died in poverty, and others became insane.' No one completely mastered the problem before Heathcoat, and he, like
Arkwright, had the gifts of a man of business. Born in 1783,
the son of a small farmer, he started life as a frame-smith,
and ended it a prosperous manufacturer, deputy lieutenant
for Devonshire and colleague of Lord Palmerston in the House
of Commons.

The bobbin net lace trade, unlike the stocking trade,
early became a factory industry, the first large factory
being occupied about 1810. In these factories the machines
were gathered together, but it was not till 1816 that power
was used. At first the machines were worked by hand, and
then wheels were put in which doubled the speed.[1] Heathcoat's success was remarkable.[2] In 1811 his lace factory,
according to the estimate of a fellow manufacturer, brought
him in £15,000 a year,[3] but like Arkwright he found that his
fellow manufacturers had no scruples about infringing his
patents. The litigation he began against infringers was
sensationally stopped by the 'surprising and untoward
discovery,' not revealed to the public, that the copyist in
copying out the specification from the draft had omitted a
line, thinking that the omitted line was a mere repetition
of the line before, and had further substituted the word 'bring'
for 'put.'[4] These alterations made the issue of the case
doubtful, and hence the infringers were able to go on unchecked for some years. By 1816 there were 156 of them.[5]
It was the competition with these infringers, added to the
competition with the warp lace trade that prompted Heath-

---

[1] Felkin, *op. cit.*, p. 240.

[2] In 1813 an important improvement on Heathcoat's machine was effected by
John Levers, originally a framesmith, who took out no patent, wasted his time
and talents according to Felkin in drink and political discussions, and finally,
like the original inventor of the stocking machine, went over to France and died
at Rouen (cf. Gravener Henson's evidence before Committee on Artisans and
Machinery, 1824, p. 274).   [3] Mr. Nunn, H.O., 42. 118.

[4] See Felkin, *op. cit.*, p. 209 f.   [5] *Ibid.*, p. 245.

coat to lower his wages by a third, and thus led to the destruction of the machinery in his Loughborough factory.

The lace trade being a new and prosperous industry had attracted many of the best hands among the Frame-Work Knitters, and the wages had been good, compared with the miserable pittances of the stocking hands; they were stated by Heathcoat's solicitor to run from 30s. to 60s. a week.[1] In May these wages were suddenly reduced by one-third at the two factories in Loughborough, Heathcoat and Bodens, and Mr. Lacey's. Mr. Lacey, in answer to remonstrances, advanced his wages again, but Heathcoat and Boden were obstinate.[2]   Some of Heathcoat's men turned out and in consultation with Lacey's men and with the Nottingham warp lace hands, they determined to destroy Heathcoat's machines, in order to prevent him underselling his rivals.[3] The ' job ' was carried out at midnight on June 28, 1816, by seventeen men, all disguised with blackened faces and high cravats, whilst a guard of some hundred sympathisers waited outside and kept the streets clear. The fifty-three patent bobbin net frames in the factory were smashed in the course of half an hour, and £6000 worth of damage done.[4] The demand for goods was so great that ten of the frames were being worked by night as well as by day, and the workmen found in the factory were forced to lie down with their faces to the floor. There had also been a guard of six men provided with arms, but five of these had conveniently gone off to drink in a public house at 11.30, and remained away till the business was done. The remaining guard, John Asher, aimed a pistol at one of the intruders, and was shot in return, but not mortally, whilst a big dog who flew at them was killed. Some incidents mentioned in the confession of one of the seventeen,[5] show that they were not altogether the ' desperate villains ' they were often taken to be. ' Rodney *alias* Bill Towle was going to pocket some lace; Hill said we are not come to rob, but for the good of the trade; if ever I see you up to that again I will blow your brains out. He took it away and burnt it on the floor.' ' On going out of the factory

---

[1] H.O., 42. 151.   [2] *Ibid.*
[3] For following account see papers in H.O., 42. 151.
[4] Heathcoat and Boden estimated their losses at £10,000 : £6,000 for machinery, the rest for contracts for wages to 100 men and the loss of six months' profits (H.O., 42. 152).
[5] Blackburn, H.O., 40. 10.

several of them went to shake hands with Asher who was shot . . . he told them to be off, that he might have a doctor.'

One of the seventeen, by name James Towle, had been identified, and he was tried and found guilty of shooting at Asher, and condemned to death in August. Samuel Slater, tried at the same time, was acquitted, thanks to the fifty-six witnesses produced by the prisoners, who swore so consistently and resisted cross examination so successfully, that Towle himself would have escaped but for slips he had made when examined by the Magistrates before he was committed.[1] It was not Towle's first experience of prison; he had been tried in 1814 for frame breaking, and acquitted, to the great annoyance of Mr. Coldham, who accused the Judge, Mr. Justice Bayley, of partiality to the prisoner and even of cowardice.[2] Whilst Towle was awaiting this first trial an attack had been made, presumably by his friends, on the house of Garton, the chief witness against him, and in the affray two lives were lost.[3] Towle was now, August 1816, condemned to death, but owing to a technical point as to the correctness of the indictment, he lingered on in prison till November, when he was executed.

The general sympathy with the frame breakers was shown at Towle's funeral, at which Dr. Wylde, J.P., Rector of St. Nicholas, forbade the reading of the Burial Service. There were three thousand present, wrote the Secret Agent,[4] ' A School master, I was told, gave out the Hymns that were sung from his house to and at the Grave by Six young women. Peter Green was there and joined in the singing. Many other men also sung. Badder[5] was there with me. . . . There was a Starr or Cross upon the Coffin lid, which excited much conjecture what it could be for. Some said it was because he had died game, others because he had been hung, and some damned Dr. Wylde for not allowing the Funeral Service to be read. Badder said the Parish Parson would have read the Service, had not Dr. Wylde threatened to strip off his gown if he did it, but he said it did not signify to Jem, for he wanted no Parsons about him.' During his months in prison, every effort had been made to induce Towle to reveal

---

[1] H.O., 42. 152. [2] Ibid., 42. 143.
[3] Ibid., 42. 141. [4] Ibid., 42. 155.
[5] Badder had nearly been tried with Towle, but at the last moment the counsel for the Crown thought it inadvisable (see Lockett, August 11, H.O., 42. 152.

the names of his accomplices, but the authorities failed ' to bring him to the desired point.' The Duke of Rutland wanted his life to be spared if he would turn informer, but the poor wretch gave no information of value, though he tried to implicate Gravener Henson in the Luddite movement.[1]

The autumn of 1816 was a time of anxiety for the authorities, and of starvation for the frame-work knitters. The system of parochial relief broke down. The condition of Hinckley will serve as an example.[2] At Hinckley, inhabited mostly by Frame-Work Knitters, there were 1200 families comprising 6000 souls. Six hundred of these families were out of work, three hundred of the remaining six hundred were excused from poor rates because of their poverty, leaving three hundred families to bear the whole burden of the poor rates. Needless to say the three hundred began to dwindle, as family after family passed over into the other categories, and the burden on the survivors increased proportionately. It is no wonder that some alarm was felt, for ' the morals of the lower classes,' wrote a clergyman of Hinckley, ' are in danger of being vitiated from want of employment.'[3] Charity eked out the poor rates, but even large sums went little way amongst so many. Hinckley, like many other parishes, adopted the expedient of employing the poor in frame-work knitting and still further overstocked the market.

In Nottingham it was feared that the troops would refuse to act against the mob, and the Duke of Newcastle urged the building of barracks to keep them separate from the populace.[4] The year before (1815) Mr. Coldham had urged this measure, ' any Infantry *want Barracks here to be effective* for otherwise they are mixed up with the Mob, and cannot be kept in a state of regularity and discipline . . . the constant state of Association with the Town's People has had a very pernicious effect upon the spirit of the men if attempted to be brought into Action against the People.'[5] In spite of Towle's conviction frame breaking went on unchecked, and there were great complaints among the masters that the magistrates did not make a number of arrests. The fact that the Corporation was Whig explained their shortcomings to the other side. The Loughborough affair had overshadowed all other frame-breaking exploits, and of the

[1] H.O., 42. 153, 154, and 156 ; and 40. 10 (Towle's narrative).
[2] H.O., 42. 150, and 42. 152.   [3] *Ibid.*, 42. 152.
[4] *Ibid.*, 42. 155.   [5] *Ibid.*, 42. 144.

chief actors all but one were still at large. ' The Luddites '
wrote Mr. Lockett early in 1817, ' are now principally engaged
in politics and poaching.' [1]   It was a poaching adventure
that led to their capture.   John Blackburn, one of the seventeen, when arrested in connection with an attack on Lord
Middleton's gamekeeper, made a voluntary confession of
the names of his accomplices in the destruction at Loughborough to the magistrate, Mr. Rolleston, but Mr. Rolleston
finding that they were not the chief Luddites, told him that
his life would only be spared if he told all about the chief
Luddites ; ' this at first he positively refused, but subsequently complied with.' [2]   On Blackburn's information
warrants were issued against thirteen men ; seven were at
once taken, including Burton, who was also persuaded to
turn informer.   As a result of their evidence, six men were
executed, Mitchell, Crowder, Amos, Savage, Rodney Towle
and Whithers, and three more men were transported for life.[3]

Some of the unhappy men condemned to death tried
every expedient of disclosure and invention to save their
lives ; Savage, in particular, who had been mixed up in the
Reform movement, declared that, if his life was spared, he
could reveal treasonable correspondence between Major
Cartwright, Sir Francis Burdett and Gravener Henson.   ' He
says he thinks Gravener Henson equal to the perpetration
of anything that ever Robespierre committed.' [4]   Meanwhile the budding Robespierre had gone to London to try
to save the lives of those who were imperilling his own liberty,
and in London, on affidavits of magistrates inspired by these
' disclosures,' which gave body to the existing vague feeling
that he was a treasonable fellow, he was thrown into prison
during the suspension of the Habeas Corpus Act.   There he
remained from April 11, 1816, till November 13, 1817, long
enough to learn discretion.   He was ' a sensible fellow,' wrote
one of the magistrates, ' and very fond of talking.' [5]

Unhappy as was the fate of the condemned Luddites, the
lot of the two informers was still more wretched.   Blackburn was only twenty-three and Burton twenty-one years
old ; each had a wife and a little daughter ; shunned by
honest and dishonest alike, they did not dare to pass their

---

[1] H.O., 42. 158.   [2] H.O., 40. 9.
[3] (1) Slater, (2) ' Little Sam,' the deserter, (3) Caldwell, who was seized with
convulsions and not tried till next July (H.O., 42. 168 and 169).
[4] H.O., 42. 163.   [5] *Ibid.*

thresholds for fear of an assassin's bullet; they were afterwards shipped off to Canada, whence they soon pleaded to
return even to the bitterness of their old surroundings.[1]

As a measure for the repression of Luddism, the execution
of these men was successful. The boldest spirits who, though
they might not have planned the frame breaking, had usually
volunteered for the 'jobs,' were either dead, or transported,
or had fled the country.[2] Some of them returned when quiet
was restored, and led blameless and law-abiding lives. One
of the Loughborough seventeen, who became a faithful and
trusty servant, caretaker of valuable stock in a warehouse,
was supposed to have left behind him a full account of Luddism,
but Felkin failed to find it.[3]

Heathcoat, who sued the county for damages, was awarded
£10,000, but as it was a condition that this money should
be spent locally, and as he had determined to abandon the
Midlands, it was never paid.[4] As his solicitor represented
his affairs to be in a serious state, the Treasury agreed to pay
the £500 reward offered in the name of Heathcoat and Boden,
and they also agreed to pay the heavy costs of the prosecution, some £2261, though suggesting that, in including
Mr. Boden's own travelling expenses as an item in the bill,
Heathcoat was perhaps relying over much on the plea of
reduced circumstances.[5]

The Loughborough affair is often supposed to have driven
a good deal of the lace trade from the Midlands down to
Devonshire; Heathcoat himself about this time set up works
at Tiverton, in a disused woollen mill, where first the waters
of the Exe, and afterwards steam were used to work his lace
machines. But he had already started this manufactory at
Tiverton before the destruction of his frames at Loughborough, as is clear from his letter to the Mayor of Tiverton
on July 1, 1816, sent by the Mayor to the Home Office.[6]
After asking for protection for his manufactory at Tiverton,
and stating that he had just heard of the attack on his

---

[1] H.O., 42. 188.

[2] For example Christopher Blackburn, one of the seventeen, who was protected by a promise given to his brother, the informer, by Lord Middleton and
Mr. Rolleston that he should not be included in the arrests (H.O., 42. 164).
In spite of this, arrangements were made to take him, but he escaped in time
to safety in the fens, 'the usual resort of those' who are driven 'from this part
of the Kingdom' (H.O., 42. 169).

[3] Felkin, *op. cit.*, p. 241.   [4] *Ibid.*, p. 242.
[5] H.O., 42. 158, and 42. 168.   [6] *Ibid.*, 42. 152.

property at Loughborough, he goes on, 'I believe the real cause of this mischief being done is principally, if not wholly, owing to the offence given by our removing here.' The failure of the woollen trade in Devonshire provided cheap labour, and empty mills were available for manufacturers who wished to move.[1]

Curiously enough, the very year of the Loughborough affair the vexed question of Heathcoat's patent was decided in his favour on a side issue in another case, and he made himself as unpopular with the masters, as he had previously been with the men, by starting actions against the infringers. He won his test case, in spite of what the Lord Chief Justice described as 'the system of terror' at Nottingham, where the masters showed that they, no less than the Luddites, could when necessary use the weapons of intimidation. He waived his right to the damages of £10,000, dropped his other actions, and entered instead into a profitable arrangement for granting licences to the infringers, from whom he secured a tribute of some £10,000 a year till the expiration of his patent in 1823.[2]

After the execution of the Loughborough Luddites the lace masters were no longer troubled by fears that their frames would be broken if they lowered their pay. An intercepted letter sent at the time of the executions from a workman in Nottingham to a friend at Calais, with the object of securing work over there for a young lace hand, who had his reasons for wishing to be away for a time, shows that the masters were not slow to use their opportunities. 'All trade is better here than it As been, but they have begun to bate And to tel us that Ned [3] is at Liester now And they well can do as they like.' [4] Felkin, writing long after, when frame breaking was a legend of the past, summed up his judgment about it thus : 'The broad substratum of the whole of this wretched heap of wrongdoing was undoubtedly the hunger and misery into which the large portion of the fifty thousand frame-work-knitters and their families were fallen, and from which they never fully emerged for the following forty years.' [5]

[1] See letter from James Dean, land surveyor from near Exeter, December 6, 1816 (in H.O., 42. 156). He writes that in the previous year Heathcoat and Boden had applied to him for premises which he had secured for them, and that lately, over twenty of the chief woollen manufacturers in Devon had applied to him to sell their mills.

[2] Felkin, *op. cit.*, p. 248.

[3] *i.e.* Ned Ludd.

[4] H.O., 42. 163.

[5] Felkin, *op. cit.*, p. 239.

Frame breaking was now discredited, and the Frame-Work Knitters resorted to other expedients. The history of their later attempts to escape from their miseries shows that, however abject their conditions, they always contained in their ranks men of ideas who delighted in arguing against the economic doctrines preached by their employers. At Leicester, early in 1817, the Frame-Work Knitters held a meeting, at which they passed twelve resolutions afterwards submitted to the employers. These resolutions dealt with the evils of low wages arising from competition amongst employers to undersell each other.[1]

The Leicester masters in response to these resolutions held a meeting, on February 13, 1817, at which fifty-one of their body were present. They recognised and lamented the privations of the Frame-Work Knitters, praised their temperate and patient conduct, declared that, whilst it was impossible to lay down any general arrangements, they would advance wages as soon as the revival of trade made it possible, and attributed much of the existing distress to the ruinous practice of the parishes in competing as manufacturers, or in offering premiums. These two sets of resolutions were sent up to Lord Sidmouth ' for the serious consideration of your Lordship and the Cabinet Ministers,' on behalf of the Frame-Work Knitters by William Jackson, the Secretary of the deputation to the Hosiers.[2] Jackson's letter to Sidmouth is interesting as giving the point of view of the thoughtful workman.[3]

You will find in the enclosed, he writes, ' a statement of matters of fact, and things as they really are in this Town and Neighbourhood. The Frame-Work Knitters in consequence of the reduction of their Wages are reduced to the

---

[1] See H.O., 42. 160, quoted in *The Town Labourer*, p. 303.

[2] William Jackson gave particulars of his own circumstances two years later before the House of Commons Committee on the Frame-Work Knitters' Petition, 1819, pp. 38 ff. He had been twenty-four years in the worsted stocking trade. He had a wife and six children, aged from thirteen to two years old. He made 8s. a week himself at superfine work, working fifteen hours a day, including meal time. His wife, helped by his little boy, made 1s. 6d. more a week by ' seaming.' Three of his children had been ' put into the frame,' and earned 9s. a week between them. Children, he said, ought not to be put to the frame till they were ten years old; he put his three earlier ' because I would not go to the parish.' Till the previous year he had paid parliamentary and parochial rates. He used to possess a frame of his own, but had sold it rather than go to the parish.

[3] H.O., 42. 160.

lowest state of misery and wretchedness, and if the present
system of giving low Wages is persisted in, the whole of the
common people must soon become paupers. One cause
of this state of things is the Combination Act, which is unjust in its principles, and impolitic in its application. If
this Act had never been enforced mechanics would in a great
measure [have] been enabled to resist their employers in
reducing their Wages, and consequently the country would
have been in comparatively flourishing circumstances. All
ranks of People in this Town see and feel the evil of the
present system of giving low Wages, and we can assure your
Lordship from a personal interview we have had with the
Mayor, that he, and the other Magistrates of this Town are
anxious that our Wages should be advanced, the present
system will eat up the Vitals of the Country, and your Lordship will find that a nation of Paupers will ultimately produce an empty exchequer and a National Bankruptcy. It is
not the want of employment of which we complain but the
lowness of our Wages, the hands out of Work being comparatively few. You have legislated to keep up the price
of Corn, and it is but just that you should legislate to keep
up the price of labour, and your Lordship will ever find in
time of Peace that the Price of one is dependent on the price
of the other. If the Mechanics and artizans were well paid
for their Labour they would not hoard up their Money. It
would find its way into the shops of the Tradesmen, the Pockets
of the Farmer and into his Majesty's exchequer. If a low
price is given for Labour the price of the necessaries of life
must come down in proportion, in defiance of all attempts
that are made to keep them up, and we would ask your Lordship how a low price of Corn, [and] a low price of labour can
exist with a heavy taxation ? Your Lordship will see in
the Resolutions of the Hosiers, that they tell us they are
forced to reduce our Wages, to come into the market upon
equal terms with Parishes that manufacture goods, and those
Hosiers who receive a Premium from Parishes for employing
their Poor ; We would call your Lordship's attention particularly to this subject. Parishes manufacture goods, send
them to Market and sell them under prime cost, and the loss
sustained is made up from the poor rates ; to meet this competition, the Hosiers are obliged to reduce the wages of their
Workmen ; your Lordship from this Statement we trust
will see the necessity of some alteration in the Poor Laws.

We would humbly suggest to your Lordship that if the Poor Rates throughout the Country were collected and put into one public fund, and the whole of the poor paid from that fund there would be no inducement for parishes to manufacture or give premiums to manufacturers for employing their poor and forcing them to work for low wages as is the case at present.'

However little consideration the Cabinet might give to such proposals the men now found important allies in the parish officers. The Mayor of Leicester refused to allow a meeting of Frame-Work Knitters to be held on Whit Monday, urging the impropriety of fixing on a day 'which in general was spent on Idleness and Dissipation'; [1] but the Overseers of the Poor of Leicester took matters into their own hands, resolved not to employ any poor in the Manufacture of Hosiery, except those actually in the Poor House, and further came to the important determination described in a letter to the Home Office 'not to allow any assistance to Persons who work at what they call underprice, and claim assistance from their Parish—The Overseers have therefore at a public meeting, set a sort of rate of wages for the different kind of work, and it is to be observed that the statement of the prices they have fixed, are not speculative, but, on the contrary, are moderate and perfectly justified *by the present market prices of Hosiery.*' [2] The difference between the prices actually paid and the new prices, adds the correspondent, is as 7s. to 25s. a week. This policy, which began in Leicester itself, spread over the county. 'The dispute,' wrote Mr. Mundy, J.P., from Burton on July 22, 1817,[3] 'is a very unpleasant one. The workmen are supported by the parish officers, who are of opinion (I fear with some truth) that there exists a combination among the Hoziers, to keep down the prices of the workmen so low that the parishes are obliged to make up the earnings of the workmen, so as to enable them to support their families, and thus carry on their trade in some measure out of the poor rates. Thus far is certain that the Hoziers have agreed that a yard of work shall consist of two-and-forty inches, instead of six-and-thirty. In consequence most of the parishes in this county, and I believe all those in the Town of Leicester, have agreed to support the workmen who give up their frames in consequence of the low prices.'

[1] H.O., 42. 165.   [2] June 9, H.O., 42. 166.   [3] H.O., 42. 168.

The men gained their advance from most of the masters in Leicester [1] itself, but it was granted on the condition that a similar advance should be gained throughout the county and in Nottingham. The men in the cotton branch in Nottingham agitated vigorously, announcing that since advances had been made in Leicester, ' so as to make it more pleasant between the Employer and the employed,' similar steps must be taken in Nottingham, and the Frame-Work Knitters in Nottingham, like those in Leicester, used the opportunity to ventilate their philosophy of Trade. ' That this Meeting,' ran one of their resolutions, on July 21st ' is fully sensible of the Advantages which this Country has derived from the Spirit of Enterprise and useful Competition, as it respects Capital and Talent, but although it is acknowledged that a judicious Use of these Means must necessarily be highly beneficial to the Community at large, yet this Meeting is firmly persuaded that the same has passed the Bounds of Limitation necessary for the well-being of all, so as to become injurious to every one connected with the Frame-Work Knitting Manufacture.' And again, ' to keep any large Body of Men in Work without a proper Remuneration for their Labour is greatly to be deprecated ; as it not only enervates the Spirit of Industry, which ultimately renders them a Burthen to the Public, but creates an unfavourable Impression in the minds of the Workmen towards their Employers, which is largely participated in by most Classes of the Community.'

The employers in Nottingham held out, and meanwhile many of the houses in Leicestershire withdrew their advance. ' One who was on the Committee who drew the scale, departed from it the first Saturday but one.' [2] Early in September, however, most of the hosiers agreed to accept the higher rates provided the acceptances were general ; but a few still refused and imperilled the men's success. A letter of September 8 to a friend, from one of these employers, Mr. John Parker, ' a manufacturer of the first respectability,' who held out, was sent up to the Home Office. He laments the ' unpleasant circumstances under which he has recently been placed.' ' Presuming that you are well acquainted

[1] Some held out ; ' many of the Hoziers and those the most opulent and of the most extensive business still give the low price,' wrote Mr. Mundy on August 13, 1817 (H.O., 42. 169). For other papers quoted on the 1817 attempt to raise wages, see H.O., 42. 170.

[2] Committee on Artisans and Machinery, 1824, p. 265.

that the nature of our manufactory is that of considerable permanence in the engagements between master and workmen, you will be able to judge how very painful [is] the situa- of the employer, in being incessantly called upon to refuse gratifications which the workman is most industriously informed is really his due.' The writer's anger is excited especially against the outside sympathisers with the men, such as the signatories of a manifesto published at Ilkeston whose conduct, he writes, ' renders them in my mind parties to a conspiracy for advancing wages.' This manifesto of August 11, 1817, from Freeholders, Farmers and Tradesmen, was signed by twelve persons, including the Vicar, a Churchwarden and two Overseers. ' With deep regret,' it ran ' we behold the once Industrious, but now degraded Frame-Work Knitters of this Parish and its Vicinity, in a most forlorn and wretched Condition. Men we have seen with pleasure maintain themselves and Families in a creditable and respectable Manner, but now deprived of that Opportunity, by their Wages being inadequate to their Labour and the Necessaries of Life.' The signatories announced their willingness, whilst deprecating violence, to co-operate with the men in order to enable them to live by industry, and their further willingness to co-operate with parishes for this end.

Various Parish overseers met in Nottingham early in September 1817, and passed a resolution that ' it is the inalienable Right of every honest and industrious Man to live by his Labour ' ; but the dissentient employers still held out, and a general strike involving some eight or nine thousand persons began on September 6. The ' Philanthropic and Feeling Public of Nottingham ' was called upon to give support. It is not clear whether the men at this time utilised their old Committees or formed new ones—Gravener Henson was in prison all the time—but they seem to have been effectively organised, with a system of correspondence between Leicestershire, Derby, Nottinghamshire and Gloucestershire ; and a man called Snow from Leicester was said to have travelled about to different places. The Magistrates, as usual, were blamed by the masters as supine. At Leicester, indeed, they called up the Chairman and many of the Central Committee, and warned them of the illegality of their conduct, but they were accused by a Leicester employer of having ' a predilection for the stockingers,' so that ' it is next to impossible to main-

tain any kind of subordination.' The proceedings of the
men, adds the same gentleman, will have the effect ' of very
much cramping the trade and allowing no scope for genius.'

These fears were unnecessary, for the united efforts of
the men and their sympathisers were powerless against the
machinery of the Combination Act, which could be set in
motion whenever the employers wished. ' At the close of
1817,' said one of the workmen later,[1] ' the workmen endeavoured to keep themselves united, that they might know
how the trade was going on, and who was paying the price,
and who was not, and contributed weekly sums ; but such
was the want of information in the county, the law being
threatened against us, the combination entirely ceased, and
the manufacturers departed from their agreement to such
a pitch, that in 1818 we were in great distress, and in 1819
worse.' [2]

The state of the Frame-Work Knitters was indeed pitiable
in the extreme. The accounts of the miserable condition
of these Midland workers all through this period recall
Cobbett's observation : ' This is what logicians call *proving
too much* ; for, if this were really true, you must all have been
dead years ago ' ; [3] and yet of the main facts stated by Felkin
there seems no doubt, namely that working sixteen to eighteen
hours a day they could only make from 4s. to 7s. a week.[4] It
might be said of the Frame-Work Knitters, that the wolf
was always at their doors, and that when he pressed his way
actually in, a strike ensued. It was also no doubt the sight
of the starving men and women in the streets, that made
the upper classes distrust for once the favourite theories
of labour finding its own level, and subscribe to support the
men in their struggle for a bare subsistence.

In the early part of the year 1819, many secret meetings
took place at Nottingham ; ' it was proposed that Delegates
should be sent to every Village in the county to suggest the
ceasing to work at the present prices and apply to the Parishes

[1] Committee on Artisans and Machinery, 1824, p. 265.

[2] Cf. Committee on Frame-Work Knitters' Petition, 1819, p. 38. Some of
the Leicester manufacturers only gave the advanced prices a month, others continued them for six months, after that the regulations were totally abandoned
and wages reduced as low as ever.

[3] Cobbett, *Political Register*, 39, 77, April 14, 1821.

[4] Felkin, *op. cit.*, p. 441. Masters and men before the 1819 Committee on
the Frame-Work Knitters Petition all agree in estimates of wages for Worsted
Stocking Makers of 6s. or 7s. a week for fifteen or sixteen hours a day.

for relief.' Gravener Henson was free again now and took part in the proceedings, but the spy system had spread such suspicion that some of the workmen mistrusted him. They said, ' Beware he does not turn Oliver.' [1]

The old proposal to abolish ' Cut Ups,' was also revived this year; some of the Leicester hosiers as well as the great body of workmen favoured it, and a Committee of the House of Commons recommended a three years' trial of the prohibition in the case of the Worsted Stocking Trade.[2] A Bill to this effect actually passed the Commons, but, like its predecessor, was rejected in the Lords.[3] Its rejection was followed by a large and well-organised strike of the stocking hands of the three counties, Nottinghamshire, Leicestershire, and Derbyshire, who demanded a return to the 1817 statement and refused to work under these prices. Men harnessed themselves together with ropes and drew cartloads of frames along, depositing them at the hosiers' doors.[4] It was estimated afterwards that fourteen thousand men stopped work.[5] The hosiers were divided; most were willing to give the advance provided all others did the same; some even subscribed to help the men.[6] Some of the parishes again supported the men's cause; at Hinckley, for example, ' the inhabitants at large considering their demands reasonable, agreed to support them by parochial relief altogether, rather than compel them to work for reduced prices, and then make up what they might require out of the poor rates.' [7] The most remarkable feature of this 1819 strike was the extent of the sympathy and help that the men received from the public.

It was in Leicester that the men found the greatest

---

[1] Secret agent's report, H.O., 42. 187.

[2] See Report from Committee on Frame-Work Knitters' Petition of 1819. The Report stated, 'That Your Committee are satisfied that the deteriorated condition of the workman is, in a considerable degree, owing to the introduction of the article complained of, the inferiority of which has brought the Worsted Stocking Trade into disrepute in the Foreign and Home Markets, and has thrown a great number of Hands out of employment without conferring any advantage on the Community.'

Your Committee further report : ' That both the Hosiers and Frame-Work Knitters (the Masters and Workmen) express an equal desire for the prohibition of this Article . . .'

[3] June 23, 1819. The voting was 27 to 25.

[4] H.O., 42. 194, and Felkin, *op. cit.*, p. 441.

[5] Committee on Artisans and Machinery, 1824, p. 271.

[6] *Ibid.*, p. 270.

[7] H.O., 42. 193.

support. One of the men's leaders said afterwards : [1] 'The Lord Lieutenant [2] and the gentlemen of the neighbourhood assisted us . . . the parishes combined, the theatre afforded us relief, the parish churches preached in our favour, and subscribed to us ; the dissenters afforded us relief from their pulpits, and we had it from every source.' The Leicester men again challenged publicly their masters' economic doctrines ; [3] after declaring that the workers are entitled to live by their industry, and lamenting the bad disposition of the hosiers, they resolved : 'That if the demand is not equal to the supply, an advance of wages, to an amount that will enable single men at least to obtain a livelihood by labour of twelve hours will tend to remove this evil, as therebye the hours of labour will be considerably diminished, and consequently employment afforded to a greater number of hands, while reducing the wages increases the hours of labour, and throws a proportionate number of hands out of employment.'

At Leicester a new and interesting experiment was started in disregard of the Combination Acts. A Union or Friendly Relief Society for the three Counties was constituted, largely by the exertions of the Rev. Robert Hall ; the funds, consisting of subscriptions from the gentry and contributions from the workers, were managed by trustees and a Committee of gentlemen. Men paid 6d. a week, women and boys 3d. Relief was paid out to those who could not obtain the standard prices ; the relief being 6s. a week for men, 3s. a week for women and boys. At the end of the year no less a sum than £6000 had been paid out, of which £4400 had been contributed by workers. [4] Felkin notes the great effect of this enterprise on the Poor Rates. At Nottingham the authorities do not seem to have been quite so friendly to the men. 'The people are orderly,' wrote the Lord Lieutenant, the Duke of Newcastle, 'peaceable, and I must say reasonable, but still they have enter'd into a Conspiracy, and therefore cannot be entitled to any legal assistance.' He had issued an address to them counselling patience. 'Let me beg of you to bear up manfully, and make the best of even what you may consider an indifferent lot.' [5] The people indeed showed no disposition to riot, and three hundred families

---

[1] Committee on Artisans and Machinery, 1824, p.266.
[2] The Duke of Rutland.   [3] H.O., 42. 192.
[4] Felkin, *op. cit.*, p. 443.   [5] H.O., 42. 193 and 194.

accepted the opportunity offered them of emigration to the Cape of Good Hope.[1]

On September 13, 1819, the men seemed to win a victory. The hosiers of the three counties met at the Exchange Hall in Nottingham, and drew up a statement of prices satisfactory to the men.[2] Unfortunately, however, there was no method of compelling all masters to adhere to this ; in Nottingham sixty-seven agreed to the prices, twenty-three refused. Funds in Nottingham were getting low, and the men had to go back to work, even at the houses who refused to give the statement prices. The other employers kept to the statement for six or eight months, and then wages fell as low as ever.[3] In Leicester, owing no doubt to the stronger position of the Union, prices were kept up longer, even till 1822, according to one witness before the Committee on Artisans and Machinery.[4] But there too, complaints arose that though prices might be kept up work was sent to Nottingham to be done at the cheaper rates. The Rev. Robert Hall's Friendly Society lasted less than five years. The drain on its resources proved too great. In 1821 of the eight thousand persons connected with the society over two thousand were out of work.[5]

It would be wearisome to recount the long series of disputes, sectional and general, between masters and men, that revolved round the 1819 statement. They all present the same features. Starvation causes the men to strike, thereupon the public and many of the masters help the men ; the masters all meet and agree to return to the 1819 statement ; they keep their agreement for a few months, then wages fall again, and preparations for a new struggle begin. The chief strikes of this character were in 1821 [6] and in 1824. It seems at first sight remarkable that so little use was made of the Combination Act in these disputes. Perhaps it was difficult to prosecute a Combination openly favoured by the Lord Lieutenant, to which the Corporation of Leicester had

[1] Felkin, *op. cit.*, p. 441, and H.O., 42. 193.

[2] H.O., 40. 16.

[3] Committee on Artisans and Machinery, 1824 (Benjamin Taylor), pp. 270-71.

[4] William Brown, p. 268.

[5] See Report from Commissioner on Frame-Work Knitters, 1845, pp. 95, 96.

[6] Cobbett made a violent attack in 1821 on the attempt of the men to obtain the 'statement' prices, arguing that their distress was due solely to excessive taxation for which the only remedy was a Reform of Parliament (see *Political Register*, April 14, 1821).

voted £100,[1] though the story of the Coventry Ribbon Weavers[2] shows that the participation of 'respectable persons' did not always secure immunity; but no doubt the real cause lay in the division of opinion amongst the hosiers. A further point arose about the legality of the Frame-Work Knitters' Union; when fourteen of the Committee were prosecuted in 1821 for combining to raise wages, their Counsel, Mr. Hopkinson, fortified by the opinions of J. Chitty and T. Denman, denied that the case came under the Combination Act, seeing that the men were merely relieving each other when they failed to obtain a Tariff fixed by the masters themselves. The Magistrates on this occasion let the Committee off with a caution 'not to attend nor to hold any more meetings, for that probably the next time the consequence would be imprisonment.' A later conviction was quashed for informality.[3]

A long strike, lasting from thirteen to eighteen weeks in 1824, which resulted in the return to the higher prices for a few months, left such memories of suffering, that the spirit of the Frame-Work Knitters seemed finally broken. Contributions to the Union failed at the very time when the repeal of the Combination Act caused such activity in other trades. The more spirited and enterprising workers had no doubt been drawn off into the lace manufacture, whilst frame-work knitting, like hand-loom weaving, being easily learnt, became the refuge of the destitute from other callings. It is indeed a remarkable fact, considering the circumstances of the industry, that the frame-work knitters had been able to combine, and to combine, as we have seen, on occasions with considerable effect.

It was not till long after the time discussed in this volume that frame-work knitting became a factory industry. The factory system had hardly begun in 1844, and was not in full force in 1867.[4] So miserable was the condition of these domestic workers, 'easily distinguished by their careworn, anxious faces from other handcraftsmen,' that few could regret the change. Felkin, who lived through the time, gives it as his opinion that the suffering and privation during the Lancashire famine of 1863-6, was far less than the distress

[1] H.O., 52. 2.
[2] See Committee on Artisans and Machinery, 1824, p. 603.
[3] Benjamin Taylor, Committee on Artisans and Machinery 1824, pp. 271-2, and H.O., 52. 2.   [4] Felkin, *op. cit.*, p. 464.

in the Midland hosiery district between 1810-45, ' where it became a long and widely spread practice to still the cravings of hunger in the adults by opium taken in a solid form, and by children in that of Godfrey's cordial.' [1] In 1833 Felkin estimated that there were some seventy-three thousand work-people in the industry.[2]

This starving population presented a new and larger programme in a petition sent from Basford to the House of Commons in 1833,[3] praying for the enactment of a minimum of wages, for the abolition of wide frames and cut-up work, for an allotment of crown or waste lands, to which they might transfer their families, and for the repeal of taxes on the necessaries of life.[4] In the same year the Union of the three counties was revived, and Felkin quotes from statements put into his hands in hopes that he would act as an intermediary with Government.[5]

' They think God made man to inherit the earth. Persons having property and capital should use them for the benefit of their fellow-citizens as well as themselves. A workman's property is his labour. . . . They were good subjects, and hoped by reforming themselves, their trades and wages, to make this England a paradise in regard to the state and morals of the labouring class, and by rendering bad government and general misery impossible.'

The lace trade meanwhile was becoming more and more distinct from the stocking trade. Between 1820-22 water or steam power was largely applied to the bobbin net machinery, and machines were being drawn into factories, whilst increasing numbers of women and children were employed for subsidiary processes, both in and out of the factories. In the year 1823 Heathcoat's patent expired, and a season of wild speculation began in Nottingham.[6] Capital and labour poured in, the population of Nottingham rose from 47,300 in 1810 to 79,000 in 1830, mechanics received fabulous wages,

---

[1] Felkin, *op. cit.*, p. 458. For evidence on the miserable conditions in the industry, see Report of Commissioner on Frame-Work Knitters, 1845.

[2] Felkin, *op cit.*, p. 449.   [3] See Felkin, *op. cit.*, p. 447.

[4] In 1843 a similar petition was sent to the House of Commons asking for the abolition of cut work and the fixing of a minimum wage. Felkin, writing in 1867, says, that a legal minimum wage is still thought by the majority of workmen 'to be not only right and desirable but feasible' (Felkin, *op. cit.*, pp. 468 and 477).

[5] Felkin, *op. cit.*, p. 448.   [6] See Felkin, *op. cit.*, pp. 331 ff.

building land was sold for £4000 an acre ; the whole district
went mad with what was popularly known as the ' twist
net fever.' Machines that worked and machines that did
not work fetched equally high prices. But the days when
blacksmiths and watchmakers turned bobbin and carriage
makers for the occasion and coined money in their garret
workshops, whilst the improvident journeymen lace workers
' would ride on horseback to and from labour, and having
taken their shift at their machines refresh themselves with
a pint of port or claret on their return,' ended in 1826, and
the collapse brought with it the usual train of misery. In
1826 there were 2469 [1] bobbin net machines as against 970
in the year 1818. The making of machines had become an
important industry employing separate capital and skill,
and this industry continued to pour out machines in spite
of the collapse, so that in 1829 there were some 3842 of them.[2]

Although bobbin lace-making had become predominantly
a factory industry, down to 1831 there were still numerous
small owners with hand machines. The figures indeed are
surprising. Felkin in that year found that there were twenty-
two factories with 1000 power lace machines, and in addition there were 3500 hand machines.[3] The number of owners
of machines is equally surprising—1382 in all, of whom not
less than 700 owned one machine apiece. It is noteworthy
that with the exception of eight, all the owners of bobbin
net machines in 1828 had been originally working artisans.[4]
The small owner disappeared rapidly soon after; in 1834
narrow and slow machines were sold as scrap iron in Nottingham, and a street cry ran 'Old rags, bones, and twist machines
to sell.' The evil legacy of long hours and night shifts, dating
back past the ' fever ' to the time when Heathcoat and his
licensees used every precious moment before the patent expired, remained with the trade after prices had fallen. How

---

[1] Of these 1792 were in the Midlands, and 480 in the South-West.

[2] Felkin, *op cit.*, p. 340, gives the number employed in the lace trade in 1831
as follows :

Preparing the material for the lace in 35 factories, 13,000 persons.

Power lace machines	. 3000	Pearlers, drawers, and	
Hd. lace machines .	. 5000	finishers (women) .	. 30,000
Winders (women and chil-		Embroiderers (working at	
dren) . . .	. 4000	home) . . .	. 150,000
Menders (women) .	. 6000		

[3] Felkin, *op. cit.*, p. 340.   [4] Felkin, *op cit.*, p. 339.

long these hours were is shown by the attempt made by the
owners of bobbin net machinery in 1828 to check over-production, by reducing the hours of working from eighteen or
twenty to twelve hours a day. The attempt was successful
for some nine months, but then failed, as so many agreements between employers and men in the hosiery trade failed ;
a minority of owners refused to be bound, and the majority
could not coerce them. The old unlimited hours were resumed
in Nottingham, in spite of remonstrances from the journeymen, but in the South-West several manufacturers, including
Heathcoat himself, refused to return to the long hours owing
to the demoralisation they caused among the workers.[1] The
horrors of the conditions under which women and children
worked both in the factories and at home falls outside the
scope of this chapter. They were fully exposed both by the
1833 Factory Commission, and many years later in 1861 by
the Commission on Children in Lace Manufacture.

[1] Felkin, *op. cit.*, pp. 265, 338.

CHAPTER IX

THE NOTTINGHAM LUDDITES

THE outbreak of Luddite disturbances in the Midlands in 1811-2 is an episode in the long and varied history of the relations between masters and men in the frame - work knitting trade, and as such can only rightly be understood in connection with what comes before and after. Since, however, it coincided with disturbances elsewhere and assumed a definite character of its own in the public eye, it will be convenient to treat it separately, only referring to the history of frame-work knitting when it is necessary to explain the conditions of the trade.

The main feature of the disturbances in Nottinghamshire and the adjoining counties was the organised destruction of stocking frames by small bands of workmen. A wrong impression of the motive and origin of this campaign is widely prevalent, an impression that is largely due to the Report of the Secret Committee of the House of Lords on the disturbed state of certain counties. This Report announced that ' the disposition to combined and disciplined riot and disturbance . . . seems to have been first manifested in the neighbourhood of the town of Nottingham, in November last, by the destruction of a great number of newly invented stocking frames, by small parties of men, principally stocking weavers, who assembled in various places round Nottingham.' Again, the Committee described the ' spirit of discontent ' as ' called into action,' amongst other causes, ' by the use of a new machine, which enabled the manufacturers to employ women, in work in which men had been before employed.' [1] Hence it has often been assumed that the Nottingham Luddites were venting their anger against new and improved machinery, whereas, in truth, there was no new machinery in use, although, amongst other grievances, there was a new and, as it seemed to the men, an illegitimate adaptation

[1] *Annual Register*, 1812, p. 385.

of an old machine, in the making of what were technically known as ' cut-ups.' This adaptation of machinery has been described in the chapter on the frame-work knitters.

In their campaign against ' cut-ups ' the men had the support of many of the more far-sighted employers. These worthless cut-up stockings were glutting still further an over-stocked market, and as continental trade was at a stand-still, the hosiers' only expedient was to force a demand by cheapening production. Wages went down and grievances of payment in truck became acute. Thus the men's anger was directed against ' cut-ups,' not only as evils in them-selves, but as exercising an evil influence over the whole trade. ' For some time before these troubles broke out,' reported Messrs. Conant and Baker, the two London police magistrates sent up to Nottingham by Government to report on the disturbances,[1] ' in many places, a fifth of the frame workers were out of employ, and this naturally induced some Hosiers (not perhaps of the first Reputation) to give them particular kinds of work at reduced prices ; and the Hosiers who were giving the higher prices found themselves undersold in certain articles at the London market. This again brought about new arrangements, which soured the whole body of workmen, and the scarcity of Corn occurring at the same time a general discontent prevailed. The first emotion was resentment against the Hosiers who paid the under price, and the unemployed and ill-disposed went about disguised to break the frames belonging to these particular persons, and also all frames that facilitated the work by being made wider than the old ones.' According to the Rev. J. T. Becker, the energetic magistrate of Southwell who wrote a long account of the origin of the dispute to the Home Office,[2] when the prices were lowered and the market over-stocked with cheap goods, ' representations were urged by the workmen, and the example of many respectable trades-men, who discharged their supernumary men and continued the remainder on full work at equitable prices was urged as a model for imitation ' but without effect.

Conferences between masters and men, or hosiers and stockingers as they are often called, were a common practice in the frame-work knitting trade, and one of these con-ferences had been held just before the first outbreak in 1811, when Messrs. Brocksopp and other hosiers had agreed ' to give

---

[1] H.O., 42. 120, February 6.   [2] H.O., 42. 120, February 11.

the men unabated wages, provided they would join in bringing up the under-paying masters to the same standard and to put down cut-up work.'[1]   The men set about this in a more violent fashion than their friends among the masters desired, by destroying the obnoxious frames.

The frame-breakers called themselves Luddites, and signed their proclamations Ned Ludd, sometimes adding Sherwood Forest.   The original Ned Ludd, according to the *Nottingham Review*,[2] was a boy apprenticed to learn frame-work knitting at Anstey, near Leicester.   Being averse to confinement or work, he refused to exert himself, whereupon his master complained to a magistrate, who ordered a whipping.   Ned in answer took a hammer and demolished the hated frame. His later fortunes history does not relate.

The aim of the frame-breakers is grandiloquently expressed in a curious declaration from ' Ned Ludds Office, Sherwood Forest,' sent up to the Home Office, where it received the official endorsement :   ' This letter cannot be answered.'[3] The declaration explains that by the Charter granted to the trade by Charles II., the frame-work knitters were empowered to break and destroy all frames and engines that fabricate articles in a deceitful manner, and to destroy such articles ;[4] that the Act passed in 1788, making frame-breaking a felony, is null and void, and that it is the intention of the frame-work knitters to break all frames that make spurious articles or fail to pay the regular prices agreed to by masters and men, and ' all Frames of whatsoever description the workmen of whom are not paid in the current coin of the realm will invariably be destroyed.'   Banditti, robbing under pretence of frame-breaking, are denounced, and a reward of £1000 offered for their detection.

A song, entitled ' General Ludds Triumph,'[5] expresses even better the frame-breakers ideal : some of it runs thus :

> ' The guilty may fear, but no vengeance he aims
>   At the honest mans life or estate
>   His wrath is entirely confined to wide frames
>   And to those that old prices abate.

---

[1] Felkin, *History of Machine Wrought Hosiery and Lace Manufactures*, 1867, quoting Henson, p. 240.
[2] December 20, 1811 (see H.O., 42. 118).   [3] H.O., 42. 119.
[4] The Charter empowered deputies appointed by the Company to examine goods, and if they were badly made, or of deceitful stuff, to cut them to pieces.
[5] H.O., 42. 119, January 27.

These Engines of mischief were sentenced to die
By unanimous vote of the Trade ;
And Ludd who can all opposition defy
Was the grand Executioner made.

' And when in the work of destruction employed
He himself to no method confines,
By fire and by water he gets them destroyed
For the Elements aid his designs.
Whether guarded by Soldiers along the Highway
Or closely secured in the room,
He shivers them up both by night and by day,
And nothing can soften their doom.

' He may censure great Ludd's disrespect for the Laws
Who ne'er for a moment reflects,
That *foul Imposition* alone was the cause
Which produced these unhappy effects.
Let the haughty no longer the humble oppress
Then shall Ludd sheath his conquering sword,
His grievances instantly meet with redress
Then peace will be quickly restored.

' Let the wise and the great lend their aid and advice
Nor e'er their assistance withdraw
Till full fashioned work at the old fashioned price
Is established by Custom and Law.
Then the Trade when this ardorous contest is o'er
Shall raise in full splendour its head,
And colting [1] and cutting and squaring no more
Shall deprive honest workmen of bread.'

The promise that Ludd's wrath should be ' confined to wide
frames, and to those that old prices abate ' was strictly kept
except in one or two instances where mistakes were made,
as, for example, at Lenton in Nottingham, where the indignant owner complained in a handbill (January 25) [2] that five
stocking frames had been broken, ' all of which were working
at the FULL PRICE,' and gave affidavits from the workmen
employed on them to prove this. The cut-up goods made
on the wide frames were destroyed,[3] and on at least one
occasion the rioters searched the bags of a carrier as he was
coming into Nottingham, and burnt all the cut-up hosiery,
leaving the goods with proper selvedges.[4]

[1] For ' colting ' see p. 227.   [2] H.O., 42. 119.
[3] In the lace trade the obnoxious article that held an analogous position to
cut-ups was what was termed ' single press lace,' see p. 228.
[4] H.O., 42. 119, January 31.

It would be a mistake to suppose that frame-breaking was a new device in the hosiery trade. The distinguishing mark of the frame-breaking in 1811-12 was that it was not a wild outburst of popular anger, but a well-planned and organised policy. The nature of the machinery and the structure of the trade lent itself to the practice. The frames for the most part belonged to the master hosiers, who hired them out to their workmen, charging a frame rent of from 1s. to 2s. per week.[1] This rent, as we have said, was a perpetual source of grievance.

The first outburst of frame-breaking at this time took place early in March 1811, when over sixty frames belonging to an obnoxious employer were destroyed in one evening at Arnold. As the month went on a few other frames were broken, and then there was a cessation till November 4, when the campaign started afresh with the destruction of frames at Arnold, Bulwell, Basford, and other villages. The destruction continued throughout November in Nottinghamshire, spread to Leicestershire and Derbyshire early in December, slackened in the latter part of December, revived in January, and died away in February 1812. In all, about one thousand frames were broken; one hundred of these were silk frames used for fine cotton work; a very few were lace frames. The total damage was estimated at from £6000 to £10,000.[2]

It was impossible to protect the scattered frames. The number of actual frame-breakers was small, but the mass of the people sympathised with them, and the workmen who hired the frames were not concerned to defend the master's obnoxious property. Troops and special constables patrolled the villages, orders were issued that no one should be out of his house after 10 P.M. under pain of arrest, but a handful of men, when the soldiers backs were turned, could quietly enter a house, break the machines, sparing any frame that belonged to the occupant, and leave again when their work was done, without fear of detection. The magistrates resorted to the device of arresting the persons in whose houses frames were broken, but the suggestion that they should be held responsible for damage was rejected as illegal by the Law

[1] H.O., 42. 120, February 9.
[2] For account of frame-breakings, see H.O., 42. 119; H.O., 42. 131. Blackner, the historian of Nottingham, estimated the total number of frames in Notts, Leicester, and Derby in 1812 as 25,218, including some 1400 lace frames. Felkin, *op. cit.*, pp. 437-8.

Officers, unless gross negligence could be proved.[1] At Basford
it was said that some frames were broken within ten yards
of a magistrate and a party of Dragoons,[2] and Felkin tells
the tale of a frame-breaker surprised by a patrol of soldiers
and special constables, of whom Felkin was one, in a house
in Rutland Street, who quietly ran along the roof, jumped
from the eaves of a three-storied house further on to some
newly turned earth, walked through the kitchen where the
family were at dinner, and escaped.[3]

On November 10 there was an affray over some frame-
breaking at Bulwell. The owner of the frames, in whose
house they were, defended his property by barricading windows
and doors, and in an attack on the house a young man, John
Wesley by name, was shot dead.[4] His funeral on November
14 was made the occasion for an orderly and impressive
demonstration of popular feeling. This was the only life
lost in the disturbances ; most of the frame-breaking took
place, as we have seen, quietly, in the workmen's cottages.
In Nottingham itself few frames were broken, and the owners,
where possible, brought their property into the town for
protection.

The first request of the magistrates for military aid was
answered by the despatch of a squadron of the 15th Dragoons,[5]
but these proving inadequate, all the local corps were called
out by the sheriff,[6] and application for more troops made
to the Government. By December 9, from 800 to 900 cavalry
and 1000 infantry of the Regular Militia had been sent into
the disturbed districts,[7] but the frame-breaking still continued. Even the hard-pressed and unorganised women,
employed at home in lace-running, i.e. in embroidering
patterns and designs on net, embarked, to the scandal of a
Loughborough parson magistrate, on a campaign to better
their lot. On December 19 the Rev. R. Hardy, J.P., writes : [8]

[1] H.O., 42. 120, February 18.   [2] H.O., 42. 117, November 27.
[3] Felkin, op. cit., p. 234.   [4] H.O., 42. 119.
[5] H.O., 42. 117.
[6] The Annual Register (1811, Chron., p. 130) says that the sheriff called out
the posse comitatus and the local Militia. In his own letter the sheriff talks of
the local corps (H.O., 42. 117, November 17). The Duke of Newcastle, Lord-
Lieutenant, was much annoyed because the sheriff acted without communicating
with him. Some fear was expressed by the Duke as to the trustworthiness of
the local Militia (H.O., 42. 117, November 16), but he reported on November
28 that they had behaved very well.—Ibid.
[7] H.O., 42. 119.   [8] H.O., 42. 118.

' A Spirit of Combination to dictate to their Employers, and to raise the price of their Wages, has within these few days shown itself among the *Women* who are employed in what we call *running Lace*. Meetings have been called and emissaries sent into all the neighbouring Towns and Villages to unite, and to collect Money for their Purpose. I have thought proper to issue a hand Bill to warn Persons against such illegal Meetings. I have reason to hope that the impression I have made upon this Town will soon spread abroad, so as to put a stop to their proceedings in this way in places adjoining.' Mr. Hardy's handbill seems to have had the desired effect. It is interesting to notice that Mr. Haynes, the lace manufacturer, estimated the number of ' runners ' (women, girls and children from five upwards) at this time as some twenty thousand working in their own houses throughout the Midland counties. The common payment for a good hand is 2d. an hour. Their earnings he estimates, in the case of girls and women at from 7s. to 12s. a week, or, for the best work, from 15s. to 21s., obviously an employer's roseate picture. He adds, however, that the girls and women often receive two-thirds of their earnings in articles of dress.[1]

A vivid account of the frame-breakers' systematic methods in outlying districts is given in a letter of December 25, 1811, to Sir Joshua Banks from his steward,[2] describing what took place at Pentridge in Derby: ' . . . on Thursday two men came to this place who called themselves inspectors from the Committee, they went to every stockinger's house, and discharged them from working under such prices as they gave them a list of, and said they should come again in a few days, and in case any of them were found working without having a ticket from their Master saying that he was willing to give the prices stated in their list—They should break there frames. They summoned all the Stockingers about twelve or fourteen in number of Master Men to a Publick House, with as much consequence as if they had had a mandate from the Prince Regent. When they got them thither all I can learn at present, was for the purpose of collecting Money from them for the support of those families, who where deprived of getting their bread by having their frames broken.— Where they found a frame worked by a person who had not served a regular apprenticeship, or by a Woman, they discharged them from working, and if they promised to do so,

[1] H.O., 42. 131.   [2] H.O., 42. 118

they stuck a paper upon the frame with these words written upon it : " Let this frame stand, the colts removed."— Colt is the name given to all those who have not served a regular apprenticeship.'

How far the existing men's organisations took part in frame-breaking or gave it their countenance it is difficult to determine. There was clearly some organisation formed to support the persons deprived of work by the destruction of their machines. Some of the leaders, for example Gravener Henson, disapproved of the whole policy of frame-breaking, but it seems probable that most of the members of existing trade societies, without joining in the policy of destruction themselves, were not ill pleased to have the work done for them. There is scarcely a stockinger,' wrote the Rev. J. T. Becker of Southwell,[1] ' who will not give half his victuals or his money to those " friends of the poor man " as they are styled, who beg in the evening from house to house, exposing for sale the Frame-Work Knitters Act, as a protection against the vagrant laws.'

It must be remembered that whilst frames were being destroyed, negotiations were taking place between masters and men, and addresses of thanks or appeal to employers were being inserted in the press, often with signatures attached. Thus we learn from the *Nottingham Review* of November 29, 1811,[2] that the gentlemen hosiers of Nottingham had agreed by November 27 to give an advance of 6d. per pair on black silk hose ; an advance, as the secretary of the plain silk stockingmakers puts it, which arouses in the men that gratitude which is imprinted on the human heart by the deity. Again on November 29 the frame-work knitters appeal to the gentlemen hosiers of Nottingham for ' Advice, Aid, Direction and Support,' with regard to ' an Address to Parliament, for the better Regulation of our Trade, and means of defence against future Impositions.' They point out their miserable state ' Destitute of all the Comforts of Life, our only acquaintance is pinching Poverty and pining Want. We wish to live peaceable and honestly by our Labour, and to train up our Children in the paths of virtue and rectitude, but we cannot accomplish our wishes. Our Children, instead of being trained up by a regular course of Education, for social life, virtuous employments and all the reciprocal advantages of mutual enjoyment, are scarce one remove from the

[1] H.O., 42. 120.   [2] H.O., 42. 117.

Brute, are left to all the dangerous Evils attendant on an uncultivated Mind, and often fall dreadful Victims to that Guilt which Ignorance is the parent of. . . .'

Some houses made their own terms with the men, as is shown in the tale told by Felkin.[1] In the ' last week of November 1811, . . . the writer of these lines, then a youth of scarcely seventeen, was required by his masters to get into the saddle and make a long round, to convey the information that if their frames, of which they employed about three thousand, were spared from the destruction with which they were threatened, one shilling per dozen advance would be paid the following Saturday, and be continued whether others paid it or not. It was a dreary afternoon with heavy rain and winter sleet. He rode hard, and at Basford, Bulwell, Eastwood, Heanor, Ilkeston, Smalley, Sawley, Kegworth, Gotham, and Ruddington, delivered to their head frame-work knitters the joyful news of the offered advance.' The promise, it may be added, was faithfully kept, and not one of the frames was destroyed. A curious advertisement in the *Nottingham Journal* for February 1, 1812,[2] throws some light on the relations between masters and frame-breakers. An employer, C. Shipley, explains that he has not removed to Mansfield in order to set the trade at defiance, or to make unlawful work, but simply because he has heard that the men intended to break all lace frames in country villages ' without regard to what they were making.' He regrets the false reports, assures them that he is stopping the obnoxious work, and hopes that they will offer him no further violence.

On December 4, the Nottingham employers and men were engaged, under the auspices of the magistrates, in negotiations that came to nothing.[3] On December 13 the hosiers agreed to raise wages, but not enough to satisfy the men ;[4] by December 21 the hosiers were reported to be coming into the workmen's terms.[5] On December 28 a list of prices agreed to by the hosiers and lace manufacturers was published in the *Nottingham Journal*,[6] and the Duke of Newcastle reported that matters had been arranged satisfactorily round Mansfield, though there was still discontent in the Nottingham district.[7] In Derby the hosiers were early inclined to revert

[1] Felkin, *op. cit.*, p. 233.   [2] H.O., 42. 120.   [3] H.O., 42. 119.
[4] H.O., 42. 119.   [5] H.O., 42. 118.   [6] H.O., 42. 118.
[7] H.O., 42. 118, December 29.

to the old prices. The Derby Committee of Plain Silk Hands addressed an earnest appeal to the Gentlemen Hosiers in the columns of the *Nottingham Review* of December 20, 1811.[1] ' Galled by the pressure of unprecedented times, we cannot any longer remain indifferent to our common interest as men. As a body of ingenious artizans employed on materials of great value, pent up in a close shop fourteen or sixteen hours a day (a confinement prejudicial to many constitutions), having under our constant care a machine confessedly difficult, from the construction of its principles, to preserve in good condition, and allowed to be one of the first productions of British genius ; devoting our time and abilities alone, to adorn the rich and great, we conceive ourselves entitled to a higher station in society : and that, in point of emolument we ought to rank with mechanics of the first eminence. If the position be admitted that one calling is more respectable than another, surely the making of Silk Stockings is an employ- ment, both in point of value and elegance of the article, highly respectable ; and considering our manufacture is consumed alone by the opulent, it ought to produce a competence adequate to the just wants of our families.' ' Hedged in by a combina- tion act,' they continue, ' we cannot say to you as a public body, that we demand an advance of wages, but we can say that JUSTICE DEMANDS that we should receive a remuneration for extra labour.'

Felkin estimates that the rate of wages was raised 2s. a dozen by the Luddite commotions, though it relapsed after- wards.[2] It seems reasonable to suppose that the cessation of frame-breaking was chiefly due to the fact that the men had, at any rate for the time being, attained a good part of their objects. Added to this the interests and energies of the more orderly portion were soon engrossed in promot- ing a bill in Parliament to abolish truck and to prohibit the making of obnoxious articles. The story of this bill and of the Union that succeeded its failure are told elsewhere.[3] As early as February 14, an advertisement to frame-work knitters in the *Nottingham Review*,[4] announces that as the legislature is taking notice of the disturbances the workmen had better furnish information about the causes, and the workmen in every town and village are asked to send two creditable persons to a meeting which will communicate with

[1] H.O., 42. 118.   [2] Felkin, *op. cit.*, p. 439.
[3] See Chapter VIII.   [4] H.O., 42. 120.

Lord Holland, the Recorder of the Town, with the two M.P.'s of the town and the county, and with Mr. Whitbread.

The notice taken by the legislature of the disturbances took the form of two bills. The first, for the preservation of peace in the county of Nottingham, enabled the county authorities to select special constables from the male inhabitants above twenty-one years of age, and to establish watch and ward in disturbed parts. The second made frame-breaking, which was at that time a minor felony, punishable by fourteen years' transportation, a capital felony. The Frame-Breaking Bill was criticised in the House of Commons with great vehemence, Sheridan, Whitbread, Romilly, Hutchinson, Pigott, and Curwen among others opposing it; [1] but the second reading was carried on February 17 by 94 to 17. Lamb, afterwards Lord Melbourne, supported it with two ominous sentences in which he declared that it was a delusion to suppose that the distress ' could receive any relaxation under the present unavoidable system,' and that ' the fear of death had a powerful influence over the human mind.' [2]

In the Lords the Bill was in the charge of Lord Liverpool, three months later to become Prime Minister. There was a considerable discussion, Holland, Lauderdale, Grosvenor, and Grenville all opposing the Bill; but the most interesting event of the debate was the maiden speech of Byron, who opened the attack on the Bill [3] with his famous declaration that he had never seen under the most despotic government such squalid wretchedness as he had seen since his return in the very heart of England. He described the frame-breakers as men convicted of the capital crime of poverty, said that capital punishment had been the favourite remedy of legislation since the days of Draco, and added an argument that was more likely to touch the heart of the Government—the argument that juries would refuse to convict. In spite of this warning the House of Lords passed the Bill. It received the Royal assent on March 20. It is interesting to notice that the Bill was not popular with the Nottingham authorities; indeed, the Town Clerk, Mr. Coldham, wrote up in strong terms against it. [4] ' It is as I feared, I have had a long conference with those who have given me most important Information, and kept a Watch upon the Motions of the frame breakers,

---

[1] See Cobbett's *Parliamentary Debates*, February 14, 17, 18, and 20, 1812.
[2] *Parliamentary Register*, February 18, 1812.
[3] February 27. [4] H.O., 42. 119.

and they will do so not a moment longer than the Law is as
it now remains. They cannot they say consent to act where
the death of a Fellow Creature must be the consequence of
their giving such Information as may lead to his Conviction. It is revolting to their Feelings and in their Judgment
increases in a tenfold degree the danger of their Employment. . . .'

The death penalty did not, of course, apply to such frame-
breakers as were in custody awaiting the March Assizes,
unless burglary could be proved against them. The Government, after some demur, agreed to pay the costs of the
prosecution.[1] The prosecutors were, for the most part, unwilling to proceed, and the witnesses had an unpopular part to
play. Mr. Coldham reported that, as the trials approached,
men were turning informers in order to obtain money to
pay for the defence of their comrades at the Assizes;[2]
an ingenious method of spoiling the Philistines. There were
many rumours that prisoners were to be rescued during the
Assizes, and after much correspondence on the subject, caused
by Mr. Justice Bayley refusing to give directions though
not withholding his consent, the military were retained in
the town during the trials.[3]

The Assizes took place before Mr. Justice Bayley in March.
Nine prisoners were tried; two were acquitted (one of them
of sending a threatening letter), and the remaining seven were
sentenced to be transported for either seven or fourteen years.
The judge aroused great indignation by what was described
as his ' temporizing and timid Conduct '[4] in not insisting
on a conviction for burglary instead of frame-breaking. Had
Mr. Coldham seen Mr. Justice Bayley's private letter of March
18 to the Secretary of State,[5] in which he suggested that
Government might like to exercise discretion in the case of
the seven youths sentenced to transportation, that indignation would have been stronger. William Carnell, aged twenty-
two, and Joseph Maples, aged sixteen, who were both acquitted
on the charge of burglary, had been sentenced to fourteen
years' transportation for breaking into a house in company
with a party of twelve and destroying seven frames. Carnell

---

[1] They pointed out in vain to the local authorities that in the Wiltshire Riots
of 1802, £10,000 had been raised by local subscription (H.O., 42. 119, January 9
and January 20).

[2] H.O., 42. 120, February 27.   [3] H.O., 42. 121.

[4] Mr. Coldham, H.O., 42. 122, April 6.   [5] H.O., 42. 121.

had been leader, but, the judge pointed out, 'he had the
merit of protecting the occupier of the House, an old Man
of 70, from any personal violence.' Maples called witnesses to prove an alibi, 'and though the Jury disbelieved
them I am not quite sure that the verdict was right. However Maples was apprehended the next night with a pistol
about him.' Benjamin Poley, aged sixteen, pleaded guilty,
so the particulars of his case were not detailed. Benjamin
Hancock, aged twenty-two, a youth of good character, had
been ringleader of a mob which destroyed £400 worth of
frames, and George Green, aged twenty-two, Joseph Peck,
aged seventeen, and Gerves Marshall, likewise aged seventeen,
had been members of the same mob and had helped to break
frames. 'They were probably drawn into the outrage without
considering the consequences,' wrote the kindly judge, 'and
Marshall and Green had very good characters.'[1] The Government's answer was promptly to remove the felons for transportation, without relaxing a single sentence, a firmness
for which the Town Clerk thanked them heartily. John
and Elizabeth Braithwaite, who by their evidence had secured
the conviction of Carnell and Maples, received a reward of
£50 each, but were forced for safety's sake to move to a distant
part of the kingdom.[2]

We have said that no violence was done in the disturbances
save to frames, but an exception must be made of the attempted
assassination of Mr. William Trentham, the hosier, which took
place in April, after the other disturbances had stopped.[3] Mr.
Trentham was knocked down outside his house and wounded,
and in spite of the offer of six hundred guineas reward the
assailants were never discovered. Probably this was the
work of private vengeance, and the key to it seems to lie in
a curious threatening letter to Mr. Trentham, now amongst
the Home Office Papers.[4] As it deals with the subject of women's
work, about which as a rule so little is recorded, we will quote
from it at some length :

'Sir,—I have received instructions from the Captain from his
Head Quarters at Grinds Booth in which he orders me to

---

[1] Enclosed in Mr. Justice Bayley's letter is a pitiful scrap of paper sent by
Carnell after he had been sentenced, asking to see the judge. '. . . tell him,'
it runs 'that i have something to say to him of more importance than eather
Life or Death God says them that them that shewes mercy shall find it.' The
judge refused to see him.   [2] H.O., 42. 123, May 3 and May 8.
[3] H.O., 42. 122, April 28   [4] H.O., 42. 120.

represent to you the conduct of a Person of the name of Haywood who takes chevening [1] from your Warehouse.   This woman gives her Girls but half a Crown a Week tho' they chevene six pair of Hose a Day for which they work a great number of Hours the Captain has written himself to a House of Nottingham respecting this Woman and he informs me that the result has been most satisfactory the Captain desires me to represent to you in the strongest terms his detestation and abhorrence of your conduct if you are privy to this Womans transactions as you must be sensible that no human being capable of work can be maintained with 2/6 a Week.

'You must be sensible Sir that these unfortunate Girls are under very strong temptations to turn prostitutes, from their extreme poverty.

'The Captain authorizes me to say that these People being defenceless he conceives them to be more immediately under his protection as his believes their Wages are the lowest in England. He hopes you will endeavour to alleviate their misfortunes by giving the employ to each of these Individuals at an equitable Price.'

The letter ends with a threat of an attack on Mr. Trentham and his property unless these demands are complied with.

[1] Embroidery.

CHAPTER X

THE LANCASHIRE LUDDITES

The Government, already alarmed by the organised frame breaking in the Midlands, saw in the disturbances which broke out early in 1812, in Cheshire, Lancashire, and Yorkshire, proof that the working classes were meditating not only the destruction of machinery but a general revolution. The narrative of what occurred in Lancashire and Cheshire, as coloured by their alarm, is best given in the words of the Report of the Secret Committee of the House of Lords on the Disturbed State of certain Counties : [1]

'The discontent which had thus first appeared about Nottingham, and had in some degree extended into Derbyshire and Leicestershire, had before this period been communicated to other parts of the country. Subscriptions for the persons taken into custody in Nottinghamshire were solicited in the month of February at Stockport, in Cheshire, where anonymous letters were at the same time circulated, threatening to destroy the machinery used in the manufactures of that place, and in that and the following months attempts were made to set on fire two different manufactories. The spirit of discontent then rapidly spread through the neighbourhood, inflammatory placards, inviting the people to a general rising, were dispersed, illegal oaths were administered, riots were produced in various places, houses were plundered by persons in disguise, and a report was industriously circulated, that a general rising would take place on the 1st of May, or early in that month.

'The spirit of riot and disturbance was extended to many other places, and particularly to Ashton-under-Line, Eccles, and Middleton; at the latter place the manufactory of Mr. Burton was attacked on the 20th of April, and although the rioters were then repulsed, and five of their number were killed by the military force assembled to protect the works, a second attack was made on the 22d of April, and Mr. Burton's dwelling house was burnt before military assistance could be brought to his support; when troops arrived to protect the works, they were fired upon by the rioters, and before the rioters could be dispersed, several of them

[1] *Annual Register*, 1812, pp. 386-8.

were killed and wounded; according to the accounts received, at least three were killed and about twenty wounded.

'On the 4th of April riots again prevailed at Stockport; the house of Mr. Goodwin was set on fire, and his steam-looms were destroyed. In the following night a meeting of rioters, on a heath about two miles from the town, for the purpose, as supposed, of being trained for military exercise, was surprised and dispersed; contributions were also levied in the neighbourhood, at the houses of gentlemen and farmers.

'About the same time riots also took place at Manchester, and in the neighbourhood; of which the general pretence was the high price of provisions. On the 26th and 27th of April the people of Manchester were alarmed by the appearance of some thousands of strangers in their town, the greater part of whom however disappeared on the 28th; part of the local militia had been then called out, and a large military force had arrived, which it was supposed had over-awed those who were disposed to disturbance. An apprehension, however, prevailed, of a more general rising in May, and in the neighbourhood of the town many houses were plundered. Nocturnal meetings for the purpose of military exercise were frequent; arms were seized in various places by the disaffected; the house of a farmer near Manchester was plundered, and a labourer coming to his assistance was shot.

'The manner in which the disaffected have carried on their proceedings, is represented as demonstrating an extraordinary degree of concert, secrecy, and organization. Their signals were well contrived and well established, and any attempt to detect and lay hold of the offenders was generally defeated.

'The same spirit of riot and disturbance appeared at Bolton-in-the-Moors. So early as the 6th of April, intelligence was given, that at a meeting of delegates from several places it had been resolved that the manufactory at West Houghton, in that neighbourhood, should be destroyed, but that at a subsequent meeting it had been determined, that the destruction of this manufactory should be postponed. On the 24th of April, however, the destruction of this manufactory was accomplished. Intelligence having been obtained of the intended attack, a military force was sent for its protection, and the assailants dispersed before the arrival of the military, who then returned to their quarters; the rioters taking advantage of their absence, assailed and forced the manufactory, set it on fire, and again dispersed before the military could be brought again to the spot.'

It is possible a hundred years later to examine the papers on which the Reports of the Parliamentary Secret Committees were based, and from these and other sources to piece together a more or less coherent account of what actually happened.

The tale is an intricate one, and the material on which to base it disordered. Four main factors stand out : (1) a general discontent with power-looms, (2) deliberate but unsuccessful attempts to destroy the obnoxious looms fomented if not originated by spies, (3) food riots, beginning in anger at high prices and ending in the destruction of power-looms or buildings, (4) rumours of a ' general rising ' started as far as can be gathered solely by spies.

The use of power-looms, originally invented in 1785, had been first made profitable by the supplementary invention of a dressing machine, patented by William Radcliffe of Stockport in 1803 and 1804.[1] They were not found yet in many factories, but the hard pressed hand-weavers saw in these machines a fresh menace to their livelihood and a fresh cause of their misery. The definite movement against steam looms began in Stockport, the place where they were most in use.[2] The weavers first waited in an orderly manner on the Rector of Stockport, Mr. Prescott, J.P., to complain of the want of employment through steam weaving. He advised them to apply to Mr. Ryder, the Secretary of State, on whom accordingly two of their number waited, only to receive from that gentleman the cold comfort of an assurance that ' the Steam Looms were of great Service to the State.' [3]

Their next step, early in February 1812,[4] was to ask the same friendly rector to arrange meetings between them and the manufacturers on the subject of their wages. In this they seemed at first more successful, the manufacturers agreeing in the magistrates' presence to raise their wages 2s. a cut, but the meeting over, the manufacturers met again at Manchester, thought better of their promise, and told the workmen's chief representative that they were only making game of the men.[5] Negotiations thus broke down, and a few of the more violent spirits amongst the weavers, discontented with their leaders, determined to take matters into their own hands [6] and to

---

[1] See p. 71.

[2] Besides William Radcliffe several other firms had steam looms, Goodairs, Marsland, Hindley (H.O., 40. 1).

[3] H.O., 42. 128 (Oliver Nicholson).

[4] H.O., 42. 120, February 11.

[5] Report of Committee on Artisans and Machinery, 1824, p. 417 (Joseph Sherwin's evidence). He instanced this as a case of combination of masters.

[6] 'The workmen became clamorous and blamed those who had acted on their part as wanting spirit or abilities ' (Thomas Whittaker, H.O., 42. 121).

destroy the obnoxious power-looms; but though several meetings were held 'little was done,' as one of them expressed it, 'save differing in opinions.' Meanwhile threatening letters about the destruction of power-looms reached the Stockport authorities, a rumour went abroad that subscriptions were being collected for the Nottingham rioters,[1] and a general feeling of uneasiness was engendered.

Mr. Lloyd, the energetic clerk to Mr. Prescott, of whom we shall hear more afterwards, was prepared for active measures as early as February 11. He made no distinction between the law-abiding and the violent weavers. As soon as the weavers do anything irregular, he wrote,[2] I shall act decisively; 'shall a set of obscure Individuals who possess no interest or feeling for their Country's honour dare to dictate to a Government or to the proprietor of a Manufacture of this sort what they shall do or what Machinery they shall use?'

Into this atmosphere of rather incoherent discontent came a mysterious man from Manchester, 'with something of Importance to communicate.' Our evidence for this part of the proceedings rests on the confession of Thomas Whittaker of Stockport, afterwards convicted at the Chester Special Commission, who hoped by revealing all that he knew to save himself from transportation. 'When the conversation began,' he says,[3] 'I found that the scene was changed, advance of wages was not the topic as usual, and I never was more surprised in my life when I heard the Manchester Delegate lay down the plans and communications with other towns.' Whittaker gives a long account of the report of the Manchester delegate, who detailed an elaborate oath, explained that companies of tens were to be formed for drilling at night, declared 'that a fixed time would be appointed for a general rising of the People,' and announced that Yorkshire and Nottinghamshire were very forward, that London would secure the Tower, Bank, and Woolwich, and that 500,000 men were ready to rise in the North and Midlands.

Now nobody who has read through the Home Office Papers for this period can fail to recognise in the report of what the Manchester delegate said, the voice of 'B.,' alias Mr. Bent.[4] Mr. Bent was a buyer and seller of cotton waste, much in

---

[1] H.O., 42. 120, February 11. This rumour was translated by the Secret Committee into a fact.

[2] *Ibid.*   [3] H.O., 42. 121.   [4] See p. 67 above.

the confidence of the working-class reformers in Manchester and the neighbourhood; as ' B.' he was also the trusted confidant and informer of Colonel Ralph Fletcher, the active Bolton magistrate. ' B.' specialised in a ' general rising.' The Home Office Papers contain numbers of illiterate communications from him, full of lurid hints of the approaching outbursts of the lower orders, encouraged by mysterious beings in high stations. The general rising, with the number of thousands who have taken the oath in different parts of the country, is his constant theme. About this time he sends up particulars of the oath and announces that **40,000** had already been sworn in in Nottingham, Leicester, and Derby.

It is not unreasonable to suppose that the particular Luddite oath, of which we shall hear a good deal more, originated in ' B.'s fertile brain, and it is clearly he who visited Stockport and urged the weavers to action. They were not attracted by his elaborate programme and preferred to form a Secret Committee ' to destroy all steam looms, to collect money and to repel force by force if hindered '; [1] apparently, however, they adopted the form of oath he suggested. [2] This oath ran as follows : [3]

' I A. B. of my own voluntary will, do declare, and solemnly swear, that I never will reveal to any person or persons under the canopy of heaven, the names of the persons who compose this Secret Committee, their proceedings, meeting, places of abode, dress, features, connections, or any thing else that might lead to a discovery of the same, either by word or deed, or sign, under the penalty of being sent out of the world by the first brother who shall meet me, and my name and character blotted out of existence, and never to be remembered but with contempt and abhorrence ; and I further now do swear, that I will use my best endeavours to punish by death any traitor or traitors, should he rise up amongst us, wherever I can find him or them, and though he should fly to the verge of nature, I will pursue him with increasing vengeance. So help me God, and bless me to keep this my oath inviolable.'

[1] H.O., 40. 1 (Yarwood).

[2] It must be remembered that by 37 Geo. III. c. 123, an Act passed after the Mutiny at the Nore, the giving or taking of unlawful oaths was punishable by seven years' transportation. Practically any secret oath would come under the Act.

[3] See Report of House of Lords' Secret Committee, *Annual Register*, 1812, p. 391. For variants of oath, see p. 336 below.

In tracing the actions of such Secret Committees it must
be remembered that all workmen's meetings and committees
for any trade purpose, however legitimate, were, owing to
the Combination Law, necessarily secret, and that organisations for Parliamentary Reform were also compelled to work
underground. Hence any workmen's meeting was liable
to misinterpretation by spies, and it is often difficult to understand what really took place. General Maitland's shrewd
observation [1] ' that the present state has originated, and
that it now exists without either, any definite Object, or
distinct End ' seems often applicable to the proceedings
of these committees.

The Stockport Secret Committee entered into negotiations
with other towns in the latter part of February and the beginning of March, in the hope probably of starting an organised
campaign against machinery. Overtures were made to
Bolton, where six weavers met two delegates from Stockport at the ' Gibralter Rock.' The Stockport delegates
proposed an oath, but all but one of the Bolton men disapproved of it, and nothing further seems to have come of
this meeting.[2] The next place approached was Manchester.
Here many meetings of weavers had taken place in connection with the attempts now being made all over the kingdom
to enforce against their masters the existing laws about apprenticeship and regulation of wages.[3] Delegates from Nottingham, Carlisle, and Glasgow were noted as present in Manchester
on February 13.[4] The meetings produced no result, but into
the ears of some of these disillusioned weavers came a whisper
of a vague ' advantageous plan,' which culminated in the
arrival from Stockport one Sunday, by the morning coach,
of a delegate who met four weavers, Humphrey Yarwood,
John Buckley, George Royles, and George Howarth, and
persuaded them to form a Secret Committee consisting of
the last three. The Stockport delegate administered the
oath and solemnly arranged tallies by means of which they
were to communicate with Bolton and Stockport.[5] There
were now two Secret Committees, Stockport and Manchester.

Meanwhile at Bolton, although the proposal to form a Secret
Committee had come to nothing, the discontented weavers

[1] H.O., 42. 124.
[2] H.O., 42. 128 (Oliver Nicholson and James Lyon).
[3] See p. 86.   [4] H.O., 42. 130.
[5] H.O., 40. 1 (Yarwood's statement).

decided on March 2 'to meet every Evening after they had
done their work by Daylight and before they lighted up
Candles and by that means they thought they could frighten
their Masters to give them more Wages.'[1] At these meetings their shouts were to inspire terror. Unfortunately
the masters were not as much impressed by their demonstrations as the weavers had expected, and a more active
organiser now stepped on the scenes to rescue the Bolton
weavers from futility. This was John Stones, a protégé
of Adjutant Warr of the Bolton local militia. Adjutant
Warr was employed by Colonel Fletcher, 'Bolton Fletcher'
as Cobbett used to call him, to obtain information by means
of 'confidants,' and in John Stones he struck a rich vein.
'The Adjutant of the Local Militia under my command,' wrote
Colonel Fletcher on March 23,[2] 'has got a confidential person
to join apparently in the schemes.'

Stones alias /S/ must have begun operations at the end
of February or early in March, and with a creditable family
feeling he soon enlisted his father in the service. His regular
rate of pay seems to have been £1 a week and out-of-pocket
expenses; occasionally clothing was given him as well, for
amongst the items of Cash for Secret Service[3] we find :

			£	S.	D.
March	9.	Cash to /S/	3	0	0
,,	16.	Cash to /S/ and old /S/ . .	1	7	0
,,	21.	Cash to /S/ to buy Shoes and Breeches	1	0	0
,,	21.	Expenses at Isherwoods, Meat, Liquor, etc., for the above and others concerned . .	1	7	7

By May his father was sharing in his allowances :

May 21.	Cash to old /S/ and young /S/ .	3	2	8
,, 22.	Hitchins Bill for Clothing Old /S/ and young /S/ . .	2	5	0

Thanks to Stones' energy a Secret Committee was now
formed in Bolton, one genuine member of which, curiously
enough, was Robert Waddington, afterwards to become
notorious as a spy in 1817.

[1] H.O., 42. 128 (Robert Waddington and William Makin).
[2] H.O., 42. 121.　　　　　　　　　　[3] H.O., 42. 124.

There were now three Secret Committees, one for Stockport, one for Manchester, one for Bolton. Whether they
represented any one but themselves is doubtful. The business of destroying machinery hung fire all through March,
except for an attempt to burn William Radcliffe's factory
in Stockport on March 20 between 2 and 3 A.M.[1] Torches
were thrown into the building, but the owner was able
to save it from destruction. Whether this attempt was
the work of the Stockport Secret Committee or of private
malice it is impossible to say. Stones at Bolton meanwhile
was doing his best to enliven proceedings by writing about
meetings at which the firing of factories was planned and
resolutions taken to murder any magistrate who arrested
an incendiary.[2] He was also busily engaged in persuading
people to take the oath, but no definite steps for organised
action were taken till a meeting on Sunday, April 5, at the
King's Arms, Oldfield Lane, Manchester, of delegates from
various towns.[3] With his picturesque touch Stones reports
that at this meeting it was said that Lord Cochrane, Burdett,
and Whitbread were to join the movement, when the country
was ready, the aim of the movement being ' to put the great
Men down that had trampled them under foot so long.' As
a practical step it was suggested that ' something serious
in the way of destruction ' should take place at Bolton, Manchester, and Stockport on Thursday night, April 9, but this
was to be contingent on the consent of Manchester.

Manchester, however, according to Yarwood, would have
nothing to do with the plans : ' When it was proposed by
some of the Secret Committee to the Districts it was rejected
and nothing but discord reigned amongst them that night.'
The Manchester organisation, in fact, was in anything but
a flourishing condition : the districts (whatever they consisted of) would not even subscribe enough money to pay
for ' the trifle of liquor ' consumed by the Secret Committee,
and when it came to paying the coach fares of two men to
Bolton and Stockport to announce that Manchester refused
to act in concert, and would not join in any work of destruction, the committee had to fall back on Mr. Bent, alias ' B.,'
who, as we have seen, had in all probability originated the
whole thing himself. Mr. Bent lent the Secret Committee
£1 for the journeys, and here, on April 6 or 7, the existence

---

[1] H.O. 40. 1, March 21.   [2] H.O., 42. 121.
[3] See Stones' own reports and Yarwood's account, both in H.O., 40. 1.

of any Secret Committee in Manchester connected in any way with the destruction of machinery comes to an end.

Manchester having failed, the destruction planned for April 9 was whittled down to a plan to fire the steam-weaving factory at West Houghton, and this plan was in due course communicated to the magistrates by the informers.

Of the Stockport committee we have no further information. Possibly they stirred up the mob who attacked Mr. Goodair's house and steam looms and broke the windows of Mr. Marsland's, Mr. Hindley's, and Mr. Radcliffe's houses on April 14.[1] Nobody was tried for these disturbances, so that their history is obscure. Mr. Prescott, the magistrate, some years later, described them as unpremeditated.

It is of Bolton, the scene of Stones' activities, that we have the fullest accounts. These come not only from Stones himself, Colonel Fletcher, and other ' trustworthy sources,'[2] but also from the depositions of a number of Bolton weavers, some of them Stones' victims, made when they afterwards took the oath of allegiance,[3] and lastly from a series of affidavits and statements, which, amongst other things, reveal the part taken by spies in fomenting the disturbances.[4]

From these papers we learn that before the West Houghton factory was finally burnt on April 24, there had been two other attempts to induce people to burn it down, attempts that had failed in spite of the indefatigable efforts of Stones and his associates. We will now deal with the first of these attempts.

It has already been mentioned that plans had been laid at a meeting of delegates to fire West Houghton factory on the night of Thursday, April 9. The project kept Stones very busy. ' /S/,' we read in Warr's report to Colonel Fletcher, ' is to go over to his father's to see how many he has got for they did not know but they might want them Thursday night.' Again, on April 7, Warr reports that a delegate

[1] H.O., 40. I.   [2] H.O., 40. I, *passim.*
[3] H.O., 42. 128, October 18, 1812.
[4] See bundle of papers in H.O. 42. 132, headed 'Trials and Proceedings at Lancaster, etc., received from Lord Sidmouth 4 Jan. 1813.' In these papers it is mentioned that the affidavits are left with Mr. Whitbread. These papers are probably the evidence collected by Dr. Taylor and Mr. Crook in order ' to prove a case before Parliament' (Colonel Fletcher in H.O., 42. 129, June 29). For Whitbread's and Brougham's speeches on the subject in the House of Commons, see *Parliamentary Debates,* July 10 and 13, 1812. See also Prentice's *Manchester,* pp. 55 f.

(presumably father Stones) has gone to Chowbent to 'instruct' them : there are between thirty and forty in Chowbent, these with two from Bolton to instruct them will be enough ; they want /S/ to be one of the two. The plans are carefully laid ; on Thursday morning at 1 A.M. there is to be a general meeting of all those sworn in, and those not attending will be dragged out of bed. Some are to go to the master of the factory or the overlooker and ask him to come on particular business, to demand his keys, to put a pistol by his head and keep him secure till the business is done. /S/ is to go to his father's to ask him to attend the general meeting, and if his men be not properly arranged, they will instruct him in matters relating thereto. ' /S/ hath been round to collect 1s. 2d., but only got 10d. which he gave to Ratcliff.'

/S/'s own account, given through Warr, is corroborated by the deposition in October of Peter Gaskell, one of the men who afterwards took the oath of allegiance.[1] He told how early in April, Stones and another called asking for subscriptions for the Secret Committee. Gaskell gave 2d. ; Stones then warned him to attend the meeting that night ; the reluctant Gaskell replied that he had no arms, Stones retorted that ' those who did not attend would be in greater danger than those who did attend and would be torn out of their Beds.' However, in spite of all the efforts of Stones and his father, Simeon, it was impossible to beat up enough recruits to fire West Houghton on Thursday night, April 9. So ended the first attempt. Colonel Fletcher solemnly wrote that the attack was postponed because London was not yet ready.

Stones, however, was not discouraged, and he now devoted his energies to starting a quasi-military organisation among such weavers as he could get together. He held secret meetings at the Brick Kiln on Bolton Moor, and divided his forces into classes, appointing captains of tens to whom he gave the appropriate names of Oliver Cromwell, Sir Francis Burdett, Lord Grey, even Lord Grenville ; for himself he usually reserved the name of Whitbread, and his own class was Whitbread's class, though occasionally he indulged in further flights of fancy, dubbing himself Colonel Wardle, then at the height of his popularity for exposing the connections between the Duke of York, Mary Anne Clarke, and the British army. At these meetings the attendance was usually twenty or thirty ; even Colonel Fletcher, whose informants naturally

[1] H.O., 42. 128, October 18.

wished to magnify them, gives only sixty or seventy as the number.

The descriptions of their farcical proceedings would be merely amusing, were it not for the shadow of coming doom over some of the foolish actors. John Hurst, for example, who was afterwards transported, entered into the spirit of the drill with great zest, acting as generalissimo with a mask, a false beard, and a long staff. On one occasion Hurst, after putting his army through their facings and marchings ' in order to try their Courage suddenly ordered them to disperse saying the Horse were approaching, which they did in such a Trepidation that several got immersed in a Pool of Water near the place of Meeting in the darkness of the Night.' Stones in vain attempted to rally his men by ' damning their soft souls,' and pulling out a pistol vowed ' he would have shot the first Man who offered to take him.'

' Old /S/ ' all this time was busily swearing people in, saying ' you can have a big loaf for little money, you must take the oath first, and then I will tell you how,' assuring his foolish victims that the whole country had joined and taken the oath, and that factories were to be destroyed and the nation plunged in confusion.

The second attempt to get West Houghton factory burnt was fixed for the night of Sunday, April 19, ten days after the first effort. This second attempt went by the name of the Dean Moor Meeting, and is not mentioned in the reports of the Parliamentary Secret Committees. It is interesting to see what Colonel Fletcher, no doubt on the authority of Stones, expected on this second occasion. ' One the 18th,' he writes on April 22, ' news came of an expected assembly in a field near my house of from 200 to 300 persons. One division was to assail my house, a second division was to burn Mr. Thomas Ainsworth's house and warehouse, a third division was to do the same at Mr. Hewett's and the disaffected from Chowbent, with the aid of a delegate from here were to burn down the Weaving Factory at West Houghton 5 miles from here.' So much for the ambitious programme revealed to Mr. Fletcher.

Of the actual events we have remarkably full evidence. The dramatis personæ were certainly not more than thirty or forty. Ten of these afterwards appeared in court charged with administering an illegal oath to militia Sergeant Holland Bowden. Ten others, namely Stones and his confederates,

who by their own and their employer's admission had acted
as spies, also appeared in court as witnesses against the
other ten.   In addition to these twenty, five other persons
gave accounts of the meeting afterwards in depositions.   So
far as destruction went the events of the night fell very flat.
The fiasco Colonel Fletcher ascribed to the fact that he had
called out the local militia, which alarmed the conspirators
so much that they did not attempt the whole programme.
Instead of the expected three hundred, 'some 30 or 40
mustered in the said Field, who were soon however ordered
to repair to Dean Moor (another situation two miles distant),
where the General caused them to pass in Review (about
11 o'clock) by their several Companies of Tens. . . .'   He
describes how they then moved off to Chowbent, meeting
on the way with Sergeant Holland Bowden, whom they
insisted on 'twisting in'[1] before they would allow him
to go.   This, Colonel Fletcher adds, will enable us to bring
conviction home to many of them, 'as we had several
confidants present.'   Only two persons, he says, joined
before Chowbent, although the General had expected about
three hundred, who were to burn West Houghton.   He
then describes how a proposal to break church windows
was made, and declined, how they gave three cheers, fired
off three pistols and dispersed.   'In the Interval I had
taken a party of 36 Local towards West Houghton to inter-
cept any Straglers, but they having passed along Byeways
eluded us.'   He does not mention the unpleasant episode
alluded to afterwards by one of the spies in court : 'as we
returned some of our own men took us into custody.'[2]
Though their blackened faces were no protection, the spies
obtained their release on showing their foraging caps.[3]

We have from one of the men present, John Heys, who
was afterwards tried and acquitted for his share in the night's
work,[4] a remarkably vivid description[5] of the Dean Moor Meeting, valuable as illustrating the desultory and rather inconsequent discontents of the men whom the governing class
credited with deep-laid schemes of rebellion.   John Heys,
who was out of work at the time, returned home about 10

---

[1] Making him take the secret oath.   [2] H.O., 42, 132.

[3] Prentice says the spies generally blackened their faces.

[4] According to Brougham he was acquitted because the spies 'buzzed round'
him too obviously (see *Parliamentary Debates*, July 13, 1812).

[5] See depositions in H.O., 42. 128.

P.M. that night by Dean Moor; he was stopped by two men with blackened faces who made him go to the meeting, saying that the military were out, and that they could not let him go lest he should give information. Two 'white faced' men came and conducted him to the meeting, which consisted of about twenty persons; after an hour or so ten or twelve blackened and disguised men came and joined them. He relates:

'That on his arrival at the Meeting they were discoursing on the Act of Queen Elizabeth which empowered the Magistrates to raise Wages to the price of Provisions, on the bad government of the Town particularly the management of the Overseers, who kept the Poor waiting twenty or thirty hours a week for their allowance.

'That the Orders in Council and the Conduct of several manufacturers were reprobated, the price of Provisions and the future prosperity of Trade were discussed.

'That on the arrival of the Blacks or Persons with their Faces blackened, the whole were formed in a Circle and one of the Blacks addressed the Meeting, asking what was to be done, recommending good Order, wishing all to speak freely but only one at a time. When he ended, a Man with a clean Face began a speech describing the Situation of the Country, the Hardships and Miseries of the industrious Weavers and Mechanics, which he attributed to the War, the Orders in Council were reprobated, and also the System of reducing Wages instead of diminishing the quantity of work in a given time, he recommended likewise a Subscription to apply to Lord Ellenborough for a Mandamus to compel the Magistrates to do their duty.

'That he was answered by one who was disfigured who said it was *all damned Nonsense to talk of Law as no Justice would be done except they did it themselves*, that they had lost time and spent Money enough to no purpose, he noticed the Proceedings at Nottingham, Yorkshire, Stockport and Middleton and hoped they would do their part which was to burn the Weaving Factory at West-houghton but this was rejected by all but the Blacks.

'That the Majority wishing to go home they were told the Military and the Constables were on the roads, and that it was impossible to get to Bolton without being arrested.

'That they were also told there were 200 Men waiting at Chowbent wishing to be joined by Bolton, and if they went to Chowbent by the time they got back the Military would be dismissed. That it was agreed to go, and being cold with standing so long on the Moor, he walked pretty sharp on passing the Four Lane Ends in Hulton there was only three in his Company.

'That he met only three drunken Men, that he stopped at the Bridge near Chowbent till the rest came up which was more than half an Hour.

'That they then proceeded to the Cross where a Pistol was fired, three Cheers given and then they were ordered to disperse.'

So ended the second attempt to fire West Houghton factory. That half hour, during which John Heys waited at the bridge near Chowbent, was eventful for the rest of the party, for it was in this interval that they came upon Sergeant Holland Bowden, whom, as we have seen, they forced to take the oath. How far this was done at the instigation of the ' confidants ' it is impossible to say, but it is difficult to believe that Stones could have allowed any one else to take the leading part.

The Dean Moor project was thus a failure, but next day at the Monday market there were lively scenes at Bolton, as well as in Manchester, Ashton, and Oldham. Oatmeal and potatoes, as Colonel Fletcher wrote shortly afterwards, were at nearly double their usual price—' the distresses consequent upon it,' he adds, ' are and must be very great until it shall please Heaven by a plentiful Harvest to relieve them.' Meanwhile the crowds of starving operatives menaced the farmers so seriously that the military had to protect the market, and the Riot Act was read. Next day, April 21, several hundreds again assembled and shouted, and at midnight an attempt was made to set fire to a Rope Walk,[1] an attempt possibly not unconnected with the report sent in by ' our confidential men ' of a settled plan to disturb the peace of the country by secret fires. Nothing seems to have happened on the 22nd or 23rd, but on Friday, April 24, 1812, John Stones' efforts were at last crowned with success, and Messrs. Rowe and Duncough's weaving factory at West Houghton was attacked and burnt.[2] Unfortunately the materials for the inner history of this third and successful attempt are wanting. Colonel Fletcher himself was absent from Bolton on private Enclosure business on the 23rd and 24th, and either did not receive or did not transmit any reports from his ' confidants.' Probably Stones found in the mob who had started food riots the Monday before better material for his purpose than in the meagre companies of tens, whom he had drilled so diligently. The outer history is clearly

[1] Charles Clark was afterwards tried for this fire and acquitted (*Manchester Mercury*, May 26, 1812).

[2] See for later history of W. Houghton some interesting figures in Cooke Taylor's *Tour in Manufacturing Districts*, p. 169.

told by Colonel Fletcher and in the documents for the prosecution, amongst the Treasury Solicitor's papers.[1]

On the nights of the 20th, 21st, and 22nd April a guard of
the local militia had remained in the building ; on Thursday
night, the 23rd, a guard of employees furnished with arms
by the local militia sat up all night, ' but on Friday the 24th
April, the reports of the Mob coming being very prevalent,
the Men who worked in the Building thought it not *prudent*
to Protect it as their Families might suffer. . . .'   The mill,
in fact, was not working that day.   On the morning of the
24th, the long-expected mob assembled at Chowbent and went
to West Houghton.   Application was made from the mill
to Bolton for soldiers to protect them, and a party of the
Scots Greys under Captain Bullen arrived at noon to find
no rioters there.   Captain Bullen, imagining himself to be
the victim of a hoax, took his men back to Bolton, declaring that he would only move again on the order of Mr. Hulton
the magistrate.   As soon as he had gone off, the same or
another mob, consisting of not more than fifty persons (most
witnesses said forty or fifty) assembled at Chowbent at
1 o'clock, and left Chowbent for West Houghton at 3 or 4 P.M.
The manager of the mill, hearing of their approach, went
off in person to Bolton, to summon the military again, but
by the time he arrived back at the factory with soldiers the
mob had completed their work of destruction and had left.
They had broken the windows, fetched straw from the stable,
piled it inside and set fire to it.   About £6000 worth of damage
was done.

That night the Bolton local militia were busy.   When
Colonel Fletcher returned home he sent off eighty men at
9 P.M. under Adjutant Warr to arrest rioters against whom
he had what he called ' *secret* or *open* information.'   The ways
of these local militia men and of the authorities who employed
them are amply exposed in the bundle of papers mentioned
above,[2] which contain many affidavits showing how, without
any excuse or warrant, they would break into the cottages,
seize the occupants with every circumstance of insolence,
and haul them before Colonel Fletcher, who in many cases
sent them home uncharged, adopting in other cases the
ingenious plan of exacting bail ' to answer any charge which
might hereafter be made.'

[1] H.O., 40. 1, and Treasury Solicitor, General Series, 3580 (Record Office).
[2] H.O., 42. 132.

West Houghton having been satisfactorily destroyed, Stones seems to have rested on his laurels, and we hear of no more disturbances in the Bolton district. Meanwhile in Manchester and its neighbourhood much had been happening. As we have seen, the movement, if it deserves that name, for the destruction of machinery in the Manchester district had collapsed early in April, but another movement amongst the working classes was rapidly gaining ground, the movement for Parliamentary Reform. The two movements were linked together in the person of John Buckley, weaver and Calvinist preacher, apparently a fussy consequential fellow with a great aptitude for quarrelling. When the original Secret Committee of three, of which he had been the moving spirit, came to an untimely end, he set to work to induce representatives from different trades to join together. The history of this new Secret Committee is rather obscure. Parliamentary Reform was clearly the main object, but Buckley seems to have used wild language, which led Yarwood at any rate to think that there was something more behind it.

Buckley was connected with the more respectable movement for Parliamentary Reform in the following way. For the 8th of April a meeting had been arranged by the leading men in Manchester to thank the Regent for retaining in office his father's Ministers; 'a few gentlemen of the town,' as Prentice describes them, determined to get up some opposition to the passing of the resolutions, and in connection with this invited Buckley, as representing no doubt a working-class organisation for Reform, to meet them at the Bridgewater Arms,[1] a fact of which he afterwards boasted a great deal. The sequel of the proposed Exchange meeting and the riot to which it gave rise are fully described by Prentice in his *History of Manchester*.[2] The promoters of the meeting determined to abandon it, but on the day a disorderly mob of men and boys appeared round the building, and were allowed to pass unchecked from sitting in mock solemnity on the chairs of the grand room and reading the news aloud, to damaging the furniture and smashing the windows.[3] The most interesting point about the riot was the fact pointed

[1] H.O., 40. I (Yarwood); H.O., 42. 121 (Whittaker).
[2] See pp. 48 ff.
[3] Colonel Clay corroborates what Prentice says of the slackness of the magistrates (H.O., 42. 122, April 11).

out by Prentice that the Manchester mob was no longer a Church and King mob.

Into the doings of Buckley's new Secret Committee, their failure to pay subscriptions, their squabbles and recriminations, it is unnecessary to enter. We have full accounts of them from Yarwood, who had been associated with Buckley in his former enterprise, and from Bent, alias 'B.,' who succeeded in getting himself appointed General Treasurer.[1] From these accounts it is abundantly clear that the new organisation had nothing to do with the two events that caused so much alarm to the Manchester authorities, namely the food riots on April 18 and 20, and the attack on Burton's factory and house at Middleton on April 21 and 22. Of these food riots the House of Lords' Secret Committee gravely said : ' the general pretence was the high price of provisions.' What this high price meant to the retail buyers is succinctly put by General Maitland, sent by Government shortly after this to take command in the disturbed districts. General Maitland, it must be observed, was a shrewd and independent observer, ready to criticise the ways of local authorities and employers.[2]

Potatoes, he reports,[3] which are much eaten, have risen from 7s. to 18s. the load : at retail prices they have risen from a penny for three pounds to a penny for one pound Other articles have also risen, some more and some less. Wages, on the other hand, have fallen, and whereas the common weaver used to get $1\frac{1}{2}$ guineas or 30s. a week, ' ten shillings I am well informed is the outside they now earn, and for that they must work six days in the week and hard. Under such Circumstances,' he naïvely adds, ' it must naturally be expected that great sourness and irratability will exist.'

Some of this ' sourness ' found play in the food riots on April 18 and 20. ' The potato market in Shudehill,' wrote the *Manchester Mercury* (April 21, 1812), ' was on Saturday morning the scene of great disorder and confusion, owing

[1] H.O., 40. 1.

[2] Thus he writes on one occasion : ' If we were to give way to individual feeling every Manufacturer in this part of the Country would have wished to have his own Property defended by the Military, and have made the Military probably the means of lowering the labour of His Workmen even below their present level ' (H.O., 40. 1, May 9).

[3] H.O., 42. 123, May 6.

to the much increased price on that indispensible part of the sustenance of the poor. Between the hours of ten and eleven o'clock, a number of ignorant, unthinking people, most of whom were women, failing in their endeavours to purchase the potatoes at the reduced rate [at] which they required them, immediately put themselves in possession of most of the produce in the Market, and never did we behold industry more conspicuous than in the seizure and conveyance of this spoil to the various abodes of the busy depredators.' The contents of the carts, we learn from another source, were sold by the rioters at 8s. the load.[1] The *Mercury* account adds that the military came up and took several persons, mostly women, into custody. 'B.' alias Bent, in one of his letters,[2] describes how some of the delegates of the newly formed 'association of trades'—that is, his Secret Committee No. 2 — 'saw the people seize the potatoes, which was high glee for them, as it was the opinion of the country people that our folks durst not do anything of the kind, and indeed it was done by the women and large boys, and since the business of the Exchange [3] it has been done by the above.'

On Monday, the 20th April (market day), there were food riots, not only in Manchester and Bolton, but also in Ashton and Oldham and all along the part of Cheshire northeast of Stockport that lies between Lancashire and Derby. In all these places mobs seized provision carts, and in some cases they broke open shops and appropriated food with or without payment. At Tintwistle on April 21, after selling flour, meal, bacon, and groceries at what they considered a fair price, they destroyed some of the machinery in Rhodes' woollen cloth mill, and also in some cotton mills.

The Oldham food riot had a serious sequel in the attempt to destroy Messrs. Burton's power weaving factory at Middleton. There is no reason to connect this attack with any secret organisation. It seems to have been an unpremeditated outburst of popular resentment. 'B.' is very explicit on this point. 'The Executive,' he writes,[4] 'recommends the people to be peaceable and not to disturb the peace on any account—those people who do are not of those who are twisted in, there may be a few who mix with the others but they are few.' The Boardman Square district, he reports,

---

[1] H.O., 42. 122, April 18.   [2] H.O., 40. 1.
[3] The Exchange riot.   [4] H.O., 40. 1, April 18.

wished to go to Middleton, but their leaders forbade them.[1]

What happened in Middleton is clearly told in several reports.[2] Oldham on the market day, Monday, April 20, was crowded with colliers from Hollinwood, who 'united with the rude uncultivated savages of Saddleworth formed an assemblage of the most desperate cast.' These rough visitors went to the meal and provision shops and presented a list of prices at which they forced sale : the best flour 3s. a peck, meal 2s. a peck, and potatoes 8s. a load. Elated by success they discussed and rejected a plan to attack the local militia depôt, going off instead to Middleton, where they joined forces with a Middleton mob in attacking Burton's power-loom factory. The Saddleworth and Oldham contingent were from all accounts the most active. When the crowd arrived at the factory Mr. Burton warned them, 'if you dare to attack this factory I will resist with force of arms.' They continued to throw stones and to use clubs, and Burton and his servants fired from the factory. Five rioters were killed and eighteen wounded, and the mob retired with imprecations, vowing that they would burn down Burton's dwelling house as a punishment for what they considered as a cold-blooded murder.

Next day, Tuesday, April 21,[3] a mob about two hundred strong, consisting chiefly of local miners, with fowling-pieces and picks, reappeared and carried out their threat of setting fire to the house. When the military arrived the mob received them with some irregular shots, on which the soldiers opened fire, killing or wounding about six. According to 'B.' ten rioters in all were killed in the two affrays.

It is in connection with the attack on Mr. Burton's house that we hear the most explicit particulars of a supposed 'general rising' on May 1, which caused a great deal of terror to the Manchester magistrates. As a rule it is only mentioned as bare information coming from 'those on whose

[1] Again on May 12, 'B.' reports 'Our Town [*i.e.* Manchester] hath done all in their power to do away with such business as Breaking and Burning Machinery and attempting to take Men's Lives' (H.O., 40. 1).

[2] See William Chippendale in H.O., 40. 1, April 23; Colonel Clay, H.O., 42. 122, April 21; a lieut.-colonel of Oldham militia, H.O., 42. 122, April 23; Treasury Solicitor, General Series, 4766.

[3] The Lords' Secret Committee gives the date as the 22nd. This is clearly a mistake for the 21st.

veracity I can depend ' or ' respectable channels ' or ' a respectable source.'   In this instance a colonel of the Oldham local
militia sent up a much more circumstantial story,[1] told him
by some anonymous person, of how whilst the Middleton
riot was in progress ' active delegates amongst the revolutionary Jacobins ' were stationed all along the roads and in
the public-houses with ruled sheets of paper which they
urged passers-by to sign. At the head of the paper was
a ' rebellious oath,' and the signatories bound themselves
to attend a general rising on May 4. The colonel's mysterious informant was told ' that the rising would be general
in London and all over the kingdom on that Day, that there
would be Leaders and Money in Abundance and nothing
would be required but resolute Hearts, as there would be
Numbers to overturn and overwhelm every Thing.' Had
Middleton been a scene of Stones' activities it would be tempt-
ing to see his hand in this story, but as the account is quite
uncorroborated, and no mention was made of this episode
at the trial of the rioters, it seems probable that it originated
in the lively brain of the unnamed informant.

May 1 and not May 4 was the date usually fixed on by the
' respectable sources ' for the general rising. By April 26
the magistrates were worked up into a state of panic.
The magistrates Hay and Silvester on April 26 sent to
the Home Office a petition against sinecures offered for
the signatures of weavers, spinners, mechanics, and other
inhabitants of Chorley, with the comment that the fact that
the signatures may be affixed till May 1 coincides with the
information about a general rising.[2] Again on April 27 [3]
their fears were enhanced by a mysterious notice of hiero-
glyphic figures stuck up in Prestwich churchyard, which 'being
deciphered by a trusty man ' proved to mean ' You are hereby
required to be ready on the shortest notice to join our army,
fail not at your peril. Amen,' and by a still more alarming
scrap of paper presented to them by the same ' respectable
source,' containing amongst other blood-curdling directions,
' Mode of Attack. Each Sett to murder the Affluent in their
own Neighbourhoods ; also such poor as will not join them
in taking their property and uniting with them in the work :
Its supposed this will be done in the space of three Hours.'

' On the 26th and 27th April,' reports Mr. Hay [4] on April
29, ' some thousands seemingly strangers, resorted to this

[1] H.O. 42. 122,   [2] Ibid,   [3] Ibid,   [4] Ibid,

town—they were all of awkward, description, yesterday
these people . . . totally disappeared.' May 1 passed, and
May 4 passed, and the affluent were still allowed to sleep
quietly in their beds. 'For my own part,' wrote General
Maitland on May 6,[1] 'I am a total disbeliever that either
such rising was seriously intended or that they were in a state
of organisation to admit of it.'

All disturbances in Lancashire and Cheshire had now ended,
and numbers of the rioters were fast in prison, awaiting their
trial, but the terror of deep-laid schemes of revolution still
haunted the authorities, and the flame was carefully fanned
by ' B.' and other ' respectable sources.' Their efforts culminated in the arrest and trial of ' the thirty-eight,' which
we discuss later. We must first describe the trials of the
rioters.

At Chester, the Special Commission to try the Cheshire
offenders sat during the last week of May.[2] Mr. Justice
Dallas and Mr. Justice Burton were the Judges. Forty-
four prisoners awaited trial, but of these, one was admitted
evidence, three were acquitted, and twelve, most of them
charged with rioting, were let off on their own recognisances,
leaving twenty-eight to receive sentence. Of these twenty-
eight no fewer than fourteen received the death sentence,
but though five of these fourteen were reserved for execution,
in the end only two were hung, Joseph Thompson, a weaver of
thirty-four, who had stolen some silver and set fire to a house
at Edgeley, and John Temples, a weaver of twenty-seven,
who had stolen silver spoons and clothes at Adlington. Of
the other twelve sentenced to death and respited, only three
were convicted of attacks on machinery : these were James
Crossland, a shoemaker of forty-five, John Heywood, a carder
of eighteen, and John Ellis, occupation not stated. They
were found guilty of breaking machinery at Tintwistle. The
other capital convictions were for riots and obtaining money
or flour at various places. In addition to the capital convictions, eight men were sentenced to transportation for seven
years, six of them for stealing flour at corn mills, and two
for illegal oaths. These last two were John Bradshaw and
Thomas Whittaker,[3] the latter a ' man of superior ability

[1] H.O., 42. 123.
[2] See *Manchester Mercury*, June 9, 1812; and H.O. 42 123, May 30.
[3] See p. 274 above.

and education,' for whose conviction the prosecution were
particularly urgent.[1]

The case against these men and against three others who
were acquitted or not proceeded against rested on the sole
evidence of one John Parnell.[2]   Mr. Lloyd of Stockport had
gone out, in his capacity of captain of the local militia, on
April 15 to disperse an assembly, and in the course of proceedings John Parnell was caught.   Afterwards, under Mr. Lloyd's
care, he confessed that he had on April 6 received an illegal
oath from Thomas Whittaker.   'None of the persons in
custody sworn at the same time are inclined to corroborate
the Testimony of Parnell, because it is evident they are so
ignorant as to conceive themselves under the obligation
imposed by the diabolical oath not to tell of one another.'
Mr. Lloyd, however, managed to scrape up corroborating
evidence of ' various minute circumstances ' and Whittaker's
conviction was secured.   Six more prisoners, one of them a
woman, were sentenced to terms of imprisonment of one
or three years for rioting or stealing flour.   Of the various
prisoners, it may be noticed that a good many were colliers,
one of whom, William Walker, who had incited a mob to
disorder and tumult at Gee's Cross, was dignified by the
name of General Ludd.   Thompson and Temples were not
executed till June 21.   Thompson gladdened the hearts of
the authorities by making a rambling dying confession, declaring that a rebellion existed and that things were to be like
Oliver Cromwell's time.[3]

The trials for offences in Lancashire took place before a Special
Commission at the end of May and beginning of June 1812.
The Judges were Baron Thomson and Mr. Justice Le Blanc.
It seems possible that their selection was one of Perceval's
last acts before his assassination.   ' Mr. Perceval,' he wrote
on May 6,[4] in a private letter to the Home Secretary who
had written to him on the subject of the Special Commission for Lancashire, ' does not conceive that it is or can be
his *official* Duty to *select* the Judges, as would appear to be
implied by the terms of Mr. Ryder's letter.'   He adds, however,
that if on inquiry he finds that he ought to do so he will make
the selection.   Whoever was responsible for the selection

[1] See Treasury Solicitor's letter from Chester (H.O., 42. 123, May 30).
[2] Treasury Solicitor, General Series, 1160.
[3] H.O., 42. 124, June 25.   [4] H.O., 42. 123.

made sure that the rioters in Lancashire should not meet with the leniency for which Mr. Justice Bayley had been blamed elsewhere.

The question of the necessity of using the evidence of spies to convict the prisoners from the Bolton district had much exercised Colonel Fletcher. 'We are *shy* of bringing these Witnesses forward,' he wrote on April 30,[1] 'being desirous to cover over our Intelligence even with a *Shadow* rather than exhibit the Sources to *open Day*.' A week later it was decided to use evidence from what might be termed the piece-work spies, in contrast to Stones and his father who were employed on a time-work system.[2] By May 21, however, it was evident that the testimony of the 'main Informants' would be necessary, but the informers themselves had fallen under suspicion. 'His' [that is John Stones'] 'Father, Simon Stones,' wrote Colonel Fletcher,[3] 'who was the Leader of those Ten Men—amongst whom some others of our Confidents were introduced to the Meeting of the 19th April—has since the Committals to Lancaster become suspected, and the suspicion has been extended also to his son—who as he resided in one of the most seditious parts of this Neighbourhood has requested to have his Family removed to a Place of greater Safety—which has been promised on our part and will be carried into Effect during his absence at the Assizes.' He adds that they have requested the solicitors for the prosecution to make as little use of Stones as possible, and that it is hoped the Government will think him deserving of some remuneration, even if the fact of his giving open testimony makes him useless for the future.

The prosecutions before the Lancashire Special Commission [4] can be divided into four main categories: (1) those for the food riots at Manchester, (2) those for arson at Middleton, (3) those for arson at West Houghton, (4) those for illegal oaths. In addition there were some minor charges for various riots and one for arson at Bolton.[5] For the first category, the food riots at Manchester, eight persons were tried, six men, two women: four were acquitted and four were found guilty and received the death sentence. Of the four condemned, three—John Howarth, John Lee, and Thomas Hoyle—

---

[1] H.O., 40. 1.   [2] *Ibid.*   [3] *Ibid.*

[4] See *Manchester Mercury*, May 26; and Treasury Solicitor, General Series, 3580, 3582, 4766.

[5] See p. 284 note above.

were found guilty of riotously assembling at John Holland's house in Deansgate, breaking his door and windows open, and stealing bread, cheese, and potatoes. The fourth, Hannah Smith, a woman of fifty-four, had played a violent part in the riots.[1] When the mob had seized ten bushels of potatoes and decreed to sell them at 8d. a score, Hannah Smith was heard to say, ' damn them we will have them for nothing,' and she afterwards helped to shovel them out, filling her own apron. She had also headed another mob and forced George Lomas to sell his potatoes at a loss, and here too her language was violent; ' we will not be satisfied with Potatoes,' she cried, and ' she threatened to stop Butter Carts and horses bringing Milk to Town, she would have Butter at 1s. per lb. and Milk at 2d. per Quart and if the Owners would not take that price she would have both Butter and Milk for nothing.' She carried out her threat about the butter, and the charge for which she was tried first and condemned to death was for jumping on a butter cart at Ardwick and selling twenty pounds of butter, worth 36s., at 1s. the pound.

The rioters at Burton's at Middleton, charged with arson, had a more fortunate fate than the Manchester rioters. Six men were tried for setting fire to Burton's house. There was no evidence to prove that they were concerned in the actual arson, but it was pretty clear that they had been in the mob, and Mr. Justice Le Blanc charged the jury, that even if the prisoners were not guilty of actually setting fire to the house, yet, if they were guilty of a riot alone, they were guilty of the whole charge.[2] What happened is best told in the words of the prosecuting counsel, Mr. J. A. Park, Attorney-General for the County Palatine, in his description of the proceedings to the Home Office :[3] ' There were six others acquitted of the clearest case of Arson, to the utter dissatisfaction of the whole Court, Mr. Ewart, a Merchant of Liverpool, the foreman of the Jury, and the *sole* cause of the Mischief, having kept the Jury out an hour, before he could bring them over to his opinion. But I immediately to the great satisfaction of the Sheriff and Grand Jury, presented a fresh Bill against them for the Misdemeanour of rioting, etc., and would have proceeded instantly to try and openly said so. But when brought up they chose to traverse—however the Judges

[1] Treasury Solicitor, 3582.   [2] *Ibid.*, 4766.
[3] H.O., 42, 124, June 2.

required two sureties for every Prisoner in £100 each, which bail they probably will not obtain, so that there has not been the triumph expected [1]—and Mr. Ewart was so looked down upon, that he never was seen in Court or at Lancaster afterwards.' It does not occur to Mr. Park that Mr. Ewart, having saved six persons from the hangman, might shake the dust of the Lancaster Special Commission off his feet for other reasons.

For arson in the successful attack on the West Houghton factory, thirteen prisoners were tried—nine were men, two were boys of fifteen and sixteen, two were girls of fifteen and nineteen. It was not necessary to bring forward the evidence of any ' confidants,' as the prisoners could be identified by persons from the mill. Outside the Brief are scribbled some notes that show the lines of the prosecution:[2] 'Lowness of wages —and dearness of provisions—the ground for the objection— Will of Providence—Is the [word illegible] mended by destroying property—one hundred people thrown out of employment. The Means of Charity destroyed—Never was so charitable a country. The Poor shall never cease out of the land—The poor ye shall have always with you,' etc. It is satisfactory to learn from the Minutes of the trial that the prosecuting counsel, Mr. Park, after pointing out that ' provisions being scarce was the dispensation of God,' alluded to the girl and boy prisoners ' with feeling,' but added ' neither the tender sex of the one or the youth of the other could excuse them.' The evidence for the defence consisted of rather weak alibis or of testimony to character. The jury deliberated for an hour, and found only four out of the thirteen prisoners guilty. They seem to have made a selection of those whom they thought most deserved hanging. Clearly the ' tender sex ' of the two girls, Mary and Lydia Molyneux, saved them from death, for they had played an active part ' with Muck Hooks and Coal Picks in their Hands breaking the Windows of the Building and swearing and cursing the souls of those that worked in the Factory,'[3] while John Brownlow, the boy of fifteen, was saved by his mother, whom two witnesses described as having pulled him away against his will. The four who

[1] Four of the prisoners managed to find sureties. They were sentenced to two years' imprisonment at the August Assizes. The two who had failed to secure bail were sentenced to eighteen months. Brougham was counsel for four of the prisoners (Treasury Solicitor, 4766).

[2] Treasury Solicitor, 3580.   [3] Ibid.

were found guilty were condemned to death.   Their names were
Job Fletcher, Thomas Kerfoot, James Smith, and Abraham
Charlson, aged sixteen.   Abraham Charlson, who had three
soldier brothers, had played the soldier to his own undoing.
He had acted as sentinel, pacing up and down with a scythe,
and calling out encouraging remarks.

For the fourth category of offences, namely, administering, receiving, or being present at the administration of illegal
oaths, fifteen men and boys were sentenced to seven years'
transportation.   The question of the Luddite oath is discussed elsewhere ; [1] it is enough to mention here that six
of these men [2] were sentenced on the evidence of Holland
Bowden, who could not identify the prisoners, and of nine
spies, for the oath to Sergeant Holland Bowden on the famous
Dean Moor evening, April 19.[3]   The rest [4] were sentenced in connection with the administration of oaths to Isaac Crompton
and others at Bolton Moor, mainly on the evidence of Isaac
Crompton himself, who purchased immunity by disclosing
what had passed.   In the notes for the case [5] the sinister
fact is mentioned that the only corroborative evidence comes
from John Stones.

Two more men were sentenced to seven years' transportation for breaking into a mill at Worsley, and stealing grain
and flour, and six women and girls and one man received
the light punishment of six months' imprisonment for rioting at
Middleton or elsewhere.   The result of the trials was briefly

8	Death and hung.
17	Transported seven years.
7	Imprisonment six months,
6	Traversed to next Assizes.
20	Acquitted.

58

The eight capitally convicted were executed on Saturday,
June 12. 'Their conduct throughout confinement,' wrote
the *Manchester Mercury*,[6] ' manifested the greatest indiffer-

---

[1] See p. 336 below.

[2] A seventh, Samuel Radcliffe, was afterwards convicted.

[3] There is an imperfect copy of the report of this trial in the bundle in H.O.,
42. 132, mentioned above.

[4] With the possible exception of John Burney, sentenced for administering an
oath to Isaac Clayton, which looks like a misprint for Crompton.

[5] Treasury Solicitor, 3580.   [6] June 16, 1812.

ence and unconcern, as to the awful state in which they were
placed ; and all the pathetic exhortations of the Rev. the
Chaplain were frequently repeated before signs of repentance
of their crimes or necessity of preparation to meet their God,
appeared in any wise to awaken their benighted minds.'

Abraham Charlson, the boy of sixteen was childish for his
age, and at the time of his execution ' called on his mother
for help . . . thinking she had the power to save him.' [1]

We must now describe briefly the incident of the arrest
and trial of ' the 38,' not only because they are often called
' the 38 Luddites,' but because it explains the temper which
could exact such cruel penalties from the rioters.[2] John
Buckley, as we have said, had tried to organise a committee
of representatives from different trades, which was called
the second Manchester Secret Committee,[3] and many quarrels
had ensued.   John Buckley seems then to have dropped into
the background, and the association of trades for Parliamentary Reform was taken over or restarted by more reputable
persons.   Of this new organisation of working-class reformers
' B.' or Bent was chosen treasurer, and he writes reports [4]
of a meeting of the delegates on May 18 for the business of
Peace and Parliamentary Reform, but the ' other business,'
he adds significantly, must not be lost sight of.   That Bent
ever seriously tried to induce any of his colleagues to work for
violent measures is unlikely, as otherwise men of the stamp
of John Knight would not have continued to trust him, but
his own report fits in well enough with the account given
later by Yarwood,[5] who, hoping to save himself by a full
' confession,' did not scruple to implicate Bent, ignorant of
course that he was a spy.   ' One Observation of Mr. Bent's
strikes me, he said if this Business had been or was to be
carried on under the pretence of a Petition for peace and
Parliamentary Reform, many persons would contribute
under that pretence, as would not under any other, and It
would be a safer plan too.'

Meanwhile the new organisation decided on May 26 to
prepare an address to the Prince Regent and a petition to
the House of Commons.   On June 11 they met again to

---

[1] Prentice, *op cit.*, p. 57, quoting John Edward Taylor.

[2] For following account, see Report of *Trial of Thirty-Eight Men*, with intro-
ductory narrative by John Knight, Manchester, 1812.

[3] See p. 286 above.   [4] H.O., 40. 1, May.   [5] H.O. 40. 1.

consider these documents, moving from one public-house to a second, because they were warned that Nadin, the deputy constable, would disturb them. But they did not escape, for their meeting at the second public-house was interrupted by Nadin, who came in followed by soldiers, and arrested the thirty-eight occupants of the room. They were charged, and afterwards tried on August 27 at Lancaster for the felony of administering or being present at the administration of an illegal oath to Samuel Fleming.

Now Samuel Fleming was an unemployed weaver, who acted under Nadin's charge, as one of the ' respectable sources ' of the magistrates' information. He had been ordered by Colonel Silvester, J.P., and by Nadin, to get himself ' twisted in,' and his story was that at this meeting William Washington and Thomas Broughton administered the approved Luddite oath to him and to one or two others, whilst the rest looked on. After taking the oath he went off to fetch Nadin, who promptly arrested the miscreants. There was no corroboration of Fleming's tale from any source, but this did not trouble the Lancashire magistrates. Indeed compared with the evidence on which men had already been transported, Samuel Fleming's story was ample for conviction.

General Maitland, however, was uneasy. ' Since I addressed you yesterday,' he wrote on June 17,[1] ' I have grounds for thinking the Men taken up here lately, will not be liable to severe Punishment, unless the fact of their administering Illegal Oaths can be brought home, which at present is extremely doubtful. I am endeavouring to try to get some of them to inform, and am not without hopes this may be accomplished, with the Aid of some money and a little management.' The money and the management were alike fruitless. Higgins, the gaoler, did his best to help by intercepting all letters and setting other prisoners on to glean information, but all he could produce was the fact that one of the thirty-eight had a father-in-law who was said to have made gunpowder for the Irish Insurrection in 1803,[2] and a rambling communication[3] from a convict in Lancaster gaol which connected Dr. Taylor and Mr. Hulme, well-known reformers of the professional class, with the thirty-eight, and asserted that three of the prisoners were alarmed lest Stones, who came to the prison one day with Colonel Fletcher, should identify them as having once been present at a meeting in Bolton.

[1] H.O., 42. 124.   [2] H.O., 42. 125, July 4.   [3] *Ibid*, July 26.

General Maitland's uneasiness grew. ' I am much afraid,'
he wrote on July 30,[1] ' unless new Evidence can be procured,
most of these will be acquitted, which would be a thing infinitely to be regretted, for though we might not be able to
get legal Proof I have no doubt of their Guilt.'

The event proved even worse than Maitland's anticipations.
After more than ten weeks in prison, on August 27, 1812, the
whole thirty-eight were triumphantly acquitted. The verbatim
account of the evidence, published afterwards with the introduction by John Knight, one of the defendants, is of
absorbing interest. The thirty-eight were fortunate in their
Judge, Baron Wood, fortunate also in their counsel, Scarlett,
Brougham, and Williams,[2] who though unable, as it was
a case of felony, to speak on behalf of the prisoners, conducted
a merciless cross-examination of Fleming and his employers.

Fleming had made some serious blunders : indeed he seems,
so far as one can judge from his later reports, to have been
a man of poor capacity. In this case he fixed on Washington
as one of the men who gave him the oath, an unfortunate
choice, for Washington, as it happened, unlike the others
had not come to the meeting till after Fleming had gone,
and could produce satisfactory evidence to show this. Again
Fleming, when called on after the arrest of the prisoners to
identify one of the men who had taken the illegal oath with
him, had pointed out one of the turnkeys. The turnkey,
it must be mentioned in Fleming's excuse, was sitting in the
place into which Nadin had pertinaciously tried to force John
Knight. Nadin too had made his mistake ; in the excitement of the evening he had overlooked one of the conspirators
on the staircase and failed to arrest him, and this man was
able to appear as a witness to the evening's proceedings.
No Bible on which to administer the illegal oath was found
in the room, and the only documents discovered were the
address to the Prince Regent, the petition to the House of
Commons, and some resolutions already printed in the *States-
man*. Baron Wood in summing up put the case to the jury :

[1] H.O., 42, 125.
[2] The ' Manchester Luddities,' as Colonel Fletcher called the Reform party,
had been busy raising money for their defence ; possibly, he adds, there is a
secret fund for them 'from Quarters yet undiscovered ' (H.O., 42. 124, June
30). The occupations of the thirty-eight are given in Treasury Solicitor, 4766.
Twelve were weavers, five cotton spinners. There was one manufacturer (John
Knight), one broker, and the rest belonged to various trades such as hatters,
fustian-cutters, bricklayers, etc.

'You have the single oath of Fleming to support the case against the prisoners, and you have the evidence of five or six witnesses, whose credit is unimpeached, all of them contradicting what Fleming has sworn.' The jury, as we have said, returned a verdict of 'Not Guilty,' and the 'thirty-eight bundles of Blue,' as Mr. Lloyd of Stockport facetiously called them, were, to the deep and unconcealed regret of the Manchester authorities, allowed to return home instead of being transported across the seas.[1]

The trial of the thirty-eight ought to have made a career like Oliver's impossible, for it brought into daylight the methods in use in Lancashire, and it called the attention of Parliament to the machinations of spies. Unfortunately the discussion in Parliament in which Whitbread and Burdett exposed the part spies had played in the affair of Dean Moor and other events, that had seemed so terrifying to Ministers, seems to have made no impression on Castlereagh and Sidmouth. The immediate effect of the trial in Lancashire was apparently to discourage the Reform movement. Everybody saw that the accused men, who had spent three months in prison, had owed their escape to a lucky combination of circumstances, and it was not likely that the next set of victims would be equally fortunate. Of the thirty-eight on whom Nadin had pounced the only one who took an active part afterwards was the indomitable John Knight.

[1] Mr. Becket, from the Home Office, writes to Lloyd on September 2: 'Any new Information against the 38 from Lancaster should be taken and sent up for consideration' (H.O., 42. 127). Fleming was rewarded in spite of his failure. On February 28, 1813 (H.O., 40. 2.) Mr. Hay writes to General Acland that the magistrates have at last settled with Fleming and paid him for his trouble. He can settle with his family where he likes. 'His wishes were ridiculous—wanted an ensign's commission, etc. etc.' According to the official endorsement of a letter on the best mode of getting Fleming off the hands of Government, the Treasury were asked to advance £100 for the purpose (H.O., 42. 132, January 26).

CHAPTER XI

THE YORKSHIRE LUDDITES

THE Luddite disturbances in Yorkshire began about the same time as those in Lancashire, but lasted into the summer, and the trials for the offences that were committed did not take place till January 1813. The scene of the disturbances, which at first were the work of a small band of highly organised and skilled workmen, was the woollen district of the West Riding, and the form the destruction of shearing frames— that is, the machinery for cutting off the nap that had been raised in the previous process. The process of cutting the nap was called ' shearing ' or ' cropping ' or ' cutting ' the cloth. The raising of the nap, as we have seen, was originally done by hand, but by this time hand work was practically super- seded by those gig mills against which the shearmen had put up so persistent a fight.[1] The shearmen seem now to have acquiesced more or less reluctantly in the use of gig mills,[2] and to have concentrated their efforts on retaining the shearing of cloth as a hand industry.

This work of ' cropping ' or shearing the cloth under the old system was carried on in small shops where master dressers employed three or four highly skilled shearmen, called in Yorkshire ' croppers.' These croppers each worked one pair of shears by hand, and it was said that a cropper could always be identified by the hoof formed on his right hand from holding the shears. The new machinery, by which one man could do the work of four, was in the form of a frame in which two or more pairs of shears were fixed and worked by power at the same time.[3] This machinery had been in-

[1] See pp. 168 ff. above.

[2] On January 12, 1812, a gig mill in Leeds was burned down (H.O., 42. 119, January 22). Cf. p. 189 above.

[3] For account of the old and new systems, see *The Risings of the Luddites*, by Frank Peel, 2nd edition, pp. 10 and 29 ; Reports of Assistant Hand-loom Weavers' Commissioners, 1840, part ii. pp. 439 ff.

troduced in various small shops in or near Huddersfield and at a few bigger establishments.[1]

It was an unfortunate time for the introduction of labour-saving machinery. There had been a bad harvest the year before; the Orders in Council had crippled the woollen industry; there were numbers of unemployed apart from those turned adrift by the introduction of new machinery. The croppers, as was perhaps natural, attributed all the evils that beset them to these new machines, and determined to destroy them. Their proceedings were at first as well organised and thorough as those of the Nottingham Luddites. They started by destroying the obnoxious shearing frames in some small establishments in the Huddersfield district in the latter part of February 1812. ' General Snipshears ' and his men, for so they styled themselves, would send a warning letter, telling the owner of the frames to take them down under pain of having not only his frames but his premises destroyed. If any owner, or servant of the owner, opposed them when they appeared, they used to tie him down and guard him till the work was done. Shearing frames, shears, and cloths were destroyed : in one instance where the owner had taken his frames down they agreed at his request to spare the shears, but took out the frames from the barn where he had put them away, and smashed them to pieces.[2]

By March 15 Mr. Joseph Radcliffe, the energetic magistrate of Huddersfield, reported that eleven houses had already suffered these depredations.[3] Relations between magistrates and military were strained. Mr. Radcliffe complained of the supineness of the commander at York, General Grey, who had refused to send one hundred infantry to protect property at Huddersfield. General Grey's case was, that it was impossible to send to Huddersfield infantry which he had not got : in fact with the troops under his command he could not furnish the aid which the magistrates seemed to expect, and he in his turn complained that the squadron at Huddersfield was reduced to nothing because the magistrates required so many detachments to guard particular houses. Were the force ten times as great as it is, he wrote,[4]

---

[1] Shearing frames had been used in Yorkshire certainly as early as 1806 (see Committee on Woollen Manufacture, 1806, p. 367).

[2] H.O., 40. 1, March 14.   [3] H.O., 42. 121.

[4] H.O., 42. 121, March 16.

it could not furnish 'separate guards for every individual who may be under apprehensions for the safety of his property.'

Whatever the responsibility of the different authorities, the result was that the machine breakers, meeting with no check, grew emboldened to attack larger establishments with their 'Enoch,' for so they called the big hammer used in the work of destruction, after the firm of Enoch and James Taylor, who made not only the shearing frames but the hammers that destroyed them. The last verse of the croppers' rollicking ballad ran :

> 'Great Enoch still shall lead the van.
> Stop him who dare ! Stop him who can !
> Press forward every gallant man
> With hatchet, pike and gun !
> Oh, the cropper lads for me,
> The gallant lads for me,
> Who with lusty stroke
> The shear frames broke,
> The cropper lads for me.'[1]

On March 15, in Mr. Vickerman's establishment at Taylor Hill near Huddersfield, ten frames and thirty pairs of shears were broken.[2] On March 24 Messrs. Thompson's mill at Rawdon near Leeds was attacked and the machinery destroyed ; the next day Messrs. Dickinson's premises in Leeds were entered and the cloths cut to pieces.[3] Consternation spread amongst the owners of the unpopular machinery ; troops were applied for on every side but could not be provided. One of the magistrates at Horbury urged the owners to pull down their obnoxious machinery ;[4] some complied. Mr. Joseph Foster, proprietor of a big mill at Horbury, refused to adopt the suggestion, and on April 9 his mill where his four sons, Thomas, John, Josiah, and Joseph, were sleeping, was visited by the frame breakers at midnight.[5] Thomas and Joseph were kept in bed, guarded by men told off for the purpose, John and Josiah were forced to come downstairs to open the doors. Josiah opened the scribbling mill door, but the rioters, declaring those were not the machines they wanted, broke into the cropping shop and destroyed all the shears and some of the machinery. John and Josiah mean-

[1] Peel, *The Risings of the Luddites*, p. 47.   [2] H.O., 42. 121, March 17,
[3] H.O., 42. 121, March 25.   [4] *Ibid.*   [5] H. O., 42. 122, April 22.

while were ordered to lie down, their legs were tied, and they were closely guarded. When the work of destruction was finished they were bidden to stand up ; one man guarded them till the rest had gone, and he then passed out of the door himself wishing them good night. Identification of the rioters was impossible, for in these midnight raids they were always disguised by blackened faces or masks.

Two nights after this Horbury affair, on Saturday, April 11, 1812, occurred the attack on William Cartwright's mill at Rawfolds in Liversedge, immortalised in the pages of *Shirley*. It was here that the frame breakers met with their first and their final rebuff. The Rawfolds mill was a large mill for finishing cloth. Two or three years earlier, Mr. Cartwright had begun to introduce shearing frames and to economise in labour. The effects of his new machinery were felt not only by his own men, but by the various small cropping shops in the neighbourhood, who found their work being taken from them. Cartwright, a man of courage and resolution, but of a cold and unsympathetic temperament, continued to introduce new machinery in spite of the depression of trade. Two waggon loads of frames destined for his mill had been broken up on the Hartshead Moor shortly before this time, but the incident had merely sharpened his determination. Knowing that his mill was singled out for attack, he fortified it with every precaution, and for six weeks before April 11 he had slept there every night.

The attack was carefully organised.[1] Contingents from Halifax, Huddersfield, Liversedge, Heckmondwike, Gomersal, Birstall, Cleckheaton, and other places, numbering about 150, met in a field belonging to Sir George Armytage near the 'Dumb Steeple' or obelisk, some three miles from the mill, between 10 and 11 o'clock. They were armed with guns, pistols, stakes, hammers, or whatever weapon came to hand, and after being mustered by numbers into companies of musket men or pistol men or hatchet men they marched to the mill, which they reached rather more than half an hour after midnight. A contingent from Leeds was expected to meet them above the hollow, but this reinforcement only arrived when firing had already begun, and their hearts failing them, they turned back home again. What happened when the rioters reached the mill is best told in a private

---

[1] See for account of attack the Report of Proceedings at York Special Commission, January 1813 ; and *The Risings of the Luddites*, chaps. ix. and x.

letter to a friend from Cartwright himself. This letter was
sent up by Lord Fitzwilliam to the Home Office:[1]

'From the friendly Interest you take in my Concerns I am sure
the particulars of the recent infamous attempt to destroy my
property will be interesting to you. In consequence of the sick-
ness of two of my men and of some symptoms of Fear manifested
by a third immediately after the affair at Mr. Fosters which
induced me to discontinue him as part of my Guard at my Mill,
I apply'd for five soldiers of the Cumberland Militia which made
us Number 10 Men, we retired to rest about ½ past twelve, in less
than ¼ of an hour after which we were rous'd by the most dreadful Crash of the Windows and at the same instant a heavy Fire
was given into the Windows of the Floor upon which we were;
we immediately flew to arms, our Fire was given with much
Steadiness and rapidity and continued as our Neighbours state
nearly 20 minutes during which Time we discharg'd nearly 140
Shots. The assailants being driven back we found they had left
behind them two Men wounded mortally who however from untoward circumstances made no Disclosure of their associates.
Many are certainly wounded the Traces of Blood being very
heavy in different Directions; We can form no idea of the Number
of our assailants, their fire was however very heavy and well
directed, providentially no man within was hurt. Our guards
without state that the Men closed upon them very silently and
took their arms from them which prevented their alarming us by
the Discharge of their Blunderbusses, they make the Number
between one and two hundred that some of them had military
uniform, But as I myself am not satisfied that they did their Duty
I suppress their Statement entirely. On looking over our Damage
we found a large Door so much cut by Hatchets as to make it
useless and eight Windows on the Ground Floor completely
destroyed Glass and Frames and above Stairs nearly 50 Squares
of Glass by single Shots.—The Iron Stanchions of the Ground
Floor which I have recently put in for the Purpose kept them
from making any Impression or getting in. In their Flight they
threw away large Hammers Hatchets and Mauls, 14 of which we
have found.

'You will I am sure regret under my Circumstances the
Expenses I must have incurred for the preparations for my
Defence as also in my subsequent expenses: they cannot have
been less than £80 exclusive of the Damages done. My Door
is replaced by a new one but the Windows I shall not put in
until there is a certainty of no further attack mean Time I have
made light Frames and cover'd them with oil'd paper which
as the warm Weather is coming will answer very well. My
Family nothwithstanding the small Distance say ¼ mile were

[1] See H.O., 42. 122, April 23, 1812.

unconscious of the proceedings which gave me much Happiness, they are now well. The public papers have been very circumstantial and correct in the Detail of the affair. But I could not refrain from handing this to you.—I am, my dear Sir, Yours truly,

W. CARTWRIGHT.

'I wish I knew the Way to get the name of one of my men who serv'd 9 years in the 11th L D and was discharged in Consequence of a thigh broken in the Service without pension to the notice of the Government he behaved most galantly. Two of the Cumberland Men behaved ill one of them was brought to Court Martial and punished; our Effectives were thus only 8.'

Cartwright in this letter, it will be noticed, makes mention incidentally of two men mortally wounded who 'from untoward circumstances made no Disclosure of their associates.' The charges against Cartwright in connection with the treatment of these dying men must be mentioned here as they explain to a great extent the passionate desire for vengeance which diverted the movement from attacks on machinery to attacks on men, resulting later in the attempted murder of Cartwright and the assassination of Mr. Horsfall. One of the wounded men was Samuel Hartley of Halifax, a man of twenty-four, formerly a cropper in Cartwright's employ, turned off when the new machinery was introduced. The other was John Booth, a boy of nineteen, son of a neighbouring clergyman. Booth's father, once himself a cropper, had been ordained by the help of the Vicar of Huddersfield, who had noticed his scholarly disposition.[1] He had been given the living of Lowmoor but eked out its scanty stipend by a partnership in a small cropping business. The son John, who was apprenticed in Huddersfield to a harness-making ironmonger, had studied the doctrines of Owen, and in his enthusiastic desire for the regeneration of society had been drawn into the Luddite schemes by his friend George Mellor.

These two young men, Hartley and Booth, lay in agony outside Rawfolds mill in the cold hours before dawn on that Sunday morning. Cartwright left them untended till neighbours arrived, afraid, so it was afterwards asserted at the trial to explain his inaction, 'lest it should be said that he had murdered them.' At last various neighbours including the Rev. Hammond Roberson, well known as Mr. Helston in *Shirley*, arrived on the scene, and the party from the mill came out. The story goes that Cartwright, with Roberson's

[1] *The Risings of the Luddites*, p. 14.

approval, refused help to the wounded men except on condition of their disclosing the names of their associates, but that Dixon, manager of a neighbouring chemical works, in spite of Cartwright's prohibition, moistened the lips of the miserable Booth, whilst Billy Clough, the tipsy bon-vivant of the neighbourhood, insisted on placing a stone under the head of Hartley, who was choking. A crowd then began to gather, Cartwright gave up his attempt to enforce confession, and the wounded men were brought into the mill and doctors summoned. Afterwards they were taken off to the Star Inn at Robertown, where soldiers rode up and down to keep back the excited throng, amongst whom sinister rumours soon spread of cruelties practised on the dying men in order to induce them to reveal the names of their accomplices.

The belief that torture was applied lived long, and it was strengthened by the fact that two beddings at the inn were known to have been destroyed by aqua-fortis, used probably in hopes of stopping the bleeding by the surgeons, for Booth's leg was shattered and had to be amputated. Without supposing that any deliberate cruelty was shown, it is easy to see how in those days before anæsthetics, a clergyman who hung over patients suffering at the surgeons' hands, urging them and urging them in vain to reveal the names of their accomplices, might seem little removed from an official hovering over his victims in a torture chamber. By six in the morning Booth's agony drew to an end; as 'he lay at the point of death he signalled to Mr. Roberson, who instantly went to his side. 'Can you keep a secret?' gasped the dying man. 'I can,' eagerly replied the expectant clergyman. 'So can I,' replied poor Booth, and soon after calmly expired.'[1] Hartley, who had been wounded in the body, lingered on all through Sunday, and died at 3 o'clock on Monday morning. No word had passed his lips. The 'untoward circumstances' of faith and loyalty had prevailed.

Hartley was buried at Halifax on the Wednesday amidst an immense concourse of people from all sides.[2] Booth's funeral was arranged for midday on Thursday, but when

[1] *The Risings of the Luddites*, p. 104.

[2] The Rev. Jabez Bunting, superintendent of the Wesleyan Methodists, roused great hostility by refusing to perform the burial service, and leaving it to a junior preacher (see *History of Wesleyan Methodism in Halifax*, by T. U. Walker, Halifax, 1836, p. 254).

the thousands who wished to attend it arrived, they found
that the authorities in alarm had hastily buried the body
early in the morning. Forbidden to pay the last honours
to their young comrade, whose steadfastness had roused
their deepest emotions, the bolder spirits grew embittered,
and ' Vengeance for the Blood of the Innocent ' was chalked
up on many doors.[1]   A week later, on Saturday, April 18,
Cartwright rode over to Huddersfield to give evidence at the
court-martial on the soldier who had refused to fire.   The
man was sentenced to three hundred lashes. Cartwright
asked for mercy, which was refused.   As Cartwright galloped
home he was fired at by two men, both of whom missed their
aim.[2]   Who these men were was never known ; tradition
says that twelve men drew lots for the task of the two 'avengers.'
On the same day a stone was thrown at the house of Mr.
Armitage, a magistrate at Lockwood, to draw him to the
window, and a shot fired.[3] The unhappy soldier was brought
to be flogged a few days after (Tuesday, April 21) close to
Rawfolds mill, but Cartwright, the ' bloodhound ' as he was
now commonly called, to the crowd's astonishment, inter-
ceded with such fervour that after twenty-five strokes the
man was unbound.[4]

Although the number of those who actually took part
in the attack on Cartwright's mill or in the destruction of
shearing frames elsewhere was comparatively small, popular
feeling was on their side, and there was hardly a man or a
woman in the West Riding who would have hesitated to protect one of the rioters from the gallows. The croppers, it
must be remembered, had formed as it were the aristocracy
of labour, and sympathy is perhaps more easily roused by
neighbours who have been prosperous and are now, through
no fault of their own, begging their bread, than by men and
women who live perpetually on the brink of destitution.
In addition to this, the small masters, who were themselves
suffering from the competition of machinery, could hardly
be expected to look too harshly on proceedings that might
bring the work back to their own shops.[5]

---

[1] H.O., 42. 122.   [2] *The Risings of the Luddites*, pp. 127 and 128.
[3] H.O., 42. 122.   [4] *The Risings of the Luddites*, p. 132.
[5] Mr. Vickerman described the 'spirit of rebellion' as 'promoted in this
neighbourhood chiefly by men called Master dressers who Imploy from 4 or 5
to twenty men who can in general get great wages and spend more money at
the Alehouse than all the other Inhabitants' (H.O., 40. 2).

' A confidential servant,' wrote a magistrate from Headingley
in a letter sent up to the Home Office,[1] ' tells me that it is
surprising how much the opinions and wishes even of the more
respectable part of the Inhabitants are in unison with the
deluded and ill-disposed of the population with respect to
the present object of their resentment Gig Mills and Shearing
Frames and this extends also to persons having Mills of a
different description employed in the Manufacturing branch,
[and] will account for the rioters constantly escaping detection.'   The adventures of the rioters preserved by tradition
or revealed at the trials amply bear this out.   Hence the
authorities had no easy task before them.   One or two men
whose share in the affray was betrayed by wounds they could
not conceal, were arrested, but no evidence against them
was forthcoming, nor did it seem likely that any would be
produced.   A woman, Betty Armstrong, suspected of giving
information against one of these men, was roughly handled
by a mob in Huddersfield.[2]   The offer of £1000 reward for
information about the attacks at Leeds and at Rawdon mill
had brought no response, and it did not seem likely that the
similar offer in respect of Cartwright's mill would be more
successful.

Just after the Rawfolds mill affair, some alarm was created
by a food riot at Sheffield on April 14, in which a mob, chiefly
composed of women and boys, seized potatoes and other
vegetables and attacked the storehouse of local militia arms,
taking away seventy-eight stands of arms out of 864, and
damaging some 200 more.   ' It is evident, however,' wrote
General Grey on April 18, ' that this affair was without plan
or system, and I should suppose totally unconnected with
the proceedings at Leeds, Huddersfield, etc., particularly as
everything has since been perfectly quiet at Sheffield.'[3]   In
the Leeds and Huddersfield districts the organised destruction of shearing frames had come to an end, but all was not
quiet.   Cartwright, as we have seen, was fired at on April
18; ten days later, on April 28, Mr. William Horsfall of
Marsden, another manufacturer who had made himself prominent by the introduction of new frames, and by his outspoken determination to defend them, was shot by four men
as he rode home from Huddersfield market, and died thirty-
eight hours later.

Horsfall was a man of hot temper and violent language.

[1] H.O., 42. 122.   [2] *Ibid.*, 40. 1.   [3] *Ibid.*, 42. 122.

In his exasperation at the destruction of shearing frames
he had once uttered a wish, according to report, that he could
ride up to his saddle girths in Luddite blood, and his hostility
was so well known that children would tease him by running
in front of his horse, calling out ' I 'm General Ludd.' [1]   He
had taken an active part in the formation at Huddersfield
of a ' Secret Committee for preventing unlawful depredations
on Machinery and Shearing Frames ' [2] which had tried to
instill more energy into the masters, and he had been busily
employed in the endeavour to track down the assailants on
Cartwright's mill.

The leading spirit amongst the murderers was George
Mellor, the friend of John Booth, a young man of twenty-
two, who had been prominent among the machine breakers.
He was no hardened ruffian, but a youth of a passionate temper,
whose mind had been darkened by the affair at Cartwright's
mill.   One story, handed down by his cousin, relates that
he cherished a deadly hatred against Horsfall as an oppressor
of the poor, and that once before as Horsfall was riding past
the plantation where he was afterwards to meet his death,
Mellor held up before him, with a bitter taunt, the dead
starved baby of a cropper's wife, whilst the woman lay faint-
ing by the wayside.   Horsfall's only answer was to cut Mellor
across the face with his whip.[3]   Whatever the truth of this
tale, the murder of Horsfall was a cold-blooded crime, and
perhaps the most significant fact is that besides the four
murderers, at least five other men, fellow workers in the
cropping shop of John Wood, Mellor's stepfather, knew of
the deed and were sworn to secrecy.   Many others must
have had more than a suspicion of the identity of the murderers,
yet all through the spring and summer of 1812 the offer of £2000
reward brought no response.   Panic prevailed among the
authorities, and they began to blame each other.   The magistrates thought the military useless : the military declared
the magistrates to be incompetent and slack.

The disorders had now taken the form of nocturnal visits
to houses by small bands of men, for the purpose of seizing
whatever weapons there were in the house.   They did no

---

[1] *The Risings of the Luddites*, p. 134.   [2] H.O., 40. 1.
[3] See *Ben o' Bills, The Luddite*, by Sykes and Walker, pp. 167 ff.   Colonel
Campbell in command at Leeds wrote that when Horsfall was shot he was
surrounded and reproached with having been the oppressor of the poor (see
H.O., 42. 123), but there was no mention of this at the trial of his murderers.

damage, though they occasionally demanded food, but later on in the year these nightly visits were turned into sheer excuses for robbery, and gangs of men, who had nothing to do with the frame breakers, worked different districts, to the great terror of the inhabitants. The military wished the magistrates to march about with them and lay traps for the collectors of arms : the magistrates retorted that they were not prepared to act as police officers, and that unless the Government gave them special powers to search for arms, they could do nothing.[1] Sidmouth at first was unfavourable to this proposal. 'The Magistrates and Inhabitants,' he wrote,[2] 'seem to be Panic-struck, and Government is reproached for not resorting to measures the most rash, and, under present Circumstances, unwarrantable, because those who are on the spot will not employ the Means which the Law has placed in their hands.'

Meantime, rumours, usually second-hand, of men drilling at night increased the uneasiness. Alarmists were not wanting. The Clerk of the Peace at Wakefield, for instance, wrote up at the end of April to say that the local powers of defence were connected with the insurgents, and that the enforcement of the Watch and Ward Act, 'so far from aiding, would be putting arms into the hands of the most powerfully disaffected.'[3] Sir Francis Wood, the Vice-Lieutenant of the County, declared that the disaffected out-numbered the peaceable.[4] When the General Sessions was held at Huddersfield for executing the Watch and Ward Act, most of the townships had asked to have the Act suspended, on the ground that their present poor rates were very burden-some, and the want of trade and the high prices made it impossible to put the Act into execution. They were answered that the court had not power to suspend it ;[5] but the town-ships seem to have suspended it themselves, for on June 17 Sir Francis Wood reported that in only two places in the district round Huddersfield and Kirkstall could the Act be carried into effect.[6] At a County Meeting at Wakefield on May 14 it was decided to form Voluntary Associations, instead of enforcing the Watch and Ward Act, and this seemed to Lord Fitzwilliam quite satisfactory. Fitzwilliam refused to surrender to the general alarm, and declared that he believed

[1] H.O., 40. I.
[2] Ibid., 42. 124, June 20.
[3] Ibid., 42. 122.
[4] Ibid., 42. 124, June 17.
[5] Ibid., 42. 122, April 22.
[6] Ibid., 42. 124

'the mass of the people to be sound, though complainant under occasional suffering.'[1] Colonel Campbell also, in command at Leeds, although himself attacked by some mysterious assailants as he was returning home one night, refused to believe with the magistrate, Mr. Scott, that the people round Huddersfield were 'desperately disposed.'[2]

General Grey, as we have mentioned before, was in command of the West Riding, but General Maitland, who was in command of the inland and north-west district, where disturbances had practically ceased, and punishments been exacted early in June, was in confidential communication with Sidmouth about Yorkshire as well as his own district, and by the middle of June was arranging for the services of spies there. His relations with Grey are puzzling. When Major Searle at Sheffield wrote to him about a would-be informer, Thomas Broughton, he administered a sharp rebuke to him for not communicating with General Grey;[3] on the same day he sent a confidential letter to Sidmouth,[4] saying that this business about Major Searle was a delicate matter, as Yorkshire had been left under General Grey, when he, Maitland, took command of the inland and north-west district; that they were on the most friendly terms, but that no doubt it would be better to have all the disturbed districts under one head. 'I need not state,' he added, 'the Reasons in regard to Grey, that makes it to me a most unpleasant subject to enter on.' Whatever the reasons, all difficulties were overcome by General Grey tactfully asking for three months' leave of absence to get married.[5] When his leave was up, he was given the command of the western district, and the two districts previously divided between him and Maitland were united under Maitland.[6]

Maitland introduced into Yorkshire the practice of keeping small bodies of soldiers moving constantly about at night, a practice previously employed with success on the borders of Lancashire, Cheshire, and Yorkshire. This movement of troops naturally caused a good deal of annoyance to the peaceable inhabitants, and a letter to the Home Office describes how General Maitland would knock up householders at 2 A.M. and make them quarter his troops.[7] He also intro-

[1] H.O., 42. 123, May 16.   [2] Ibid., 42. 123, May 10.
[3] Ibid., 42. 125, July 18 ; 42. 127, September 6.
[4] Ibid., 42. 125.   [5] Ibid., 42. 125, July 19.
[6] Ibid., 42. 129, November 10.   [7] Ibid., 42. 124.

duced an extensive use of spies, largely supplied by Nadin
of Manchester, and enrolled amongst the military. Revelations about the proceedings of these bodies of soldiers were
afterwards published by Captain Raynes of the Stirling militia
and caused a considerable sensation.[1]

Among the Home Office Papers [2] are various bundles of
military reports on the disturbances, considering largely of
the letters of this Captain Raynes and of others to their
commanding officers. From them we learn that Captain
Raynes employed various 'S.C.s,' or Special Constables,
to act as a ' medium of intelligence.' ' The S.C.s have applied
to me for money,' he writes ; he asks if he is to attend to
them, as Nadin fails to supply it, adding that he has given
each of them £1. These S.C.s apparently enrolled themselves as members of the Stirling militia, and he complains
that the Norfolk men [3] have circulated the report that the
Stirling men are sent to get intelligence, which has caused
a check to their operations. They did not confine themselves to acting as spies, but arrested whomever they pleased
in an entirely arbitrary fashion. The best plan, observes
Raynes, is to take up men on suspicion, and then others
' tumble in ' through fear. There are long descriptions of
hunts for evidence against different suspects. ' I find,' naïvely
complains Raynes, ' nothing will procure information but
money ' ; another letter from Colonel Nelthorpe at Ashton
describes how they seized a man, Charles Faith by name,
and threatened him with ' swinging ' unless he gave evidence
against others. It is not surprising to read that the people
were very angry with soldiers going about in this secret
manner and that ' our parties were all hissed into Stockport yesterday on their return.' By October 9 General
Maitland was suggesting the curtailment of the use of these
Special Constables as much as possible in order to avoid
unpopularity, as ' there exists a feeling of detestation against
us that makes its appearance even in the middle of their fears.'

The rate of pay for these military S.C.s seems to have
been one guinea a week. Raynes reports to General Acland
that he promised the active Thomas Braddock 5s. a day
for expenses, and the same salary as the other Special Con-

[1] See Bennet's speech in debate on Spies and Informers (Hansard, February
11, 1818). The book is not in the British Museum.

[2] In H.O., 40. 2.

[3] Among the officers of this force was the father of George Borrow.

stables. But the money expended was strangely unproductive ; perhaps the methods of the S.C.s were too rough and ready, and after the trials at Lancaster men were more alive to the dangers of intercourse with spies. Even William Cooper, alias Strapper, who had won his laurels by achieving single-handed the transportation of Daniel Garside for an illegal oath at the Chester August Assizes,[1] was a failure. He was, indeed, as Captain Raynes regretfully wrote, not a man to be trusted with much £ s. d., but his plans, if unsuccessful, were ingenious. He was made a constable on the Halifax station, and we learn that ' he thinks he shall get a number of Ludds to attend his dancing school.'

Two of Raynes' men, posing as Luddites, succeeded in entrapping a carpet weaver of Millbridge, James Starkey by name, aged twenty-two, into an opinion on the best method of destroying Cartwright's mill. Starkey had no connection with the Luddites, and he suggested a barrel of gunpowder, only to find a few hours later that he was charged with inciting two soldiers of the Stirlingshire militia to blow up the mill. Starkey, however, luckily for him, had influential friends, one of them the Rev. Hammond Roberson, and they succeeded in getting his trial postponed several times, until the tale of victims was judged complete without him.[2]

The S.C.s were not the only spies let loose in Yorkshire : to mention only the successful, there were MacDonald and Gossling, of whom we shall hear later, and Thomas Broughton, who offered to obtain information about Barnsley.[3] General Maitland, before he took over the command in Yorkshire, suggested to Government a plan for procuring information by means of men from the clothing districts in Wiltshire : [4]

[1] See Treasury Solicitor, General Series, No. 1160. The only corroborating evidence was that of a man who had seen accuser and prisoner together. See also for Cooper, H.O., 42. 126, and 42. 127.

[2] For Starkey see *The Risings of the Luddites*, pp. 116-8 ; Proceedings at York Special Commission ; and H.O., 42. 129, November 28 and 29.

[3] See p. 312 above ; also H.O., 42. 127.

[4] See H.O., 42. 124, June 17. The idea of employing persons from the west of England clothing districts had originally been suggested by some Huddersfield merchants, who asked that one or two of the dragoons stationed at Huddersfield, who happened to have been cloth-dressers in the west of England, should be dressed up as countrymen, and employed to find out the plans of the frame-breakers, but Major Gordon, in command at Huddersfield, doubted the propriety of a soldier becoming ' a disguised spy ' (H.O., 42. 120, February 4). Maitland, on May 9, had suggested getting ten or twelve men of ' the lower orders of the Community ' from London (H.O., 40. 1).

two were to be sent to Huddersfield, one to Halifax, one to Bradford, one to Saddleworth, two to Leeds. They were to become ' Active and Efficient Members of these Committees, to conceive merely being sworn in is nothing.' Each was to be known by a letter in the alphabet, beginning at M, ' as I hope the other previous letters will be filled up.' Sidmouth in answer was not hopeful. ' It will not be possible, I fear,' he wrote,[1] ' to find in Wiltshire such a number of *competent* Persons as you have named,' though he added that possibly Gloucestershire might supply the deficiency, ' but the Inhabitants of those parts have not the sharpness of Understanding nor the determination of character which belong to those of the North.' The search, even in Gloucestershire, apparently proved unsuccessful, though possibly it was there that the Government picked up a certain mysterious ' party ' called Playfair,[2] whom they suggested sending down to Yorkshire in company with another man. Maitland, however, wrote strongly, ' I am a total Enemy to Copartnership,' and urged that Playfair should be sent down alone and be put entirely in some one person's hands, for unless he is put under a strict rule, a gentleman of his disposition ' will infallibly become a general Operator under Government '—a warning, it may be remarked, which Maitland might well have taken to heart with regard to his other informants. Playfair was not despatched after all, and only one man came from Wilts and he was useless. Maitland's attempts to procure men from Scotland also failed. ' Those who are willing to undertake mixing with the Disaffected are generally of a Character whose information must be received with extreme Caution, and certainly in the instance of those on whom we could rely, they very much to their Credit feel extreme difficulty in going the lengths they must necessarily do, to be of any real Utility.' [3]

The West Riding during the summer and autumn of 1812 presented a curious spectacle of the methods of justice in tracking down offenders. The military were at work with their spies, of whom the magistrates knew nothing; Mr. Lloyd of Stockport, clerk to Mr. Prescott, J.P., was also taking an active part in operations : he held some sort of curious semi-official

---

[1] H.O., 42. 124, June 20.
[2] For Playfair, see H.O., 42. 124, June 25, July 18.
[3] H.O., 42. 125, July 18.

position, being employed by the Crown,[1] corresponding constantly with the Home Office and managing his own set of spies. Last came the magistrates, the most notable amongst whom was Mr. Joseph Radcliffe of Huddersfield, a bluff, straightforward, irascible gentleman, who seems to have had no hand himself in gaining information by questionable methods. His general attitude is shown by an inquiry addressed by him to the Home Office, as late as August 16. I wish to know, he wrote,[2] ' how I am to act, in case of an informer being an accomplice, but supported by no other evidence ; shall I send him about his business, saying such persons are not to be attended to, or in what manner am I to act ? ' The official endorsement on this letter is interesting in the light of the subsequent trials. ' Acquaint Him that He may proceed as a Justice of Peace in the same manner upon the information of an Accomplice as He would upon that of any other Person. It is to be observed, however, that it is very desirable in all such Cases to procure corroborative Evidence—as upon the trial of the party informed against, the Judges will not direct a Jury to Convict upon the Evidence of an Accomplice only unsupported by confirmatory Evidence of some sort.'

Complications arose from the quarrels of these different authorities ; nor were the magistrates themselves a homogeneous body, for General Maitland complained bitterly of their ' teazing ' jealousies. Mr. Hay, the Lancashire magistrate, was also a justice of the West Riding, and tended to interfere in what Mr. Radcliffe naturally regarded as his own sphere of operations. The relations of the different authorities were illustrated in the amusing case of Joseph Barrowclough, a man on whose seizure and confession the highest hopes were built early in July.[3] Barrowclough was reported to be a valuable mine of information by Whitehead, one of Mr. Lloyd's special informants, sent by him from his own district to the West Riding. Barrowclough was arrested at Holmfirth, under a warrant from Mr. Hay, by Maitland's aide-de-camp, with whom were Mr. Lloyd, Mr. Lloyd's clerk, and Whitehead. It might naturally be expected that he would be taken before a magistrate to be examined ; instead of this his examination was conducted by Mr. Lloyd and by Mr. Allison, the solicitor for the Hudders-

[1] H.O., 42. 132, January 13.   [2] H.O., 42. 126.
[3] For Barrowclough see H.O., 42. 125, and 42. 129.

field Society for Prosecuting the Luddites.[1] General Maitland described himself as unwilling to interfere in the matter of Barrowclough's examination, ' but I believe Lloyd and a very zealous Officer indeed having no such Delicacy, went into him and got out of him all the Information we had.'

Meantime Mr. Hay spirited the prisoner away into Lancashire, to the intense annoyance of Mr. Radcliffe. The battle for the body of the living Barrowclough resembles the quarrels among medieval cities for the bodies of dead saints. Barrowclough, in Mr. Lloyd's hands, did his best to give satisfaction, and the susceptible Mr. Hay confessed himself to be ' a good deal agitated ' by the disclosures. The general rising, or the marriage feast of Mrs. Ludd, was postponed, said Barrowclough, till July 24, 1814, twenty-four years from the beginning of the Luddite system. French officers were drilling the Luddites and managing the whole affair : roads were being mined and powder laid for blowing up opponents. Pressed for concrete details Barrowclough warmed to his task, revealed the name (a wrong one) of Horsfall's murderer, and gave a circumstantial and detailed account of fifteen small depôts of arms near Holmfirth, conveniently placed in fields, so that no search warrants were necessary. In vain did General Maitland make long and earnest search for all fifteen : not a firearm, not even a pike, could be found. Barrowclough was much disturbed at this and asked leave to point out the places himself. Accordingly Mr. Radcliffe received him once again into his jurisdiction. But confidence was shaken, and though nine men were kept in prison on his information, and though the stories that French officers on parole were drilling Luddites were believed, and the question of supervising them more closely considered, Barrowclough himself could not recover his prestige. Even Mr. Lloyd, though still convinced that Samuel Haigh, whom Barrowclough had denounced as Horsfall's murderer, was the criminal, for he had exhibited symptoms ' very convincing to me of his guilt,' reluctantly admitted that Barrowclough's manner was ' sufficiently equivocal to induce a stranger to suppose him flighty.'

Barrowclough no sooner faded from the scene than a man of stronger inventive powers took his place. This was Sergeant

[1] Mr. Allison seems also to have been employed by the Crown either now or later (H.O., 42. 132, January 13).

Lawson,[1] alias Montgomery, of the 1st Royal Surrey militia, stationed at Chelmsford, who confessed to Brigade-Major Chamberlain at that place that he was involved in a terrible and far-reaching plot, fostered by French prisoners, the ultimate object of which was to establish a Republic, the immediate programme to fire all big towns and to assassinate Castlereagh. One of the leaders, 'Lord Lovat' by pseudonym, corresponded with France, and Lawson had seen a letter to him from Talleyrand beginning 'My Beloved Couzin.' The conspirators were active round Manchester and in the West Riding, the plot extended to Ireland, and they calculated on mustering some 150,000 followers. Week after week did Lawson pour out his fresh revelations. Maitland, to do him justice, was occasionally sceptical with regard to his part of the country, but no doubt seems to have been cast on Lawson's more important revelations : indeed on September 21 warrants were issued by Sidmouth to apprehend Lord Lovat, otherwise Russel, and twenty-one others for high treason, and Maitland, in spite of the dissuasion of the Law Officers, was ordered not to restrict himself to the persons named in the warrants, if there seemed occasion to arrest others. 'I am confident,' wrote Sidmouth, 'that you will assume an Authority for that purpose, if the Occasion should appear to you to call for it, and I need not add that in that case, you may rely on the support of the Government.' But the warrants were never executed, for the culprits were not to be found, and Lawson himself fell under a cloud. He crossed over into Ireland, and Peel's searching eye [2] noted serious inaccuracies in his tales of operations there. His stories, it must be confessed, presumed on his hearers' powers of credulity. Amongst other items he professed to have travelled 1078 miles in eleven days. Disillusionment progressed rapidly after this, and outside the last of innumerable bundles of documents about him runs the inscription, 'Papers relating to Lawson, a fabricator of false intelligence.'

At the end of July 1812 the Bill for which the Yorkshire magistrates had asked was passed. They were given power to search for arms in any place where they suspected them to be, without waiting for a deposition on oath that arms were there. They were also empowered to demand the

[1] For Lawson see H.O., 42. 126, 42. 127, 42. 128, 42. 129, 42. 130.
[2] Peel was Irish Secretary.

surrender of any arms not secure from seizure, and to disperse without the formality of the Riot Act, tumultuous assemblies by day, or suspicious assemblies of ten or more by night.[1]

The provisions of the Bill were to expire on March 25 next year. Another Bill was passed earlier in July, which made the penalties for giving or taking illegal oaths more stringent, death being decreed for the former, and transportation for life for the latter.[2] One section of the Act promised indemnity within three months to any one coming forward to confess that he had taken an unlawful oath, and to take the oath of allegiance.

Little resulted from the new powers given to the magistrates, whom Maitland accused of slackness, but as summer advanced and trade showed some improvement the raids for arms became less frequent. The Orders in Council had been repealed on June 23,[3] five days too late, as America had already declared war, but Napoleon's disastrous invasion of Russia broke up the continental system.[4]

No want of zeal could be alleged against the indefatigable Mr. Lloyd, but he worked under certain difficulties, as Mr. Radcliffe's ways were not his ways. 'In the case against the Murderer of Horsfall,'[5] he writes from Wakefield,[6] 'and other Depredators committed to York, I have obtained a material piece of Information, which if the zeal of Mr. Radcliffe the Justice has not marred, I shall avail myself of here—but the doubt I have is that Mr. Radcliffe has been taking some steps upon the same information which was unfortunately laid before him—and now if I make anything out of the Witnesses, it must be by suddenly taking them up and *running away with them to a Distance* a measure I shall certainly take the responsibility of doing, and therefore I am not asking your advice, but informing you of the resolution I have formed. I find Mr. Scott a valuable Justice —I fear Mr. Radcliffe *talks too much.*' ' I see no great objec-

---

[1] The Preservation of the Public Peace Bill, 52 Geo. III. c. 162. In Lancashire and Cheshire the magistrates had not waited for the legal permission (H.O., 42. 124, 40. 1).

[2] 52 Geo. III. c. 104. In the original Bill both giving and taking were made capital offences (see Hansard, May 5, 1812).

[3] Maitland, on June 19, declared that the suspending the Orders in Council had already had a good effect on trade (H.O., 42. 124).

[4] Smart, *Economic Annals*, i. p. 332.   [5] The wrong one.

[6] H.O., 42. 126, August 31.

tion to this Step' (of running away with the witnesses), answered
Mr. Becket of the Home Office,[1] but he warned Mr. Lloyd
to leave Bent alias ' B.' alone, for Lloyd, with inconvenient
zeal, had got hold of a letter from ' B.' written in his character
as reformer, and had asked what should be done about him.

A startling example of Mr. Lloyd's methods was given
in the case of John Schofield of Nether Thong.[2]   John Hinchcliffe of Upper Thong, parish clerk of Holmfirth, told the
Rev. Mr. Keeling, whether correctly or not it does not appear,
that John Schofield was implicated in Luddism.   Schofield
accordingly was arrested, but as there was no evidence
against him he was released.   Shortly after, Hinchcliffe was
visited at night, according to his own story, by two men,
who abused him for informing against Schofield and shot
him in the left eye.   Hinchcliffe was unable to identify either
of them.   Next day, John Schofield, hearing that Hinchcliffe accused him of the attack, made off for America via
London.   In London he was caught and taken before a magistrate, where he foolishly denied that he knew any one of
the name of Hinchcliffe.   He was then brought back to Yorkshire, much to the annoyance of the Home Office authorities,
who were considering the question of offering him a pardon
in return for disclosures.   Mr. Lloyd now set to work to prove
that Schofield, against whom there was no particle of evidence,
beyond the fact that he had run away, was the culprit.   At
last he met with success.   ' By a particular mode of examination,' he writes, ' which I made use of in this neighbourhood
where I have met with Hinchcliffe (the person shot at Nether
Thong) I have now prevailed over Hinchcliffe to identify
Schofield as one of the two men concerned in that outrage.'
The case, he remarks complacently, will cause a great sensation.   Hinchcliffe, after his complaisant identification,
might well wonder whether he were accuser or prisoner.   ' Hinchcliffe is now safe at a Gentleman's House in the neighbourhood, not to be seen by any except myself and Mr. Allison
the Solicitor of this place.'   Later on, Hinchcliffe, like many
others, was spirited over the County borders to Congleton.
' I placed [him] here in retirement under the inspection of
Mr. Watson, a county Magistrate, who is my relation ; and
consequently to be trusted with such a business.'

In spite of all the exertions of Mr. Lloyd information came

[1] H.O., 42. 127, September 2.
[2] For Schofield see H.O., 42. 126, and 42. 128.

in but slowly. Culprits were arrested in plenty, but no evidence against them could be obtained. At last, early in September, Mr. Lloyd succeeded in gaining information against one of what General Maitland called the ' gangs of plunderers.' His method was circuitous ; he started by arresting a man at Flockton for being out of his house at an unreasonable hour. Now this man was known to have been in company with a man of bad character, and the man of bad character was examined to such good effect that warrants were issued against two other men for burglary or incitement to burglary. One of these last men, Earl Parkin by name, a collier, ' impeached (by good management[1]) many others of capital offences.'[2] General Maitland was clearly a little uneasy about these methods of obtaining information. ' There is no doubt,' he wrote,[3] ' much of it is out of the strict letter of the Law, though I believe perfectly in the Spirit both of the Law and of the Constitution, when fairly understood. It does not appear,' he continued, ' that the Gang here have ever taken the Oath regularly, and I rather think it will turn out, what I heard for the first time three days ago, that an accumulation of Villains, had come into this part of the Country, finding that the Terror, and the Timidity was such, that by knocking at a Door, and stating themselves to be Luddites, they could obtain the same Ends, in a much more quiet manner, than they had heretofore done, by House breaking or any such Practise.'

In spite of the arrest of this gang, the results, from the point of view of cases to try, were still poor. In the middle of September the Law Officers, consulted on the advisability of resuming the Assizes at York on October 19, for trying such cases as were already to hand, answered that in the absence of confirmatory evidence it was better to postpone the trials rather than risk an acquittal.[4] The magistrates meanwhile were asking for a Special Commission. Their motives were not so much the desire for the greater pomp and impressiveness of a Special Commission, as the wish to avoid having the lenient Mr. Justice Bayley as Judge.[5] At the August Assizes at York, when the Sheffield rioters [6] were tried, he had deeply pained the county authorities by his treatment

---

[1] ' By good management ' is scratched out in original but still legible.
[2] H.O., 42. 127, September 4.   [3] *Ibid.*, 42. 127, September 13.
[4] *Ibid.*, 42. 127.   [5] *Ibid.*, 42. 129, November 2.
[6] See p. 309 above.

of the offenders.[1] ' I could have wished,' wrote Mr. Radcliffe,[2]
' Judge Bayley had not so lightly held forth the conduct
of Sykes of ——'s forcibly taking arms (to the jury) as to
deem it a frolic. I am very glad to hear,' he writes later,[3]
' there is no chance of the prisoners being tried by Judge
Bayley whose determinations at the last assizes have in my
humble opinion done much harm.' Unaware of the strong
prejudice against him, Mr. Justice Bayley wrote in November,
offering to resume the Assizes in York, in December, if required.[4] But Government had decided otherwise.

Late in October, six months after Horsfall's death, his
murderers were apprehended. Two of them, Mellor and
Benjamin Walker, had been in custody on suspicion shortly
before, but had been released for want of any evidence. Two
other men had also been in prison on suspicion of being the
murderers, one on the information of Barrowclough, the
second, Joshua Haigh, who had probably taken part in the
attack on Cartwright's mill, and had certainly run away,
on the information of an inaccurate aunt. Both were guilt-
less of the murder. Benjamin Walker's mother, afraid that
one of the other murderers might turn King's Evidence,
confided her fears to a friend, through whom Mr. Lloyd heard
of the affair. He applied his usual methods,[5] and in the
end Benjamin Walker agreed to give information. A visit
by Mr. Lloyd and Mr. Allison to Wood's workshop, where
the prisoners had been working, in order ' to prevent their
proving alibi,' resulted in information from William Hall, one
of the most prominent of the frame-breaking croppers, who
had lent Mellor the pistol with which he shot Horsfall. Hall
further informed against sixteen men for the attack on Cartwright's mill, and against ten for breaking Mr. Vickerman's
shearing frames.[6]

Much to Mr. Lloyd's chagrin, it was decided to send down
the solicitor for the Treasury [7] on behalf of the Government
to manage the prosecutions. General Maitland had long been
' ill at ease in regard to the effect of over Zeal which is frequently

---

[1] The heaviest sentence was fifteen months' imprisonment.

[2] H.O., 42. 126.   [3] Ibid., 42. 128, October 1.

[4] Ibid., 42. 129, November 6.

[5] e.g. October 20 : ' I have run away with one of the witnesses to prevent
her being tampered with and have placed her in my own House where she will
more fully and freely give her Examination.'

[6] See H.O., 42. 128, for above,   [7] Mr. Henry Hobhouse.

worse than doing nothing at all.'[1] and had urged that the cases needed sifting. It was decided to hold a Special Commission in January. The evidence against the men in custody for the attack on Cartwright's mill, and for the breaking of Vickerman's frames was still unsatisfactory, resting entirely on William Hall, the accomplice : indeed the Law Officers, who seem to have been more strict than many Judges in their views as to the value of the testimony of accomplices, gave it as their opinion, as late as November 11, that there was 'no evidence whatever' in these cases.[2] Efforts were now directed to obtaining some sort of corroboration of William Hall.

Early in December some more arrests were made : Job Hey, John Hill, and William Hartley for stealing arms in August ; James Hey, Joseph Crowther, and Nathan Hoyle for demanding firearms and taking a £1 note, as late as November 29. The first three seem to have been part of the original Luddite organisation, the latter group a mere plundering gang, whose object, as an accomplice euphemistically put it, was 'to receive or get some property to better their circumstances, by going into people's houses and plundering them.'[3] It may be remarked here, that whatever their threats, in no instance did these gangs do any bodily harm to the persons whose property they took, nor does there seem, after the early days of searching for arms, any concerted action. General Maitland, early in November, pointed out that there was 'no real bottom in all this Luddite system.'[4] Had the harvest been better and the American ports open, the 'unpleasant scene' as he called it would end, but whilst provisions were high and wages low, the situation must be anxious

The Special Commission opened at York on Saturday, January 2, 1813.[5] The Judges were Mr. Baron Thomson and Mr. Justice Le Blanc, both of whom had already figured at the Lancaster trials. The Grand Jury, we are told, was 'highly respectable.'[6] The first trial was of four men, Swallow, Batley, Fisher, and Lumb, members of a plundering gang, against whom Earl Parkin had 'by good management' informed. Three of them, as well as the informant, were coal

---

[1] H.O., 42. 127, September 28.   [2] *Ibid.*, 42. 129.
[3] Proceedings at York Special Commission, p. 198.
[4] H.O., 42. 129.
[5] See Proceedings at York Special Commission, January 1813, 3rd edition.
[6] H.O., 42. 132, January 4.

miners. The case was clear, and was strengthened by the fact that the prisoners had talked incautiously to a debtor in York Castle. All four were found guilty. 'The Court,' we read, ' was extremely crowded throughout the day, and with an audience for the most part of a very ill Complexion. But the Verdict was received with perfect Silence.' [1]

Next day, Wednesday, came the trial of George Mellor, William Thorpe, and Thomas Smith for the murder of Horsfall, made dramatic by the evidence of their fellow murderer, Benjamin Walker. Here again the case was clear. The defence consisted in attempts to prove alibis for all three. A curious light is thrown on the value of these alibis and on the administration of the gaol by a letter smuggled out by Mellor, which afterwards fell into the hands of the Government.[2] In it he urged a friend to impress on his cousin that he must stick by what he had sworn before Mr. Radcliffe, ' remember a Soul is of more value than work or Gould.' All three were found guilty and condemned to death. Thursday was spent over the trial of John Schofield for shooting at John Hinchcliffe. He was acquitted. Not only was the difference between Hinchcliffe's statements a strong point in the prisoner's favour, but his alibi was a good one. There had been a Methodist meeting in his father's house, where he lived, the evening that Hinchcliffe was shot, and he had been seen in the house by persons who attended the meeting though he had not been present at it himself. At the close of the day a curious little scene was enacted. The Grand Jury stated that they had no more bills before them. Mr. Park, the prosecuting counsel, thereupon made a solemn short speech to the effect that finding that the persons involved in certain cases had been misled by those already convicted, the prosecution had decided to exercise leniency and to forbear to press the charges by presenting bills against them, at any rate for the present. He hoped that they would return to a better course of life, through fear if not from ' gratitude for the mercy extended to them.' ' The Effect of this step,' wrote the solicitor for the prosecution, ' is to release about six Prisoners without Prosecution against whom the Evidence was next to nothing.' [3]

On the Friday morning before the court opened the three murderers of Horsfall were executed. To the last they refused

[1] Letter from Solicitor for Treasury, H.O., 42. 132.
[2] H.O., 42. 132.   [3] *Ibid*, 42. 132, January 7.

to acknowledge their guilt. 'They were young men,' wrote the *Leeds Mercury*, ' on whose countenances nature had not imprinted the features of assassins.'

Friday's sitting of the court was taken up with charges of administering illegal oaths. First John Eadon, a weaver of Barnsley, was convicted of administering in May an illegal oath to Richard Howells. This case was one of the fruits of the exertions of Thomas Broughton, who had offered his services to Major Searle of Sheffield. Richard Howells was a young man whom Broughton persuaded to produce information. Howells' story was that Eadon had persuaded him to take the oath when they were alone in the fields together, and had given him a paper on which the oath was written out. This paper he professed to have given to Broughton, and it then passed through various hands. Howells explained that he himself took the oath as a sort of joke. The case rested on the evidence of Howells, and on that of Broughton, who had no hesitation in swearing that the paper was in Eadon's handwriting, on the strength of having once seen Eadon writing some names of delegates. Broughton also described an interview with Eadon, in which Eadon had talked of forming an organisation in the country to overthrow the tyrannical system of Government. Eadon denied the whole story. Whether he was a Parliamentary Reformer, as seems possible, does not appear. At any rate he was sentenced to seven years' transportation. It was arranged afterwards that Broughton and Howells should receive £10 each for this piece of work, as well as their expenses which amounted to £27. Broughton went to settle in Dublin, and Howells enlisted.[1] Another case of Broughton's against the same John Eadon and a certain Craven Cookson for administering an illegal oath to him was dropped, as it was too weak. There was no Howells to corroborate. Cookson was exhorted to return to the course of honest industry.

The next case, also one of administering an unlawful oath, excited great interest. It was against six prisoners from Halifax : John Baines the elder, a hatter of sixty-six ; his son, Zachariah Baines, a boy of fifteen ; his nephew, John Baines the younger, a shoemaker of thirty-four ; William Blakeborough,

---

[1] H.O., 42. 133, April 28; but from Mr. Stuart Wortley's letter, October 30, 1813 (H.O., 42. 135), it seems as if only Broughton got the £10. Mr. Stuart Wortley complains bitterly of not having had the money he advanced for the purpose repaid by the Treasury.

a shoemaker of twenty-two; George Duckworth, a shoemaker of twenty-three; and Charles Milnes, a cardmaker of twenty-two.   John Baines the elder was leader of such democratic or republican party as existed in Halifax, and the other prisoners were all his close associates.   For three-and-twenty years, so he said, his eyes had been opened, and when the Luddite movement began he hailed it with joy.   At a meeting of his democratic club at the Crispin Inn he made a fiery speech, so impressive to the listeners that it was handed down by oral tradition.[1]   'Oh that the long suffering people of England,' he cried, ' would rise in their strength and crush their oppressors in the dust.   The vampires have fattened too long on our hearts' blood. . . . They have filched from us our natural inheritance, and by usurping the House of Commons, have got the purse strings of the nation into their hands also.   They have provoked wars and lived and fattened upon them.   They have sent us to fight anybody and everybody, to crush French liberalism and to maintain despotism all over Europe. . . . All the offices in the land are held by them and their friends ; salaries and pensions are showered upon them from the national treasury, and still like the horse-leech they stretch forth the greedy, ravenous maw, and cry, " Give ! give ! "

' For thirty years I have struggled to rouse the people against the evil and, as some of you here know, have suffered much for my opinions in body and estate.   I am now nearing the end of my pilgrimage, but I will die as I have lived ; my last days shall be devoted to the people's cause.   I hail your rising,' he ended, ' against your oppressors and hope it may go on till there is not a tyrant to conquer.   I have waited long for the dawn of the coming day, and it may be, old as I am, I shall yet see the glorious triumph of democracy.'

With the actual destruction of machinery Baines seems to have had nothing to do, though he was present at Hartley's funeral.   He regarded that destruction as a mere preliminary to the people's ' rising in their majesty.'

Such a man was naturally an object of suspicion to the authorities, but for several months no evidence against him was forthcoming.   Early in July two police spies were sent over to Halifax from Manchester by Nadin at the request of General Maitland.[2]   Their names were John MacDonald

[1] Preface to second edition of *The Risings of the Luddites*, and pp. 54 ff.
[2] See Nadin's letter, H.O., 42. 138, March 26, 1814.

and John Gossling. 'I've got two men at Halifax,' wrote Maitland,[1] 'doing well, if they will only be quiet; they think it a great thing to get twisted in whereas that is only the beginning.' MacDonald, who was sent on this errand, had a chequered career, best described by Mr. Evans, the stipendiary magistrate at Manchester some years later, when a question came up, in another connection, as to the value of MacDonald's testimony.[2] 'John MacDonald is a person who actually was formerly in the habit of uttering base coin, and was afterwards employed in detecting offenders in the same line and in the passing of forged Notes, and taken into the general employment of the Police of which he has been a useful Assistant. . . . In October 1812, MacDonald was convicted at Manchester Sessions, of an assault upon a Woman of the name of Harriet MacOwen, who swore that he had put some base money into her basket for the purpose of charging her with the possession of it.[3] He was sentenced to be imprisoned a year, but had previously been instrumental in detecting some of the persons guilty of administering unlawful oaths at Halifax and was examined as a witness at the Special Commission at York in January 1813, and in consequence of that evidence received a pardon.' Such was the man on whose unsupported evidence (unless the tale of his assistant, Gossling, who did not profess to have been present at the administration of the oath, can be counted as support) John Baines the elder and the four other men were found guilty of administering or assisting at the administration of an illegal oath.

John MacDonald's story was that on arriving in Halifax he made the acquaintance at the Crispin Inn of Charles Milnes, who took him that same night to John Baines' house to be sworn in; John Baines the elder administered the oath in the presence of the other prisoners. Gossling's story was that four of the prisoners had afterwards admitted the 'twisting-in,' and that Baines the elder had declared that his eyes had been opened for three-and-twenty years and had held forth on the meaning of the words Aristocracy and Democracy. Some qualms were felt at first even by Mr. Lloyd.

---

[1] H.O., 42. 125, July 20.   [2] *Ibid.*, 42. 152, August 18, 1816.
[3] This crime was a common one because the Bank gave a reward of £7 on conviction. Alderman Wood said in the House of Commons (April 13, 1818) that a great many poor Germans, Swedes, and Irishmen who were ignorant of the English language were entrapped into passing bad coin.

' With respect to the oath,' he wrote on September 17,[1] ' none but MacDonald and the committed persons were present, but some of those afterwards admitted the fact to Gossling —who will not appear implicated as to the oath—And John MacDonald going for the purpose of taking it, will be in better credit than being connected with them in all matters. He gave information of it immediately. The only thing I dislike is his Character. He had done too much in the like sort of manner. But I hope to God he has not been base enough to swear a lie. The other man appears to be a very decent respectable man, and I shall be happy to find upon an examination that there is confirmation such as will dissipate every doubt.' No confirmation was forthcoming, and on November 11, by which date MacDonald was himself in prison for his more recent escapade, the Law Officers remarked that there were ' some singular circumstances ' in the case.[2]

When the Commission opened, scruples had disappeared, though fears were felt that the case might be weakened by the cross-examination of MacDonald.[3] A month or two of prison, and the knowledge that his own liberty was at stake, seem to have sharpened MacDonald's wits. In a eulogy of his conduct at the trial the Rev. Mr. Hay (Chairman of the Quarter Sessions that had convicted MacDonald in October) wrote,[4] ' He certainly rose powerfully in proportion as he found how weak Mr. Brougham was on his cross examination.' Against the evidence of the police spies the prisoners produced what certainly seem to the reader satisfactory alibis. The jury disbelieved them. Probably the obviously false alibis of Mellor and the other murderers two days before had brought this species of defence into disrepute. Mr. Baron Thomson, in summing up, did his best to quiet any misgivings the jury might have as to the part played by MacDonald.[5] ' And there really never can be any injustice done in such a case to an innocent man, for if the person applied to (as in this instance) is not one of that description, that is, in the habit of administering unlawful Oaths and binding persons to the wicked purposes of such associations, it is impossible that he should in any way be trepanned into any such unlawful act.'

One of the accused was acquitted, Zachariah Baines, the

[1] H.O., 42. 127.   [2] *Ibid.*, 42. 129.
[3] *Ibid.*, 42. 132, January 9.   [4] *Ibid.*, 40. 2.
[5] Proceedings at York Special Commission, p. 120.

boy of fifteen, whose alleged offence was that he had held the door whilst his father gave the oath. The jury refused to listen to the plea of the prosecution, in the mouth of Mr. Park, ' you will find (and the humanity of the Law of England every man is acquainted with) that malice supplies age, *malitia supplet aetatem*.' [1] ' A smile lighted up for an instant the wrinkled face of old John Baines as he heard that his son Zachary was acquitted, and then he turned with a defiant air towards the Bench to hear his own sentence.' [2] This was given four days later, when Baines and his four companions were sentenced to seven years' transportation, the heaviest sentence possible. As Mr. Baron Thomson pointed out to Baines the elder, had the oath been administered only two days later (perhaps it would be more correct to say, had Mac-Donald fixed on a later date), the offence under the new Act would have amounted to a capital felony.[3] The Judge indeed hinted that the sentence of transportation was unduly light for a man of John Baines' record.[4] ' You, John Baines the elder, have made it your boast that your eyes have been opened for three-and-twenty years ; and you also declared your sentiments with respect to Government, and with respect to no Government, plainly, according to what we have collected from the evidence, preferring anarchy and confusion to order and subordination in society.'

The trial of eight prisoners for the attack on Cartwright's mill was taken on Saturday, and lasted the whole day. All the prisoners were croppers of good character, in the prime of life. Cartwright and the others in the mill were unable to identify any of the assailants, but they were betrayed by their accomplices, helped by a few shreds of corroborative evidence. William Hall, Joseph Drake, and Benjamin Walker, Horsfall's murderer, all of whom had taken part in the attack on Cartwright's mill, were the chief witnesses, helped by Sowden, another worker at Wood's shop, who had been privy to all the frame-breaking plans. Five of the prisoners were found guilty and three acquitted. There was little to choose between the cases. Of the acquitted, John Hirst was popularly supposed to have owed his life to the unwillingness of William Hall to bring to the gallows his old

[1] Proceedings at York Special Commission, p. 118.
[2] *The Risings of the Luddites*, p. 236.
[3] See p. 319 above.
[4] Proceedings at York Special Commission, p. 207.

shopmate who had often concealed his own irregularities.[1]
Hence Hall's memory failed him when asked if he had
seen Hirst at the mill, though Hirst himself admitted that
he had under compulsion gone there and seen some firing.
Hirst lived to old age, but refused ever to speak about his
Luddite days, till he fell into his dotage, when he would
re-enact the scenes to himself, and rock his grandchildren to
sleep with a Luddite ditty :

> 'Around and around we all will stand
> And eternally swear we will,
> We'll break the shears and windows too
> And set fire to the tazzling mill.'

James Brook, another of the acquitted, probably owed his
life to the fact that his next-door neighbour, a woman who
came forward to give evidence against him, was proved to
have borne him a grudge. Against John Brook there was
hardly any evidence.

Among the condemned, Thomas Brook had sealed his fate
by borrowing a hat from the gossiping wife of a fellow-
Luddite, as he returned from the attack. His own hat had
fallen off into the mill dam. James Haigh had been badly
wounded in the shoulder by a musket ball, and was forced
to go to a surgeon with a story that he had been injured by
falling into a quarry. The surgeon discreetly asked no questions, and held his tongue, but Haigh was too ill to return
to work. His master did his best for him by taking him to
a distant friend's house, but suspicion was aroused and he was
arrested, though no evidence against him was forthcoming
till William Hall turned informer. John Ogden had gone
home from the mill in company with George Mellor, Thomas
Brook, and the two accomplices Benjamin Walker and Drake.
On the way they had stopped at a woman's house in Clifton
and got some muffin bread and a pitcher of water, for which
they paid her 3d. The woman herself corroborated Drake
and Walker's story, though unable to identify the persons.

Jonathan Dean, like James Haigh, had been wounded at
Rawfolds mill. Dean's wound was in the hand. He disappeared after the affair, only returning in June when his
hand was healed. He was then arrested, but was rescued
by the well-meant perjury of his master's two apprentices,
who swore that Dean had by his master's orders helped them

---

[1] For Hirst, see *The Risings of the Luddites*, p. 284.

to 'harden up' the night of the Rawfolds affair, and that his hand had been injured in doing so. His master corroborated the tale, though he did not profess to have seen Dean himself.[1] Dean was released and went quietly back to work, thinking that his troubles were over, till William Hall betrayed him at the end of October. He was again arrested, and under the expectation that it might be to his advantage, signed a voluntary confession. It is noteworthy that the prosecuting counsel read this confession in his opening speech, although when Mr. Allison, the solicitor, was called on to prove it, and the question raised of the circumstances under which it was made, he agreed to drop it.[2] The recital of it, however, had done its work. The fifth of the condemned, John Walker, had left the neighbourhood and had enlisted in the Royal Artillery at Woolwich, where he lived in fancied security till William Hall's disclosures. The evidence against him in addition to that of the accomplices came from Sowden. The witnesses called by the various prisoners to prove alibis were numerous, but unconvincing. After an hour's deliberation the jury found the last five prisoners guilty and acquitted the first three.

After the trial of the Rawfolds rioters a few cases remained, and they were disposed of on the Monday and Tuesday. In the first of them, the trial of Joseph Brook for being a party to one of the regular raids for arms and money, the evidence of identification was so weak that in spite of the obviously concocted alibi of the prisoner, the jury acquitted him. Job Hey a waterman, John Hill a cotton spinner, and William Hartley a tailor, were next found guilty of stealing arms ; James Hey a woollen spinner, Joseph Crowther a cotton spinner, and Nathan Hoyle a weaver, of robbing a dwelling house. In both cases an accomplice, Joseph Carter, gave evidence. Pathetic tales have been handed down[3] of the starving William Hartley, who joined the Luddites in a fit of desperation, against the entreaties of his wife, who fell dead at the time of his arrest. These trials were the last. There were indeed other prisoners in plenty, but the cases against them were dropped. Seventeen men indicted capitally for the destruction of shearing frames or the stealing of arms

---

[1] See H.O., 42. 128.
[2] Proceedings at York Special Commission, p. 141 ; *The Risings of the Luddites*, p. 257.
[3] See *The Risings of the Luddites*.

were discharged on bail, to appear and answer when required : thirteen were not indicted ; three were acquitted by consent.

It only remained to pass sentence. The six men convicted of administering illegal oaths were, as we have said before, sentenced to seven years' transportation. The ten men found guilty of taking arms or money received the death sentence : one only, John Lumb, was reprieved and transported for life. The five men found guilty of the attack on Cartwright's mill were also condemned to death, making with the three murderers of Horsfall, already executed, a death-roll of seventeen. Cartwright refused to interfere on behalf of the Rawfolds prisoners, unless they first made full disclosures of all they knew. ' I can have none other than fulness of compassion,' he wrote on January 12,[1] ' for the unfortunate and misguided Men and I deplore as much as any man their Delusion, but a sense of Duty only having guided me up to the present moment I cannot step out of that Line by interfering with the course of Justice until after the most satisfactory disclosure—you will then find me ready to aid you in the best manner I am able.' Belief in the existence of mysterious stands of arms of which the condemned men could tell if they would, still survived, though it seems difficult to understand why the accomplices were not supposed capable of making the required disclosures.

The fourteen condemned men were executed the following Saturday, seven at a time. ' A grim joke of the Judge survives. After the Baron had passed the sentence of death the counsel for the prosecution asked his Lordship if he thought that the fourteen men should all be hanged on one beam. Baron Wood revolved the question and then in his grave conscientious way replied quaintly, " Well, no, sir, I consider they would hang more comfortably on two." '[2]

It is perhaps worth while to glance at the subsequent history of a few of the actors in the Yorkshire Luddite drama. Mr. Joseph Radcliffe, in return for his exertions, was, to General Maitland's annoyance, offered through Lord Fitzwilliam a Baronetcy, which he accepted.[3] Mr. Lloyd's operations

---

[1] H.O., 42. 132.

[2] *Annals of a Yorkshire House*, by A. M. W. Sterling, vol. ii. p. 131. It is, of course, a mistake to attribute the saying to Baron Wood, who had nothing to do with these trials, and was not at all the sort of man to show such brutality.

[3] H.O., 42. 130, December 23.

were brought rather abruptly to an end by the Treasury
Solicitor after the trials. General Maitland, wrote Mr. Hobhouse, the solicitor,[1] thinks that the severe example here
together with an amnesty will ensure tranquillity. ' I conceived it would be right to prevent the Effect of these Measures
being endangered by any Indiscretion on the part of the
Attornies who have been employed for the Crown at Huddersfield. I have therefore taken upon myself to inform Mr.
Lloyd and Mr. Allison that they cease to be employed from
this time, and that they are to take no step whatever on the
part of Government without express orders for which however they are at liberty to apply if they shall see occasion.'
For pecuniary reward Mr. Lloyd received a handsome purse
from some gentlemen manufacturers, though it was suggested
in vain by his friends that the office of clerk to the magistrates
at Manchester would be very acceptable.[2]

If William Cartwright caused much suffering, he also
suffered much himself. Financial ruin stared him in the
face. About twelve months before the attack on his mill
he had been nearly ruined by the dispute with America, but
friends had stepped in and averted the catastrophe.[3] After
the attack on his mill, his fellow millowners did not at once
given him the help he considered his right ; in a letter he
talks of ' the miserable prospect of Ruin, in Consequence
of the Desertion of those, whose best Interests had been
promoted by my successful stand against a lawless and Blood-
thirsty Banditti.' [4] His difficulties were relieved in December
by a gift of money (the amount not stated) from the Government, handed him by General Maitland.[5] Later on, in May
1813, others came to his assistance, and at a public meeting at Halifax addresses were presented to Sir Joseph Radcliffe and to William Cartwright,[6] and it was resolved to share
Cartwright's expenses and losses and to give him handsome
compensation for his services, settling the balance of the
money subscribed on his family.[7] This subscription is said
to have amounted to £3000.[8] Two years later, in November
1815, the Government gave Cartwright a gratuity of £300.[9]

---

[1] H.O., 42. 132, January 13.   [2] Ibid., 42. 136, 42. 134.   [3] Ibid., 40. 1.
[4] Ibid., 42. 130, December 2.   [5] Ibid., 42. 136, December 2 and 23.
[6] There is an original of a testimonial to Cartwright in the Brontë Museum at
Haworth.   [7] H.O., 42. 123.
[8] The Risings of the Luddites, p. 153.
[9] H.O., 42. 147, November 27 and December 12.

Benjamin Walker, who had brought his fellow murderers to the gallows, applied but applied in vain for the blood money of £2000. He had been supplied by Mr. Lloyd with money to go to some distant part, but in 1816 we find him still hoping for the reward, though reduced to beggary in London. This reward had been promised not by the Crown, but by the committee for prosecuting the Luddites at Huddersfield. The committee evaded their obligations, by saying that Walker was not the first informer, and turned a deaf ear to Walker's plea that the £2000 had been held out as an inducement to him to reveal the names of his accomplices. Probably the committee agreed with the Treasury solicitor in thinking that Walker should consider himself sufficiently fortunate in escaping a halter.[1]

Of William Hall we hear no more; he and the other accomplices were not again required to give evidence on behalf of the Crown, in spite of the fact that there were many outstanding cases depending on their testimony, in which the plaintiffs claimed damages. ' I mentioned to you and to Lord Sidmouth,' wrote Mr. Park in June 1813,[2] that I had prevented certain cases from being brought on at the last Assizes at York, from a desire not to have the witnesses, who had given evidence, particularly the accomplices, upon the Special Commission again submitted unnecessarily to public inspection. I communicated this to Mr. Baron Thomson, who highly approved of my motives.' Mr. Park adds that a further inducement to drop these cases was the fact that at the trials there would be a discussion of what cases fell within the Riot Act and what did not, ' and how far rioters might go in the execution of their plans, without incurring the guilt of felony. It did not appear to me to be wise to have this too generally known, especially in the County of York.' Hence he suggested that Government should pay the monies claimed rather than proceed with the trials.

It cannot be said that the instruments used by Government were satisfied with the treatment meted out to them. Joseph Nadin[3] in particular complained bitterly in February 1814 that not a penny of his long bills sent up to the Government had been paid. He detailed his many services and sacrifices to the cause of law and order. In addition to the

[1] See H.O., 42. 153, October 18, 1816.   [2] *Ibid.*, 42. 134, June 17.
[3] For Nadin's claims, etc., see H.O., 42. 137, February 17; 42. 138, March 26 and 28.

exploits for which he sent up accounts, he claimed to have achieved at the Derby Spring Assizes the capital conviction of five men, three of whom were hung and two transported for life. The Treasury solicitor in his comments on the bill remarked shrewdly that ' the Amount of some of those Items which are charged as Disbursements, leads to a strong Suspicion that a considerable Profit on them must have accrued to himself.' Nadin, he remarks, is ' a very useful Police Officer, whom it is desirable to render *chearful* in the Execution of his Duty,' but the Derbyshire cases must have been sufficiently profitable to him without further payment, since the five convictions entitled the prosecutor to five rewards of £40 each, besides the Tyburn Tickets [1] out of which Nadin probably had a considerable share. Nadin, indignant at this close scrutiny of his accounts, declared that the rewards and Tyburn Tickets at Derby had all been taken by the prosecuting solicitor, and as for his other accounts, he had paid out £60 in excess of his charges, not to mention the sum of £37 spent in experiments in getting people twisted in round Manchester for which he made no charge as the attempts were not successful. Nadin's actual bill is not preserved among the Home Office Papers, but we learn that £300 was disbursed to him in March 1814 for his expenses during the riots.   This included some payments for expenses and loss of time to MacDonald and Gossling, who had been out of work for six months after the trials. MacDonald sent up his own plea for a reward and was given £50.[2] MacDonald, it must be remembered, had also been liberated from prison in reward for his exertions. He was again employed under the Manchester Police, and there are many tales in the *Manchester Observer* of 1818 of his ways and methods, from which it does not seem that he had altered his character. The last we hear of him is a recommendation from various Manchester magistrates in 1822 that he should be employed in the London Police Force.[3]

Much has been said in these pages of the Luddite oath, a feature of the disturbances that caused more uneasiness to the Government than any overt act. ' The object of this oath,' said the House of Lords' Secret Committee,[4] 'is to prevent

---

[1] The right of exemption from service in parish offices.
[2] H.O., 42. 139, May 12, 1814.   [3] *Ibid.*, 52. 3, January 22.
[4] See *Annual Register*, 1812, p. 391.

discovery, by deterring through the fear of assassination those who take it from impeaching others, and by binding them to assassinate those by whom any of the persons engaged may be impeached.   These oaths appear to have been administered to a considerable extent; copies of them have been obtained from various quarters, and though slightly differing in terms, they are so nearly the same, as to prove the systematic nature of the concert by which they are administered.'

What was the origin of this oath, and how widely was it in use? The trials for illegal oaths at Lancaster, Chester, and York, as we have seen, throw little light on the subject.   They prove that Government spies, or prisoners who could obtain their own freedom by doing so, were ready enough to give circumstantial,' if uncorroborated, accounts of the administration of the oath, but nobody who has followed the trial of the Thirty-eight at Lancaster will be inclined to put much faith in this species of evidence.   That an oath was administered in some cases in Lancashire and Cheshire seems clear.   This we know from the depositions of those who took it, and of those who were solicited but refused to take it : the real point to determine is whether that particular oath was ever administered except by spies or their dupes.   'Under the Combination Laws,' Mr. and Mrs. Webb have pointed out, ' oaths of secrecy and obedience were customary in the more secret and turbulent Trade Unions,' [1] and apart from the natural love for mystic and secret rites, it was imperative to impress on all new members the need for secrecy, since a careless tongue might involve others in heavy penalties.   Hence the mere fact of an oath being administered would cause no surprise to any workman.

The particular Luddite oath was stated by a correspondent to the Home Office to be ' by no means dissimilar ' to one of the Freemasons' oaths.[2]   There were several variants of it sent up by ' B.': in one of them the taker swore that rather than betray the secrets I will have ' my head cut off with both my hands, and all my Family served the same if any I have, so help me God.' [3]   The form most commonly used, and quoted by the House of Lords' Committee, was sent up by Colonel Fletcher on March 23,[4] some time after the mysterious Manchester delegate, whom we saw reason to identify with ' B.,' had paid his visit to Stockport.[5]   As we have said before, it is not

---

[1] *History of Trade Unionism*, p. 113.   [2] H.O., 42. 125, July 21.
[3] *Ibid.*, 40. 1.   [4] *Ibid.*, 42. 121.
[5] See p. 274 above.

unreasonable to suppose that ' B.' started this particular oath on its career when he visited Stockport, and that it was administered by the members of the Secret Committees formed Bolton is the place about which we have the fullest information, and there Stones and his father and one or two dupes were for some time very busy ' twisting in.'

The Act passed on July 9 (52 Geo. III. c. 104) which increased the penalties for giving or taking illegal oaths, also gave indemnity during the next three months to those who confessed to having taken them. The question arose whether the indemnity extended to the ' twisters in ' as well as the ' twisted,' and the Law Officers replied that, although strictly speaking only the latter could claim the indemnity, yet as ' a measure of discretion and prudence ' it would be well to extend the benefits to the former also.[1] After the York trials this pardon was renewed until March 1, 1813, by Royal Proclamation, and was extended not only to those who had taken illegal oaths, but also to those who had stolen firearms.[2]

What light does the information about the numbers who availed themselves of this indemnity throw on the subject of the oath ? The chief influx of persons to purge themselves, in the three months after the passing of the Act, was at Stockport, where, by the end of August 1812, Mr. Prescott the magistrate reported that upwards of five hundred had come in.[3] General Maitland looked at these numbers through a magnifying glass, and inserted in the *Leeds Mercury,* ' a very mischievous Paper universally read among them ' (*i.e.* the disaffected), a paragraph to the effect that a thousand had come in, at and near Stockport.[4] Now the surprising thing about the people who took the oath of allegiance at Stockport is that not one of them came from Stockport itself or from any other town, but all lived in the small district harried by Captain Raynes and his ' S.C.s,' the district where Lancashire, Cheshire, Yorkshire, and Derbyshire meet.[5]

Maitland deduced from this the conclusion that the numbers for the whole country must be enormous. It did not occur to him that a close acquaintance with the ' S.C.s ' and their methods might lead any reasonable being to purchase indem-

---

[1] H.O., 42. 126.
[2] Proceedings at York Special Commission, pp. 212 f.
[3] H.O., 42. 126.   [4] H.O., 42. 126, August 29.
[5] H.O., 42. 126, August 27 ; see for Raynes, p. 313 above.

nity from a charge of taking an illegal oath, whether he had
actually taken one or not. Early in September, thirty-two
of the Duke of Bridgewater's colliers came in,[1] whether to
confess to the Luddite or simply to a trade oath does not
appear. No man from Manchester or all that neighbourhood
had yet taken advantage of the Act, but on September 13
the magistrate from Didsbury reported that fifty-eight
Manchester men had come in and confessed to having been
twisted in.[2] ' They profess that in some cases motives of
curiosity to know the secret attached to it,' in many fear
or terror or persuasion induced them to take the oath, ' but
in all no information was given to them as to what must
be done, but they were told " to be ready when called upon."
It appears that the men who administered the oath to these
people were either Strangers or Men who have left this part
of this Country.' It is impossible not to connect this description with Nadin's abortive attempts, over which he spent
£37, at ' getting people twisted in ' round Manchester.[3]

On October 7, almost the last day to which the indemnity
extended, twenty Bolton weavers went—not to Colonel
Fletcher be it noted, but—to Sir Richard Clayton at Adlington,
and there made depositions of all that they knew, and took
the oath of allegiance. Fortunately these depositions are
preserved, and we have drawn on them largely for the account
of what happened at Bolton. Seven of the twenty professed
to have actually taken the oath, most of the others had seen
copies of it. In all cases the business can be traced to the
machinations of Stones and a few dupes.

In Yorkshire the results of the offer were surprisingly
small. On February 18, 1813, General Maitland reported
that not more than fifty had availed themselves of the Royal
Proclamation.[4] According to Mr. Scott, the magistrate, those
who took the oath of allegiance denied that they had taken
an illegal oath.[5] A few individuals are mentioned separately.[6]
Altogether, so far as the Home Office Papers show the offer
of the indemnity produced less than 700 confessions of one
kind or another. It is, of course, impossible to say how many

---

[1] H.O., 42. 127.   [2] *Ibid.*, 42. 127.   [3] See p. 335 above.
[4] H.O., 42. 132.   [5] *Ibid.*, February 7.
[6] *e.g.* James Knott, hatter, of Hyde, one of the Thirty-eight, whom Mr.
Lloyd hoped to prosecute after their acquittal. Knott, however, had already
secured indemnity by abjuring (H.O., 42. 129, November 8). Also the two
principal witnesses for the Thirty-eight (H.O., 42. 128, October 2).

of these professed actually to have taken the oath, or how
many had taken Trade Union oaths, and thought it safer
to confess to them, for it is only in the case of the twenty
Bolton weavers that we have the actual depositions, but
on the most liberal interpretation, there is no evidence to
show that the oath was widespread, or that it was ever administered except in districts where spies were busy at work.

One last question remains : what evidence is there of any
correspondence between the different disturbed districts ?
This correspondence was, as we have seen, usually assumed
by the authorities. ' The general persuasion,' reported the
Secret Committee of the House of Lords,[1] ' of the persons
engaged in those transactions appears . . . to be, that all
the societies in the country are directed in their motions
by a Secret Committee, and that this Secret Committee is
therefore the great mover of the whole machine ; and it is
established by the various information to which the committee has before alluded, that societies are formed in different
parts of the country ; that these societies are governed by
their respective secret committees ; that delegates are continually dispatched from one place to another, for the purpose
of concerting their plans ; and that secret signs are arranged
by which the persons engaged in these conspiracies are known
to each other.'

Early in 1812 suggestions were made that the Nottingham
rioters were having arms prepared for them in Birmingham,
and the Birmingham magistrates forwarded a communication
from a ' respectable inhabitant ' to this effect.[2] Mr. Conant,
one of the London magistrates sent down by the Government to Nottingham, summed up these rumours thus : [3]
' The intercourse with Birmingham and Manchester, similar
to that named with Birmingham in your inclosure, continually
are spoken of here . . ., but no one ever has any authority
for what they surmise, or can give any clue to any quarter
in which anything from authority can be had or the report
be traced,' and of the Birmingham communication he says
scathingly, ' though the writer may be respectable he may
also be credulous . . . it is a pity the gentleman endured
ten sleepless nights before he unbosomed himself.'

Tales of delegates going to Manchester are sent up by

[1] *Annual Register*, 1812, p. 391.   [2] H.O., 42. 119, January 30.
[3] *Ibid.*, 42. 120, February 5.

an anonymous correspondent at the end of February 1812,[1] but it must be remembered that delegates were by no means necessarily connected with the disturbances. All this time communications were passing between different trades in different districts on the subject of enforcing the existing laws on apprenticeship and the rating of wages against employers,[2] the crop of actions that sprang up necessitated concerted arrangements, and these arrangements had necessarily to be kept secret, on account of the Combination Act. There were also delegates sent up to London on Parliamentary business, who would naturally visit different towns on their way; such, for example, were the delegates from Manchester and the three delegates from Scotland sent up to London with the petitions of the cotton weavers for a minimum wage,[3] or the delegates sent up from different Midland towns in connection with the Frame-work Knitters' Bill.[4] Thus when delegates from Nottingham are reported by Lord Bulkeley and other magistrates to be meeting the delegates of the weavers at Stockport in December 1811, or when delegates from Nottingham, Carlisle, and Glasgow are said by a commercial house to be present in Manchester in February 1812,[5] there is no reason to connect their visits with the disturbances, and when Colonel Fletcher, in March 1812, announces that delegates from Nottingham have been in Bolton administering the oath,[6] it seems necessary to know from what ' respectable channel ' he obtained this piece of information, before deciding as to its truth, for no suggestion that the Luddite oath was ever administered in the Midlands is made elsewhere.[7]

[1] H.O., 42. 121.   [2] See Webb, *History of Trade Unionism*, pp. 52 ff.
[3] See p. 83 above.   [4] See p. 229 above.
[5] See H.O., 42. 118, and 42. 120.   [6] *Ibid.*, 42. 121.

[7] The only evidence of connection that we have been able to find comes in an account of a visit from a Nottingham delegate to Halifax, and his speech (see *The Risings of the Luddites*, pp. 51 ff.) and this does not fit in with the evidence of the Home Office Papers.

CHAPTER XII

THE ADVENTURES OF OLIVER THE SPY

'Close by the ever-burning brimstone beds,
Where Bedloe, Oates, and Judas hide their heads,
I saw great Satan like a Sexton stand
With his intolerable spade in hand
Digging three graves.   Of coffin shape they were,
For those who coffinless must enter there
With unblest rites.   The shrouds were of that cloth
Which Clotho weaveth in her blackest wrath:
The dismal tinct oppress'd the eye that dwelt
Upon it long, like darkness to be felt.
The pillows to these baleful beds were toads,
Large, living, livid, melancholy loads,
Whose softness shock'd.   Worms of all monstrous size
Craw'l round; and one, upcoil'd, which never dies.
A doleful bell, inculcating despair,
Was always ringing in the heavy air;
And all about the detestable pit
Strange headless ghosts, and quarter'd forms did flit;
Rivers of blood from dripping traitors spilt,
By treachery slung from poverty to guilt.
I ask'd the fiend for whom those rites were meant?
"These graves," quoth he, "when life's brief oil is spent,
When the dark night comes, and they're sinking bedwards,
I mean for Castles, Oliver, and Edwards."' [1]

THE reader who took his history of the year 1817 from the
Reports of the Secret Committees of the House of Lords and of
the House of Commons,[2] reports which the authors described
as 'substantiated, in almost every particular, by depositions on oath taken before magistrates,' would picture the
manufacturing districts of the North and the Midlands
as seething with revolutionary fury only held in check by
the powers given to the executive under the suspension of
the Habeas Corpus Act.   The first proof of the 'traitorous

---

[1] Lamb, 'The Three Graves.'   [2] See Hansard, June 12 and 20, 1817.

conspiracy for the overthrow of our established government and constitution, and for the subversion of the existing order of Society' he would find in the plan for a great march from Manchester to London with the avowed intention of presenting petitions to the Prince Regent, with the real intention of using force if their petition was not granted. But no sooner was this attempt mercifully frustrated by the vigilance of the authorities than the rebels proceeded to 're-organise the party,' and a general insurrection was planned to take place in Manchester on March 30, in the course of which magistrates were to be seized, factories were to be set on fire, soldiers were to be overpowered. 'This atrocious conspiracy,' he would learn with relief, 'was detected by the vigilance of the magistrates, and defeated by the apprehension and confinement of some of the ringleaders a few days before the period fixed for its execution.'

In spite of this blow to their plans, delegates from Manchester, Birmingham, Nottingham, Derby, Leeds, Sheffield, Wakefield, Huddersfield, and elsewhere continued to meet in secret and 'to combine some general plan of simultaneous, or connected insurrection; the object of which was, after consolidating a sufficient force, to march upon London, and there to overturn the existing Government and to establish a republic.' Thanks however to the timely arrest of these assembled delegates on June 6, 'the final arrangement of the plan which was there to be settled, was thus happily frustrated,' though the spirit which had been excited could not be wholly suppressed and showed itself first in an outbreak at Huddersfield on the night of June 8, where, in spite of the retreat of the insurgents, 'guns fired as signals, in different directions, and lights shown on the heights throughout the country, sufficiently proved the extent of the confederacy, and the concert with which it was organized,' and secondly in 'a more open insurrection' on June 9 in Derbyshire, when two hundred insurgents armed with pikes or firearms marched towards Nottingham, but were cut off on the way 'by detachments of cavalry (under the orders of active and intelligent magistrates).' The reader would learn, finally, that in spite of the successful repression of 'the late insurrection on the borders of Derbyshire and Nottinghamshire,' the committee who had access to all the reports on the subject considered the ordinary powers of the law insufficient to cope with the grave spirit of disaffection.

What relation does this lurid picture bear to the actual course of events ? It will be best to answer this question by giving a narrative of what happened, a narrative based mainly on the Home Office Papers, which contain the documents on which the Reports of the Secret Committees are based. We shall find the main actor in the latter part of the story to be a certain Mr. Oliver, alias Richards, alias Hollis, celebrated by Lamb in the verses quoted at the head of this chapter, who, although his activities pass unrecorded in the Reports of the Secret Committees, figures extensively both in the Home Office Papers and in subsequent debates in the House of Commons.

The earlier events at Manchester, in which Oliver had no share, fall into two divisions : first, the march of the Blanketeers on March 10 ; second, that ‘ most daring and traitorous conspiracy ’ for March 30. We will take these two episodes in order.

The unfortunate Blanketeers’ march was organised by two of the more hot-headed amongst the working-class reformers, Bagguley and Drummond.[1] The other leaders dissuaded or, as Bagguley considered, deserted them.[2] The spinners were also connected with the plan.

To understand the material of misery on which Bagguley and Drummond worked for their scheme, it is worth while to glance at some statements about weavers’ earnings and deductions, published in the Manchester *Political Register* for January 4 : [3]

(1) Weekly receipt for 1s. 5d. of particular kind of warp which a man weaves in 5 weeks	*s.*	*d.*	Week's Expenses—	*s.*	*d.*
			Rent . . .	1	9
			Fire . . .	1	0
	6	**4¾**	Sizing warp . .	0	3
			Looming ,, . .	0	3
			Size or Sowan for do.	0	3
			Soft soap, tallow, oil	0	2
			Candles . . .	0	4
			Soap for family and washing . .	0	4

Leaving 2s. 0¾d. for support.   4   4

[1] See p. 101 above. Bamford says that the scheme of the march came from London (*Passages in the Life of a Radical*, p. 32). Prentice mentions a story that it was approved of by Cartwright and Cobbett (Prentice, *op. cit.*, pp. 93-94).

[2] H.O., 42. 164.   [3] See H.O., 42. 158. Some technical details are omitted.

(2) Journeyman doing same work—

	s.	d.
Weekly receipt	6	4½

Weekly deductions

	s.	d.
for loom room, &c., one-fourth	1	7¼
Sizing warp	0	3
Looming „	0	3
Candles	0	4
Lodging, cooking, and washing	1	6
	3	11¼

Leaving 2s. 5¼d.

(3) For another sort of warp—

Aged man weaves a cut a week, and his wife winds the picking.

Weekly receipts for weaving and winding

	s.	d.
	4	0

Weekly deductions—

	s.	d.
Rent	1	9
Fire	0	10
Sizing warp	0	3
Looming „	0	3
Size or Sowan for do.	0	3
Candles	0	4
Soft soap, tallow and oil	0	2
Soap for family washing	0	2
	4	0

The *Political Register* declares that these budgets far exceed the average earnings of any considerable number. How do such people subsist? it asks. The answer is that they do not pay outgoings such as rent, and that they depend on parochial and private relief.

The plan of the great march was carefully organised. It was to be all open and above board, and the constables were invited to attend. Bagguley had unearthed some Act of the time of Charles II.,[1] from which he had got the idea that it was legal for ten out of every twenty petitioners to go and present their petition. Hence the idea of a great march to London to present petitions to the Prince Regent. There would be a leader for every ten, and a leader for every hundred, and if any man wanted anything he was to apply to his leader of ten, who next applied to the leader of the hundred, who in turn would apply to the 'provisioners.' It was calcu-

[1] H.O., 42. 164.

lated that in six days they would reach London and that they would have to sleep on the ground or in churches on the way, hence the need for blankets. The question of support on the way had to be considered. It was suggested that those remaining behind at work should contribute 2s. 6d., 3s., even 5s. a week—or what they could afford—either to the families of the marchers or to the marchers themselves. The arrangements for commissariat were perhaps a little vague. 'A gentleman,' Bagguley told the would-be marchers, 'has calculated that you can do it on oatmeal and water.' [1]

The spinners took an active part in the organisation of the march. To the surprise of the magistrates, though exempt from the pressure of the times, they were discontented. This is perhaps less surprising to others, seeing that their wages are said to have fallen by one-third from 1814 to 1817. [2] They were said to have given 5s. each in addition to the donation of £20 from the box of a Friendly Society. [3] About this donation full particulars were sent to the authorities from a firm of employers two of whose men had been deputed to give the sum. [4] The Society was a Sick Club composed of the spinners from nine or ten mills, and founded only the previous Whitsuntide with the sole ostensible object of relieving the sick and burying the dead. [5] The club had about £30 in hand, and out of this the majority of subscribing mills had voted about £22 'towards defraying the Expenses of carrying Petitions to be presented to His Royal Highness the Prince Regent begging Redress of grievances.' The men, however, who were appointed to present the money arrived too late at the meeting. One Meldrum was sent by the spinners by coach to London, to look after the proceedings, but he was arrested on the way at Nottingham as a suspicious character. [6]

Each petitioner was to carry his petition wrapped in a bit of brown paper and tied round his right arm with a bow of white tape. [7] Some well-thumbed copies of the petition, written or printed, lie amongst the Home Office Papers. [8] It

---

[1] H.O., 42. 164.
[2] Committee on Artisans and Machinery, 1824, p. 411.
[3] H.O., 40. 10.   [4] *Ibid.*, 42. 161.
[5] It is, of course, impossible to say how far the statements about these clubs are true.
[6] H.O., 42. 164, and 42. 161.   [7] *Ibid.*, 42. 164.   [8] *Ibid.*, 42. 162.

is difficult enough to understand how the authorities could connect this pathetic and futile outcry with any 'traitorous conspiracy.' Before the last war, say the petitioners, we neither felt nor feared difficulties and privations, our repeated applications have been disregarded, taxation has been quadrupled, rent has doubled, the whole produce of the Kingdom is absorbed and nothing is left for us. Had the House of Commons been appointed by the people at large these evils could not have happened, nor would the Corn Bill nor the Libel Law nor the suspension of the Habeas Corpus Act have been passed. Hence we pray you to dismiss your Ministers. Our lives are in your hands ; if you will not relieve us, ' we can neither support you nor ourselves.' The marchers were far from being the active revolutionaries pictured by the Secret Committee. To judge from their subsequent depositions few had clear ideas of their object or the meaning of the petition. They only knew that times were bad and that this plan might bring some help. When one of them who said he was going to London about the Habeas Corpus was asked what the Habeas Corpus was, he answered, ' he could not tell but it was to mend the trade.' [1] Another was going ' to petition the Prince to make a better living.' A childish belief in the power of the first gentleman in Europe to redress their wrongs was held by many of the marchers. ' All I was to say,' said one of them, ' when we were to go down on our knees before the Prince was to ask him for help—the most miserable looking of us was to kneel down and the others to take the petition and the Prince would then tell us why trade was so slack.' [2]

The 10th of March was the day appointed for starting. There was to be a ' send off ' from a meeting in St. Peter's Fields. The majority of the marchers were weavers, few were over thirty, many were under twenty.[3] Their womenkind seem to have used some violent language. ' The Women of the lower Class,' wrote Mr. Evans, the stipendiary magistrate, afterwards, ' seem to take a strong part against the Preservation of good Order, and in the course of the morning of the 10th it was a very general and undisguised Cry amongst them that the Gentry had had the upper Hand long enough and that their turn was now come.' [4]

No dangerous sentiments are reported to have been uttered

[1] H.O., 42. 161.
[2] Ibid., 42. 162.
[3] Ibid., 40. 19.
[4] Ibid., 42. 162.

by the would-be marchers themselves. The plan, however, seemed full of danger to the authorities. Nadin, writes Mr. Hay, J.P., says that ' as they go through the country they will breed a Commotion in the towns as they go along and by that they will have a heavy body together and try at a Revolution.' [1] It was decided that the desperadoes must be stopped. The meeting was allowed to take place, but a detachment of dragoons under General Byng rode up and surrounded the hustings, whilst the civil authorities (special constables) arrested twenty-nine persons including Bagguley and Drummond.[2] This had the effect of dispersing the meeting, but several hundred marchers had already set out. The dragoons, yeomanry, and special constables set off after them and came upon the main body as they were stepping quietly along, before they reached Stockport; one hundred and sixty-seven were taken prisoners and sent back to Manchester. Only one man, John James, was killed, and he had nothing to do with the Blanketeers. He was watching the procession from his garden in Heaton Norris when some one near threw a stone, whereupon one of the regular soldiers came into his garden and killed him by cutting his head open.[3] The marchers were not all stopped near Stockport. Some four or five hundred straggled into Macclesfield tired and footsore.[4] Five hundred were said to have got as far as Leek, but as they marched on towards Derby they found the Hanging Bridge over the river Dove near Ashborne occupied by yeomanry, who expected some thirty thousand men to march upon them. Most turned back, some twenty-five were taken into custody.[5] A few, in spite of the force at the Hanging Bridge, got as far as Derby whence they were persuaded to return, some were said to have reached Loughborough ; [6] one, at any rate, Abel Couldwell of Stalybridge, reached London and presented his petition to Lord Sidmouth for the Prince Regent on March 18.[7]

The ' knapsack ' prisoners, as they were called, were a serious embarrassment to the magistrates, and the prospect

[1] H.O., 42. 161.

[2] *Ibid.*, 42. 161. Was the Riot Act read? J. E. Taylor thinks probably not (see Prentice, *op. cit.*, p. 93). Cf. Peterloo.

[3] At the coroner's inquest a verdict of Wilful Murder was returned but no one was brought to trial (see H.O., 42. 162).

[4] H.O., 42. 162.

[5] *Ibid.*, 42. 161.

[6] *Ibid.*, 42. 162.

[7] *Ibid.*, 42. 163.

of the arrival of twenty-five more sent back by the magistrates of Staffordshire and Derbyshire was not greeted with enthusiasm. 'They might have made cases of Vagrancy very well against them in Staffordshire and Derby,' wrote Mr. Lloyd of Stockport, who was playing a zealous part in the affair, ' and,' he adds, ' it may be running no risque to have them convicted in acts of Vagrancy here.' [1] Not only were the prisons already overcrowded, but awkward questions as to the legality of the arrests began to be asked. The Home Office advised on March 5 that those who were deluded by others and were now contrite should be set free.[2] The magistrates acted on this advice, but there were some who were not contrite ; what was to be done with them ? Five at least were such stubborn Britons that they refused to find sureties, declaring they had done nothing wrong. One of them, George Grimshaw, would not allow his employer to offer bail; another, Thomas Leigh, a boy of seventeen, was ' very obstinate in maintaining the Propriety of his Conduct,' and would not let his friends give bail. These five with four others were committed for trial at the August Assizes.[3] Mr. Evans thought some prosecutions for misdemeanour essential —otherwise actions might be begun against the magistrates and municipal officers. It might indeed be ' desirable to be provided with certioraries for removing the cases into the King's Bench at the discretion of the gentleman who may be employed as counsel,' though if the case could be brought to trial with a strong expectation of conviction it would be very beneficial ' for the Jury of this County who feel the situation which we are in will I apprehend not be indisposed so far as is fairly consistent with the Merits of the case.' [4]

It is worth while to record what the prisoners themselves, whose conviction was to be so beneficial, were thinking as they lay week after week in prison. In May they sent a letter written by one of them, William Wood, to Lord Sidmouth : [5]

' In behalf of Myself and fellow Prisoners, 8 in number, who humbly crave your Assistance, in our present Distress, we was taken by the Military and Civil Powers on Monday, March 10th last, nearly at Noontide, betwixt Manchester and Stockport, on our Journey for London with an Intent of presenting a Petition

[1] H.O., 42. 161.   [2] Secret Letter Book, H.O., 79. 3.
[3] H.O., 42. 162.   [4] Ibid., 42. 165.   [5] Ibid.

to the Prince Regent, for a redress of our Grievances which was dreadfull in the extreme, our Familys being nearly in a state of Starvation, and haveing no means of paying our Rent, and nearly Naked, as such we thought it a duty incumbant there was upwards of Two Hundred Persons taken that Day, and Lodged in the New Bailey Manchester the rest was Liberated, in a few Days, excepting Nine as mention'd above, we was detained in the Lockups, five of us Nine Days and Nights the other four of which I was one 13 Days and Nights with nothing but bare flaggs, to sleep upon, which I found affected my health being nearly 61 Years of Age, when Committed to Lancaster Castle, we was sent in Irons, some of our property was detain'd at the New Bailey, amongst which was a Sum of Money, advanc'd by our Relations and Friends to defray our expences on the Journey, wee made Application to the Governor of this Castle he advised us to Apply to the Magistrates of Manchester, as such we wrote a Petition to them which was presented, by a friend, We did so, and by them order'd to apply to Mr. Nadin Deputy Constable, we apply'd to Mr. Nadin, but he would not deliver the Money. My Lord we hope you will take our case into Consideration and as we trust in your Clemency we rest in hopes we shall not be disapointed, as We do assure your Lordship, we really thought we was doing our duty, as real Friends to the Laws & Constitution of our Country. . . .'[1]

The last incident in the tragic comedy of the Blanketeers is the sending of a confidential letter from the Under-Secretary of State to Mr. Fletcher of Bolton. This letter is fortunately preserved in the Secret Letter Book.[2] 'The only Government prosecution at Lancaster,' writes that gentleman, ' is that against a few of the obstinate Blanketeers. It is an extremely difficult case to deal with, and I am very much disposed to think that after the prisoners have sustained about five months Imprisonment it will be more prudent to make a merit of letting them off, than to run the risque of a Verdict after an inflammatory speech of Mr. Brougham or some such Orator.' The eight prisoners were accordingly discharged without trial.[3]

[1] Mr. Evans' comment on this is the characteristic official assurance that every attention was paid to the prisoners. Since, however, there were only 140 sleeping cells in the prison and there were already 560 prisoners before the conspirators came in, the accommodation was necessarily rough. As for the property, all had been returned except the money collected round the hustings, of which £1, 3s. 6d. had been found on Grimshaw, one of the prisoners. It would be interesting to know the ultimate destiny of this money. £20 had also been taken from Bagguley and Drummond.   [2] H.O., 79. 3.

[3] See petition from Manchester, Hansard, February 9, 1818.

We must now return to the day after the Blanketeers had started on their expedition, the 11th March, when the dark plot for a general insurrection at Manchester was first broached. The information obtained by the Government on the subject came from five sources: (1) A certain Michael Hall, alias Dewhurst, known as No. 1 ; (2) a certain James Rose, known as No. 2 : these were both convicts returned from Australia employed by Nadin, and they had for some time been reporting on the doings of the Reform party to the Manchester authorities ; (3) 'A. B.,' or Robert Waddington, a weaver of Bolton, who figured in the Luddite business,[1] but had now for some time been the confidential informant of Colonel Fletcher ; (4) an 'informant,' name unknown, employed by Mr. Chippendale of Oldham ; (5) William Lomax, a barber, whose position is more difficult to understand.

On the 11th of March Lomax began going round to various persons, with wild talk of factories blazing, and of Manchester becoming a Moscow that very night ; amongst others he, or an emissary of his, applied to Bamford, who describes how the Middleton reformers rejected his mad proposals.[2] Lomax in fact met with no success in his mission ; those whom he addressed thought him at best a foolish young man, at worst a spy ; but it is not the habit of Englishmen to rush to the police to denounce wild talk, and hence nothing was said to the authorities. On March 17 Lomax wrote up to Lord Sidmouth to inform him as a loyal subject that ' there Egzists a Conspiracy to overturn Government by force of Arms,' and promising to give every information in return for protection. He would like, he adds, to see Sidmouth, but his wife is ill and his clothes are in rags.[3] No notice was taken of this letter, and beyond a perfectly futile attempt to induce two men to fire some factories on March 24,[4] Lomax seems to have engaged in no further operations, nor had he any knowledge of the great plot for a rising on Sunday night, March 30.[5]

The credit for this plot must go to No. 1, No. 2, ' A. B.' and Mr. Chippendale's informant, but No. 1 deserves the lion's share. On March 17 there was a gathering of some ten or twelve men at the house of John Lancashire (in Middleton), called for the purpose of collecting money for the men

[1] See p. 277.   [2] *Passages in the Life of a Radical*, p. 37.
[3] H.O., 42. 164.   [4] Philip's speech, Hansard, February 9, 1818.
[5] H.O., 42. 164.

who were already in prison. At this gathering No. 1 was a prominent figure.[1] There was a good deal of incoherent and some wild talk, no business was transacted, but another meeting was fixed for the 23rd at Chadderton. Here again the attendance was so small that this meeting was adjourned till the 28th. For the meeting on the 28th, No. 1, No. 2, and ' A. B.' were indefatigable in whipping up recruits, but they only succeeded in procuring an attendance of ten, excluding spies, and one of them, Redeings of Failsworth, had come expressly to protest against suggestions of violence. How far the others were implicated in any wish for violence it is of course impossible to say. We have their word on one side, the spies' word on the other. The only corroborative evidence on the spies' side is that of Richard Flitcroft, one of the men arrested and thrown into prison. After a few weeks of prison he wrote an abject letter [2] offering to give information. His information,[3] which describes the meeting on the 17th, shows that there was some wild and futile talk, and that Flitcroft himself had gone as a delegate to Birmingham, but as he had no credentials nobody would listen to him. Bamford, with the self-righteousness that made him unpopular with his associates, thought that they had become compromised by mixing with the spies.[4] However this may be, the formidable meeting that was to engineer the general rising in Manchester two nights later [5] was adjourned that same evening, on Dewhurst's suggestion, to the George and Dragon at Ardwick ; Dewhurst himself stayed behind, ostensibly to bring over late comers ; Waddington went with the ten,[6] and with them was arrested by the police officers that same night, an inconvenience which Dewhurst managed to escape.

Mr. Hay, who figures largely in these proceedings, which resemble his exploits in saving the State in 1812, was full of activity and excitement that night. ' I feel in a very responsible situation,' he wrote,[7] and he dwells on the ' dreadful

---

[1] See H.O., 42. 168, for No. 1's account.   [2] H.O. 42. 165.   [3] *Ibid*.

[4] About as bad a case could be made out against Bamford himself for listening to Lomax or Lomax's emissary without denouncing him, and this Robinson did not fail to point out in the House of Commons (Hansard, March 5, 1818).

[5] Chippendale's informant went further and said that simultaneous risings were arranged for in Sheffield, Nottingham, Leicester, and Birmingham (H.O., 42. 162).

[6] The movements of No. 2 are uncertain ; Philips did not know of him.

[7] H.O., 42. 162.

intentions' and the 'loss of life' imminent but for his preparations. In addition to the men arrested at the actual
meeting, a few more dangerous characters were seized, including William Lomax, of whose overtures to Sidmouth
the spies were clearly ignorant. 'William Lomax,' wrote
Mr. Hay, '. . . is inclined to give evidence, and has disclosed several circumstances, stating that his intention was
to give Evidence, he acknowledges having written to your
Lordship.'

The conspirators from the meeting were not a very formid-
able-looking band. 'All these,' wrote Mr. Hay, 'are miserable objects, but I fear, desperate incendiaries.'[1] Lomax
and Waddington (alias A. B.) were released next day. Lomax
died soon after;[2] Waddington's career as a spy was cut short
by his unfortunate arrest. A certain awkwardness arose
in his case for, so wrote Mr. Hay,[3] Colonel Fletcher had stipulated that he should not be brought forward as a witness,
'but inasmuch as he is now blown upon, he can never
again be employed as an informer. Our informer,'[4] he adds
proudly, 'stands unsuspected and may be of further use.'

The arrests of March 28 were followed by many others
under the suspension of the Habeas Corpus Act, Bamford,
Knight, and Benbow being among the victims.

No suspicion fell on No. 1 for many months, till November,
when Sellars, one of the men whom he had helped to entrap,
wrote to his wife from prison saying that Hall had always
been ready to treat those without money, and had proposed
the change in the place of meeting on March 28. This of
course cannot be true, says the borough-reeve naïvely,[5] since
the instructions given to No. 1 and No. 2 from the very first
were, not to push forward the plans of reformers, but only
to engage so far as was necessary to discovery under pain
of dismissal. However, Hall was now suspected, a distinction he shared, it may be mentioned, with most of the
genuine working-class reformers, and it was thought wiser to
remove him from Manchester before the prisoners returned.[6]

[1] H.O., 42. 164.   [2] He was dead by November (H.O., 42. 171).
[3] H.O., 42. 164.   [4] No. 1.   [5] H.O., 42. 171.
[6] H.O., 42. 171, and 79. 3.   After Dewhurst's and Lomax's doings were
unmasked by Mr. Philips, February 9, 1818, the Government (F. Robinson) on
March 9 declared that no man of the name of Dewhurst was known to Government. It was true that he was not known under that name, but on February 13
Mr. Hay had written 'Most *private*. We consider that by Dewhurst is meant
No. 1' (H. O., 42. 174).

No. 2 was not suspected till later, but according to the *Manchester Observer* of March 7, 1818,[1] where he is called Roe, both he and No. 1 had fled by that date. His last contribution to the great plot was to hold a meeting on March 31, after the arrests, with five notorious characters and to decide that it was useless to attempt a general insurrection since the military force was too strong.[2] The great Manchester plot was in fact over, and we now come to the more extended operations connected with the name of Oliver, operations compared with which the achievements of No. 1 and No. 2 are reduced to very slight proportions.

Mr. Oliver, alias W. J. Richards, was described by an acquaintance as ' a person of genteel appearance and good address, nearly six feet high, of erect figure, light hair, red and rather large whiskers, and a full face, a little pitted with the small-pox. His usual dress . . . was a light fashionable-coloured brown coat, black waistcoat, dark-blue mixture pantaloons, and Wellington boots.'[3] According to his own account he was born in Shropshire.[4] By the time he came into public notice he had already lived thirty years in London, where he pursued the callings of carpenter and builder, and also latterly of surveyor. Business had not prospered with him, and he declared that he had lost a large sum as a builder. The Opposition in the House of Commons afterwards ferreted out some inconvenient details about his past life,[5] such as the fact that he had committed bigamy, and the more relevant story of a rather ugly transaction with a Mr. Restall, formerly his master, a carpenter who accused Oliver of fraud.[6]

Oliver's first communication to the Government seems to have been made on March 28, when he brought an unsigned letter to the Home Office requesting an interview.[7]

---

[1] H.O., 42. 175. [2] H.O., 42. 165.

[3] Sir F. Burdett, House of Commons (Hansard, June 16, 1817).

[4] Examination on June 15, 1817 (H.O., 42. 166). The *Manchester Courier*, March 3, 1818, said that he was a native of South Wales.

[5] Hansard, February 11 and March 5, 1818.

[6] William Smith, in the House of Commons, March 5, 1818, declared himself ready to substantiate charges of gross fraud against Oliver. Mr. Bathurst retorted that the affair alluded to had been referred to arbitration, and that though the arbitrator directed Oliver to pay a sum of money he acquitted him of criminality. Mr. Smith adhered to his story, said the arbitrator was deceived, and asked for an inquiry. [7] H.O., 40. 10 (Bundle 9).

At this time he was mixed up with a certain Pendrill, one of the more violent London reformers, and whether it was for his own safety, as he himself avowed,[1] or for the sake of gold, that he asked to see Sidmouth and promised communications, is unimportant.   His activities in the provinces began on April 23, when he started out for a tour in the North and the Midlands, in company with Mitchell, a hot-headed and unbalanced enthusiast, ostensibly for the purpose of obtaining petitions for Parliamentary Reform. Birmingham, Derby, Sheffield, Wakefield, Huddersfield, Dewsbury, Leeds, Halifax, Royton, Middleton, Manchester, Barnsley, Nottingham were all visited, many of them twice.[2] Mitchell was got out of the way by arrest on May 4,[3] but Oliver's own tour lasted till May 16, when he arrived back in London and consoled his friend Mitchell by paying him several visits in Cold Bath Fields prison.[4]

During this first tour Oliver wrote reports to the Home Office.[5] He is ' obliged to appear as a Liberal patriot,' he writes from Birmingham, and Mitchell believes him sent, he says in another letter from Wakefield, by the London patriots ; ' every nerve of mine,' he adds with considerable truth, ' has been at work since I left London.' His task indeed was arduous.   To the more staid reformers he represented himself as the friend of Burdett and Cartwright, introducing himself ' with Sir F. Burdett's compliments,' [6] bent on obtaining a monster petition for Reform, but insinuating that stronger measures might soon be necessary.   To the more violent spirits, chafing under the suspension of the Habeas Corpus Act, he represented himself as delegated by the physical force party in London, where seventy thousand men were ready to rise as soon as plans were matured over the country.

[1] H.O., 42. 166.

[2] His own time-table is given in H.O., 40. 9.   Bennet's history of him, which coincides, though all the dates are not filled up, is in Hansard, February 11, 1818.

[3] The arrest took place rather sooner than Oliver intended.   See Oliver's own letter, H.O., 40. 10.

[4] Mitchell was afterwards accused of being a spy himself, but there is no evidence of this.

[5] H.O., 40. 10.

[6] When Burdett complained of this, Castlereagh's answer was characteristic : ' If the hon. baronet's name had been mixed up with any of the proceedings of the individuals to whom he had alluded, it was himself that he had to thank for it, and not his Majesty's government ' (Hansard, June 19, 1817).

At each town, the other towns were reported to be ready
for action, eager to begin the great fight for liberty, provided only that the town he happened to be visiting at the
moment would make its arrangements. The object of all
these machinations was to gather together recruits, or ' delegates ' as he called them, to attend meetings, and he worked
hard for this purpose, generally with less success than his
exertions deserved.

His second and more important mission to the Midlands
and the North began on May 23 and ended rather abruptly
on June 7, but in that fortnight he achieved a great deal.
He was in an even more responsible position now, for he
brought with him credentials from the Home Office, in the
form of a private letter dated May 22 from Whitehall,[1] to
four or five individuals in positions of trust.

'Sir,—A Person well acquainted with the Designs of the
Disaffected at —— and other Places in the Midlands and
Nothern Counties, will leave London Tomorrow Evening, and
will visit —— previous to his Return. It is possible that he may
obtain some Information while at that Place, the early communication of which to a magistrate on the spot may be of material
importance. He will accordingly be entrusted with this Letter
which he will make use of as his Introduction to you, in case
such a Communication should become necessary during his Stay
at ——

' He is an intelligent Man, and deserving of your confidence.
I am, &c.,   J. H. Addington.'

This letter was sent to Mr. Hamper, a magistrate of Birmingham, to the Mayor of Leicester, to Mr. Lockett of Derby,
to General Byng, and to Mr. Hay the parson magistrate
at Manchester. The secret was kept from other magistrates
with embarrassing results. At Sheffield the justices had
their own private informant, Thomas Bradley by name,
a silver plater. Now Bradley in his reports made such constant mention of the London delegate, Oliver, and of his
doings, that the magistrates naturally thought that Oliver's
arrest was most desirable. At Sheffield, Oliver had found
good if scanty material on which to work, including a certain
James Westenholme, who seems to have been whole-hearted
in his desire to use any means ' to effect the delivrance of
our common country from the greatest Slavery and Despotism.'[2]

[1] H.O., 42. 165.   [2] *Ibid.*

On May 21, Bradley relates [1] that Mr. O——, the London delegate, was in Sheffield last Wednesday and agreed that ' the concern ' should be put off from May 27 to June 10, and that Oliver recommended that accounts of this postponement should be sent by post to Manchester, Birmingham, and Nottingham. Again on June 3, [2] Bradley deposes that when he went to Wakefield on June 1 at the request of the magistrates, there was much talk about Oliver, the London delegate, and the landlord of the inn asked if Bradley ever doubted that Oliver was a man of good faith, saying, ' if he is not, I and many more must be hanged.' Bradley goes on to say that on May 28 he was in the company of Oliver in Sheffield and Oliver ' urged Sheffield on,' saying that he could raise seventy thousand men in East London and seventy thousand more in West London. The Sheffield party, he adds, have no other knowledge of the strength and numbers of partisans in Nottingham, Birmingham, and elsewhere, ' but what they were told by Oliver. Oliver is the Chief Agent and promoter in the business.' Elsewhere he states of Oliver, ' He was considered by all the Party as the Man who communicated and directed things from London, and as they directed, so he acted.' [3]

The Sheffield justices wishing to nip the plot in the bud went in person, on the information of Bradley, to surprise a secret meeting at the Grinding Wheel on May 29. [4] The conspirators received the alarm and took to their heels, but four men, including Westenholme, were arrested as they came away. Mr. Parker, a Sheffield justice, who communicated with the Home Office, wrote to Lord Sidmouth to describe the arrests, adding casually in a postscript the remark that as he had a full description of Oliver he would, if time allowed, send a constable to take him at Leeds ; if missed at Leeds he might be arrested when he went to visit Mitchell in Cold Bath Fields prison. This official zeal caused consternation at headquarters ; and in the Secret Letter Book is a copy of the letter Sidmouth wrote to Mr. Parker on May 31. [5] After praising his activity, I must tell you, he proceeds, ' that O. is employed by me, that He is travelling under my directions at this time, and that I have reason to confide in his disposition and ability to render Himself eminently useful, under

[1] H.O., 42. 165.   [2] H.O., 42. 163.
[3] Bradley, June 6 (H.O., 40. 10).   [4] H.O., 42. 165.
[5] H.O., 79. 3.

present circumstances, I accordingly shall be anxious till I hear again and should be much relieved by hearing that He has not been apprehended.'

'It was purely accidental,' wrote Mr. Parker in return,[1] 'that Oliver did not fall into our hands at Sheffield, and from a letter yesterday from the Mayor at Leeds I find he had a similar escape there.' He added that the persons engaged in the affair in Sheffield were 'of the lowest order and not so numerous as I stated in my letter of the 31st Ult^{o}.'

The number then suggested as a maximum was 230, calculated on the unlikely supposition that each man who came to meetings had ten others behind him.[2]

Mr. Parker was a second time rather too energetic to allow the plans to ripen properly. Oliver, as we have said, worked indefatigably to gather meetings of so-called 'delegates' from different places together. He had contrived one such meeting at Wakefield on May 5, another at Mill Bridge near Wakefield on May 11, and he was now busily engaged arranging for a third at Thornhill Lees on June 6. He spared no pains to obtain a good attendance. He did his best to get a delegate from Birmingham, even sending over Crabtree, a foolish young man who had entered heart and soul into his schemes, to persuade one of the members of the Reform party to come, but his efforts were useless.[3]

Manchester was equally cold, and Oliver expended his eloquence there in vain.[4] The only persons, in fact, whom he managed to collect at his meeting on June 6 at the Sportsman's Arms, Thornhill Lees, were ten obscure individuals from Leeds, Bradford, Wakefield, and the surrounding districts.[5] The attempts in this part of the world, wrote

[1] H.O., 42. 166.   [2] H.O., 42. 165.

[3] Mr. Jones, a respectable jeweller in Birmingham, head of the Reform party there, had been one of the first people seen by Oliver on his former mission. Rather reluctantly a delegate had been sent from Birmingham to the meeting at Wakefield on May 5, but finding that instead of petitions physical force was discussed, the Birmingham reformers had no more to do with Oliver's schemes (see Bennet's speech, Hansard, February 11, 1818).

[4] On June 4 General Byng wrote that he heard that Manchester had given up the rising as hopeless, and that Oliver who had just come from Manchester corroborated this information (H.O., 42. 166). All the inflammable material had already been used up by No. 1 and No. 2 and A. B. Prentice, *op cit.*, pp. 108-9, says that a small band of middle-class reformers in Manchester had exposed the spy system too thoroughly for Oliver to get any footing (cf. Prentice, *op cit.*, p. 111).

[5] H.O., 42. 166.

General Byng on June 4,[1] after seeing Oliver, will be decided
on at a meeting of delegates next Friday, ' which He will
attend, and then see me, and immediately afterwards proceed
to Birmingham. . . .' It is clear that Oliver had not meant
these delegates to be arrested that day, nor did General Byng
wish it. Byng wrote [2] that as Mr. Parker, after a meeting
of magistrates, proposed arrest, he could not very well object,
but he accompanied the magistrates and yeomen in person
to give aid, and ' that I might take Care and dispose of the
Person introduced to me by your Brother, who I knew was
to be there.' ' The Person I alluded to,' he adds later, ' I
was forced to seize upon, but I contrived his escape and sent
him off by the Mail tonight for Nottingham and Birmingham,
from whence he proceeds to town.' This slight incident
was to have very important consequences.

The ten dangerous delegates safe in prison, Oliver went
on his way to Nottingham.[3] Oliver's first visit to Nottingham was on May 15, just at the end of his first tour; his
second visit was on May 26, when he stayed till the 28th
visiting the villages round; his third visit, when he came
from Thornhill Lees, was on June 6. At Nottingham he
found an enthusiast ready to fall in and forward any proposal however wild, in the person of Jeremiah Brandreth,
a half-starved, illiterate, and unemployed frame-work knitter,[4]
of swarthy and what is commonly called ' foreign ' appearance. Probably he had a strain of gipsy blood. Brandreth,
to whom leadership and excitement were attractive, entered
heart and soul into the scheme. On May 23 Mr. Enfield's
secret agent reports [5] that Brandreth came to see him and
talked of the ' general strike ' to take place in London, Manchester, Sheffield, Derby, Nottingham, Leicester, Yorkshire,
and other places the following Sunday or the Sunday after.
Part of the plan was to seize soldiers' arms wherever they
could get them, to march together to London, and in London
to contend for a change in Government. On May 25 he reports [6]
a meeting at Brandreth's house in the morning of five persons,

---

[1] H.O., 42. 166.   [2] *Ibid.*

[3] In the case of Nottingham, as of Sheffield, there are reports from another
'secret agent' employed by the local authorities and ignorant of Oliver's
position.

[4] He was receiving parish relief at the time, and with his family had been
'removed' from Sutton Ashfield to Wilford (see *Trials of Brandreth and
Others*, vol. i. p. 211).

[5] H.O., 42. 165.   [6] *Ibid.*

when there was a good deal of incoherent conversation about the Brunswick family, the people's cause and pikes. Another meeting took place at the Three Salmons the same afternoon, of the same persons joined by five others, including a delegate from Bradford, identified in the margin by the Home Office authorities as Crabtree.[1] This delegate discoursed, after Oliver's fashion, on the theme that it had been resolved to petition no more but to arm themselves, and a vague discussion followed on the time of the rising and the Brunswick family and the expectation that the London delegate would come next Tuesday.

There are no more reports from Nottingham till June 5,[2] by which time plans had matured, and Brandreth had been given, or had assumed, the command of the contingent from Pentridge in Derby which was to march out and join the other forces at Nottingham. Brandreth told the Nottingham secret agent that the London delegate was well known. ' I asked him if they had any communication with any other person than the London Delegate. He said they had not but some of the Chaps had.' Birmingham, where they had trusty friends, was to send a delegate. From other sources the secret agent learned that arms were expected from London, that the London delegate was to visit Nottingham shortly, that the rising was fixed for Monday night, June 9, when Mansfield and Sutton were to rise at 9 P.M., Bulwell at 10 o'clock, Nottingham at 11 o'clock, whilst the London delegate was to go to Chesterfield, Sheffield, Leeds, Manchester, Liverpool, Derby, Leicester, Birmingham, London, and then back to Nottingham. Next day, June 6, the secret agent reported [3] that the villages of Arnold and Bulwell, which he had been asked to rouse, refused to take part in the plan ; that refusals to join came from many quarters, but that all was said to be ready for action on Tuesday at Birmingham, where Jones the jeweller was to head the rising. Those who were not killed were to be put in a coal pit.

We now come to Oliver's arrival in Nottingham on June 6,[4] fresh from Thornhill Lees and from his interview with General Byng. He brought word that they were to begin at Sheffield, Huddersfield, Wakefield, and Leeds on Sunday the 8th, and the Nottingham people decided that their operations should begin on Monday the 9th and sent word to Derby and Birmingham to that effect. But now a curious situation arose.

[1] H.O., 42. 165.   [2] H.O., 42. 166.   [3] Ibid.   [4] Ibid.

News had reached Nottingham of the Thornhill Lees arrests and of Oliver's strange escape. One of the small band at Nottingham, Holmes by name, began to suspect Oliver, or Hollis as he now called himself. Was he perhaps a traitor in disguise? Would it be as well to decoy him into the fields and there shoot him?[1] Some favoured this policy, others opposed it. Finally a meeting was held at the Punch Bowl of about twenty persons, and Oliver was subjected to perhaps the most searching ordeal he ever had to face. He must have been a man of considerable nerve, for he stood the cross-examination well, declared, what was after all the truth, that he was an ex-builder paid by a mysterious friend to travel about in the cause of Reform, and persuaded them —also the truth—that his activities were essential to the success of the scheme. They let him go and he returned to London, visiting Birmingham again on his way, where, as was suitable to the type of reformers he visited there, he made free use of the names of Burdett and Cartwright.[2] When he reached London his part in the rising was over. It only remained for the rising itself to take place.

The story of this rising which was to embrace the North and the Midlands is soon told. In only two places were there persons foolish enough to translate words into action, first at Huddersfield, and secondly in the Derbyshire villages round Pentridge. At Huddersfield, Sheffield, Wakefield, and Leeds the rising as has been said was to begin on Sunday night, June 8.[3] On Sunday night a mob gathered at Huddersfield, demanded arms at several houses, met six of the yeomanry at the bridge, exchanged shots and forced the yeomanry to retire. When, however, the yeomen came back in stronger force the mob was gone, and the rising, so far as the West Riding was concerned, was over, though a few of the so-called insurgents were recognised and arrested.[4]

That Sunday Brandreth was sitting in a public-house at Pentridge discoursing very openly of his plans to an audience,

[1] H.O., 42. 166.

[2] Bennet's speech, Hansard, February 11, 1818.

[3] H.O., 42. 166. Byng writes on June 10 from Wakefield: I want to find out ' why the Rising was not attempted last night, for of the intention *there cannot be a doubt.*'

[4] See Fitzwilliam's letter of June 17, H.O., 42. 167. Also see H.O., 42. 166 (Briefs of Evidence).

which included two special constables, who were so far from taking him seriously that they contented themselves with mild remonstrances. Brandreth and his friends threatened to put them up the chimney if they were not quiet. Brandreth recited some verses, probably of his own composition :

> ' Every man his skill must try,
> He must turn out and not deny ;
> No bloody soldier must he dread,
> He must turn out and fight for bread.
> The time is come, you plainly see
> The Government opposed must be.' [1]

It is possible that in spite of his enthusiasm Brandreth would have obtained no following had not local indignation been stirred by the fact that some men from Mr. Jessop's foundry at Butterley had been discharged on the Saturday night ' in consequence of their Jacobinical principles, and calling themselves Members of an Hampden Club.' [2] As it was, a small number of workmen, at the most two hundred, probably fewer, from Pentridge, Wingfield, and Ripley were induced to join in a march towards Nottingham. Some thought that when they got to Nottingham there would be plenty of rum and a hundred guineas,[3] others more vague ' wanted a bigger loaf and the times altering,' [4] and they all thought that something important was happening everywhere else. England, Ireland, and France, said one enthusiast, would rise that night at 10 o'clock, and there was much talk of a ' cloud of men ' sweeping down from the North and carrying all before them.[5]

Encouragement indeed was needed, for the rain poured down, it was fourteen miles to Nottingham, and the expected reinforcements were nowhere to be seen. At Nottingham that night there was a good deal of agitation in the streets —not an unusual occurrence in that town—and about one hundred men were said to have gathered on the racecourse, but nothing more happened. On their way the Pentridge party stopped at nine or ten houses and demanded arms, and in some cases forced a man from the house to go with them. The insurgents were armed in motley fashion, mostly with what witnesses afterwards called ' spikes ' or

---

[1] *Trials*, vol. i. pp. 75 f.
[2] See letter from Derby Post Office, June 11 (H.O., 42. 166).
[3] *Trials* , vol. i. p. 78.   [4] *Ibid.*, vol. i. p. 113.
[5] *Ibid.*, vol. i. p. 87.

'sticks with things in them,' though the Government preferred to describe them as 'pikes.' There was one act of
violence. At the house of a Mr. Hepworth, Brandreth, in his
wild excitement, shot and killed a manservant. There is
nothing to show that the deed was intentional, but firing
through windows to impress the people within is a dangerous
game to play.

With dwindling numbers and sinking spirits the rebels
marched on in the early morning hours as far as Eastwood
on their way to Nottingham.   There at about 6 A.M. they
met two magistrates who had come out with eighteen men
of the 15th Light Dragoons and two officers to oppose them.
What happened is best described by one of the magistrates,
Mr. Mundy :[1] '. . . about a mile before we reached Eastwood we came in sight of the mob who though at near three
quarters of a miles distance from us no sooner saw the Troops
than they fled in all directions dispersing over the fields and
throwing away their arms they were pursued for a considerable time and finally driven out of this County into Derbyshire . . . they did not fire a single shot and seemed only
intent on escape.'   Some were captured at once, others were
beaten out of the woods and hedges like pheasants ; in all
about forty-eight were taken.[2] Never was war levied against
the King in more spiritless fashion.

Hitherto to those ignorant of the part played by Oliver,
the outbursts, however futile in themselves, might seem
signs of a grave state of affairs, but on June 14 the most sen-
sational revelation that ever newspaper published appeared
in the second edition of the *Leeds Mercury*, on the subject
of Oliver and his share in the late disturbances : a revelation that caused a profound change in public opinion.   It
so happened that amongst the persons with whom Oliver
had got into touch were Mr. Willans a bookseller of Dewsbury, and Mr. John Dickenson a linen-draper of the same
town, both members of the local Reform party.   Oliver had
come several times to Mr. Willans' house, where Mr. Dickenson had seen him, but Mr. Willans had grown suspicious of
Oliver's hints about the need for employing force, and had

[1] H.O., 42. 166, June 10.
[2] H.O., 42. 166 and 167. Brandreth escaped at first, and after vain attempts to
obtain a passage to America from Bristol sought refuge in the 'secret agents'
house in Nottingham where he was taken (July 22, H.O., 42. 168).

ceased communications with him, thinking him a dangerous
fellow.   On the morning of the meeting at Thornhill Lees,
Oliver had come not once but twice to Mr. Willans' shop
to press him to attend the meeting as a delegate from Dewsbury. His friends in London, he told Mr. Willans, ' were
almost heartbroken that the people in the country were so
quiet.' Mr. Willans, however, refused. Later in the day,
after the arrest of the delegates, Mr. Dickenson chanced
to be in an inn at Wakefield and there to his surprise he saw
Oliver, and asked him how it was that he had escaped when
all the other reformers had been seized at the Thornhill Lees
meeting. Oliver was hard put to it, and could only give the lame
reply that no papers had been found on him. Mr. Dickenson knew enough of the ways of justice to think this a very
insufficient explanation of Oliver's escape, and his suspicions
were at once aroused. Unfortunately for Oliver, Dickenson
was the witness a few moments later of an incident that turned
his suspicions of Oliver's real character into conviction. For
a manservant in livery came up to speak to Oliver and as
he came to him he touched his hat. Dickenson making in-
quiries found that the man was the servant of General Byng
and had driven Oliver in a tandem from his master's house
to catch the coach. Dickenson and Willans put these facts
before the *Leeds Mercury*, which published them with a strong
article demanding an explanation of Oliver's position, and
declaring him to be ' a green bag maker.' [1]

This article saved Oliver's Yorkshire victims. It caused
great excitement, and everywhere the reformers began to
put two and two together and to reconstruct the story of
Oliver's operations. On the 16th Mr. Dickenson and Mr.
Willans attended before the magistrates to lay charges against
Oliver.[2] On the 17th Fitzwilliam sent an important letter
to the Government, round which controversy afterwards
raged.[3]

[1] See also *Leeds Mercury* for June 21, 28, July 5, 12, 19, etc. ' I believe the
Leeds Mercury has done much more harm to the political morals (if I may allow
the term) of the labouring classes in this part than ever Tom Paine's trash did
—it is a most villainous publication' (Correspondent to Home Office, February
1818, H.O., 42. 174).

[2] Mr. Dickenson's deposition was taken (H.O., 42. 166, June 16). Mr.
Willans could not be heard because though not yet formally admitted as a
Quaker he had conscientious scruples against taking an oath (H.O., 42. 167,
June 17).

[3] See p. 373 below.

After giving particulars of the Willans and Dickenson revelations he wrote :

'There certainly is very generally in the Country a strong and decided opinion that most of the events that have recently occurred in the Country are to be attributed to the presence and active agitation of Mr. Oliver. He is considered as the main spring, from which every movement has taken its rise. All the mischievous in the country have considered themselves as subordinate Members of a great leading Body of Revolutionists in London, as co-operating with that Body for one general purpose, in this view to be under its Instructions and Directions communicated by some Delegate appointed for the purpose. Had not then a person, pretending to come from that Body, and for that purpose, made his appearance in the Country, it is not assuming too much to say that probably no movement whatever would have occurred. It does not follow that a dangerous spirit could not have been found lurking in any Breast, but that that Spirit would not have found its way into action.'

He then gives his opinion as to recent occurrences :

'First then at Sheffield it appears that when the Delegate from London had made his appearance and sanctioned by his approbation the measures taken there, and had urged them to press forward and not to be more backward in preparation than other places, when therefore a Meeting of Delegates or Leaders of Tens was summoned for the important purpose of finally arranging matters for a Rising, and the consequent measures of operation, eighteen Leaders only, with four excuses, were present.

'Again, when the grand effort in the Manufacturing District was made Sunday June 8th when actual Insurrection was resorted to ; when the Insurgents came out in Battle Array, took post at the Bridge near Huddersfield, and had their Sentries at their Outposts, who brought prisoners, or attempted to do so, to Head Quarters, they are not reported to have exceeded a *few Hundreds* ; and such appeared their want of order, or their want of Arms, that having come into Contact with Six Yeomen upon whom they fired, and forced back, nevertheless in less than an hour, on the return of the Yeomen in force, not a Vestige of a Body, or even of a Man in Arms, was to be found.' [1]

The revelations of the *Leeds Mercury* had an immediate effect on the treatment of the prisoners in Yorkshire. Of

[1] H.O., 42. 167, June 17. Sidmouth wrote in answer to Fitzwilliam's letter and Dickenson's declaration : ' The Statement is to me incredible but I think it so important as to require immediate and minute Investigation' (H.O., 42. 167). The only investigation, so far as one can judge, was an examination of 'the Person known by the name of W. J. Richards' by Home Office officials on June 15 (H.O., 42. 166).

the ten Thornhill Lees delegates, met to arrange the final plans for the rising, two were sent up to London under warrants from the Government.[1] The magistrates discharged seven others on their own recognisances or on bail, and detained one in hopes of further evidence.[2] The prosecution of the Huddersfield rioters had been even more of a fiasco. Here Fitzwilliam's influence was clearly shown. On June 23 he writes [3] that he has recommended the magistrates not to try to procure further evidence against others from the prisoners ; he dislikes the evidence of accomplices and there is no hope of getting ' witnesses less objectionable.' It is better to restore public confidence and not leave every one with the uneasy feeling that they may be arrested. In spite of this the Government solicitor (Wm. Le Blanc) hoped to obtain capital convictions against six men for shooting at a constable and against eight men for burglary of arms.[4] He had reckoned without the Judge, Mr. Baron Wood, who shared Fitzwilliam's dislike of accomplices' evidence. The prisoners charged with burglary were all acquitted ; for the Judge treated the evidence of accomplices as valueless unless confirmed, and the only confirmation came from a woman who happened also to have told some people that she knew no persons implicated. After the summing up the jury could not fail to acquit. The riot charges were dropped when it was seen how the Judge treated such evidence. Next day (July 26) the prosecution met with no better fortune in their charges connected with the shooting of the constable.[5] Here again the only witnesses for the Crown were accomplices, and one of these was, according to the prosecution, tampered with, and so told the Grand Jury that the yeomen fired first when he ought to have said the mob fired first. According to his own story [6] what he said was true, but the prosecution had tried to bribe him by 1s. worth of oranges to say that the mob fired first. However that might be, he was rendered useless, and grave doubt being thrown by the Judge on the truthfulness of the other witness, here again the prisoners were all acquitted.[7]

[1] H.O., 42. 166.   [2] H.O., 42. 167.
[3] *Ibid.*   [4] H.O., 42. 169.
[5] The Grand Jury had thrown out a bill for firing at the constable, but found a true bill for rioting and abetting in the shooting.
[6] See Sherwin's *Political Register*, August 9, 1817 (H.O., 42. 170).
[7] The Government in June had met with another disagreeable check. Watson, Preston, Thistlewood, and Hooper were all arraigned for High

' How little do those who triumph on such occasions, see that the Jurors neglect of his oath has a direct Tendancy to the subversion of a Public Liberty.' So wrote an official of the Home Office on Lord Sidmouth's behalf to Mr. Fletcher of Bolton after the verdicts.[1] The comments of the *Annual Register* form an interesting contrast: ' Against all this weight of power and influence, seconded by the public purse, a few obscure men and boys, principally in the very lowest ranks of society, had to defend themselves. The odds were terrific ; but with the zeal and intelligence of their professional advisers and advocates, and the presiding presence of a righteous Judge, who knows no distinction between the lofty and the humble in the administration of justice, the trial by jury obtained another distinguished triumph, and the prisoners after a period of deep anxiety were restored to their liberty and to their friends.' [2]

The prisoners at Derby were to meet with a less happy fate. There was no Fitzwilliam in Derbyshire, and they were not tried before Baron Wood. A repetition of the fiasco at York had to be avoided by the Government, and some careful stage-management was needed. A Special Commission with four Judges was issued and the prisoners were charged, not with such simple counts as burglary or shooting, but with High Treason itself. Mr. Lockett, solicitor of Derby, who helped prepare the cases for the Crown, wrote that it would not do to have the trials before the harvest was over, for ' we shall want at least 400 common Jurors from parts of the county in which crops are backward, and if they have to come before crops are nearly housed, they will make every possible excuse, and come, if obliged, with reluctance, and out of humour. This temper would be prejudicial to us.' [3] He adds advice, which was taken, to brief Mr. John Balguy for the Crown, for he is popular with Derbyshire juries and might be briefed for the other side ; advice reiterated by Mr. Mundy, J.P., who added : ' As it will be necessary in selecting the jury to avoid those parts of the County that border on Nottinghamshire, as

Treason in London. The Government case rested on an accomplice, Castles; the jury acquitted Watson, and in consequence the Crown dropped the other prosecutions.

[1] H.O., 79. 3, August 9.   [2] *Annual Register*, 1817, Chronicle, p. 73.
[3] H.O., 42. 169, August 11.

also those parts in which the insurrection broke out, and
also those parts that are much connected with Manchester,
the summoning the jury will of course fall heavily on the
other parts.' [1]

Mr. Lockett afterwards came in for a good deal of criticism
for having acted as if he were under sheriff as well as solicitor
to the Crown, by using his influence with the under sheriff
to name and pack juries.[2]   The criticism would have been
strengthened had his critics seen his letter to the Home Office
on October 11 : [3] 'I am happy to inform you that we are
prepared for the trials. I have intelligence upon which I
can depend as to every Juror. The list throughout is most
respectable. There will be but few challenges on the part
of the Crown.'

For four months, till the harvest was over and suitable
jurors were ready to try them, the prisoners lay in gaol.   They
had some friends, among them Joseph Strutt, the curate of
Pentridge named Wolstonholme,[4] and a Presbyterian clergyman, Mr. Higginson ; and a solicitor was engaged for their
defence.   Their solicitor wrote after they had been eight weeks
in prison to ask if they were not 'intitled to some other allowance as state prisoners besides *Bread and Water,* on which
alone the greater part of them are now subsisting; not having
the means of procuring any thing better or more substantial.'
The answer given was that the prisoners were to have an allowance ' adapted to the Situation in life and the ordinary mode
of living of the respective Prisoners.' [5]   Mr. John Cross and

[1] H.O., 42. 169, August 23.
[2] H.O., 42. 173.   On July 24 (H.O., 42. 168) he writes up to say that as the
Derby gaol is overcrowded and insecure he has ordered Brandreth to be ironed
and asks to be authorised to iron the other High Treason prisoners.
[3] H.O., 42. 170.
[4] H.O., 42. 171.   Joseph Strutt, manufacturer, was third son of Jedediah
Strutt of Derby-rib machine fame. Joseph was a patron of art and literature ;
for his princely liberality to the town, see Felkin, *op. cit.*, p. 100.   Lockett
wanted to have Wolstonholme arrested on the general charge of treasonable
practices, and he wrote to the Home Office pointing out that it was undesirable
to confine him in the Derby prison where he might get into communication
with the other prisoners.   The Attorney-General evidently thought that
Wolstonholme might be able to defend himself and that a general charge would
be risky. Lockett accused Wolstonholme of sheltering Weightman. Wolstonholme was a man of great courage and independence.   His licence, so Lockett
wrote, enabled him to 'bid defiance to the loyal party.' Lockett hoped something might be done by pressure from Sidmouth on Wolstonholme's bishop
(H.O., 42. 170 and 172).   [5] H.O., 42. 169, August 9.

Mr. Thomas Denman were counsel for the prisoners. Much clearly turned on the question whether Oliver's doings could be kept out of the proceedings. The suggestion that Crabtree should be tried or used as a witness was soon vetoed by Mr. Lockett.[1] 'I do not want Crabtree. He will let in Oliver's proceedings upon us. We will confine ourselves to the *Derbyshire* traitors if you please.' When the trials began it looked as if it might prove impossible to keep Oliver out altogether. 'Oliver must come to be produced in court if necessary,' wrote Mr. Litchfield, the Treasury solicitor;[2] 'please send him *at once* with Raven, disguised and under the name of Maule to the George Inn.' Oliver came, but his services were not required. Mr. Litchfield frankly describes the line pursued by the prosecution, 'avoiding all questions about O——, and not ever giving them an opportunity of introducing his name.'[3] A few days later they decided to send Oliver back, for 'we have resolved not to bring forward any prosecution in which his name can be brought in question.'[4]

Five-and-thirty traitors[5] were brought up for trial on October 16, 1817, charged by a stroke of grim irony with having been 'moved and seduced by the instigation of the devil' to levy war against the King, and to compass to depose him. The case of Brandreth was taken first. Evidence as to his actions on June 8 and 9 was clear and conclusive. The defence tried to show that what had happened was a riot, not treason. Could the jury say that 'the five and thirty miserable paupers . . . arraigned here did levy war against the King?' The jury instructed by the Judge saw nothing grotesque in so deciding, and Brandreth was found guilty. 'A crime is not less a crime,' said Lord Chief Baron Richards in summing up, 'because the man who commits it is poor.' After Brandreth's conviction the other cases were taken one by one and the evidence given again with wearisome repetition. First, William Turner a stone mason, formerly a soldier, was tried and found guilty; second, Isaac Ludlam the elder, also a stone mason; third,

---

[1] H.O., 42. 169, August 11.   [2] H.O., 42. 171, October 15.
[3] H.O., 42. 171, October 19.
[4] H.O., 42. 171, October 22. Oliver's journey to Derby had become known, and particulars were published in the papers causing considerable sensation.
[5] Forty-six were indicted on July 26. The charges against eleven were evidently dropped.

George Weightman a sawyer. Denman pressed inconvenient questions as to the motive for drawing a veil over everything that had occurred before June 8, but he received no answer. He employed all the arts of his eloquence to persuade the jury that the others were merely led on by Brandreth whose influence, ' the influence of an eye like no eye that I ever beheld before,' he magnified until he was even led to quote the description of Conrad in Byron's *Corsair* as a portrait of Brandreth, beginning :

> ' Who is that chief ? his name on every shore
> Is famed and feared ; they ask, and know no more.' [1]

When it came to George Weightman's case, his counsel merely asked for mercy without attempting any defence. ' Here,' wrote the Postmaster of Derby to the General Post Office in London, ' the finger of Providence was perceptable for upon this Jury one Endsor of Parwick had got in who would if his word is to be taken have starved the whole sooner than have found him guilty.' As it was, he adds, it was difficult to persuade Endsor to acquiesce in the verdict of guilty with which however a strong recommendation to mercy was joined. [2]

The prosecution meanwhile was hoping for overtures from the prisoners' representatives seeing that ' each case as we proceed will be gradually weaker.' [3] These overtures were made. As a result the charges were dropped against twelve of the younger prisoners and they were set free, whilst the remaining nineteen pleaded guilty and received formal sentence of death. One of them, Thomas Bacon, had been much associated with Oliver and had acted as a delegate at meetings arranged by him. His name came first in the original indictments, but his determination to plead that he was Oliver's dupe ensured the postponement of his trial. [4] ' Old Bacon,' wrote a correspondent from Derby during the trials, ' has been telling the prisoners they are not tried by their Peers, but by men of property. I name this to show you what dreadful principles these men have taught their unfortunate children.' [5]

---

[1] The tone of Brandreth's last letter with its pitiful prayer, ' A Prayer in trobel of Sin,' and his adjurations to his wife remind the reader of a local preacher rather than a Corsair (H.O., 42. 171).

[2] H.O., 42. 171, October 25.   [3] H.O., 42. 171, October 23.
[4] H.O., 42. 170, September 2.   [5] H.O., 42. 171, October 21.

Including the four tried at the beginning there were twenty-three men found guilty of High Treason. 'Your object was to wade through the blood of your Countrymen, to extinguish the Law and the constitution of your Country, and to sacrifice the property, the liberties, and the lives of your fellow subjects, to confusion and anarchy and the most complete tyranny. God be praised, your purpose failed.' [1] Six of the prisoners had their death sentence commuted to various terms of imprisonment, three were transported for fourteen years, eleven, including Thomas Bacon and George Weightman, were transported for life.[2] Jeremiah Brandreth, William Turner, and Isaac Ludlam were left for execution. On Friday, November 7, 1817, they were drawn on a hurdle round the yard in front of the felons and debtors, hanged on a platform in front of the gaol till they were dead, and their heads severed from their bodies. The rest of the sentence as to quartering was graciously remitted by the Prince Regent. 'God bless you all and Lord Castlereagh too,' said Brandreth. 'I pray God to bless you all, and the King upon his Throne,' said Isaac Ludlam, but William Turner, in a manner described by Mr. Lockett as 'malignant and deceitful,' uttered as his last words, 'This is the work of Government and Oliver.' [3] This declaration created a painful impression, which even the chaplain's certificate that neither Ludlam nor Turner had ever seen Oliver or heard of him at meetings failed to dispel.[4] Mr. Enfield, the Town Clerk, and Mr. Carpenter-Smith, who was on the committee that managed the police at Nottingham, asked that they might see Oliver's statements in order to answer the questions put to them as to the truth of Turner's assertion.[5] 'Lord Sidmouth,' ran the letter in answer to this application, 'would have great satisfaction in complying with the Request of those respectable Gentlemen if he could do so consistently with His Public Duty but at this period when it is the Wish of H.M.'s Government to throw a Veil over the Scenes of Turbulence which have passed ; His Lordship deems it impolitic to extend the Knowledge of Oliver's statements which (as you are

[1] Lord Chief Baron Richards in passing sentence.

[2] Twenty years later, when a Whig Government was in power, Prentice started a successful agitation for their return (Prentice, op cit., p. 112).

[3] H.O., 42. 171, November 7.

[4] Oliver, of course, dealt with the principals, Brandreth and Bacon.

[5] H.O., 42. 172, December 13.

aware) relate to a great Variety of Facts and implicate a large Number of Persons not connected with the Counties of Derby and Nottingham, and convey much Information unnecessary for the Object which Mr. Enfield and Mr. Smith have in vi   [1]

Oliver's career is important in history because these methods of government were rapidly growing into a system. Probably no English Government has ever been quite so near, in spirit and licence, to the atmosphere that we used to associate with the Tsar's government of Russia as the Government that ruled England for the first few years of the peace. Oliver's adventures were the most daring example of methods that had become habitual in the treatment of the poor by several magistrates, but the employment of spies, and of the kind of spies that pass readily into *agents provocateurs*, had become very common in the last few years, as part of the political system ; Tierney declared in 1818 that there was no subject that demanded the attention of Parliament so urgently. The system was checked by two forces : the independence of the London juries and the protests of the Whigs in Parliament. No writer on the subject of this volume is likely to run into a dangerous enthusiasm over the conduct and achievements of the Whig party as a whole, but it is clear that it was the rally of the Opposition to the call of Bennet and Philips that scared Castlereagh and Sidmouth and successive Governments from developing these practices. The debates of 1818 on the demand for an inquiry into Oliver's conduct, though they ended as all party debates end, displayed a spirit and excited a spirit that made Governments more cautious in the future.[2]

The Whigs were in many respects as indifferent to the claims and conditions of the working classes as the Tories, but they had preserved the tradition of the Englishman's way of looking at this particular species of injustice. Men like Fitzwilliam, Grosvenor, Tierney, and Althorp, though they had

[1] H.O., 79. 3, December 17.
[2] There were debates in the House of Commons on February 11 and March 6, 1818, on motions for inquiry. On the first occasion the motion was rejected by 111 votes to 52 ; on the second by 162 to 69. There was a debate in the House of Lords on February 18 on the grievances of the Habeas Corpus prisoners which took largely the character of a debate on espionage. The motion was negatived without a division. The Opposition were exceedingly active in both Houses throughout the months of February and March.

the general point of view of their class, had a sense of honour that was revolted by the spectacle of wretched and ignorant men tempted to their ruin in some wild scheme by a Government spy. Moreover as politicians, they saw the dangers of such a system ; as it was, a Government that wanted an excuse for suspending the Habeas Corpus Act had found the machinations of their spies a most convenient pretext, and it was obvious that the temptation to use them deliberately as *agents provocateurs* might be too much for terrified and unprincipled Ministers. Consequently the men who often had only the support of half a dozen friends when denouncing injustice in Parliament had on this occasion the support of the Opposition.

The issue was a simple one. The Government had persuaded Parliament to suspend the Habeas Corpus Act after submitting to Secret Committees a mass of evidence tending to show that the working classes in the North and the Midlands were preparing a rebellion. By the time that Parliament met in 1818 it was known that this report was an absurd exaggeration, a good deal of Oliver's history had come out, and it was everywhere noted that disturbances ceased when he ceased to look for them. There had been the exciting discovery of Dickenson of Dewsbury, and the prompt action of the *Leeds Mercury*. The middle-class reformers of Manchester, who were by this time a powerful body, had been exasperated by the machinations of the Lancashire spies, and their demand for an inquiry was voiced by Philips, who presented a petition from Manchester merchants and manufacturers on February 9 and made a damaging speech about the Lancashire spies. Meanwhile the facts of Oliver's journeys and conduct had been gradually collected with infinite patience and trouble by the most active of the little set of men who tried to expose and prevent the ill-treatment of the unsheltered classes. Henry Grey Bennet[1] was the John Howard of his day, and his visits to the prisons had taught him a good deal about the spy system. In the House of Commons he defended the poor as the Seventh Beadman in Spenser's holy hospital defended orphans and widows :

---

[1] Bennet (1777-1836), son of the 4th Earl of Tankerville, and Radical M.P. for Shrewsbury, 1806 and 1811-26, was one of the half-dozen most useful men in Parliament, but by a strange omission he does not find a place in the *Dictionary of National Biography*.

'In face of judgement he their right would plead,
Ne ought the powre of mighty men did dread
In their defence ; nor would for gold or fee
Be wonne their rightfull causes downe to tread !'

His speech on this occasion [1] was a model of discretion
and judgment. The Government's critics had a stronger
case than they knew, but even without the conclusive evidence contained in the Home Office Papers they were able
to construct an argument that was unanswered because it
was unanswerable.[2]

The Government's reply only made matters worse. In the
House of Lords Sidmouth called Oliver a 'much injured
individual.' Lord Holland retorted that he could make out
a better case against Oliver than Sidmouth could make out
against the people of England from whom he had taken the
Habeas Corpus, and Grosvenor promised to bring overwhelming evidence to show that Oliver was at the bottom of the
whole business. In the House of Commons [3] Canning cited
the first letter written by Fitzwilliam, in December 1816,
and omitted to mention the fact that there had been a second
letter. This disingenuous conduct provoked a sharp nemesis,
for Fitzwilliam's son, Milton, who had felt that as a member
of the Secret Committee, he was not at liberty to disclose
what had happened at its deliberations, considered that as
his father's first letter had been brought into use by the
Government it was his right and his duty to tell the full story.
It was thus that the House learned that the Government
had withheld from the Secret Committee what was perhaps
the most important document in their possession.[4] Wilberforce made two unhappy speeches, for which Romilly reproached
him with obvious pain, protesting at once his attachment to
the God of Truth and his attachment to Lord Sidmouth. As
a follower of the God of Truth he abominated spies : as a
follower of Lord Sidmouth he disliked the proposed inquiry.
His vote went to Lord Sidmouth. Tierney brought the subject home to his audience by a simple analogy, making no

[1] February 11, 1818.

[2] Any one who compares the facts set out by Bennet in his speech with the
information disclosed in the Home Office Papers must admire the success with
which he had pieced the story together. The difficulties are obvious, for of
course to admit that one had been in Oliver's presence was inviting danger.
He made a slip or two but was on the whole singularly accurate.

[3] Debate on Spies and Informers, Hansard, February 11, 1818.

[4] See p. 364 above.

wild demand on their imagination. ' Suppose one of these artful informers persuaded a gentleman who kept five horses, to return only four, and afterwards not only made the fact known to the commissioners, but participated in the reward; if the matter were brought before parliament, would not every gentleman start from his seat, and demand an instant and a strict inquiry ? Yet where was the distinction, except that here the lives of poor men, and not the pockets of rich men were concerned ? '

It is probable that the Government fell under graver suspicion than they deserved in consequence of their refusal of an inquiry and the line of their defence. There is no reason to suppose that Sidmouth deliberately employed Oliver for the diabolical purpose of fomenting an abortive rebellion, and this view was undoubtedly held at the time. The guilt of the Government was grave enough but it was not this. They took Oliver into their employment without knowing anything of his character. Their own correspondents sent them information, early in his career, that would have put any Home Secretary, who had the slightest sense of responsibility for the lives and liberties of his countrymen, on his guard. Then came the disclosures of the *Leeds Mercury*, which were brought to the notice of Parliament at the time by Burdett. When Brandreth and his fellow victims were on their trial the Government knew enough about Oliver to make them suspect that these foolish ranters had been drawn into their ludicrous escapade by the craft of the man who was receiving the money of the taxpayers and acting as their servant. The temptation to produce something that looked like a spontaneous disturbance was strong, for hitherto the life of the country had borne no resemblance to the pictures drawn by the Government in the House of Commons. Moreover if Oliver's part in the Derbyshire rising had been made public, the part he had played elsewhere could scarcely be hushed up. Sidmouth never professed to put a high value on the liberty of a working man, and he would easily satisfy himself that Oliver's miserable victims were better out of the world or at any rate out of the country. His conduct accordingly seemed less shocking to him than to many of his contemporaries, and the alternative of a possible exposure of the entire system of espionage would have appeared to him a far greater catastrophe than a miscarriage of justice.

The history of the Oliver affair is important because it influenced English opinion on the whole subject of Reform. In Lancashire and in some other parts of England spies were constantly shadowing the lives of working men. This system had attracted little notice until 1817, when Oliver, thinking to take rather more valuable prizes than his fellow spies, entered into relations with the middle-class reformers, and made the mistake of trying to draw into his toils men whose education and position enabled them to defend themselves. If Oliver had been less ambitious and contented himself with the ordinary working-class victims, this great exposure would probably never have come about, and his career would have continued. Bennet pressed the obvious moral in the House of Commons, that Fletcher of Bolton ought to be removed from the Commission of the Peace. Sidmouth was not likely to punish a man for acting as he acted himself, and there is nothing to show that Fletcher modified his practices in consequence. But the revelations of this debate were an important element in the conversion of the middle classes to Reform.

One other comment is suggested by the affair. To many historians the odium that surrounds the memory of Castlereagh is a mystery. As modern investigation has revised the traditional accounts between him and Canning, he has gained in reputation as a Foreign Minister. Recent military history has awarded him the palm of comparative success in a sphere where all his contemporaries reaped unqualified failure.[1] In both these fields he has deserved the distinguished reparation that has been made to him. How comes it then, some historians ask, that Castlereagh went to his grave amid a hatred that death itself could not abate for a single hour, and that his memory was pursued with a bitterness unique in the history of public men ? The answer is that of the three men whose government of England is symbolised in the two words, Oliver and Peterloo, Sidmouth was saved by his comparative obscurity, and Canning was saved by his later life, and thus Castlereagh stands out in the popular mind as the type of methods that are odious to the English nature. Historians who only think of England as an aristocracy in mortal conflict with Europe's tyrant attribute to spontaneous malice the hatred that haunted the Minister who defended her with such resolution and courage. But

[1] Fortescue, *History of the British Army*.

the mass of his countrymen remembered the War Minister who sent the armies to the Peninsula as the Minister who employed German mercenaries at the public flogging of English peasants, and the diplomatist whose heart never failed him in the dark hours of the war with Napoleon as the politician who regarded the poor of his own country as he regarded the Jacobins of France. Hence in the Mask of Anarchy Sidmouth passes riding on his crocodile, and Eldon weeping big tears that turn to millstones, but Castlereagh is followed by seven bloodhounds and throws them the hearts of his countrymen to chew.

CHAPTER XIII

CONCLUSION

‘ Education . . . would teach them to despise their lot in life,
instead of making them good servants in agriculture, and other
laborious employments to which their rank in society had
destined them.’

DAVIES GIDDY, President of Royal Society,
House of Commons, July 1807.

‘The poor man is esteemed only as an instrument for the
creation of wealth.’

Voice of the People, January 29, 1831.

THE system on which modern industry is conducted has two
aspects : in one aspect it appears as the organisation of capital ;
in the other as the organisation of effort.

Men and women are engaged in producing : they produce by
applying energy of mind and body to the forces of nature.
For this task they need equipment : they need machines and
they need also food, clothing, and shelter during the process of
production. This equipment is provided by the savings of
the past, *i.e.* by the excess of things produced over the things
consumed, which becomes a reserve of wealth and is called
capital. As mechanical improvements progress, the help that
capital gives to human effort in this way increases. When
it is said of some industry that it needs little capital, we know
that such an industry uses cheap and simple plant : when it
is said that an industry needs a great deal of capital, we know
that the operations performed by machinery are many in
number or complicated in their character.

The rulers of the country a century ago looking at this system
saw it as the organisation of capital. This was natural in the
case of the old territorial aristocracy, the guardians everywhere
of privilege and authority, and of the rights of inherited power.
The industrial pioneers, who were assuming a share of political
control, were free from many of the prejudices of an old order,
but their outlook on the industrial system was virtually the
same. They were struck, not unnaturally, by the vast and

377

rapid results that followed from the introduction of machinery
for which capital was necessary. They thought of capital as
the master of human energy, for they argued that it depended
on the use to which capital was put whether this or that kind
of worker was employed. The owner of capital might consume
it, or he might build a mill in Lancashire, or he might sink a
shaft in Derbyshire, or he might set up a factory in France or
Switzerland. He was then the arbiter of thousands of lives,
for his choice would determine the destinies of thousands of
men and women. He was thus the *de facto* ruler of society.
He could turn wildernesses into populous towns or populous
towns into wildernesses, for he could decide how and where
men should live and whether they should live at all.

The wise society would recognise the *de facto* ruler and adapt
its arrangements to his convenience. This involved a certain
amount of suffering, in the form of low wages and long hours,
but such suffering was inevitable, and it would only be aggravated by any interference with the authority of capital. The
test of civilisation was not the kind of life that men and women
were leading, but the encouragement and scope that it gave to
the owner of capital. Show him the opportunity of profit and
he will use his capital in your country and so enrich your people
and increase the comforts of the world. Let him expect trouble
and insubordination, and he will either consume his capital on
his own pleasures, or he will employ it in some other country
where the capitalist is free from the danger of disturbance.

Was this dependence of the world on the small class of the
owners of capital desirable and not merely inevitable ? In
the long run they would answer, yes. The world was advancing,
slowly for many centuries, rapidly to-day, from hard and
barbarous conditions of life to a standard of comfort and refine-
ment. That advance demanded the full use of capital and the
full use of energy. How were men induced to use their capital
for production instead of consuming it on their pleasures, and
how were the workers induced to work instead of idling or
drinking ? The great incentives were the love of gain and the
fear of hunger. Remove the hope of gain from the capitalist,
and he would enjoy his wealth instead of using it : remove the
fear of hunger from the worker and he would work less diligently or cease to work at all. The capitalist system gave
order and method to these commanding motives : it organised
the leading impulses of human nature for the general good of

mankind. For it guaranteed the two essential conditions of progress : production and accumulation, industry and thrift.

A society concerned only with this aspect of the industrial system made the security of property the object of its existence. What was the chief danger to property ? The discontent of the poor. The basis of this system was an inequality of wealth, education, political and civil rights, that was not softened but intensified with the progress of mankind. Inequality breeds envy and hatred : men and women who found that it was their lot to live in poverty and ignorance and to bring up their children to the same prospect would be tempted to rebel against their circumstances. It was therefore essential that they should never know their power. Education was one way of teaching them their power : combination was another : political discussion was a third. The judge, the magistrate, the parson, every one who occupied a responsible position in society was to look at every question from the point of view of this danger. Seneca said that a great fortune was a great servitude, hard to acquire and harder still to guard. The wealth the nation had acquired imposed this servitude on its politics. The philosophers of an earlier and a poorer age, living in an atmosphere of hope, had talked of the good life as the object to be pursued by a civilised State; the ruling class a century ago, living in an atmosphere of fear, had made the State into a police system, existing for the protection of capital.

Let us now turn to the other aspect of the system on which modern industry is conducted. A thousand men are working in a factory with machines and appliances provided by capital. Their enterprise, which looked to our forefathers as the organisation of capital, might be regarded in a different light as the organisation of effort. This body of men is producing something with the help of capital. Should capital in such an arrangement be regarded as master or servant ? On the one view we ask, as our ancestors asked, how capital can make the most out of the labour of the thousand men : on the other we ask how the thousand men can make the most out of the help of that capital. On the one view we argue, as they argued, that the profit of capital would be imperilled if these men did not work long hours and live on a bare minimum of comfort : on the other we should argue that the power of those men to turn the help they got from capital to the best account, would be impaired if they were stinted of food or leisure, and if their natural faculties of mind and body were left undeveloped. So with society as a whole. Looking first at the importance of preserving and developing a small rich class, men like Sidmouth could argue that it was more dangerous to have an educated than a servile population.[1] But if we regard property as a means to the full life of the community, it is clear that the better the health of men and women, the happier their homes, the more thorough their education, the more beautiful their towns, the greater the advantage they will derive from the help of the capital they employ. This was the unconscious instinct behind the revolt of the workers in all industries against the new tyranny. They wanted men to be the masters of this power, whereas their rulers believed that men could find no higher destiny than to be its servants. For those rulers had converted every new engine that man invented into a new tyrant over man, and now they had made the greatest engine into the greatest tyrant. The spinner or weaver, the comber or cropper, the frame-work knitter or the miner were all rebelling on behalf of human nature against a new and universal slavery.

If an aristocrat who had ever thought about the society which he found so agreeable had been asked to justify its inequalities, he would have said that a small class preserved the traditions of culture, giving shelter to art and literature and the spiritual light of mankind, while the mass of men and women did the hard work of a world to whose finer treasures they must inevitably remain blind. The hands of the many produced the necessaries of life that the minds of the few might give it the beauty of form and colour. The sacrifice of the many was thus the price paid for the self-expression of the few who could enrich the world with their ideas. The Industrial Revolution gave a new turn and a new stimulus to this view of society from the scope it offered to special genius. The great inventions dazzled the age. The mass were to live and labour in ignorance that the few might invent. It was painful to think of tired children toiling to the mill in the dusk before the dawn, and struggling to keep awake in the dusk after sunset, but the human mind was comforted by the thought of the new spinning machines that had made the arrangements of yesterday seem almost savage in their primitive simplicity. The cotton industry, if it presented the most terrible sacrifices, presented also the most intoxicating triumphs of the new system. The

[1] See Wallas, *Life of Place*, p. 338.

temptation to measure civilisation by railways and steam power alone, always strong, was irresistible, and even critics of the political abuses of the time overlooked the sacrifices of that system in their admiration of its triumphs.

For in an age of such rapid invention and development it was easy to slip into the belief that the one task of the human race was to wrest her secrets from nature, and to forget how much of the history of mankind is the history of the effort to find a tolerable basis for a common life. Man has been more successful in learning to control his environment than in learning to control his social relationships; in learning to co-operate with wind and water than in learning to co-operate with his fellow man. It is not the obstinacy of nature but the discord of human wills that has been the chief obstacle to progress. So it was easier to invent the spinning machine than to construct the human associations that could make that machine a help rather than a hindrance to human fellowship. The effort to find such a basis has thrown up a hundred social forms, from the Greek City-State to the modern Empire. In the greater moments of his history man has aimed at something more than outward order : he has aimed at a society in which men can live and work together in a spirit of freedom and mutual respect; he has thought of the State, in the words of Aristotle, as a community of free men. That desire, breaking against the old world of custom and authority, had given to mankind in the French Revolution a generous hour of hope, followed by a bitter hour of despair. From this spectacle the rulers of England had derived one set and fixed idea : the idea that the art of government was the maintenance of discipline ; the power to imprison beneath an inexorable system of force all those spiritual discontents that disturb the life of habit. Hence their unquestioning welcome to an industrial system that seemed to answer their own purpose and to answer the purpose of nature as well : to reinforce at once the law of authority and the law of progress. In their terror of the French Revolution they treated the sovereign hope that has inspired its best minds throughout the long pilgrimage of the race as an overwhelming illusion : in their confidence in the unchecked rule of capital they made law, order, and justice the sentinels of a new and more terrible inequality between man and man. The life of a society in which violence so deliberate as this is done to the instincts and the passions of mankind turns inevitably into civil war.

APPENDIX

OLIVER'S LATER HISTORY

Mr. A. C. G. Lloyd, the Librarian of the South African Public
Library, was kind enough to write to us after reading *The Town
Labourer* to say that there was good reason to believe that Oliver
turned up afterwards in Cape Colony as William Oliver Jones,
Inspector of Buildings during the Governorship of Lord Charles
Somerset, and he directed our attention to documents that were
likely to throw some light on the point.

From these documents it seems quite clear that Jones was
Oliver. Lord Charles Somerset is described by Dr Theal as a
high-handed and extravagant Governor, and his administration
provoked a great deal of discontent. Some of his critics roundly
accused him of corruption. Certain of these allegations were
examined by a Commission of Inquiry which was sent to the
Cape. One of the complaints urged against Somerset was that
he treated Jones as an intimate and confidential adviser and
that Jones had received advances from the Public Treasury for
buildings for which he gave no account. The Commission of
Inquiry found fault with these financial arrangements, and both
Lieut.-Colonel Bird, who was Secretary to the Government at the
Cape from 1818 to 1824, and Somerset made statements to the
Commission about Jones which bear on his history.

Bird, who was very hostile to Somerset, said: ' Lord Charles
Somerset may now affect to regret having placed so much confidence in W. O. Jones, but was Lord Charles Somerset ignorant of
the character of W. O. Jones? did he not know who W. O. Jones
was? and may it not be inferred that therefore he gave him confidential employment?' (Theal, *Records of the Cape Colony*, vol. xxi.
p. 168).

Somerset gave some important evidence about the circumstances
under which Jones originally found public employment. 'I have
now only to add that the employment of W. O. Jones did not
originate with me. When I returned from England I found him
superintending the repairs of the wharf and doing the duty of
inspector of government buildings, the inspector having had a
long leave of absence from the acting Governor. Lieut.-Colonel
Bird informed me, that Mr. W. O. Jones brought out a letter from
Mr. Goulburn, under date 10th January 1820, recommending
him for employment here, and it was in consequence of such

recommendation of him that I confirmed him in the appointment of inspector of government buildings on the resignation of Mr. Melville' (*Ibid.*, vol. xxiii. p. 475).

Mr. Goulburn was Under-Secretary for the Colonies from 1812 to 1821. This statement explains how it is that Jones was able to enter Cape Colony without the usual formalities, which at the time were very strict. There is no record of his receiving any permit.

Jones was more than once publicly identified with Oliver and the allegation was never directly denied.

Thus a colonist of the name of Bishop Burnett, who brought several charges against Lord Charles Somerset, accused Jones of writing and posting up a libellous placard attacking the Governor in the hope of incriminating Burnett. This charge was not proved, but in his petition to Parliament Burnett calls Jones 'Oliver the spy,' and Brougham when presenting that petition referred to this allegation (Hansard, June 16 and 22, 1825).

Jones died in August 1827 without ever accounting for the public money that had passed through his hands (Bird's statement, Theal's *Records*, vol. xxxiii. p. 392.) Compare Somerset's statement, *ibid.*, vol. xxxi. p. 275:

'It has long been matter of more regret and vexation to me than I can find words to express, that the inspector neglected to keep his accounts in the form required, which has rendered it impossible to ascertain with precision the exact expense of each distinct service on which the artificers and labourers were employed under him.'

He left a will, dated 10th December 1824 (Cape Archives Orphan Chamber Wills, vol. ciii. of 1827) in which he described himself as a native of Ponsonbury in the County of Salop, aged about fifty, and married to Harriet born Dear of Fulbourn, Cambridgeshire.

INDEX

A. B. *See* Waddington, Robert.
Accrington, 127.
Acland, General, 300 *n.*, 313.
Addington, J. H., 355.
Adlington, 291, 338.
Agriculture, Annals of, 136, 144 *n.*, 147 *n.*, 150, 210.
Aiken, Mr., 127 *n.*
Ainsworth, Richard, 74.
Ainsworth, Thomas, 66, 281 ; and regulation of wages, 75, 76, 77, 83, 84, 90, 91 ; on cotton trade, 122, 123.
Albion Mills, 200.
Allison, Mr., and Yorkshire Luddites, 316, 317 *n.*, 320, 322, 331, 333.
'Alpha,' 126.
Altham, 54.
Althorp, Lord, 371.
America, North, 49, 189.
—— South, 111.
American wars, (1775-1783) 53, 55, 141, (1812) 319, 323.
Amiens, Peace of, 110, 172.
Amos, 241.
Anglesey, 144 *n.*
Annual Register, on Spitalfields executions, 208 ; on trial of Huddersfield rioters, 366.
Anstey, 259.
Apprentices, 340.
—— woollen trade, 168, 170, 177, 180, 184, 185 ; woolcombers, 198 ; Spitalfield weavers, 209 ; Coventry ribbon weavers, 211 ; Macclesfield silk weavers, 214 ; framework knitters, 221, 222, 223. *See also* Colting.
Arbitration Acts, cotton, 62-64, 67-69, 72, 87.
Arden, Lord, 89.
Ardwick, 294, 351.
Arkwright, Richard, 49, 50, 55, 237 ; his patent machinery, 51, 53, 54, 56, 57. *See also* Water frame.
Armitage, Mr., J.P., 308.
Armley, 154.

Armstrong, 44.
—— Betty, 309.
Armytage, Sir George, 304.
Arnold, 261, 359.
Arrowsmith, William, 130 *n.*
Artisans and Machinery, Committee on (1824), 62, 93, 154, 164.
Ashborne, 347.
Ashburton, 197.
Asher, John, 238, 239.
Ashley, Professor, 2.
Ashton, Thomas (1808), 80.
—— (1831), murder of, 134, 135 *n.*
Ashton Moss, 113 *n.*, 116.
Ashton-under-Lyne, 111, 112 *n.*, 116, 120 *n.* ; spinners' strike (1830), 131-135 ; Luddite disturbances, 271, 284, 313.
Ashwellthorpe, 193.
Atherstone, 197.
Atkinson, Richard, 17, 18.
Auckland, Lord, 73 *n.*, 186.

'B.,' alias Bent, 67, 73 ; on 1818 strike, 99, 100, 106 *n.* ; and Luddite disturbances (1812), 274, 275, 278, 287-289, 291, 297, 320, 336, 337.
Bacon, Thomas, 369, 370.
Badder, 239.
Bagguley, John, 89 *n.* ; and 1818 strike, 95 *n.*, 101, 107, 108 ; and Reform, 113 *n.*, 116, 120 ; and Blanketeers, 343-345, 347, 349 *n.*
Baines, *History of Cotton Manufacture,* 72.
—— *Yorkshire Past and Present,* 139, 155 *n.*, 169 *n.*
—— John, the elder, trial and sentence, 325-329.
—— the younger, 325, 329.
—— Zachariah, 325, 328, 329.
Baker, Mr., 258.
Balguy, Mr. John, 366.
Ballance, Mr., 220 *n.*
Bamford, Samuel, 3, 7 ; on Thorpe reformers, 9 ; and Blanketeers,

343 *n.*; and 'general insurrection' (1817), 350, 351; arrested, 352.

Bancroft, Rev. Mr., 67.

Banks, Sir Joshua, 263.

Baring, Mr., M.P., 77, 216, 217.

Barnsley, 314, 325, 354.

Barnstaple, 197.

Barrowclough, Joseph, 316, 317, 322.

Barton the Weaver, 181.

Basford, 254, 261, 262, 265.

Bath (meeting of Clothiers, 1802), 174, 177.

Bathurst, Mr., M.P., 353 *n.*

Batley, John, 323.

Bayley, Mr., J.P., 62, 64, 65.

—— Mr. Justice, and Notts Luddites, 239, 268, 269, 293; and Sheffield rioters, 321, 322.

—— Samuel, 79.

Beaver, Mr., 127.

Becker, Rev. J. T., on frame-work-knitters' wages, 225; on Luddites, 258, 264.

Becket, Mr. (of H.O.), 300, 320.

Bedford, 144.

Bedlington, 35.

Bedworth, 214.

Belloc, H., *The Servile State*, 2 *n.*

Beloe, Arthur, 193.

Ben, Big, 196.

Benbow, 352.

Benefit Club, 183; miners on, 29. *See also* Friendly Societies.

Bennet, Henry Grey, 372 *n.*; on spies, 313 *n.*, 354 *n.*, 360 *n.*, 371-373; on Fletcher of Bolton, 375.

Ben o' Bill's, The Luddite, 310 *n.*

Bent. *See* 'B.'

Berks, 211 *n.*

Berlin Decrees, 8.

Berry, Rev. Mr., 9.

Bethnal Green, 208, 216.

Betts, 133.

Bilston, 37.

Bird, Lieut.-Colonel, 377.

Birkacre mill destroyed, 54.

Birley, Mr., 105.

Birmingham, 108, 339, 342; and Oliver, 354-360.

Birstall, 304.

Bischoff, *History of Woollen and Worsted Manufactures*, 138 *n.*

Bisley, 159.

Black Book, the, 26.

Black Dwarf, the, 26.

Blackburn, 53, 54, 59, 81, 120 *n.*, 123 *n.*; in 1818, 111, 118, 119;

and minimum wage, 121, 124; destruction of power-looms (1826), 126, 127; weavers' manifesto (1810), 82.

Blackburn, Vicar of, 127.

—— Christopher, 242.

—— John, 241, 242.

Blackburn Mail, 127.

Blackner, 261 *n.*

Blaize, Bishop, festivals, 201, 203.

Blakeborough, William, 325, 329.

Blanketeers, march of (1817), 92, 101, 342-348; arrests, 347; prisoners' letter, 348-349; discharge of prisoners, 349.

Bleachers, 118.

Blyth, 23, 35.

Bobbin-net trade, 237, 254-256. *See also* Heathcoat.

Boden (Heathcoat's partner), 238, 242.

Boldon Fell, 35, 45.

Bolton, 52, 54, 59, 65, 66, 67; weavers' petitions, (1811) 83, (1813) 69, 87, 88; and regulation of wages, 72, 74, 75, 86, 87, 91, 120; ridicule of soup, 89; loyal weavers, 90; and 1818 weavers' strike, 111, 112, 113, 115, 117; and 1830 spinners' strike, 131, 134; and Luddite disturbances, 272, 276, 277, 279-286, 293; and Luddite oath, 337-340.

Bolton Moor, 280, 296.

Bond, yearly, of miners, 12, 25, 26, 29, 30; disputes over, (1765) 12-17, (1810) 21-24; refusal to bind members of Union (1832), 41.

Boot and Shoe Makers, 103.

Booth, John, 306, 307, 310.

Borrow, George, his father, 313 *n.*

Bouverie, General (Sir Henry), 36 *n.*; and 1830 spinners' strike, 132, 133.

Bowden, Sergeant Holland, 281, 282, 284, 296.

Braddock, Thomas, 313.

Bradford (Wilts), 149, 159 *n.*, 162; disputes about gig mills, 171-173, 181, 188.

Bradford (Yorks), 2; worsted centre, 143, 145, 150; steam engines in, 152; attack on power-looms (1826), 194, 195; wool-combers' strike (1825), 201-203; Luddite disturbances, 315; and Oliver, 357, 359.

Bradley, Thomas, 355, 356.

Bradninch, 196.

Bradshaw, John, 291.

Braithwaite, John and Elizabeth, 269.
Brandling, Rev., 39, 40.
—— R. W., 40, 45 *n*.
Brandreth, Jeremiah, 358, 359, 367 *n*.; and Pentridge rising, 360-362; trial and execution of, 368-370, 374.
Bricklayers, 181.
Bricksetters, 96.
Bridgewater, Duke of, his colliers, 20, 21, 54, 338.
Bristol, 179.
Broadhurst, Nathan, 69 *n*.
Brocksopp, Messrs., 258.
Bromsgrove, 197,
Brontës, the, 4.
Brook, James, 330.
—— John, 330.
—— Joseph, 331.
—— Thomas, 330.
Brooke, Mr., M.P., 184.
Brookes, Thomas, 106.
'Brother to No. 2,' 116.
Brougham, H., 71 *n*., 189, 217; on spies, 279 *n*., 282 *n*.; as counsel, 295 *n*., 299, 328, 349.
Broughton, Thomas (of 'the 38'), 298.
—— —— (the spy), 312, 314, 325.
Brownlow, John, 295.
Brunswick family, 359.
Buckley, John, 276, 286, 287, 297.
Buddle, John, 26, 27, 31 *n*.
Bulkeley, Lord, 90 *n*., 340.
Bullen, Captain, 285.
Bulwell, 261, 262, 265, 359.
Bunting, Rev. Jabez, 307 *n*.
Burdett, Sir Francis, 241, 278, 280, 300; and Oliver, 354, 360, 374.
Burn's *Justice*, 62.
Burnett, Bishop, 378.
Burney, John, 296 *n*.
Burnley, 111, 123 *n*., 127, 144; and minimum wage, 121, 124, 126.
Burnley, *Wool and Woolcombing*, 201 *n*.
Burton, Mr. Justice, 291.
—— William, 241.
Burton, 246.
—— -on-Trent, 54, 95.
Burton's house and factory, attack on, 271, 287-289; trials for, 293, 295.
Bury, 49, 59, 66, 121; meetings of weavers in 1818, 111, 114, 117-119; handbill of meeting, 114, 115; destruction of power-looms (1826), 126, 127.

Butler, J. R. M., 132 *n*.
Butterley, 361.
Buxton, Sir Thomas Fowell, 210, 217, 218.
Byng, General, and 1818 strikes, 99, 106, 107, 116; and 1826 disturbances, 128; and Blanketeers, 347; and Oliver, 355, 357 *n*., 358, 359, 360 *n*., 363.
Byron, Lord, 267.
Byron's *Corsair*, 369.

'C.,' 73.
Cabinet-makers, 181.
Caermarthen militia, 22.
Calais, 243.
Caldwell, 241 *n*.
Calico manufacturers and minimum wage, 121, 122, 124.
—— printers, 103.
—— printing firms and minimum wage, 121, 122, 124.
Callerton, 38.
Calverton, 221.
Cambridge, 200 *n*.
Cambridgeshire, 144.
Campbell, Colonel, 310 *n*., 312.
Candid Appeal to the Coal-Owners, etc., *A*, 29.
Canning, George, 373, 375.
Cape of Good Hope, the, 252, 377, 378.
Capitalism, before Industrial Revolution, 2.
Carlisle, cotton weavers of, 93, 106, 276, 340; and minimum wage, 86, 121.
Carmen, 209.
Carnell, William, 268, 269.
Carpenter-Smith, Mr., 371.
Carpenters, 96.
Carr, Elizabeth, 42.
Carrington, Lord, 214.
Carter, Joseph, 331.
Cartwright, Edmund, invents power-loom, 71; woolcombing machine, 196.
—— Major, 71, 241, 343 *n*.; and Oliver, 354, 360.
—— William, 304, 314; attack on his mill, 304-307, 322; letter from, describing, 305, 306; attempt to assassinate, 308; trials and executions for attack, 323, 329-332; subscriptions for, 333.
Castlereagh, Lord, 189, 300, 318, 354 *n*., 370, 371; why hated, 375, 376.
Castles, 341, 365 *n*.

Chadderton, 111, 127, 351.
Chamberlain, Brigade-Major, 318.
Chapman, Professor, 58 *n*.
Charles II., 221, 259, 344.
Charlson, Abraham, 296, 297.
Charter of Frame-work Knitters' Company, 221, 259.
Chatham MSS., 169.
Chelmsford, 318.
Chester Assizes (1812), 314.
—— Castle, 96.
—— Special Commission (1812), 291, 292.
Chester-le-Street, 22, 31.
Chesterfield, 359.
Chief-Justice, Lord, on Nottingham, 243.
Children, employment of: mines, 32; woollen industry, 148-150; worsted mills, 155; frame-work knitters, 221-223, 244 *n*.; in lace trade, 254, 255 *n*., 256.
Chippendale, William, 109, 123, 289 *n*.; his 'informants,' 100, 116, 350, 351 *n*.
Chitty, J., 253.
Cholera, 38, 40.
Chorley, 54, 59, 75, 290.
Chowbent, 59; Luddite disturbances, 280-285.
Christian, Mr., 86.
Church, Edward, 212.
Clapham, J. H., 137 *n*.
Clark, Charles, 284 *n*.
Clay, Colonel, 286 *n*., 289 *n*.
Clayfield, John, 160.
Clayton, Isaac, 296 *n*.
—— Sir Richard, 338.
Cleckheaton, 304.
Cliff, Richard, 64.
Clifton, 330.
Clitheroe district, 79.
Clothiers' Delight, 156, 157.
Clough, Billy, 307.
Clutton-Brock, A., 5 *n*.
Coal Act, 36.
Coal-heavers (London), 209.
Cobbett, William, 7, 89 *n*., 277, 343 *n*.; on frame-work knitters, 249, 252 *n*.
Cochrane, Lord, 278.
Cockeymoor, 111.
Colchester baize, 192.
Cold Bath Fields Prison, 354.
Coldham, Mr. (Town Clerk of Nottingham), 229, 231, 236; and Hosiers' Secret Committee, 233; and secret agent, 234, 235; on Mr. Justice Bayley, 239, 268; on

barracks, 240; on Frame Breaking Bill, 267.
Coleman, Joseph, 207 *n*.
Colliers. *See* Miners.
Colne, 124, 144.
Colonel of Oldham local militia on general rising, 290.
' Colting,' 196, 227, 260, 264.
Combinations: Miners, (1810) 22; (1825) 27, 29, 30; (1831-1832) Chapter III. Cotton spinners, 93; (1810) 93; (1818) 103-108; (1829-1831) 129-135. Cotton weavers, (1799) 59, 60; (1801) 67; (1805) 73; (1807) 75; (1811) 83; (1818) 111-119. Cotton power-loom weavers, (1818) 95, 96. Woollen spinners, (1819 and 1822) 154, 155. Woollen weavers, (1756) 157-159; (1802 and 1803) 180, 188; (1822) 164; (1825) 165, 166; (1826 and 1829) 163. Shearmen, (1802, etc.) 172-180, 182, 183, 186, 187. Worsted weavers, 191, 193. Woolcombers, 196, 198, 199, 200-203. Silk weavers, Chapter VII., *passim*, and 212 *n*. and 215 *n*. Ribbon weavers, 215, 216. Frame-work knitters, (1812-1814) 229-235; (1817) 248, 249; (1819-1824) 249-254.
Combination Acts: passing of, 60, 61; and miners, 27; and cotton workers, 69, 93, 96, 102, 104, 118, 124, 129, 132 *n*.; and Reform agitation, 120; and woollen and worsted workers, 162, 166, 174, 176, 178, 182, 200, 202; and Coventry ribbon weavers, 215, 216; Spitalfields weavers and, 217, 218; and frame-work knitters, 234, 245, 249, 251, 253, 266; secrecy engendered by, 276, 336, 340.
Combination Laws, Committee on (1825), 164, 165.
Committees, Secret:
—— of Hosiers, 233, 234, 236.
—— of House of Lords (1812), on Luddite disturbances, 257, 271, 281, 287, 339; on Luddite oath, 335, 336.
—— of Houses of Parliament (1817), 341-343, 346, 372, 373.
—— of Huddersfield masters, 310.
—— of Luddites, 275-280, 286-288, 297, 337, 339.

Company, Frame-work Knitters', 221, 222, 227, 259 *n.*

Conant, Mr., 258, 339.

Congleton, 320.

Congress of Woolcombers, 200.

Conspiracy Laws, and spinners (1818), 105, 108, 109; and weavers (1818), 118, 119; and shearmen (1802), 174; and Coventry ribbon weavers (1819), 216.

Cookson, Craven, 325.

—— Mayor of Leeds, 177.

Cooper, William, alias Strapper, 314.

Corn Laws, 73, 85, 120 *n.*, 126, 245, 346.

Cornwall, 147, 197.

Cotton spinners, 49, 53; and new machinery, 55, 56; new class of men spinners, 57; strike of 1810, 92; help to Blanketeers, 345; strike of 1818, 94, 96-109; and Reform, 100; strikes of 1829, 1830, 128-135; general Union, 130; and female spinners and piecers, 131; attempted general strike, 134.

Cotton twist or yarn, export of, denounced, 65, 90, 91, 126.

Cotton weavers, 49, 50, 53; golden age, 58; combination (1799), 58; ask for regulation of wages (1800), 61; Cotton Arbitration Acts (1800-1804), 62-69; agitation for minimum wage supported by masters, 72-75; Rose's Bill (1808), 77; riots on withdrawal, 78; petitions to Parliament (1811), 83; and Reform, 84, 85, 94, 89-91; attempt to enforce Elizabethan Act, 86; Act repealed (1813), 87; strikes of 1818, 95, 109-119; masters propose minimum wage, (1819) 121, (1826) 124; destruction of power-looms, *see* Chapter x. and 126-128.

Couldwell, Abel, 347.

Coventry, 142, 197, 200. *See also* Ribbon weavers.

Cowpen, 23.

Coxlodge, 38-40.

Crabbe, 7.

Crabtree, 357, 368.

Crispin Inn, 326, 327.

Croft, James, 20 *n.*

Crompton, Isaac, 296.

—— Samuel, 50-52, 71.

Cromwell, Oliver, 280, 292.

Crook, Mr., 279 *n.*

Croppers. *See* Shearmen.

Cross, John, 367.

Crossland, James, 291.

Crowder, 241.

Crown lands, 254.

Crowther, Joseph, 323, 331.

Cuckney, 196, 198.

Cullompton, 162.

Cumberland, 144.

—— Militia, 305, 306, 308.

Cunningham, Dr., 227 *n.*

Curwen, Mr., M.P., 86, 267.

'Cut-ups' described, 226, 227; agitations against, (1811-1812) 228, 229, 258-260, (1819) 250, (1833) 254.

DALLAS, Mr. Justice, 291.

Danby, Mr., 20 *n.*

Daniels, G. W., 58 *n.*, 82 *n.*

Darlington, 202.

Davis, Captain, 22.

Davy lamp, 28.

Dean, James, 243 *n.*

—— Jonathan, 330, 331.

Dean Moor, 281-284, 293, 296, 300.

Defoe, 48, 139.

Delavel, Thomas, 14.

Delegates, 108, 340.

Denman, Thomas, 253, 368, 369.

Denton, 18.

Derby, 12, 56, 61, 224, 229, 369; centre for silk hose, 222; insurrection of 1817, 342; and Blanketeers, 347, 348; and Oliver, 354, 355, 358.

—— ribs, 222.

—— Special Commission, 1817, 366, 370.

Devonshire, 197, 237; (woollens) 137 *n.*, 162, 243; (lace) 242, 243.

Dewhurst. *See* Hall, Michael.

Dewsbury, 154, 155, 164, 167; and Oliver, 354, 362, 363.

Dickenson of Dewsbury, 362-364, 372.

Dickinsons, Messrs., 303.

Didsbury, 338.

Dissenters (and Woolcombers), 200.

Dixon, 307.

Dodds, Rev., 166.

Doherty, John, 129-131, 133, 135.

Dolphin Holme mill, 152, 203.

Domestic system of industry, 3, 5; (lace running) 7; (woollen) 139, 140, 151, 170, 185, 186.

Doyle, John, 208.

Dragoons, 262, 362.

Drake, Joseph, 329, 330.

Draper, James, 64.
Drummond, and 1818 strike, 95 *n.*,
    101, 107, 116; and Blanketeers,
    343, 347, 349 *n.*
Dublin silk weavers, 205 *n.*, 213 *n.*;
    frame-work knitters, 229.
Duckworth, George, 326.
Dukinfield, 104, 132.
Dumfries, 231, 232.
Durham, Chapters II. and III.,
    passim, for miners; cotton
    workers, 64; woolcombers, 197.
—— Bishop of, 21.
—— Lord, 38 *n.*, 41, 45.
Dursley, 163.
Dyeing, 142.
Dyers, 47, 96.
Dyson, 66 *n.*

EADON, John, 325.
Eastwood, 265, 362.
Eccles, 271.
Eckersley, Major, 123 *n.*, 126.
Eden, Sir F. M., 144, 147, 192.
Edenfield, 127.
Edgeley, 291.
Edinburgh Review, 54.
Edward VI. statute about gig mills,
    168, 170, 184.
Edwards, 341.
—— Nath., 182 *n.*
Eldon, Lord, 376.
Elizabeth, statute of, 5; attempts
    to use for regulating wages, 86,
    88, 283; repealed, 87; and
    woollen industry, 158, 168, 185;
    repealed, 188; relaxed for wool-
    combers, 200; attempt to use for
    silk weavers, 207.
Elleker or Hilleker, Thomas, 175,
    181, 182.
Ellenborough, Lord, 64, 283.
Ellice, Mr., M.P., 217.
Ellis, John, 291.
Ellison, Robert, 111, 118, 119.
Emigration, law against, 189 *n.*;
    cotton weavers and, 119; shear-
    men and, 189; frame-work
    knitters and, 252.
Endsor of Parwick, 369.
Enfield, Mr. (Town Clerk of Not-
    tingham), 236, 358, 370, 371.
'Enoch,' 303.
Errington (coal owner), 25 *n.*
—— (pitman), 42.
Essex: worsted, 137, 144, 153, 192;
    silk, 211.
Ethelston, Rev. G. W., 92, 116.

Evans, Mr. (Stipendiary of Man-
    chester), on MacDonald, 327; on
    Blanketeers, 346, 348, 349 *n.*
Ewart of Liverpool, 294, 295.
Exchange meeting at Manchester
    (1812), 286, 288.
Exeter, 162, 197, 200.

FACTORY COMMISSION OF 1833, 7,
    256.
Factory legislation, 108 *n.*, 156.
—— system, 3-5; cotton, 49, 53,
    56, 57, 72.
—— —— woollen industry, 146,
    148, 150, 151, 170, 171, 183, 185,
    186; worsted, 152, 153, 155, 156;
    bobbin net trade, 237, 254-256.
—— —— frame-work knitting, 253.
Fagan, Francis, 163.
Failsworth, 351.
Fairweather Green, 194
Fairles, Mr., J.P., 43.
Faith, Charles, 313.
False reed or slay, 153.
Fane, General, 236.
Fatfield, 14.
Felkin, Chapter VIII., *passim.*
Felons, prosecutions in Lancs, 65 *n.*
Felling colliery, 46.
Fielden, John, 6, 124, 128.
Fielding, James, 104.
—— Sir John, 207-209; on Spital-
    fields Act, 210.
Fines (Northumberland and Dur-
    ham miners), 27, 28, 32-34.
Fisher, 323.
Fitzwilliam, Lord, 371; on croppers
    177, 178, 190; in Yorkshire
    Luddite disturbances, 305, 311,
    332; on Oliver, 363, 364, 373;
    trials of Huddersfield rioters, 365.
Flannel manufacturers, 165.
Flax-dressers, 181.
Fleming, Samuel, spy, 103, 105;
    and 'the 38,' 298-300.
Fletcher, Job, 296.
—— Ralph, Colonel, of Bolton, 65;
    on disaffection, 66, 73, 88; his
    spies, 67, 113 *n.*, 126; on mini-
    mum wage, 75, 76, 86, 87; in
    1818, 114, 118; his spies and
    activities in Luddite disturb-
    ances, 275, 277, 279-282, 284, 285,
    293, 298, 299 *n.*, 336, 338, 340;
    his spies and activities in 1817,
    349, 350, 352, 366; Bennet on,
    375.
Flitcroft, Richard, 351.
Flockton, 321.

Flying shuttle: used for cotton, 49; wool, 159-161; worsted, 192.
Foster, John, 303.
—— Joseph, 303, 305.
—— —— junior, 303.
—— Josiah, 303.
—— Mr., J.P., 134.
—— Thomas, 303.
—— —— (Union of Cotton Spinners), 131.
Foulkes, Mr., 65.
Frame breaking in 1811, Chapter IX., *passim*; in 1814-1816, 235, 236, *see also* Loughborough; cessation of (1816), 244.
Frame Breaking Bill (1812), 267.
Frame rents, 223, 227, 261.
Frames, stocking, invention of, 221.
—— —— independent, 223 *n.*
Frame-work Knitters (*see* Chapter VIII.): early conditions, 3, 5, 222-223; and regulation of wages, 223, 224, 254; agitations against ' cut-ups,' 226, 250, and Chapter IX.; Bills against ' cut-ups ' rejected (1812, 1819), 229, 250; Society of (1813), 230-235; campaign against low wages supported by public (1817 and 1819), 244-252; later strikes and misery, 252-254. *See also* Frame breaking.
Frame-work Knitters' Petition, Committee on (1819), 225, 244 *n.*, 250.
France (and 1817 rising), 361.
Freemasons and Luddite oath, 336.
French prisoners and Luddites, 317, 318.
Freshford, 162.
Friars Goose, 42, 43.
Friendly Relief Society for framework knitters (1819), 251, 252.
—— Societies Acts, 178 *n.*
—— —— and minimum wage agitation (1808), 75; and 1808 strike, 79; and cotton spinners' unions, 93; and Blanketeers, 345.
Frome, 146, 148, 161.
Frost, James, 106.
Fustian cutters, 103.
Fustians, 48, 49, 58 *n.*
Fynes, 43 *n.*, 46 *n.*

Garside, Daniel, 314.
—— (millowner), 95.
Garton, 239.
Gaskell, Peter, 280.

Gaskell, P., *Manufacturing Population of England, 2 n.*
Gateshead, 38, 43.
Gee's Cross, 292.
General Union, of cotton spinners (1810), 93; of trades (1818), 103, 104, 108, 114; of cotton spinners (1829-1831), 130-134; of all trades (1830), 131, 134. *See also* National Association for Protection of Labour.
German mercenaries, 376.
Germany, 49.
Gibson, George, 234.
Giddy, Davies, M.P., 77.
Gifford, R., 102.
Gig mills: statute about, 168, 170, 180, 184, 185; description of, 169; introduction of, 169, 170; campaign against (1802), 170-180; Parliamentary action on subject, 180-188; declared legal, 188; extended use of, 188, 189, 301; resentment against (1812), 301 *n.*, 309.
Gisborne, Rev. Thomas, 20, 21.
Glasgow, 52, 229, 276, 340.
Glossop, 134.
Gloucestershire (woollen industry), 137, 146, 168 *n.*; woollen weavers of, 157-164, 183; frame-work knitters, 224, 248; spies from, 315.
Godalming, 224, 229-232.
Godfrey's cordial, 254.
Goldschmidts, Messrs., 75.
Gomersal, 304.
Goodairs, Mr., 273 *n.*, 279.
Goodwin, Mr., 272.
Gordon, Major, 314 *n.*
Gorgon, the, 99 *n.*
Gosforth, 39.
Gossett, 207 *n.*
Gossling, John, spy, 314, 327, 328, 335.
Gotham, 265.
Gott, Mr., 139, 177.
Goulburn, Mr., 377, 378.
Graham, James, 186.
Gray, Mr. (of Manchester), 101, 102, 105-107, 113, 116, 132 *n.*
Green, George, 269.
—— Peter, 239.
Grenville, Lord, 267, 280.
Grey, General, 302, 309, 312.
—— Lord, 73, 280.
Griffon, James, 178, 179.
Grimshaw, George, 348, 349 *n.*
—— Messrs., 71.

Grose, Mr. Justice, 81.
Grosvenor, Lord, 267, 371, 373.
Gurney, Mr., 63-65.

HABEAS CORPUS ACT, suspension of (1817), 91, 94, 100, 113, 241, 341, 346, 352, 354, 372, 373.
Haigh, James, 330.
—— John, 99 *n.*
—— Joshua, 322.
—— Samuel, 317.
Hale, William, and Spitalfields Act, 211 *n.*, 220 *n.*; on earnings of weavers, 213 *n.*
Halifax, 2; worsted centre, 143, 152 *n.*, 164; gig mills, 169; worsted weavers, 202; and Luddite disturbances, 304, 307, 314, 315, 325-327, 333; and Oliver, 354.
Hall, Michael, spy, alias Dewhurst, alias Number One, 350-353.
—— Rev. Robert, 251, 252.
—— William, 322, 323, 329-331.
Hampden Clubs, 119 *n.*, 361.
Hamper, Mr., J.P., 355.
Hancock, Benjamin, 269.
Hand-loom weavers. *See* Cotton weavers, Woollen weavers, Worsted weavers, Silk weavers.
—— —— Commissioners on, Report of, 128, 167 *n.*, 193.
—— —— Committee, (1834) 62, 128, 219; (1835) 69, 70, 128.
Hanson, Joseph, 81.
Hants, 211 *n.*
Hardy, Rev. R., J.P., 262, 263.
Hargreaves, James, 50, 53.
Harrison, Joseph, 101, 107, 120.
—— Mr., J.P., 95 *n.*
Hartley Colliery, 23.
Hartley, Samuel, 306, 307, 326.
—— William, 323, 331.
Hartshead Moor, 304.
Haslam, Richard, 55.
Haslingden, 111, 127.
Hatters, 47, 103.
Hay, Mr., J.P., 67, 92, 102, 113 *n.*; and general rising (1812), 290; and Fleming, 300 *n.*; and Yorkshire Luddites, 316, 317, 328; and Blanketeers, 347; on general insurrection (1817), 351, 352.
Haynes, Messrs., 228, 263.
Haywood, 270.
Headingley, 309.
Heanor, 265.
Heap, 80.
Heathcoat, John, 235, 237, 238;

lace factory destroyed, 238; damages, 242; move to Devonshire, 242, 243; patent, 237, 243, 254, 255; and hours of work, 256.
Heaton, 27.
Heaton Norris, 347.
Heckmondwike, 304.
Helps, Lewis, and Ray, Messrs., 75.
Helston, Mr., in *Shirley*, 306.
Henderson, Mr., 128 *n.*
Henfield, 127.
Henson, Gravener, and frame-breaking, 235, 264; and Society of frame-work knitters, 229; and truck, 236; imprisoned, 241, 248; free and distrusted, 250.
Hepburn, Thomas, 35, 39, 40, 43, 45, 46.
Hepworth, Mr., 362.
Hertford, 56.
Hetton, 35, 38, 41, 42.
Hewett, Mr., 281.
Hey, James, 323, 331.
—— Job, 323, 331.
Heys, John, 282-284.
Heywood, 111.
—— John, 291.
Hibbert, John, 111.
Higgins, 298.
Higginson, Rev. Mr., 367.
Higher Darwen, 111.
Hill (Loughborough affair), 238.
—— John, 323, 331.
—— Mr. (Spitalfields), 207.
Hilleker. *See* Elleker.
Hinchcliffe, John, 320, 324.
Hinckley, 240, 250.
Hindley, Mr., 273 *n.*, 279.
Hirst, John, 329, 330.
Hobhouse, Benjamin, M.P., 172, 173, 175.
—— Henry, 103 *n.*; as Treasury Solicitor on Luddite disturbances, 322 *n.*, 333, 334; on Nadin, 335.
Holbeck, 154.
Holcroft, James, 59, 61, 63, 64, 67.
Holdsworth, John, 195.
Holland, John, 294.
—— Lord, 229, 267, 373.
Hollinwood, 289.
Hollis. *See* Oliver.
Holmes, 360.
Holmfirth, 316, 317, 320
Honiton, 197.
Hooper, 365 *n.*
Hopkinson, Mr., 253.
Horbury, 303, 304.
Horner, Francis, M.P., 77.

Horrocks, H., 71.
—— Mr., M.P., 75.
Horrockses, Messrs., 76.
Horsfall, William, murder of, 306, 309, 310 ; his murderers, 317, 319, 322, 324, 329, 332.
Horsfalls, Messrs. (Bradford), 194, 195.
Houldsworth, Mr., M.P., 102 *n.*, 105, 106, 107.
Howard, Thomas Phipps, 170.
Howarth, George, 276.
—— John, 293.
Howells, Richard, 325.
Hoyle, Nathan, 323, 331.
—— Thomas, 293.
Huddersfield : woollen centre, 138, 150 ; woollen weavers' union, 166, 167 ; shearmen and gig mills (1802), 177, 180 ; Luddite disturbances, 302-304, 308-310, 314 *n.*, 315 ; Society for prosecuting Luddites, 316, 317, 334 ; and Oliver, 354, 359 ; and 1817 rising, 360, 364 ; trials of rioters, 365, 366.
Hull, 143.
Hulme, Mr., 298.
Hulton, 283.
—— Mr., J.P., 285.
Hume, Joseph, M.P., 210 *n.*, 217, 229.
Hunslet, 150.
Hurst, John, 281.
Huskisson, W., M.P., 216-218.
Hussars, Yorkshire, 195.
Hutchinson, Mr., M.P., 267.
—— James, of Bury, 122, 127.
Hyde, 104, 133, 135 *n.*

Ilkeston, 248, 265.
Indian cotton goods, 48.
Inspectors of woollen goods, 168 *n.*, 184 ; under Worsted Acts, 190, 191 ; Luddite, 263.
Insurrection, general,' at Manchester, of 1817, 342, 350-353. *See also* Rising, general.
Ireland : weavers from, in Lancs, 70, 78, 126 *n.* ; cotton spinners' delegates from, 134 ; insurrection of 1803, 298 ; frame-work knitters in, 230 ; shearmen in, 174 ; and rising of 1817, 361 ; supposed Luddite plot, 318.
Irwell, 127.
Isle of Man, 130.
Italy, 49.

Jackson, William, 244-246.
Jacobins, 9, 59, 66, 67, 88, 92, 290, 361 ; of France, 376.
James I., Act of, regulating wages, 86, 87.
James, John, *History of Worsted Manufacture*, Chapter VI., *passim.*
—— 347.
Jarrow, 24.
Jenny-spinners of Stockport, strike in 1818, 94, 95.
—— spinning, invented by Hargreaves, 50-53, 57 ; destroyed in 1779, 54 ; Parliamentary Committee on, 56 ; and woollens, 145 150 ; and worsteds, 152, 153.
Jesmond Dene, 35.
Jessop, Walter Hilton, 180, 181, 188.
Jessop's foundry, 361.
Jobling, 43, 44.
Johnson (reformer), 95 *n.*, 100, 107, 116.
—— and Brookes, 128.
Joiners, 47, 96, 181.
Jones, jeweller of Birmingham, and Oliver, 357 *n.*, 359.
—— John, of Bradford, Wilts, 171 *n.*, 173-176, 181.
—— William, 104, 105.
—— W. O. *See* Oliver.
Judd, Thomas, 234.

Kay, James, 167 *n.*
—— John, 49. *See also* Flying shuttle.
—— Richard, 118, 119.
Keeling, Rev. Mr., 320.
Keelmen, 19.
Kegworth, 265.
Keighley, 202.
Kenyon, Thomas, 120.
Kerfoot, Thomas, 296.
Kersall Moor, 102.
Keynsham, 149.
Kidderminster, 197.
King, Mr. (of Home Office), 62.
Kingswood, 163.
Kirkstall, 311.
'Knapsack' prisoners, 347-349.
Knight, William, 84, 94 *n.*, 100 ; one of 'the 38,' 297, 299, 300; arrest in 1817, 352.
Knott, James, 338 *n.*

Lace Industry, growth of, 228, 236-238, 253, 254-256 ; lace frames destroyed, 236, 261 (*see also* Loughborough) ; numbers employed (1831), 255 *n.* *See also* Bobbin net, Point net, Warp lace.

Lace manufacture, Commission on Children in, 256.

—— running, 7, 262, 263.

Lacey, Mr., 238.

Lamb, Charles, *The Three Graves*, 341, 343.

—— George. *See* Lord Melbourne.

Lambton, H. Morton, 36 *n.*

Lancashire, John, 350.

Lancaster, 134.

—— Special Commission (1812), 292-296.

Lascelles, Mr., M.P., 77.

—— Lord, 189.

Latham, 230.

Lauderdale, Lord, 218, 229, 267.

Law. *See* Lord Ellenborough.

Law Officers, and 1818 strike, 102 ; and shearmen, 174 ; and wool-combers, 201 ; and frame-work knitters' Society, 233 ; and Lawson, 318 ; and Yorkshire Luddites, 321, 323, 328 ; and illegal oaths, 337.

Lawson, Sergeant, alias Montgomery, 318.

Lead miners. *See* Miners.

Le Blanc, Mr. Justice, 292, 294, 323.

—— William, 365.

Lee, John, 293.

—— Rev. William, 221.

Leeds, 2, 192, 195 ; woollen centre, 138, 139, 164 ; and woollen machinery, 150, 152 *n.* ; woollen spinners, 154, 155 ; weavers, 167 ; shearmen in 1802, 172, 176, 177 *n.*, 178-180, 189 ; and Luddite disturbances, 301 *n.*, 303, 304, 309, 315 ; and Oliver, 342, 354, 356, 357, 359, 360.

Leeds Mercury, 325, 337 ; and worsted mills, 156 ; revelations about Oliver, 362-364, 372, 374.

Leek, 214, 347.

Leicester, 56 ; frame-work knitters of, 3, 5, 224, 229 ; centre for woollen hose, 222 ; spinning machinery destroyed at, 222 ; frame-work knitters' resolutions (1817), 244 ; parish authorities and minimum wage, 246 ; 1819 strike, 250-252 ; and ' general insurrection ' (1817), 351 *n.* ; and Oliver, 355, 358 ; and wool-combers, 197-199.

—— Corporation of, 252.

Leicester, Mayor of, 246.

Leigh, 112 *n.*

—— Thomas, 348.

Lenton, 260.

Levers, John, 237 *n.*

Lewis, Mr., of Brinscomb, 190.

L. F., spy, 73.

Libel law, 346.

Litchfield, Mr. (Treasury Solicitor, 1817), 368.

Littleton, 172.

Liverpool, 143, 359.

—— Lord, 189, 229, 267.

Liversedge, 304.

Lloyd, Mr., of Stockport, 90, 92 ; and Lancashire Luddites, 274, 292 ; and ' the 38,' 300 ; activities after Yorkshire Luddite disturbances, 315-317, 319, 320-322, 327, 328, 332-334 ; and Blanketeers, 348 ; and 1818 strikes, 95, 96, 101, 103, 107, 113 *n.*, 117 ; in 1819, 121.

Lloyd, A. C. G., 377.

Locke, John, 115.

Lockett, Mr., of Derby ; and Oliver, 355 ; and Derby trials, 366-368, 370.

Lomas, George, 294.

Lomax, William, 350, 351 *n.*, 352.

London : merchants and minimum wage, 75 ; juries, 119, 371 ; wool-combers, 197 ; frame-work knitters, 221, 224, 229-232 ; and Lancashire Luddites, 274, 290 ; Oliver and revolution in, 354, 356, 358, 359, 364.

Londonderry, Lord, 29, 30, 34, 38 *n.*, 41.

Long Holme, 127.

Looms, limitation of, 168, 170, 171, 180, 183-185, 187.

Losh, James, 37, 38, 43 *n.*

Loughborough, 347.

—— Lord, 214.

—— Luddites : attack on Heathcoat's factory, 238 ; trial and execution of, 241-243.

Lovat, Lord, alias Russel, 318.

Lower Darwen, 111.

Lowmoor, 306.

Ludd, General, 292, 310 ; song about, 259, 260.

—— Mrs., 317.

—— Ned, 243 *n.*, 259.

Luddite disturbances. *See* Chapters ix., x., and xi.

Luddites, Loughborough, 238-243.

Ludlam, Isaac, 368, 370.

Lumb, John, 323, 332.

MACAULAY, 140.
Macclesfield, and silk, 211 *n.*, 214-216, 219; and Blanketeers, 347.
MacDonald, John, spy, 314, 326-328, 335.
Machinery: introduced for cotton spinning, 50-53, 57; opposition of workers to, 53-55; introduced for cotton weaving (power-loom), 71, 72, 123, 124; opposition of workers to (1812), Chapter x. (1826), 126, 127, 128; introduced for wool and worsted spinning, 145-156, 222; opposition of workers to, 146, 149, 150, 222; introduced for woollen weaving, 164, 167; introduced in worsted weaving, 193-195; opposition of workers to, 194, 195; introduced for shearing, gig mills, 169, 170, 188, 189, 301; shearing frames, 169, 187, 188, 190; opposition of workers to (1802), 170-188, and (1812) Chapter xi.; introduced for woolcombing, 196, 203; opposition of workers to, 197-200.
MacOwen, Harriet, 327.
Maddocks, Peter, 131.
Maitland, General, and Luddite disturbances in Lancs, 276, 287; and general rising, 291; on trial of '38,' 298, 299; and General Grey, 312; and Luddite disturbances in Yorks, 312; his spies, 313-315, 326, 327; on magistrates, 316, 319; and Barrowclough, 317; and Lawson, 318; on Lloyd's methods, 321, 322; and Luddism, 323, 333; on Radcliffe, 332; on Luddite oath, 337, 338.
Malmesbury, 149.
Manchester, 10, 180 (*see* Chapters iv. and v., *passim*); weavers' address (1818), 117; and silk trade, 215, 216; and Luddite disturbances, 272, 276, 278, 279, 286-288, 297, 338; and Oliver, 354-359; middle-class reformers, 372. *See* also Blanketeers and 'Insurrection, general.'
Manchester Courier, 353 *n.*
—— *Mercury*, 287, 288, 296, 297.
—— *Observer*, 99 *n.*, 119 *n.*, 335, 353.
—— *Political Register*, 343, 344.
Manners-Sutton, Thomas, 175.
Mansfield, 265, 359.
—— Lord, 227.
Maples, Joseph, 268, 269.

Marriott, Mr., J.P., 116.
Marryatt, Samuel, 230.
Marsden, 309.
Marshall, Gerves, 269.
Marsland, Mr., 273 *n.*, 279.
Mask of Anarchy, 376.
Maule, alias for Oliver, 368.
May, James, 179, 181.
—— William, 180, 181.
M'Connell's mills, 134 *n.*
Medcalf, John, 105.
Melbourne, Lord, 35; on Miners' Union, 44, 45; on spinners' strike, 133; on Frame Breaking Bill, 267.
Meldrum, 345.
Melksham, 147.
Mellor, George, 306, 310, 322, 324, 330.
Mephringham, 225.
Methodists, 24, 230, 324.
Middlesex frame-work knitters, 224.
Middleton, 3, 111; Luddite disturbances, 287, 296 (*see also* Burton); reformers and general insurrection, 1817, 350; and Oliver, 354.
—— Lord, 241, 242 *n.*
Milbanke, Sir Ralph, 14.
Mile End, 216.
Military, use of, in strikes and riots: miners' strikes, 17, 22, 35; Manchester riot (1808), 78; Stockport strike (1818), 95; riots of 1826, 127; at Horsfall's mill, 195; Spitalfields, 206-208; Luddite disturbances, 262, 282, 284, 285; at Cartwright's mill, 305, 306, 308; Pentridge rising, 362; proposal to sound (1826), 126; too friendly to people at Nottingham, 240; Maitland on demands for, 287 *n.*; Grey on, 302; differences with magistrates, 310, 311.
Militia, 172; disbanded to flood labour market and break Union, 233, 235; used by unemployed workers, 82 *n.*
Mill Bridge, 314, 357.
Millwrights, 103.
Milnes, Charles, 326-327.
Milton, Lord, 77, 373.
Minchin Hampton, 159.
Miners of Tyne and Wear (*see* Chapters ii. and iii.): early conditions, 17; dispute of 1810, 21; statement of grievances (1825), 27; strikes of 1831 and 1832, Chapter iii.; dissolution of Union, 45.

Miners, lead, 37, 38, 40, 43.
—— Lancashire, 20, 103, 104, 289, 292, 338.
—— Somerset, 149, 200.
—— Yorkshire, 20 *n.*
Mines Report, 1842, 28, 43.
Minimum wage. *See* Wages, regulation of.
Mitchell (Loughborough), 241.
—— (reformer), 354, 356.
Molyneux, Lydia and Mary, 295.
Montagu, Mrs., 18, 19.
Montgomery. *See* Lawson.
Moore, Ambrose, 212 *n.*
—— Peter, M.P., 184, 215, 229 *n.*
Moorfields, 206, 209.
'Moscow, Manchester to be a,' 350.
Mule, the spinning : invented by Crompton, 50-53, 57 ; used for woollens, 149, 151.
—— spinners' addresses (1818), 97, 101.
Mundy, Mr., J.P., on hosiers, 246, 247 *n.* ; and Pentridge rising, 362; and Derby trials, 366, 367.
Murgatroyd, Nathaniel, 192 *n.*

NADIN, Deputy Constable of Manchester, 81, 88 *n.*, 105, 350 ; and trial of ' the 38,' 298-300 ; and Luddite disturbances, 313, 326, 334, 335, 338 ; and Blanketeers, 347, 349.
Napoleon, 8, 319, 376.
National Association for Protection of Labour, 42 *n.*, 131, 134.
Naylor, Mr., 105.
Need, Mr. (hosier), 224.
Needham, Richard, 79 ; and Arbitration Acts, 62, 68, 69 *n.* ; and minimum wage agitation, 72, 73, 75, 76, 120 ; as loyal weaver, 90, 113.
Nelthorpe, Colonel, 313.
Nesfield, Rev. Mr., 22, 23, 25 *n.*, 27.
Newburn-on-Tyne, 38.
Newcastle, 38 ; Town Moor, 31, 35 ; Committee of Trades, 202.
—— *Chronicle*, 36.
—— Duke of, 240, 251, 262 *n.*, 265.
—— Mayor of, 31 *n.*, 32, 33 *n.*
—— (Staffs), 103.
New Chapel, 59.
Newton, 59, 104.
Nore, Mutiny at, 176 *n.*, 275 *n.*
Norfolk : worsted centre, 137, 144, 153 ; silk, 211.

Norris, Mr., stipendiary at Manchester, 97 *n.* ; and 1818 strikes, 101, 102, 105-108, 112, 115, 116.
Northampton frame-work knitters, 224, 232.
North Riding, 197.
—— Shields, 38.
Northumberland, Duke of, 25 *n.*, 34 *n.*
—— Earl of, 14.
Norwich, 106, 108 ; worsted centre, 140-145, 152, 153 ; worsted weavers, 191-194 ; woolcombers, 196 ; silk trade, 216.
Nottingham, 5, 53, 54, 56, 108 ; centre for cotton hose, 222 ; frame-work knitters of, *see* Chapter VIII., *passim* ; riots on rejection of Minimum Wage Bill (1779), 224 ; ' system of terror ' at, 243 ; strikes of 1817 and 1819, 247, 251, 252 ; and twist-net fever, 254, 255 ; and Luddite disturbances, Chapter IX., and 274, 339, 340 ; and ' general insurrection ' (1817), 342, 345, 351 *n.* ; and Oliver, 354, 356, 358-361.
—— *Journal*, 265.
—— *Review*, 226, 259, 264, 266.
Number One. *See* Hall, Michael.
Number Two. *See* Rose, James.
Nuneaton, 214.

OASTLER, Richard, 5, 156.
Oates, Joseph, 154, 165 *n.*
Oath of allegiance, 279, 280, 319, 337-338.
Oaths, illegal : penalties for, 275 *n.*, 319, 337 ; shearmen and, 176, 181 ; Luddite oath, 275, 276, 278, 290 ; trials for, (Chester) 291, 292, (Lancs) 293, 296, 298, 299, (Yorks) 325-329 ; discussion of Luddite oath, 335-340.
Observations on Woollen Machinery, 150, 151, 168 *n.*
Ogden, John, 100, 330.
Oldham, 2, 57, 59, 112 *n.*, 135 ; weavers' manifestoes, 109, 110 ; food riots (1812), 284.
Oliver the spy, alias Richards, alias Hollis, alias Maule, alias W. O. Jones, 95 *n.*, 250, 300, 341, 343 ; described, 353 ; first mission, 354; second mission, 355-360 ; disclosures about, 362-364 ; and Derby trials, 368-370 ; debates on, 371-374 ; later history, *see* Appendix.

Orders in Council (1807), 8, 82, 83, 283, 302, 319 ; of November 1831, 156.
Owen, Robert, 3, 52 *n.*, 306.
Oxford, 200 *n.*

PADIHAM, 111.
Paisley, 52.
Palmer, George, of Leeds, 172, 178, 179.
Palmerston, Lord, 237.
Paper makers, 87, 181.
Papplewick, 57.
Parish authorities and minimum wage : frame-work knitters, 246, 248, 250 ; cotton weavers, 124-126.
—— employment of poor, 240, 244, 245.
—— relief, payment of wages from : cotton weavers, 92, 128 ; worsted spinners, 154 ; woollen weavers, 166 ; ribbon weavers, 211.
Park, J. A., and trials of Lancashire Luddites, 294, 295 ; of Yorkshire Luddites, 324, 329, 334.
Parke, Mr. Justice, 44.
Parker, Mr., J.P. of Sheffield, 356-358.
—— John (hosier), 247, 248.
Parkin, Earl, 321, 323.
Parkinson, Samuel, 55.
Parnell, John, 292.
Patten-ring makers, 181.
Paul, Wyatt and, 51.
Payne, Mr., of Burbage, 227.
Peace Preservation Bill (1812), 318, 319.
Peck, Joseph, 269.
Peel, Robert (the elder), 54.
—— Sir Robert (first Bart.), 3, 66, 100 ; and minimum wage, 75-77.
—— —— (second Bart.), 318.
Pelham, Lord, 181.
Pembroke, Lord, 175.
Pendrill (reformer), 354.
Pentridge, 263 ; rising, 359-362 ; curate of, 367.
Perceval, Spencer, 74, 175, 292 ; and minimum wage (1808), 76, 77.
Peterloo, 10, 26, 120, 122, 375.
Pewsey, 148 *n.*
Philip and Mary, statute of. *See* Looms, limitation of.
Philips, G., M.P., and spies, 350 *n.*, 351 *n.*, 352 *n.*, 371, 372.
Picketing, 105.
Pickford, Mr., J.P. *See* Ratcliffe, Joseph.

Pigott, Mr., M.P., 267.
Pilkington, 111.
—— Robert, 113, 118, 119.
Pitmen. *See* Miners.
Pitt, William, 60, 169 ; and Arbitration Act, 62, 63 ; and woollen laws, 183-186.
Place, Francis, 218.
Playfair (spy), 315.
Plymouth, 197.
Poaching, 225, 241.
Point-net trade, 228, 236.
Poley, Benjamin, 269.
Political Union (Northumberland), 35.
Poor, Society for Bettering Condition of, 20, 148 *n.*
—— Law Authorities. *See* Parish.
—— Law Commission (1834), 128.
Porters (London), 209.
Portland, Duke of, 60.
Posse comitatus, 262 *n.*
Potteries, 103.
Power-loom : invented by Cartwright, 71 ; use of, for cottons, 71, 72, 123, 124 ; effects on spinners, 124 *n.* ; campaign against (1812), *see* Chapter x., *passim* ; destruction of (1826), 126-128 ; for woollens, 139, 164, 167 ; for worsteds, 193-195.
—— weavers, strike at Stockport (1818), 95, 96.
Prentice, A.: *History of Manchester*, 78 *n.*, 81, 286, 287, 343 *n.* ; on Oliver, 357 *n.* ; and Derby prisoners, 370 *n.*
Prescott, Rev., J.P. of Stockport, 273, 274, 279, 315, 337.
Press gang, 170.
Preston, 54, 55, 75, 81, 93, 121, 134.
—— (reformer), 104, 365 *n.*
Prestwich, 111, 113 *n.*, 290.
Priestley, Dr., 9.
Prince Regent : Blanketeers and, 342, 344-347, 349 ; and Derby rioters, 370.
Privy Council, Committee for Trade, 185.
Pucklechurch, 147 *n.*
Pudsey, 139.

RACKHEATH, 196.
Radcliffe, Joseph, J.P., afterwards Sir, 9; and Yorkshire Luddites, 302, 316, 317, 319, 322, 324, 332, 333.
—— Samuel, 296 *n.*
—— William, of Stockport : on weavers' golden age, 58, 59 *n.*, 69 ;

and power-loom, 71, 273; and Luddite disturbances, 278, 279.

Ramsey (Isle of Man), 130.

Ratcliff, 280.

Raven, 368.

Rawdon mill, 303, 309.

Rawfolds mill, destruction of, 304, 307-309. *See also* Cartwright, William.

Rawtenstall, 127.

Ray, Messrs. (hosiers), 232-234.

Raynes, Captain, 313, 314, 337.

Read, Mr., 170 n., 172, 175, 176, 181, 185.

Reading, silk trade, 214, 216.

Redeings of Foulsworth, 351.

Reform Bill, 35, 45.

Reform movement, 10, 11; miners and, 26, 35; cotton weavers and (1808-1809), 80; turn to Reform, (1811) 84, 85, 94, (1816) 89-91; and Luddite disturbances (1812), 276, 286; ' the 38 ' and, 297-300; and ' general insurrection ' in 1817, 350; and Oliver, 354, 357, 360, 362, 375; connection with 1818 strikes, 100, 101, 113, 116, 119; 1819 agitation, 69, 120, 121; Loughborough Luddites and, 241; Cobbett on frame-work knitters and, 252 n.

Reformers, early, 9.

Regulation of wages. *See* Wages.

Restall, 353.

Results of Machinery, The, 4.

Revolution, Industrial, 2-8.

—— in France (1830), 132.

Rhodes, Messrs., 288.

Rhymes, doggerel, 64.

Ribblesdale, 79 n.

Ribbon weavers of Coventry, 211, 217, 218; and miniumm wage, 214, 215; prosecution of Committee, 215, 216, 253.

—— Weavers' Petitions, of Leek, 214; Committee on (1818), 210 n., 211 n., 212 n., 213 n., 214 n., 215.

Ricardo, 217.

Richards, Lord Chief Baron, 368, 370.

—— W. J. *See* Oliver.

Ridley, J. B., 14.

Riot Act, 284, 334, 347 n.

Ripley, 361.

Ripon, 197.

' Rising, general,' of 1812, 273, 275, 289-291, 317. *See also* Insurrection, general.

Rising of labourers (1816), 158.

Roberson, Rev. Hammond, 306, 307, 314.

Robertown, 307.

Robespierre, 241.

Robinson, F., M.P., 351 n., 352 n.

Rochdale: riots in 1808, 78-80; woollen weavers, 165.

Rodbury, 160.

Roller spinning, 51.

Rolleston, Mr., J.P., 241, 242 n.

Romilly, Sir Samuel, 230, 267, 373.

Rose, George, 185; and Arbitration Act, 68, 72, 74; and minimum wage, 76, 77.

Rose, James, spy, alias Number Two, 350-353.

Ross, Sir Henry, 33 n.

Rowe and Duncough. *See* West Houghton factory.

Rowland and Burrs, 75.

Royles, George, 276.

Royton, 9, 80, 354.

Ruddington, 265.

Russel. *See* Lord Lovat

Rutland, Duke of, 240, 251, 252.

Ryder, Mr. (Secretary of State), 273, 292.

/S/. *See* Stones.

Saddleworth, 180, 289, 315.

Sadler, Michael, 9 n., 156.

Salford, 59, 61, 66 n.

Salisbury Assizes (1802 and 1803), 180, 181.

' Sam, Little,' 241 n.

Sarum, New, 197.

Savage, 241.

Sawbridge (sheriff), 208.

Sawley, 265.

Sawyers, 181.

' S.C.s ' (special constables) in Yorkshire Luddite disturbances, 313, 314, 337.

Scarlett, James, 299.

Schofield, John, 320, 324.

Scotland, 67, 134, 315, 340; weavers, 83, 86; shearmen, 174; silk, 210; frame-work knitters, 230, 232.

Scots Greys, 285.

Scott, Mr., J.P., 312, 319, 338.

Scribbling, 147 n., 149, 173.

Seamen, 19.

Searle, Major, 312, 325.

Secret Agent of Nottingham, 235, 239; on Oliver, 358, 359.

—— Letter Book, 349, 356.

Seddon, John, 59.

Seend, 147.

Sellars, 352.

Serf system for miners in Scotland, 12.

Settlement, parish, 13.

Shaw, Colonel, 131, 132, 135 *n.*

Shearing frames, 169, 173, 187, 188, 190; destruction of, in 1812, *see* Chapter XI.

Shearmen or croppers, 167, 190; work of, 169; campaign against gig mills (1802), 171-180; petitions against suspending Bills, 181-188; Bill of, 146, 183, 184; ask to emigrate, 189; system of work in Yorkshire, 301. *See also* Chapter XI.

Sheffield, 312; food riots (1812), 309, 321; and general insurrection (1817), 342, 351 *n.*; and Oliver, 354-360, 364.

Sheppard of Uley, 162, 163, 168 *n.*

—— William, 149 *n.*

Shepton Mallet, 145, 146.

Sheridan, 267.

Sheriffs, and Spitalfields, 208.

Sherwin, Joseph, 273 *n.*

Sherwood Forest, 259.

Shipley, 194.

—— C. (hosier), 265.

Shirley, 304, 305.

Shoemakers, 47, 103, 181.

Sholl, *Historical Account of Silk*, 212 *n.*

Shoploom system, 163, 187 *n.*, 193.

Shudehill Market, 287.

Sidmouth, Lord, 76, 95 *n.*, 122, 235 *n.*, 244, 279 *n.*, 300, 334, 347, 348; and regulation of wages, 87, 90, 91; and 1818 strike, 116; and emigration of shearmen, 189; and Frame-Work Knitting Bill, 229; and Yorkshire Luddites, 311, 312; on spies from S.W., 315; on Lawson, 318; and Lomax, 350, 352; and Oliver, 354, 356, 364 *n.*, 370, 371, 373-376; and trials of Huddersfield rioters, 366.

Silk, prohibition of foreign, 206.

—— stocking makers' address (1811), 266.

—— weavers of Spitalfields, 47, 104 (*see* Chapter VII.); early rioting, 205-208; Spitalfields Act (1773), 209-212; societies amongst, 212, 213; wages, 213; opposition to repeal of Act, 218, 219; later history, 219, 220; of

Macclesfield, 214, 215; of Leek, 214 *n.*; of Reading, 214. *See also* Ribbon weavers.

Silvester, Colonel, J.P., 78, 290, 298.

Simcoe, Lieut.-General, 200.

Simpson, Samuel, 232, 234.

Sinecures, 89, 91 *n.*, 100, 290.

' Single press ' lace, 228, 260 *n.*

Singleton, John, 60.

Skipsey, 44.

Slater, 241 *n.*

—— Samuel, 239.

Smalley, 265.

Smart, Professor, *Economic Annals*, 8 *n.*, 88 *n.*

Smith, Mr. (writer of paper on weavers' wages), 92.

—— Adam, 63, 112, 123.

—— Hannah, 294.

—— James, 296.

—— John, 207 *n.*

—— Thomas, 324.

—— William, M.P., 353 *n.*

' Snipshears, General,' 302.

Snow, of Leicester, 248.

Soldiers, discharged, and unemployment, 70, 88, 172, 173, 188; and soup, 188.

Somerset, 197; clothing district, 137, 146, 149, 158, 159, 161, 162, 168 *n.*, 176.

—— Lord Charles, 377, 378.

Soup, riaicule of, 89.

Southwark, 197, 200 *n.*

Southwell, 225, 258, 264.

Sowden, 329, 331.

Spanish wool, 162.

Special Commissions: Cheshire Luddites, 291, 292; Lancashire Luddites, 292-297; Yorkshire Luddites, 321, 323-332; Derby rioters (1817), 366-370.

Special constables. *See* ' S.C.s.'

Speenhamland system, 128. *See also* Parish relief.

Spencer, J. B., & Co., 75.

—— Lord, 73 *n.*, 186.

Spenser, Edmund, 372, 373.

Spies and informers: first mention of industrial spies (1801), 67; Bills for, 73, 277; part in Lancashire Luddite disturbances (1812), 273 ff.; responsibility for Luddite oath, 275, 337, 338; employment in Yorkshire Luddite disturbances (1812), 313 ff.; proposal to use spies from S.W. in Yorkshire, 314; employment in Nottingham

(1815), 235, 239; protests of Manchester merchants against use of, 372 ; activities about ' general insurrection' (1817), 350-353; debates on, in Parliament, 279 *n.*, 300, 371-374; effect of, in making workers suspicious, 250. *See also* 'B.'; 'Brother to No. 2'; Broughton, Thomas; 'C.'; Fleming, Samuel; Hall, Michael; Gossling, John ; L. F. ; MacDonald, John ; Oliver ; Rose, James ; 'S.C.s' ; Secret Agent of Nottingham ; Stones, John and Simon ; 'T.'; Waddington, Robert.

Spitalfields Act, 72, 85 ; passing of, 209 ; effects of, 210-212 ; suggested extension, 68, 214-216 ; repeal of, 216-219.

—— weavers. *See* Silk weavers.

Spring looms. *See* Flying shuttle.

Stafford, 43, 56, 348.

Stalybridge, 93, 104, 347 ; spinners' strike (1830), 131-135.

Stanley, Colonel, 62.

Stanningley, 154.

Starkey, James, 314.

Steam power applied to cotton industry, 57 ; to wool, 142, 148, 150 ; to worsted, 152 ; to lace, 254.

Steeple Ashton, 172.

Stirling militia, 313, 314.

Stockport, 59, 69 *n.*, 75, 78, 120, 340 ; weavers' addresses and petitions, (1811) 83, (1816) 88, 90, (1818) 113, 114, (1819) 121 ; spinners' combinations, 93, 100 ; power-loom weavers' strike (1818), 95, 96 ; weavers' strike (1818), 111, 114-117 ; jenny-spinners' strike (1818), 94 ; spinners' strike (1829 and 1830), 129, 134 ; and Luddite disturbances, 271-279, 313, 337.

Stones, John, a Bolton spy, 277, 278 ; part in Luddite disturbances, 279-284, 293, 296, 298, 337, 338.

—— Simon, father of John, spy, 277, 280, 281, 293, 337.

Strapper. *See* Cooper, William.

Strikes: miners, (1765) 13-16, (1810) 21, 22, (1816) 25, (1831 and 1832) Chapter III.; cotton spinners, (1810) 92, (1818) 96-109, (1829, 1830) 128-135 ; cotton weavers, (1808) 78, (1818) 95, 109-119 ; woollen spinners, (1819) 155 ;

woollen weavers, Yorkshire, (1819) 164, Frome (1823) 161, Gloucestershire (1825) 162, (1828-1829) 163, Rochdale and Huddersfield (1827) 166 ; shearmen, (1802) 171 ; woolcombers and worsted weavers, (1825) 201-203 ; frame-work knitters, (1814) 233, (1817) 248, (1819) 250, (1821) 252, (1824) 253.

Stroud, 158, 159, 160, 162, 163.

Strutt, Jedediah, 222.

—— Joseph, 367.

Sudbury, 211 *n.*, 216, 217.

Suffolk : worsted centre, 137, 144, 153, 154 *n.* ; and silk, 211.

—— Lord, 210.

Summerseat, 127.

Sunderland, 19, 38.

Surrey, 224.

Surrey militia, 318.

Sutton, 359.

Swallow, 323.

Swindells, Henry, 104.

Swinton, 20 *n.*

Sykes, 322.

'T.,' spy, 73.

Tailors, 17, 47, 85, 103.

Talleyrand, 318.

Taunton, 216.

Tavistock, 197.

Taylor, Benjamin, 253 *n.*

—— Dr., 279 *n.*, 298.

—— Enoch and James, 303.

—— J. E., 297 *n.*, 347 *n.*

—— J. F., 165 *n.*

—— Richard, 84.

Taylor Hill, 303.

Temple, Colonel, 195.

Temples, John, 291, 292.

Tester (woolcomber), 201.

Tewkesbury, frame-work knitters at, 224, 230, 232.

'Thirty-Eight, the,' 291 ; arrest and trial of, 297-300, 336.

Thistlewood, 365 *n.*

Thomas, Charles, 179.

Thompson, Joseph, 291, 292.

Thompson's mill, 303.

Thomson, Baron, Lancashire Special Commission (1812), 292 ; Yorkshire Special Commission (1813), 323, 328, 329, 334.

—— Mr., M.P., 77.

Thong, Nether, 320.

—— Upper, 320.

Thornhill Lees, 357-360, 363, 365; Oliver's arrest and escape, 358.
Thorpe, 9.
—— Thomas, 63, 90, 120.
—— William, 324.
Threatening letters, 65.
'Three-days' grievance (miners), 27, 31, 33.
Tierney, George, 77; on spy system, 371; on Oliver, 373, 374.
Times, the, 78, 218, 219.
Tintwistle, 288, 291.
Tiverton, 197; Heathcoat's lace works, 200, 242.
Todmorden, 111, 124.
'Tommy-shops,' 20, 31-33.
Tooke, *History of Prices*, 88 n.
Toplis, William, 196; petition against woolcombers, 198, 199.
Tories, 121, 371.
Tottington, 111.
Towle, James, 239, 240.
—— Rodney, alias Bill, 238, 241.
Towns of Industrial Revolution, 7.
Townsend, Sheriff, 208; Lord Mayor, 209.
Trade Unions. *See* Combinations.
Trentham, William (hosier), 269, 270.
Trowbridge, 146, 188; centre of shearmen's organisation in 1802, 171, 172, 175, 178-181.
Truck system: mines, 20, 21, 26, 33; woollen industry, 157, 161, 163, 184; frame-work knitting industry, 228, 229, 235, 236, 258, 266.
Trye (woolcomber), 196.
Turner, William, trial and execution of, 368, 370.
Turnpike men, 181.
Twarton, 200.
Twist-net fever, 255.
Tyburn tickets, 335.
Tyne Main, 43.
—— *Mercury*, 24, 33-36, 38 n., 41.
—— Vale, 18.

ULEY, 162, 163, 168 n.
Undertakers in ribbon trade, 214.
Union lodges (woollen weavers), 163, 164.
Unions, Trade. *See* Combinations.
United Trades' Co-operative Journal, 131.
Unwin, Professor G., 144 n.
Ure, A., *Cotton Manufacture of Great Britain*, 50, 124 n.

VAGRANCY ACT, 43, 348.
Valline, John, 208.
Vend, the Newcastle, 24, 25.
Venezuela, 112.
Vickerman, Mr., 303, 308 n., 322, 323.
'Vindex' in *Tyne Mercury*, 36.
Voice from the Coal Mines, A, 27.
Volunteers, doubts of, 66.

WADDINGTON, Robert, spy, alias A. B., 113 n., 277; activities over 'general insurrection' (1817), 350-352.
Wages, regulation of: cotton weavers, 61, 62, 72-75, 77, 78, 83, 86, 87, 121, 124, 128; woollen weavers, 157-159; silk weavers, 207, 209-219; frame-work knitters, 223, 224, 254.
—— miners, 18, 18 n., 20, 21 n., 28, 33, 37; cotton spinners, 94, 97-99, 129 n., 131-133; cotton weavers, 70, 74, 78, 88, 92, 110, 120, 343, 344; woollen spinners, 144, 147, 154, 155; woollen weavers, 144 n., 154, 155, 158, 160, 161, 164, 166, 167; shearmen, 173; worsted spinners, 155; worsted weavers, 192, 195; woolcombers, 198, 201; silk weavers, 213, 217; ribbon weavers, 217; frame-work knitters, 223-225, 228, 244 n., 246, 249, 263, 264, 266, 270.
Wakefield, 311, 319, 342; and Oliver, 354, 356, 357, 359, 360, 363.
Waldridge, 38-40.
Wales, 43.
Walker, Benjamin, murderer of Horsfall, 322, 324, 329, 330; subsequent history, 334.
—— John, 331.
—— William, 292.
Wallas, Graham, 7 n.
Waller, Ann, 179.
Walmsley, Elizabeth, 81.
Walshaw Lane, 111.
War: with America, (1775) 53, 55, 141, (1812) 319; with France, 8, 142, 162, 193, 226; with Spain, 55.
Wardle, Colonel, 280.
Warminster, 171, 172.
Warp machine, 226, 236.
Warp lace trade, 236, 237; workers, 238.

Warr, Adjutant, 79 *n.*, 277, 279, 280, 285.

Warren, Joseph, 179.

—— Phœbe, 179.

Warrington, 59.

Warwick, 197; ribbon weavers, 214, 216.

Washington, William, 298.

Watch and Ward Act, 311.

Water frame, patented by Arkwright, 50; used for worsted, 152, 155, 222.

Watermen, 209.

Watson, Dr., 365 *n.*

—— Mr., J.P., 320.

Watt, James, and steam engine, 57.

Watts, Nathaniel, 160.

Webb, Mr. and Mrs., *History of Trade Unionism*, 86, 130 *n.*, 336.

—— Mr. (clothier), 180.

Weddle, George, 44.

Wedgwood, Josiah, 54.

Weightman, George, 367 *n.*, 369, 370.

Wellington, 162.

—— Duke of, 10.

Wesley, John, 230.

—— —— (Luddite), 262.

Wesleyan Methodists, 307 *n.*

Westenholme, James, 355.

West Houghton weaving factory, 272; plans to fire, 279-284; burned down, 285; trials and executions for, 293, 295, 296.

Westmoreland, 141.

West Riding, 4; and worsted trade, 137, 141, 143; and woollen trade, 137-140.

Whalley, 127.

Whig Ministry of 1806, 73, 186.

Whigs, 121, 240; and spy system, 371.

Whitbread, Samuel, 83, 267, 278, 279 *n.*, 280; on spies, 300.

White, George, 229 *n.*

—— Mr. (cotton master), 119.

Whitefield, 59, 63, 64.

Whitehead, 316.

Whithers, 241.

Whittaker, Thomas, 273 *n.*, 274, 286 *n.*, 291-292.

Wigan, 54, 55, 58, 59, 78, 100; and abuse of charitable at, 90.

Wilberforce, William, and woollen workers, 184, 186, 187; on Oliver, 373.

Willans, Mr., of Dewsbury, 362, 363, 364.

Williams (counsel for ' the 38 '), 299.

Wilmot, Mr., 180.

Wilton, 197.

Wiltshire, 10; clothing district, 137, 146, 158; riots of 1802, 268 *n.*; suggestion to get spies thence, 314, 315.

Wingfield, 361.

Wolstonholme, Rev. Hugh, 367.

Women: as cotton hand-spinners, 50, 53, 56; as cotton machine-spinners, 131; as cotton hand-loom weavers, 60; as cotton power-loom weavers, 72; strike of, in 1818, 95, 96; as woollen and worsted spinners, 143-156; as woollen weavers, 161, 162; as silk weavers, 209; as frame-work knitters, 222 *n.*; Luddite opposition to employment, 257, 263; as lace workers, 254, 255 *n.*, 256; lace runners try to combine, 262, 263; as embroiderers of hose, 269, 270; behaviour in strikes (pitmen's wives in 1832 strike), 42, 43; in cotton strike (1808), 80; in cotton strike (1818), 105, 115, 116.

Wood, Alderman, 327 *n.*

—— Baron, 332, and trial of ' the 38,' 299, 300; and trial of Huddersfield rioters, 365, 366.

—— John (cropper), 310, 322, 329.

—— —— (Bradford spinner), 156.

—— Sir Francis, 311.

—— William (Blanketeer), 348, 349.

Wool, export of British, 136, 137.

Woolcombers, 47, 190, 194 (*see* Chapter VI., section vi., 195); nature of work and characteristics, 195, 196; opposition to machinery, 197-200; Toplis on, 198, 199; Congress at Coventry, 200, 201; Bradford strike (1825), 201-203; superseded by machinery, 203, 204; address to masters (1840), 203.

Woollen Bill, 136 *n.*, 145.

—— industry, 136-140.

—— Manufacture, Committee on state of (1806), 181, 186, 187.

—— statutes, 168; attempt of men to enforce (1802-1809), 180-188; Bills suspending, 181-185, 187, 188; shearmen's Bill, 184; Committee of 1806 on, 186; repealed (1809), 188. *See also* Gig mills, Apprentices, Limitation of looms.

—— weavers (*see* Chapter VI., section iii.), 156; early characteristics, 156; attempt to obtain regulation of wages in S.W. (1756), 157-159; attempt to enforce woollen statutes (1802-1899), 180-188; and flying shuttle, 159-161; stability of wages in S.W., 162; organisation and strikes in S.W., 162-164; organisation and strikes in Yorkshire, 164-167; and power-looms, 167.

Wool-sorters, 181.

Worcester, 56.

Worsley, 296.

—— T., 93 *n*.

Worsted Acts, 190, 191.

—— Committee, 190, 199.

—— industry, 136-138, 140-143.

—— mills, 152, 153, 155, 156.

—— weavers, 47 (*see* Chapter VI., section v., 190); of Norwich, 191-194; of West Riding, 194, 195; and power-looms, 194, 195; join

woolcombers in 1825 strike, 201-203.

Wortley, 154.

—— Stuart, 325 *n*.

Wotten, 163.

Wright, Mr., J.P., 116.

Wyatt and Paul, 51.

Wylde, Dr., J.P., 239.

Wymondham, 193.

YARWOOD, Humphrey, and Luddite disturbances, 276, 278, 286, 287, 297.

Yates, Mr. (Peel's partner), 66.

Yeomanry, the, used (1818), 95, 119.

Young, Arthur: on woollen manufacture, 2, 136, 139, 150, 151; on worsted, 141, 152 *n.*, 192; on wretchedness of spinners, 145; on miners, 18 *n.*, 19, 20 *n.*; on silk, 211 *n*.

Young, Sir William, 184.